CAMBRIDGE GEOGRAPHICAL STUDIES

---

13. POPULATION GROWTH AND AGRARIAN CHANGE: AN HISTORICAL PERSPECTIVE

CAMBRIDGE GEOGRAPHICAL STUDIES

Cambridge Geographical Studies presents new methods of geographical analysis, publishes the results of new research work in all branches of the subject, and explores topics which unite disciplines that were formerly separate. In this way it helps to redefine the extent and concerns of geography. The series is of interdisciplinary interest to a wide range of natural and social scientists, as well as to planners.

1 *Urban analysis*, B. T. Robson
2 *The urban mosaic*, D. W. G. Timms
3 *Hillslope form and process*, M. A. Carson and M. J. Kirkby
4 *Freight flows and spatial aspects of the British economy*, M. Chisholm and P. O'Sullivan
5 *The agricultural systems of the world: an evolutionary approach*, D. B. Grigg
6 *Elements of spatial structure: a quantitative approach*, A. D. Cliff, P. Haggett, J. K. Ord, K. A. Bassett and R. B. Davies
7 *Housing and the spatial structure of the city: residential mobility and the housing market in an English city since the Industrial Revolution*, R. M. Pritchard
8 *Models of spatial processes. An approach to the study of point, line and area patterns*, A. Getis and B. N. Boots
9 *Tropical soils and soil survey*, Anthony Young
10 *Water management in England and Wales*, Elizabeth Porter
11 *Geographical change and industrial revolution: coalmining in south-west Lancashire 1590–1799*, John Langton
12 *Population and metropolis: the demography of London 1580–1650*, Roger A. P. Finlay
13 *Population growth and agrarian change: an historical perspective*, D. B. Grigg

POPULATION GROWTH AND AGRARIAN CHANGE

An historical perspective

DAVID GRIGG

CAMBRIDGE UNIVERSITY PRESS

CAMBRIDGE
LONDON   NEW YORK   NEW ROCHELLE
MELBOURNE   SYDNEY

Published by the Press Syndicate of the University of Cambridge
The Pitt Building, Trumpington Street, Cambridge CB2 1RP
32 East 57th Street, New York, NY 10022, USA
296 Beaconsfield Parade, Middle Park, Melbourne 3206, Australia

First published 1980

Printed in Great Britain at the
University Press, Cambridge

Library of Congress cataloguing in publication data
Grigg, David B
Population growth and agrarian change: an
historical perspective
(Cambridge geographical studies, 13)
1. Population – History. 2. Agriculture – Economic
aspects – History. 3. Underdeveloped areas – Population.
4. Underdeveloped areas – Agriculture – Economic aspects.
I. Title. II. Series.
HB871.G82   301.32′9′1724   79-4237
ISBN 0 521 22760 7 hard covers
ISBN 0 521 29635 8 paperback

CONTENTS

List of tables   *vii*
List of figures   *x*
Acknowledgements   *xii*

1   Introduction   1

PART ONE   METHODOLOGY   9

2   Overpopulation: definition and measurement   11
3   The symptoms of overpopulation in agrarian communities   20
4   The possibilities of increased output in pre-industrial societies   29
5   Demographic adjustments to population growth   40

PART TWO   MALTHUS JUSTIFIED   49

6   European population in the long run   51
7   Western Europe in the thirteenth and early fourteenth centuries: a case of overpopulation?   64
8   England in the sixteenth and seventeenth centuries   83
9   France in the sixteenth and seventeenth centuries   102
10   Ireland: the great tragedy   115
11   Interim conclusions   141

PART THREE   MALTHUS REFUTED   145

12   Holland in the sixteenth and seventeenth centuries   147
13   Breaking out: England in the eighteenth and nineteenth centuries   163
14   France in the eighteenth and nineteenth centuries   190
15   Scandinavia in the eighteenth and nineteenth centuries   207
16   Coda to Part three   231

PART FOUR   MALTHUS RETURNS?   235

17   The developing countries today: the demographic response   237
18   The developing countries today: the production response   261
19   Conclusions   281

Notes   296
Index   333

v

For Jill, Susan, Catherine and Stephen,
with much love

> Go, little book, and wish to all,
> Flowers in the garden, meat in the hall,
> A bin of wine, a spice of wit,
> A house with lawns enclosing it,
> A living river by the door,
> A nightingale in the sycamore!
>
> R. L. Stevenson

TABLES

1	World population increase, AD 14–1975	1
2	Regional rates of population increase, 1950–73	2
3	Staple crop yields and calorific output in Africa	35
4	Population changes in selected countries in Europe, c. 1450–c. 1600	55
5	Population changes in selected countries in Europe, c. 1600–1750	57
6	Population in Europe, 1700–1970	60
7	Population change in Western Europe, 1700–1970	61
8	The population of England, 1377–1695	84
9	Price indices, 1450–1649	87
10	The urban population of England and Wales, 1520–1851	95
11	Place of birth of apprentices in London, 1540–1640, 1690	96
12	Mean family size of British peers, 1550–1799	100
13	The population of Ireland, 1687–1971	116
14	The rate of population increase in Ireland, 1712–1851	117
15	Agricultural population densities, c. 1841	121
16	Farm size in Ireland, 1845–1911	122
17	The urban population of Ireland, 1841–1926	128
18	Emigration from Ireland, 1821–1920	132
19	Trends in Irish and English fertility, 1870–1920	136
20	Ever-married as a percentage of all females, 15–45, in Ireland	138
21	The population of the Netherlands and some of its provinces, 1475–1815	149
22	The urban and rural populations of Holland, 1514 and 1622	156
23	The population of England and Wales, 1695–1939	165
24	The rural and urban populations of England and Wales, 1751–1911	169
25	Farm size in Ireland (1845) and in England and Wales (1851)	171
26	Farm size on the Leveson-Gower estate	171
27	Major land uses in England and Wales, 1696–1866	177
28	Area and consumption of potatoes in England and Wales	178
29	Wheat yields in England in the nineteenth century	179
30	Migrational gain and loss in England and Wales, 1841–1911	186

31   Numbers employed in agriculture, England and Wales, 1851
     and 1911   186
32   Emigration from England and Wales, 1825–1909   186
33   Rate of loss by migration, 1851–1939   187
34   Crude birth and death rates in England and Wales, 1801–40   188
35   The population of France, 1700–1911   191
36   The rate of population increase in Western Europe, 1700–1910   191
37   Farm size in France, 1892   195
38   The arable area of France, 1701–1913   198
39   Area in fallow in France, 1701–1892   198
40   Rural and urban populations of France, 1811–1911   203
41   Agricultural and rural populations of France, 1700–1911   203
42   Loss by migration from rural areas, France 1856–86   204
43   Rate of natural increase in France, 1816–90   205
44   Population growth in Norway and Sweden   208
45   Trends in crude birth and death rates, Norway and Sweden   210
46   Male agricultural population: Sweden, 1751–1900   214
47   Rural social structure in Norway, *c.* 1845   215
48   Population and arable land in Sweden in the nineteenth
     century   216
49   Crop yields in Sweden 1801–20 to 1891–1900   218
50   Seed–yield ratios in Norway, 1835 and 1881   219
51   Land use in Norway (1870s) and Sweden (1860s)   220
52   Annual overseas emigration per 100 000 population   223
53   Rural and urban populations in Norway and Sweden, 1800–60   226
54   Internal and external migration from Swedish rural districts,
     1816–1900   226
55   Rural and agricultural populations in Sweden, 1800–1930   228
56   Rural and agricultural populations in Norway, 1801–1910   228
57   Average rates of population increase per annum, 1950–75   237
58   Average rates of increase in selected countries, 1900–70   238
59   Expectation of life at birth in Latin America   243
60   Agricultural densities in Western Europe in the nineteenth
     century and the developing world *c.* 1975   245
61   Total population per 100 hectares of arable land   250
62   Rates of increase of rural and urban populations in Western
     Europe, 1750–1900   254
63   Rates of increase of rural and urban populations, 1920–70   255
64   Urban and rural demographic differentials, *c.* 1960   256
65   Arable land, 1950–75   264
66   Area under major food crops, 1950–75   264
67   Long-term increases in the arable area in parts of Asia   265
68   Arable area per head of agricultural and total populations,
     1950 and 1975   266

69 Potential, actual (1962) and proposed (1985) arable areas   269
70 Indices of multiple cropping in Asia   270
71 Staple crop yields and calorific output in Asia   272
72 The rural population of Europe in the nineteenth century   291

FIGURES

1 The agricultural labour force as a percentage of the total labour force, 1975   3
2 The agricultural labour force as a percentage of total labour force, c. 1950   4
3 The average rate of increase of the agricultural population, 1965–75   6
4 Optimum population, and overpopulation   14
5 Changes in the equivalent of the wage rate of a building craftsman in southern England, 1264–1954   24
6 Symptoms of overpopulation   45
7 Production and demographic responses to population pressure   46
8 The population of Europe, AD 1000–1900   52
9 Wool and wheat prices in England, 1450–1649   86
10 Population density in Ireland in 1841   120
11 Emigration from Ireland, 1841–1921   133
12 Regional rates of emigration from Ireland during the Famine, 1846–1851   134
13 The changing rate of land reclamation in the Netherlands, 1200–1950   151
14 The chronological patterns of land reclamation in the Netherlands   152
15 Crude birth and death rates in England and Wales, 1838–1920   166
16 Crude birth and death rates in France in the nineteenth century   192
17 Crude birth and death rates in Norway and Sweden, 1750–1930   209
18 Emigration from Norway and Sweden, 1850–1920   224
19 Decline in the crude death rate in Egypt, Sri Lanka and Mexico, 1925–73   242
20 World population densities, 1975: total population to cultivated area   244
21 World population densities, 1975: total population to arable area   246

22 World population densities, 1975: agricultural population to
    cultivated area   247
23 World population densities, 1975: agricultural population to
    arable area   248
24 Dietary energy supply as a percentage of requirements, *c.* 1970   262
25 A schematic representation of population growth in Western
    Europe   283

ACKNOWLEDGEMENTS

I am most happy to acknowledge the help I have had from friends and friendly institutions during the six or seven years this book has been a-growing. Benny Farmer and Tony Wrigley encouraged me to write it, and have kept me on course during several dashes away from the theme. Professor Michael Chisholm read an early version and made many helpful comments. I was particularly fortunate to be awarded a Social Science Council Research Fellowship in 1976–77, which allowed me to spend part of the year in Cambridge. I was lucky enough to be able to live in St John's, and I am grateful to the Master and Fellows of the college for their generosity. It was pleasant to return to former haunts in the South Wing of the University Library, and equally pleasant to discover a new one, the library of the Cambridge Group for the History of Population.

In Sheffield Miss P. A. Chedgzoy, Mrs Joan Dunn, Mrs Penny Shamma, Miss Anita Fletcher and Miss Carole Dawson managed to decipher my antique hand and efficiently type the manuscript. Mr Stephen Frampton and Miss Sheila Ottewell drew the maps and diagrams with care and dispatch. Dr Verity Brack read the manuscript and greatly improved grammar and style. My thanks are due to all these friends.

Snaithing Lane, Sheffield,
Midsummer 1978

CHAPTER 1

INTRODUCTION

In the last twenty-five years the world's population has increased to an unprecedented degree, from 2486 million in 1950 to 4000 million in 1975, an average rate of increase of 1.92% p.a.; by the early 1970s the rate had risen to 2.05% p.a. At no time in the past has the world's population increased so rapidly (table 1). But population has not increased at an equal rate in all parts of the world. The rate of increase in the underdeveloped world – Latin America, Africa and Asia – has been much greater than in the developed world, where the exceptional rate for Australasia can be attributed mainly to immigration (table 2). Indeed by the 1970s there were few countries in the underdeveloped world with population increasing at a rate of *less* than 2% p.a., whilst in the developed world those countries with rates of increase *above* 1.2% p.a. were rare.

Table 1. *World population increase, AD 14–1975*

Year	Population (millions)	Average rate of increase p.a. since preceding date (%)
AD 14	256	—
600	237	−0.01
1000	280	0.04
1340	378	0.09
1600	498	0.11
1650	516	0.07
1700	641	0.43
1750	731	0.26
1800	890	0.39
1850	1171	0.55
1900	1668	0.71
1950	2486	0.80
1960	2982	1.84
1970	3632	1.99
1973	3860	2.05

SOURCES: Colin Clark, *Population growth and land use* (London, 1967), p. 64; United Nations, *Demographic yearbook 1973* (New York, 1974), p. 81.

1

Table 2. *Regional rates of population increase, 1950–73*

	Population (millions)			Average rate of increase p.a. (%)	
	1950	1970	1973	1950–73	1970–73
World	2486	3632	3860	1.9	2.1
Africa	217	344	374	2.4	2.8
Latin America	162	283	309	2.8	2.9
Asia	1355	2056	2204	2.1	2.3
North America	166	228	236	1.5	1.3
Europe	392	462	472	0.8	0.7
USSR	180	243	250	1.4	1.0
Australasia	10	15	16	2.1	2.0

SOURCE: United Nations, *Demographic yearbook 1973* (New York, 1974), p. 81.

The very high rates of population increase currently being experienced in the underdeveloped world have no precedent in the past; the rate in Holland was 0.8% p.a. in the century between 1514 and 1622; in the late eighteenth and the nineteenth centuries a number of countries in Western Europe grew very rapidly: Ireland's population doubled between 1780 and 1841, an average rate of 1.2% p.a., while England and Wales nearly tripled their population between 1750 and 1851, an average rate of 1.0% p.a. But in no decade did the average rate per annum rise above 1.6%.[1]

The very rapid increase in population in the underdeveloped world, due largely to a fall in the death rate, has caused serious economic difficulties. From 1947 constant attention has been paid to the world food problem; more recently the shortage of energy resources has attracted equal attention, as has the difficulty of providing employment for the urban populations of Afro-Asia and Latin America. But the greatest problems are in the countryside: most countries in the underdeveloped world are still primarily agrarian (fig. 1). This was even more true in the 1950s (fig. 2) when there were few countries with less than two-thirds of their working populations engaged in agriculture; although the *proportion* of the work force in agriculture has everywhere declined, the absolute numbers seeking a livelihood from the land has continued to rise, for the massive migration from the country to the towns has been much less than the natural increase in the countryside (fig. 3). Thus in the Philippines the agricultural population doubled between 1950 and 1970, in India it rose from 249 million to 365 million, while in Malawi it rose from 2 million to very nearly 4 million.[2]

Not surprisingly these great increases in numbers in such a short time have had a very adverse effect in countries where the productivity of agriculture was poor and the standard of living low even before the great upsurge in

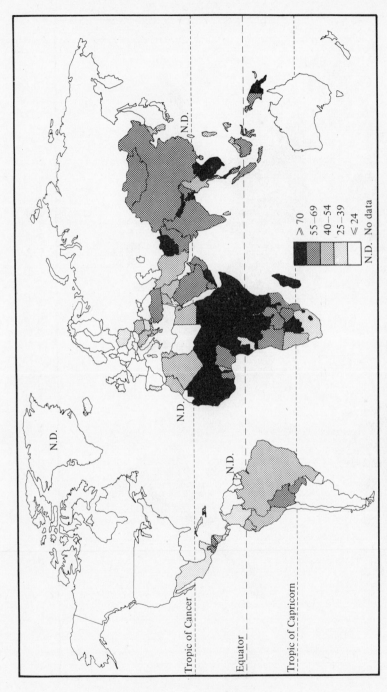

Fig. 1. Agricultural labour force as a percentage of total labour force, 1975. Source: FAO, *Production Yearbook 1976*, 30 (Rome, 1977), pp. 61–9.

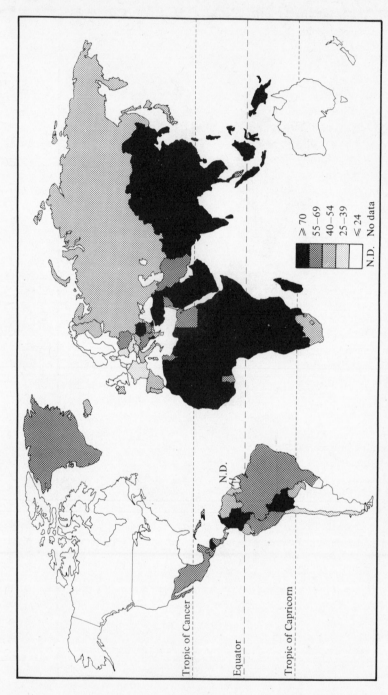

Fig. 2. Agricultural labour force as a percentage of total labour force, c. 1950. Source: D. Grigg, 'The world's agricultural labour force 1800–1970', *Geography*, 60 (1975), 194–202.

numbers. While population pressure is not the only cause of poverty in the underdeveloped world, it is of prime importance, and its adverse effects are only too apparent. Thus although there have been considerable additions to the cultivated area in most countries in the last thirty years, this increase has not been commensurate with the increase in population. As a result the average size of farm has fallen: in India, for example, from 3.0 hectares in 1953–4 to 2.6 hectares in 1960, while in western Guatemala the average size was halved between 1950 and 1964. In many countries the subdivision of farms means that many of them are now too small to provide the minimum subsistence for a family. In Pakistan it has been estimated that the minimum subsistence holding is 5 hectares; but half the holdings in the country are less than $2\frac{1}{2}$ hectares, while in southern Rhodesia in 1950 two-thirds of African holdings were less than the 2.1 hectares agronomists thought necessary to provide a livelihood.[3] Not only have farms been subdivided as population has grown, but in many countries an increasing proportion of the rural population is without any land at all, and relies on wage labour. An increase in the number of landless both in absolute numbers, and as a proportion of the rural population is a distinctive feature of most countries in the underdeveloped world over the last thirty years. It is true that in many places, particularly in Latin America, this is due to the concentration of land in a few large holdings; but in much of Africa and Asia where there is a more equitable distribution of ownership, the same growth in those dependent upon day-labour has occurred.

Rapid population growth also has adverse effects on land use and productivity. In Africa the dominant method of land use thirty years ago was bush fallowing, where land is cleared of its natural vegetation, cropped for two or three years, and then the natural vegetation is allowed to re-establish itself. Twenty or so years seems sufficient to re-establish the fertility of the soil, and the land can then be cultivated again. But such a system of farming is only possible where population densities are low; with an increase in population the length of the natural fallow is reduced and in the absence of any alternative means of maintaining soil fertility crop yields fall and in some cases soil erosion occurs.[4] In other farming communities an increase in population leads to an expansion of the cultivated area but at the expense of grazing land. Thus there is a greater concentration on food crops, less grazing land, fewer livestock, and possibly a poorer diet.

That rapid population growth has had adverse effects upon the agricultural communities in Afro-Asia and Latin America few would deny, although many would argue that population pressure is not the sole or indeed the most important cause of rural poverty. Many argue that a prime cause of rural poverty is the concentration of land in the hands of a few landowners: if land were more equitably divided and tenant farmers were made occupier owners they would then improve their methods.[5] Unfortunately where land reform has occurred it has not always led to dramatic improvements in farming

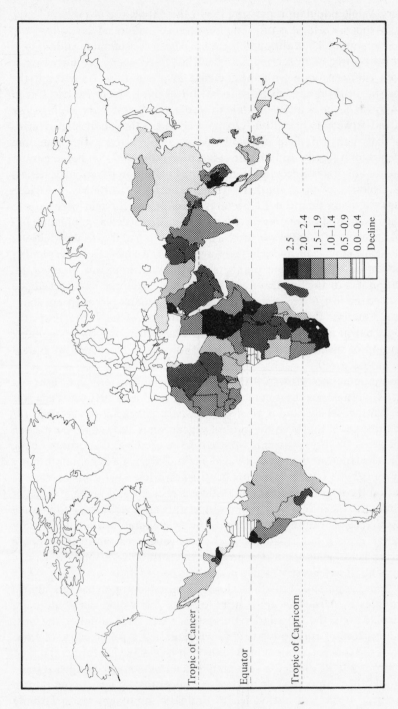

Fig. 3. Rate of increase of the agricultural population % p.a. 1965–75. Source: FAO, *Production Yearbook 1976*, 30 (Rome, 1977), pp. 65–75.

methods.[6] Others discount the role of land tenure and emphasise the need to encourage the adoption of improved techniques; again it is sometimes forgotten that the agronomy of the temperate countries of the Western world is not always suited to the tropics, nor is labour-saving machinery appropriate to countries where there is an abundance of labour and a shortage of capital.

But underlying most of the discussions of the present-day problem of the relationship between population growth and agriculture is the assumption that the problem is new. While it is true that the rate of population growth is higher than at any time in the past, there have been periods of comparatively rapid growth in the past. It is sometimes thought that the dramatic increase of the last thirty years is the culmination of a period of increase dating back a hundred years or so; before then population is assumed to have grown almost imperceptibly and at an even rate. But it can be shown that there have been alternate periods of growth and stagnation. Most countries in Western Europe for which population estimates have been made show a similar pattern of population growth over the last millennium. From about AD 1000 to 1300 there was an increase in population, and indeed in many places densities were reached in the thirteenth and early fourteenth centuries which were not reached again until the nineteenth century. The Black Death in the mid-fourteenth century led to a fall in the population, and until the middle of the fifteenth century there was little recovery. But from then population grew again and continued to do so in some countries until the late sixteenth century, and in others until the middle of the seventeenth century. The seventeenth century saw a decline in the population of some countries, particularly in the Mediterranean, and stagnation in northern Europe, and there was only a slow rate of increase in the first half of the eighteenth century. But from 1740 population grew rapidly and this growth continued – except in Ireland – to the present day, although at a lower rate in most countries in the first half of the twentieth century than in the nineteenth century.

There are few countries outside Europe where it is possible to reconstruct with any confidence population totals before this century, but in China, where reasonably reliable estimates are available, a not dissimilar sequence of growth alternating with stagnation can be traced.[7] Thus it is likely that these countries must have faced problems similar in kind if not degree to those occurring today in the underdeveloped world. Three questions immediately occur. Are there recorded instances of rural overpopulation in the past? How were these problems overcome, if indeed they were? And has the study of the past any lessons for the underdeveloped world today?

Such an enquiry must be confined to countries which have adequate records and for which there exists a body of historical writing; the investigation pursued in this book is confined to Western Europe, indeed to a few countries: England, France, the Netherlands, Ireland, Norway and Sweden. An attempt is made to see if these countries were overpopulated during the periods of population growth; this involves not only defining overpopulation and identifying the symptoms of population pressure but also considering the ways in which the problems of population growth could be overcome. What possibilities of increasing production were available, and to what extent could these pre-industrial societies control their numbers?

First to be considered are those areas which seem to have been overpopulated: Western Europe in the thirteenth century, England in the sixteenth and early seventeenth centuries, France between 1550 and 1740, and Ireland in the first half of the nineteenth century. In all these cases lack of technological advance and the nature of institutions prevented output growing as fast – or faster – than population. Attention is then turned to those countries – for the most part at a later date – which were able to match population growth with an increase in output, and in which eventually output grew more rapidly than population. The first case to be considered is the Netherlands in the sixteenth and seventeenth centuries; attention is then turned to England and Wales between 1650 and 1850, France in the eighteenth and nineteenth centuries and finally Norway and Sweden in the nineteenth century. These countries all adopted a different combination of strategies to overcome the challenge of population growth.

But before making these case studies it is necessary to have some methodology. What is overpopulation? How is it defined? Can it be measured? What strategies are available to farming communities faced with population growth? These problems are discussed in the first part of this book. In chapter 2 the attempts to define and measure overpopulation are considered; it is concluded that these are unsatisfactory. In chapter 3 the symptoms of overpopulation in agrarian communities are considered, to provide a guide to the case studies in Part two of the book. But not all periods of population growth end in overpopulation. Few societies remain supine to the challenge of population growth. All societies make some attempt to adjust to the increase in numbers that threatens their standards of living. These responses may be divided into two categories: output may be increased by technological and institutional changes, by diversification and by specialisation; alternatively, agricultural communities can attempt to slow the pace of population growth, either by controlling the number of births, or by migration. These two approaches, which are of course not mutually exclusive, are considered in chapters 4 and 5.

PART ONE
METHODOLOGY

CHAPTER 2

OVERPOPULATION: DEFINITION AND MEASUREMENT

It is useful to look at the interrelationships of population growth and agricultural change when studying pre-industrial societies, both as an aid to understanding the past and as a possible guide to present problems. It seems reasonable to assume that any society, however simple, can adopt a variety of strategies to avoid the problems which arise when population outruns – or threatens to outrun – production. They may change their methods to increase output, cultivate land hitherto uncultivated or grow different and higher-yielding crops; they may limit the number of births so that population growth slows down, or some may migrate to the towns or other countries. The choice of strategy will vary according to local conditions of tenure, custom, soil type and knowledge.

All peasant societies are constantly confronted with the problems of adjusting their way of life to changing numbers; sometimes they fail, they become overpopulated: their standard of living falls. It is often assumed that parts of present-day Asia, Latin America and Africa are overpopulated and many historians have argued that parts of Europe were overpopulated in the past – England in the thirteenth century, Ireland in the early nineteenth century or France in the seventeenth century. But overpopulation is rarely defined without ambiguity and much of the theoretical discussion of the effect of population growth upon a country has dealt not with agriculture, but with the economy as a whole.

Three definitions of overpopulation are discussed here. First is that which can be derived from T. R. Malthus; overpopulation occurs when population growth causes output per head to fall to the subsistence level and rising mortality causes population growth to cease. Second is that put forward by writers on optimum theory; overpopulation occurs whenever population exceeds the optimum for a country with given resources and technology. Third is that definition put forward by those who have tried to measure rural underemployment; overpopulation occurs when the marginal productivity of labour is zero.

Any account of the theory of overpopulation must begin with T. R. Malthus, not because his ideas were new but because, as J. A. Field has aptly remarked, people listened to what he said, and his work has influenced all subsequent discussions.[1] Malthus published *An Essay on the Principle of*

11

Population in 1798. It was a reply to William Godwin's *Enquiry Concerning Political Justice*, which argued that mankind's misery was due to the institutional imperfections of society. Malthus believed that no change in institutions could improve man's lot, for however society was organised there would always be a tendency for population to outrun the growth in the means of subsistence. This tendency was opposed by checks to population growth, all of which could be described as causing misery or vice – war, famine and disease. Malthus produced a much longer version of his essay in 1803, and there were four subsequent revised editions, the last published in 1826.

Malthus argued that population *could* increase geometrically but food output could only increase arithmetically. 'It would be contrary to all our knowledge of the property of land...it must be evident...that in proportion as cultivation extended, the additions that could yearly be made to the former overall produce must be gradually and regularly diminishing.'[2] Malthus was here near to stating the law of diminishing returns, first formulated by Turgot, and later incorporated into Malthus' system by J. S. Mill.[3] Malthus, however, went on to argue that as population rarely did increase geometrically there must exist checks that restrain population growth. The ultimate check was food supply but this rarely occurred except in cases of famine. He divided the checks into two categories: preventive and positive. The preventive check is a man's doubts as to whether he can support a family, which lead him to defer marriage, which Malthus called 'moral restraint'; the positive checks are all the causes of a shortened life, which include a variety of things but principally war, famine and disease.

Thus Malthus envisaged that when for some reason income per head rose there would be earlier marriage and an increase in population. But as population increased it would eventually outrun the means of subsistence and as income per head fell, so the death rate would rise and marriage would be deferred. The average income per head would fall again to what it had been at the start of the cycle; indeed the essence of his argument was that while population could increase, income per head would always be kept down to the subsistence level by population growth.

Malthus' system has been criticised on a variety of grounds: his expectations were not borne out in the nineteenth century because of great technological advances in industry and agriculture which, together with the import of grain from North America, led to a sustained increase in income per head in most West European countries after 1850. But Malthus' assumption of an unchanging technology was more easily assumed in 1798, and above all he claimed to be describing the present and the past, not to be a prophet.[4] Nor can he be blamed for ignoring the possibility that birth control could take place within marriage and in the twentieth century would become a major control of population growth. It is ironic that a man, who as a clergyman could not condone birth control, should have his name associated with its advocacy later in the century. What he seemed reluctant to accept was that man might defer marriage in order to increase his standard of living, although he seemed to recognise the possibility in later writings.[5] Once the possibility of limiting numbers because of what would now be called 'rising expectations' is accepted, then a chance rise in income per head need not necessarily lead to population increase and the Malthusian system collapses. But perhaps the major criticism of Malthus' system is that he never makes clear the relationship between population growth, the positive checks and the means of subsistence. By the 'means of subsistence' he appears to mean the food supply, yet most of his positive checks were independent of the food supply. Thus 'severe labour, living in towns, unwholesome occupations, exposure to the seasons, wars, bad nursing of children and excesses of all kinds' are in no way related to the food supply. Nor is infectious disease, unless it is accepted that hunger or malnutrition make people more likely to catch the disease and less able to survive it. Modern medical research has not resolved this problem. Famine, the last of his positive checks, was of course a function of the food supply, but not necessarily a function of population growth; famines were a result of harvest failure due to bad weather or plant disease and the poor communications that made it difficult to transport grain to afflicted areas. What in effect Malthus argued was that in a society incapable of technological advance and not practising any control of births, numbers will eventually outrun agricultural output and the rising death rate will halt population growth. This is the definition of overpopulation in the Malthusian system.

Yet not all writers are agreed that Malthus did define overpopulation. Indeed, A. Carr Saunders argued that overpopulation was impossible in the system for a rise in the death rate or a fall in births always reduced the population.[6] Others have seen the theory as one of a stationary population: population will increase until numbers reach the maximum which can be maintained at a minimum standard of living, and will then be maintained at that level by a combination of positive and preventive checks.[7] But it is more common to see population in Malthus' system as an oscillating equilibrium. Any improvement in the standard of living leads to an increase in numbers; as the increase exceeds the means of subsistence so the checks are brought into play, the standard of living falls, and the rate of increase falls.[8]

In the later half of the nineteenth century Malthus' theory was generally neglected – indeed rejected – by most economists, and population ceased to play much part in economic discussion. Those who were concerned with population began to consider what is the *best* population for a country to have. The economic optimum has been variously defined as that which maximises average output per head, welfare per head or economic return per head, the first definition being followed here.

Optimum theory assumes that while population changes, other factors which influence productivity are held constant: thus the amount of land does not change, capital available remains constant, technology does not advance, the working population remains a constant proportion of the population, the

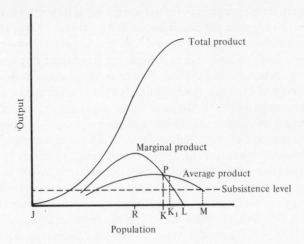

Fig. 4. Optimum population, and overpopulation.

distribution of income within the population remains unchanged, and that for analytical purposes output can be regarded as one product.[9]

Given these assumptions, the optimum is then derived from the ideas of increasing and decreasing returns. With a very small population it is not possible to benefit from economies of scale: specialisation is difficult and fixed overheads are divided amongst few people, while some factors of production cannot be used until the population is larger. Thus, during this stage not only does each increase in population give a greater average output per head but marginal output per head is above average output (fig. 4). Marginal output per head reaches its maximum when population JR is reached and thereafter declines. Total output and average output per head continue to increase as population rises from JR to JK but marginal output per head is now falling, although well above average output per head. But at population JK average output is at its maximum and marginal output per head equals average output per head. This is the optimum population. As population rises above JK total output continues to increase but average output falls and marginal output falls below the average output. In terms of optimum theory a population less than JK means a country is underpopulated for its given resources and technology, but with a population of more than JK it is overpopulated.[10] This would seem to give a simple measure of overpopulation; once the optimum population or density of a country or region is established the difference between the optimum and actual population gives a measure of overpopulation. Indeed it should be possible to give a precise measure; indices could be constructed to show comparative degrees of population pressure. Unfortunately optimum theory has grave defects both in theory and in practice.

In the first place it is an entirely static concept; it neglects the fact that as population grows, technology can change and maintain output per head.

Indeed some would argue that population growth is a spur to economic growth.[11] Secondly, neither land nor other resource will necessarily remain constant; it is often possible to increase the area under cultivation. Thirdly, it is unlikely that capital stock will remain a constant as population increases, indeed most authorities believe that the principal disadvantage of rapid population growth is that it consumes capital simply in maintaining non-productive needs such as housing, hospitals and schools for the increasing population, and reduces the amount available to invest in productive capacity. Thus, assuming a capital:output ratio of 4, in the short run, an economy whose population is growing at 1% per annum will need 4% of national income to maintain capital per head; but if population is growing at 3%, then 12% of national income will be needed. Enquiries in a number of developing countries have shown that 65% of all investment is needed just to maintain capital per head, whereas this figure is less than 25% in developed countries.[12] Fourthly, it is by no means clear to what area optimum theory is supposed to be applicable; in most discussions of the theory, it seems to be implicitly assumed that a modern industrial nation-state is being considered. Yet it can surely be argued that one part of a country can be overpopulated, another not so. Such local differences, it has been suggested, are not matters of overpopulation but are due to the imperfect mobility of labour. But there are further problems. Most discussions of optimum theory assume that the state is part of a closed economy. Thus when international trade is introduced into the argument the issue becomes even more complex.[13]

Fifthly, optimum theory refers to aggregate output per head of a country or region: it tells us nothing about the way in which aggregate income is distributed among individuals or classes within the state. It is thus perfectly possible in a country where income per head is falling due to population pressure, for the standard of living of one section of the population to be improving while that of another group or class is falling. In pre-industrial societies it was usually the ownership of land which determined this differential effect of population pressure.[14] Sixthly, there are different degrees of over-population. Any population above JK will have a lower output per head than the optimum population but population JK_1 will not experience any great fall in its standard of living, although technically it is overpopulated. At the other extreme a population at JM will be at the minimum level of subsistence and if numbers increase any further income per head will fall so low that mortality will rise so that there is no further growth; it is at this point that there occurs what is sometimes described as a Malthusian crisis.[15] However, there are clearly a wide range of populations between JK and JM which can be described as overpopulated in terms of optimum theory.

One of the assumptions of this book is that agricultural communities respond to increasing population growth by changing their farming methods or limiting their numbers. In the early stages of population growth there is little incentive to change as each increment of population increases returns per head until the maximum average output per head is reached. Once this point has been reached income per head begins to decline, and this might be supposed to trigger off either technological advance or an attempt to reduce population. But it may be that different communities will accept different standards of living, and thus there will be a time lag between the onset of population pressure and the agricultural or demographic response.

Lastly, it should be noted, it has proved very difficult to measure the optimum population and if it is not possible to do this then it is not possible to measure overpopulation. Optimum theory will then have only a heuristic value.

Attempts to measure overpopulation have been for the most part confined to agrarian communities, and were first prompted by the rural poverty found in Eastern Europe in the 1930s and in the underdeveloped world since the end of the Second World War. Two different approaches may be distinguished.[16] In the *consumption approach* the total agricultural output of the area under study is estimated and an *adequate* standard of living is postulated, measured in the same units as the total output of the area. From this it can be shown how many people could be supported in the area at the given standard of living; this figure is then compared with the actual population. In the *production* approach an attempt is made to determine the number of people required to carry out agricultural activities in the area under study during one year; this is then compared with the labour force available, and by comparison a surplus population can be calculated. This approach was first developed in Eastern Europe in the 1930s, and from this work arose the idea of disguised unemployment or underemployment in agriculture.

There have been few attempts to apply the *consumption* approach; the work of Miss Sen Gupta on India may illustrate the possibilities and limitations of this method.[17] She used data for the 335 districts of India to construct a comparative index of total overpopulation. The index of population pressure per km² was $I = (P - P_1)/A$ where P_1 was the number of rural inhabitants who could be supported at a given income (K), P the actual population in 1961, and A the total rural area of the district in km². $P_1 = X/K$ where X was the gross value of output from agriculture, fishing and forestry at current prices, K was taken as the income per head from these activities 'needed to obtain a slight improvement in standard of living for the rural population'. Thus whereas average earnings per head from the primary sector were estimated at 192 rupees in 1961, K was set at 250 rupees; this was the defined standard of living, set one fifth above actual earnings. From this data, indices were calculated for each of the 335 districts of India, and a map showing areas of underpopulation and overpopulation drawn. There are a number of obvious defects in such an approach. Actual numbers are not compared with an optimum income, but with one a little above subsistence level. Also, the gross value of primary output within a district is not an accurate guide to earnings per head. Not only will there be a difference in income accruing between say, landowners and labourers, but not all the income will be retained within the district. Thus the plantation districts of India appear on the map to be in areas of low population pressure but much of the value of output will not be retained in these districts.

The *production* approach to rural overpopulation was first attempted by a number of East European agricultural economists in the 1930s but it is the work of Doreen Warriner and W. E. Moore which is better known.[18] Both argued that if better farming methods were introduced into Eastern Europe a considerable proportion of the population would be surplus to requirements. Miss Warriner calculated the farm population densities by dividing the total farm population by the total agricultural area. She then argued that the type of farming practised in Eastern Europe was practised more efficiently in the central European states of Czechoslovakia and Hungary, where the density was 60 per 100 hectares. Densities in the countries of Eastern Europe were higher, and by comparing the densities in these Eastern European countries with the central European standard 60 per 100 hectares, a measure of labour surplus was derived.[19]

A more elaborate series of calculations was made by W. E. Moore. He began by calculating the net volume of agricultural output for each country in Europe and expressing this in Standard Crop Units. He then calculated an index of productivity by dividing the net output by the male agricultural labour force. From this he derived two measures of labour surplus. In the first estimate he calculated how many workers would be needed to produce the net agricultural output of a country if the mean European level of productivity obtained in each country. This was then compared with the actual labour force, and a surplus derived. Thus, for example, in 1930 the agricultural population of Albania was 800000, the net agricultural output was 7646000 Crop Units. If average European productivity obtained in Albania, this output could be reached by using a labour force of only 178000. Thus, 77.7% of the labour force was surplus. Moore repeated this calculation but used French productivity, which was above the European mean, and thus arrived at a series of even greater surpluses for East European countries.[20]

There have been numerous criticisms of these methods. Both Warriner and Moore used nations as the basic unit, and this may conceal very great differences within these countries. Population was related to total farm area, which included not only arable land, but also orchards, gardens, meadow and grazing land. Attempts to weight these different land uses have, however, not been very successful.[21] The total farm population also has limitations as a measure for it includes men, women and children, family labour, permanent labour and casual workers. Not all work for the same length of time in a year, or with the same effect; it would be better to express the labour available in man-hours rather than man-years.[22] Further, some of the labour surplus which is calculated in this way simply represents those parts of the year – such as the winter – when little work has to be done on the farm. Seasonal variations in labour requirements will necessarily appear as labour surplus if the surplus is calculated in this way.[23] Nor does it follow that no work is done in the slack seasons, for in simple peasant societies this time is often used in domestic industries, in maintaining farm equipment, clearing new land for cultivation or transporting and trading in farm products, activities which in more advanced societies are undertaken by specialists. Thus a labour surplus may greatly overestimate rural overpopulation. Nor does this method distinguish between the *unemployment* of hired wage labourers, and the *underemployment* of family labour, which is not made redundant and is more difficult to measure.[24]

All these points relate to the methods of measuring the available labour. More difficult are the problems of calculating labour requirements. The work of Moore and Warriner was incorporated in a number of models of economic development after the Second World War and applied to the developing countries of Afro-Asia and Latin America. It was argued that a surplus labour force existed in the agricultural sector of underdeveloped economies, that the marginal productivity of this labour was zero, and could thus be withdrawn without causing a fall in output; and that as long as the surplus labour existed in agriculture, wages in industry would not rise. This allowed industrial growth to proceed at constant and low wage levels until the agricultural surplus was exhausted.[25]

This theory has prompted many attempts to measure the amount of disguised unemployment in countries in the developing world, and apparently provides measures of rural overpopulation. Thus for example a survey of farms in part of Guatemala showed that only 38% of the available man-hours were used, in East Pakistan the surplus was put at between 15% and 20% of the total labour force, while a sample of wet-rice farms in Ceylon showed that 28% of the labour force was redundant. In Peru in 1970 it was calculated that the agricultural output could have been achieved using only 57% of the employed labour force; in Chile in the same year 33% of the available man-hours were used.[26]

Although the literature on disguised unemployment would seem to provide a guide to rural overpopulation, some qualifications must be made. In the first place Moore and Warriner argued that there would be a labour surplus in Eastern Europe if better farming methods were introduced; they did not try to measure the surplus with existing methods, possibly because of the difficulty of measuring labour requirements in a traditional system or of identifying the optimum method. Rosenstein-Roden has distinguished these two types of underemployment as *static* – without a change in methods – and *dynamic* where the surplus with improved methods is calculated.[27] Secondly, it should be noticed that disguised unemployment occurs when marginal productivity falls below zero; this point occurs when population is above the optimum, but less than that at the point where average output falls below the means of subsistence (JL in fig. 4); thus this provides a third definition of overpopulation.[28]

There is no need to pursue the long and contradictory literature on disguised unemployment, for it does not provide us with any unequivocal and simple method of measuring rural overpopulation although it does illuminate some of the agricultural consequences of overpopulation. But because it is not easy to define or measure overpopulation it does not follow that rural overpopulation does not exist. If population growth occurs in simple peasant societies without adequate technological and institutional change, then there are adverse effects on land tenure, farm size, social structure and land use. These may be called the symptoms of agrarian overpopulation and must now be considered.

CHAPTER 3

THE SYMPTOMS OF OVERPOPULATION IN AGRARIAN COMMUNITIES

Modern definitions of overpopulation do not for the most part shed much light on the problems of agricultural communities. We may agree that agricultural overpopulation is the condition where 'a greater number of people live on one unit of cultivated area than are required to work it or can possibly attain a decent standard of living from it',[1] but this does not help to identify nor measure the condition. Statements that define overpopulation in terms of population outrunning resources, or using them up at an excessive rate do not aid clarity of thought. Nor does the fact that a country cannot feed the population without importing foodstuffs mean that a country is overpopulated – unless we exclude the possibilities of international trade.[2] Optimum theory does shed some light on the problem. Overpopulation and underpopulation can only be understood in relation to an optimum number or density but in the absence of any adequate measure of the optimum, the theory loses much of its value; it is the belief of some economists that it is a sterile concept.[3]

Nonetheless optimum theory does illustrate the possibility of several types of overpopulation. As we have seen, the classical economists – Malthus and Ricardo in particular – defined overpopulation as the point where average output per head fell below the minimum subsistence level, so that mortality levels rose or marriage was deferred and population growth was halted. In contrast neo-classical writers developed optimum theory, in which overpopulation occurs whenever average output per head falls beyond the maximum. Later writers have added a third definition of overpopulation, which occurs when marginal productivity falls below zero; this lies between the optimum and the Malthusian point. It is apparent that most of the methods used to measure the degree of overpopulation are based on the classical concept, for basically they compare actual numbers with the numbers which could be supported at a minimum subsistence level or a little above it.[4]

It is not surprising that some writers have doubted the value of optimum theory in identifying conditions of rural overpopulation, or the value of the methods of measuring overpopulation, and have preferred instead to regard certain features of the agricultural land use and social structure as diagnostic of agrarian overpopulation: 'to determine even the existence of overpopulation in a given region we must...rely on the consenus of opinion', C. J. Robertson has written, 'and accept as guides what are commonly regarded as symptoms'.[5] In this chapter the symptoms of agricultural overpopulation are reviewed (fig. 6).

The subdivision of farms

In peasant societies the main factors of production are land and labour; capital plays a limited role. Few if any inputs are purchased, and equipment is simple; draught livestock are the farmer's most important capital, and in many peasant societies both past and present only the wealthier possess oxen or horses. Thus the amount of land available to the farmer is of great importance. A great many factors determine the size of farms but population density is perhaps the single most important. At present there is a close inverse relationship between average size of holding and population density for those countries which have reliable figures on farm size.[6] Not that average farm size is necessarily the best measure to show differences in farm size either geographically or over time. In countries where the bulk of the land is operated in a few large units but the majority of farms are very small – as in many Latin American countries – the average size of farm may be misleading. Modern agricultural censuses collect data on the number of farms in certain size categories, and the area occupied by these farms; this allows a more illuminating analysis of change. But such censuses were not taken in Western Europe until the second half of the nineteenth century. Before then information on farm size can only be obtained from estate records or tax returns and rarely provides convincing evidence for large areas or over a long period of time.

Nonetheless where population is increasing and no commensurate increase in the cultivated area is taking place, it is a reasonable presumption that farms will get smaller; this however depends very much on the system of land tenure. If farmers own the land they farm and have rights to determine their heirs, then subdivision will occur if partible inheritance is practised; that is to say if land passes to all the sons or all the children. Partible inheritance is the most common system in those parts of the world where the private ownership of land prevails, and it seems to have been common in most parts of Western Europe in the past. But in those systems where primogeniture occurs, and the farm passes to the eldest son, there is no subdivision; rapid population growth is not necessarily accompanied by the subdivision of farms.

Where farmers do not own the land they work, and some system of tenancy prevails, the landlord is under no obligation to divide land up to provide extra land for a growing population. In the Middle Ages landowners seem to have been under some moral duty to provide land for those who owed them dues and obligations, and subdivision did occur. But with the commercialisation of farming and the introduction of cash tenancies landlords rented land on leases to the highest bidder, to the man most likely to provide the rent and improve the tenancy. Under these circumstances, best exemplified in southern and eastern England and northern France in the nineteenth century, there is no relationship between farm size and population increase.

However, while it does not follow that rapid population growth always leads to smaller farms, there are many occasions when it does, and did. Thus in India farms of less than 2 hectares occupied 15.4% of the farm area in 1954–5, but this had risen to 19.2% in 1961–2. In South Korea the average size of farm fell from 1.2 hectares to 0.9 hectares between 1930 and 1968. In China and Java the average size of farm has been in decline since at least the beginning of this century, as it has in Egypt. Subdivision has characterised the Kikuyu lands of Kenya since the 1950s, northern Nigeria, and many parts of Latin America, where the large *hacienda* remain and the growth of the rural population has led to a proliferation of *minifundia*.[7]

The subdivision of farms does not necessarily lead to a fall in output. Modern studies of productivity in peasant agriculture suggest that output per hectare is higher on small than on large farms, as farmers are compelled to work their land more intensively or switch to high value crops to raise their income.[8] But subdivision has both in the present and in the past reduced farms below the level where it is possible to provide an adequate subsistence for a family, so that incomes have to be supplemented by working on large farms as day labourers, in domestic industry or by seasonal migration. In India in the 1950s 5 hectares was thought to be the minimum subsistence area, but 85% of all farms had less; in Galicia in the 1920s 3 hectares was thought the minimum, but only half had more, while in Ireland on the eve of the Great Famine 3 hectares was thought the subsistence minimum yet one-third of all holdings were less than this.[9]

But population growth is not the only cause of small farms; in peasant societies there is an upper limit to the area which a family can work with simple tools. In parts of Java where only hand tools are used, a man and his wife can only manage to cultivate 0.8 hectares of wet rice. In the African savannas farmers have to wait the beginnings of the rainy season before they can cultivate the hard, parched soil; weed growth is prolific in the growing season, and the area cultivated is often a function of the amount of labour available to carry out the weeding. In Iran, the farmer with the traditional wooden plough and two oxen can plough no more than 6 hectares.[10]

Fragmentation

In Britain, much of Scandinavia, North America and Australia farms usually consist of one block of land with the farm buildings on the land, ideally near the centre. But in much of Europe, Asia and Latin America the farms are fragmented, the individual fields or plots which make up the holding being dispersed among the fields of other farms. This gives rise to many problems: time is wasted going from one plot to another; land is wasted in paths and boundaries; machinery is difficult to use economically; and pests and trespassers are difficult to control. The fragmentation of farms is not a new feature of the landscape, it has existed in most of Western Europe since at least the sixteenth century. It was greatly reduced by consolidation or enclosure in Britain, Sweden, Denmark and parts of Germany in the eighteenth and nineteenth centuries; but it was not until after the Second World War that any large-scale schemes to consolidate got underway in the rest of Europe.[11]

The causes of fragmentation are far from clear, for it has few advantages to the farmer. In some cases it may have arisen because each villager sought some land on different types of soil; this is most noticeable in the wet-rice areas of Asia, where each farmer has some irrigated land, some dry land above, and a garden plot near his home. In a few cases the scattering of a farmer's fields may be a way of avoiding the risks of isolated climatic hazards, such as hailstorms, but this is hardly likely in the village communities of Western Europe, where parishes are small and climatic hazards rarely so highly localised. It may be that some scattering arises from the purchase of land. Where land is in short supply and peasants eager to purchase or rent extra land, they may be prepared to purchase plots remote from the original holding.[12] But in Western Europe scattering is often attributed to the survival of the common fields; under this system the village arable was divided into three very large fields. One was sown with winter grain, one with spring grain and one was left fallow; each field was subject to a three-year rotation. The fields were split into a large number of separate strips or plots. A farmer who had all his plots in one field would thus have all his parcels in fallow every third year, so he needed to have strips in each field.

However, it has recently been argued that the collective rules of the common-field system with the fragmentation of holdings, is a relatively modern feature in Western Europe, and was a result of population growth. In a sparsely populated area there would seem to be few advantages in a common-field system; only when grazing land and arable become in short supply would it be necessary to apply collective rules about cropping and grazing the stubble; only then would it be necessary to have parcels in each of the great fields.[13]

A further cause of fragmentation was the subdivision of farms between sons at a farmer's death; this would increase fragmentation as well as reducing the size of farm, for each son would want a share of the better soil or of the plots with the most advantageous location. Fragmentation, it might be noted, often leads to a reduction in the average size of plot as well as their dispersal. In India the larger farms – over 6 hectares – average only 3.5 parcels of farmland per hectare but the smaller – less than 0.5 hectares – average 13.1 fragments per hectare.[14]

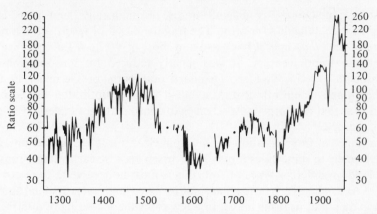

Fig. 5. Changes in the equivalent of the wage rate of a building craftsman expressed in a composite physical unit of consumables in southern England, 1264–1954 (1451–75 = 100). Source: E. H. Phelps Brown and S. V. Hopkins, 'Seven centuries of the prices of consumables, compared with builders' wage-rates', *Economica*, 23 (1956), 303–5.

Land values, rents and prices

A shortage of land has important repercussions on prices for agricultural products and for the factors of production. As population increases, the number of those seeking land grows and this affects the level of rents, the sale price of land, the price of agricultural products and the cost of labour. There are no reliable series of figures for rents and sale prices for many parts of Europe from the Middle Ages, and the only long-run figures available for wages are those for building workers, not agricultural labourers (fig. 5).[15] Nonetheless the long-run trends in this series show a fairly close correlation with population change. In the twelfth and thirteenth centuries population growth led to an abundance of labour and real wages declined. Cash rents were unusual at this time but entry fines, paid at the beginning of each tenancy, rose, as did the prices of agricultural products. In the period after 1350, when population was low after the Black Death, rents and prices stagnated, but real wages showed a great improvement on the period before 1347.

However, during the sixteenth century prices, rents and land values rose again as population increased, and real wages fell. Most of these indices changed direction again in the mid-seventeenth century, as population fell or stagnated. It was not until the second half of the eighteenth century as population increased again that prices, rents and land values rose again; so too did wages, but not on the whole as rapidly as prices, so that purchasing power fell away in the late-eighteenth and early-nineteenth centuries.

Although the trend in these indices, and their relationship to the changing demand for land and fluctuations in the numbers of those seeking paid employment on the land is clear, not all authorities are agreed that these trends are due to population pressure. The sixteenth century has been the centre of much discussion of the relative importance of monetary factors – particularly the influence of gold and silver from the Spanish Empire – upon inflation. Nor did these trends bear equally upon the well-being of all sections of the agricultural community. In periods of rising prices and rents landowners and large farmers did well; the latter could sell at increasing prices, and the abundance of labour meant that the wages of agricultural labourers did not increase as rapidly as farm prices. On the other hand farmers who produced mainly for subsistence and had little surplus to market did not benefit from rising prices and may have had their rents raised. Those without land suffered most, for they had to buy grain at high prices whilst their growing numbers kept wage increases down.

Landlessness

Most discussions of English agriculture emphasise the tripartite division of the agricultural population into those who own the land but before 1914 did not farm it themselves; the tenant farmers, who rent the land from the owners; and the agricultural labourers, who are paid wages and lack any land other than a garden and perhaps a small allotment. In the past this tripartite distinction was less clear, as it is in most parts of the world today, for there is a *continuum* between those who farm quite large holdings to those who have very small amounts of land. Indeed it is not easy to distinguish between those who are completely lacking in land, and those who have some, but need to work for wages on larger holdings. In many parts of the world, and particularly in Latin America, those who work on *haciendas* receive in return a small amount of land; they are thus both 'farmers' and day labourers, and no doubt confuse records of both farm size and labourers.[16]

There may have been a time when in Western Europe there were no farm labourers and all the land was equally divided. However, the earliest records of land holdings show marked differences in the size of holding in village communities.

This could arise in a variety of ways: a succession of small families on one farm would prevent subdivision, while in contrast a series of large families could lead to subdivision. Early death of the farmer would leave the widow and children vulnerable. Some farmers are more efficient than others, and rent or purchase extra land. Where physical and financial power was concentrated in the hands of the landowners they may expropriate land. Debt will lead to the sale of land. In these and a variety of other ways inequality in the size of holdings can arise. But a very powerful cause of inequality, and particularly of the growth of landlessness, is population growth. Whether population growth is due to lower mortality or higher fertility, it leads to competition for land. Small farms may be divided so that eventually they are too small to provide a livelihood, and so a quasi-landless population grows up, or where primogeniture occurs the younger sons swell the landless population.

Currently there has been a great increase in the landless population of the underdeveloped world, both as a proportion of the rural population and in absolute numbers, and this has occurred in spite of migration to the towns, land reform schemes which have expropriated large estates and divided them among the landless, and attempts to settle the landless in newly reclaimed areas.

In the past, periods of population growth have also seen a growth in the numbers of those without land. In England, for example, it occurred in the thirteenth century, in the sixteenth, and in the eighteenth and nineteenth centuries; while it can be argued that this was partly due to institutional processes such as enclosure, population growth seems to have been the major cause (see below, pp. 172–5).

This growth has adverse effects upon the economic condition of the landless. Their growing number leads to competition for jobs as hired labourers; periods of population growth are for the most part periods of decline in the real wages of agricultural labourers. As numbers grow, there is not always work for everyone, even at the height of the demand for labour, during the harvest, and unemployment results. Population growth affects the use of labour even on family farms; here there is no question of unemployment, but there is underemployment: as the numbers on the farm increase, work-sharing becomes more common, and each individual works less.[17] Under these conditions it is possible that a considerable proportion of the labour force could be withdrawn without any loss in output. It has been suggested that England before the Black Death and Ireland before the Famine were in this situation.[18]

Technology and labour supply

During the last thirty years there have been very marked increases in the agricultural populations of most parts of the Third World. This of course provided farmers with an abundance of labour at low cost; and it has almost certainly retarded the adoption of labour-saving machinery. Population growth has not only created surplus labour, but it has reduced the size of farms and thus has made the use of machinery uneconomic.

Prior to the nineteenth century there were few innovations in agriculture which were overtly labour-saving. The horse was faster than the ox, but this increased the number of cultivations that could be carried out – particularly the use of the harrow in late spring – rather than reducing the amount of labour that was needed. The seed drill, although designed in the early eighteenth century, was not widely adopted in England until after 1800 and in France until after 1850. The flail remained the main means of threshing grain in most of Western Europe until the second half of the nineteenth century, and in England the abundance of labour in the early nineteenth century undoubtedly delayed the adoption of the threshing machine. The reaper, imported from the United States in 1851, was only slowly adopted in Europe, and the growing harvest needs were met by replacing the sickle with the scythe.[19] Indeed the general use of agricultural machinery largely awaited the decline of the agricultural population, which began in Britain in the middle of the nineteenth century, in Belgium and Switzerland two decades later, and in France and Germany towards the end of the century.[20]

Land use

The effects of population growth are perhaps most apparent upon the economic structure of agriculture but it also has consequences for land use. One of the fundamental features of any agricultural system is that it takes more land to produce a given number of calories from livestock than from crops. Thus in any pre-industrial society with a dense population, a high proportion of the land will be under food crops – in Western Europe cereals – and little land will be devoted to crops to feed animals, and the animals will for the most part rely upon natural vegetation for their fodder. Livestock will be kept, in fact, mainly for their use as draught animals.

In Western Europe the parish was the main unit of farm organisation; within the boundaries of the parish were found: the great arable fields surrounding the village; the valuable land by the river, used for meadow, cut for hay and then open to common grazing; woodland, the source of fuel and feed for pigs; and the waste land grazed in common by the livestock of the villagers.

Any increase in population had adverse effects. It led to clearing of woodland and waste for extra arable land; much of this would be marginal land, giving lower yields and liable to soil erosion. It also reduced the amount of grazing land, which in turn reduced the amount of manure available for crops, so that yields declined. Expansion into common grazing land has always caused conflict: between peasant and landlord, between rich peasant and poor peasant, and between squatters and peasants. Attempts to control the rights to grazing both on common land and the arable stubble after harvest are generally made in periods of population growth. Thus population pressure was a problem for farming in Western Europe until the adoption of fodder crops on the fallow provided extra fodder, extra manure and higher yields.[21]

Population growth may also affect the type of crop grown. Away from the urban areas farmers in pre-industrial Europe grew mainly cereals and small amounts of vegetables. But with the rise in population in the eighteenth century there was an increase in the growth of what were then thought to be inferior food crops, potatoes and maize, which had hitherto been only grown as crops for livestock. Their advantage was their much higher yields. Similar switches to inferior but higher yielding crops can be found in densely populated areas in the developing world today: in Java sweet potatoes have replaced rice in some areas, and in Africa cassava has ousted the traditional yams.[22]

Thus there are a variety of ways in which overpopulation can be detected in rural communities. Indeed those discussed do not exhaust the list; to them may be added emigration, both permanent and seasonal, vagrancy, pauperism and banditry; in short, population pressure causes poverty. But some cautionary comments must be made. Many of the symptoms noted here may have alternative explanations. Thus many regard the rise of a landless population to be a result of enclosure; a decline in crop yields may be due to poor weather and not to the use of marginal land.

Also, it should not be thought that all these symptoms will appear in every region. What symptoms occur will depend upon, *inter alia*, the type of farming practised, the density of population, and the location of the area in relation to urban markets. If the area is one of family farms subdivision is more likely than the growth of landlessness, but in in area of large tenant farms subdivision is unlikely and an increase in the number of landless labourers is more probable. Nonetheless it should be possible to diagnose the existence of rural overpopulation by reference to the criteria discussed in this chapter.

CHAPTER 4

THE POSSIBILITIES OF INCREASED OUTPUT IN PRE-INDUSTRIAL SOCIETIES

In chapter 3 it was argued that in the absence of technological change population growth will have adverse effects upon the structure of agriculture and the pattern of land use, all of which lead to a decline in income per head. But clearly a community threatened with overpopulation, in which average output per head is beginning to decline, does have a number of possible ways of arresting this decline (fig. 7). It may reduce its population – or at least retard the rate of population increase – by limiting births, or by emigration. With no changes in technology, output per head swings back towards the optimum. Alternatively it may seek to increase its income by increasing output in agriculture and by turning to alternative sources of income, so that output rises faster than population, and output or income per head again swings back towards the maximum. Technological advance increases output and also creates a new and higher optimum density. These two approaches are not mutually exclusive. Any agricultural community may, in the face of population pressure, combine birth control, emigration, and improved farming methods to regain the optimum. In this chapter, however, we will consider the possibilities of increasing income in rural communities. As, however, this work deals with agricultural communities before, or during the early stages of industrialisation, some note must be taken of the differences between rural societies before and after the age of urbanisation and the industrialisation of agriculture.

Peasant societies and their characteristics

There is a large and contentious literature on the nature of 'peasant' societies; these are seen as societies which differ both from simple tribal communities, and from the commercialised farmers of modern North America and Western Europe.[1] Their definition will not be pursued here; we will simply note some of the ways in which pre-industrial peasants – or farmers – differ from modern farmers.

The peasant – whether contemporary or historical – is seen as having as his prime aim the provision of as much of his own consumption needs as possible without resort to the market.[2] This means that he will concentrate upon growing food crops – in Western Europe generally cereals – and will keep some livestock for milk, meat and wool, but because of the high cost of livestock, they play a minor role in his diet and the workings of his farm. However, the truly self-sufficient subsistence farmer was rare, because he has always had to pay rent, tithe and tax; and from the fifteenth century these were increasingly demanded in cash. Thus whereas it is true that as late as the nineteenth century many peasants in Western Europe were not fully integrated into a national market, the idealised 'natural economy' must have been eroded at a very early date. However, the primacy of self-sufficiency does influence the peasant's choice of crops and methods. The need to provide the family's food precludes experiments with new, non-food crops, thus early specialisation in non-food crops came only in areas with a developed transport and marketing system.

The peasant farm is identical with the peasant household; the first aim is to provide the consumption needs of the household but income comes not only from the land, but from the activities of the household as a whole. Household income includes not only agricultural goods but earnings from 'industries' carried on at home, the practice of crafts, and earnings from seasonal and temporary migrations. These non-agricultural earnings may be considerable. A sample of farmer's wills in sixteenth-century England shows that two-thirds had some 'by-employment', and a sample of Russian peasant households at the beginning of this century shows that income from crafts and other domestic activities equalled income from agriculture.[3]

Peasant farms rely mainly upon family labour to work the land, and only occasionally hire day-labour. Although this may be true of most parts of Western Europe before the nineteenth century, it must not be forgotten that most villages would have one or two richer peasants – yeomen, *kulaks* or the *coq du village* – who would need labourers. But small family farms, with less than 8 hectares, were the dominant unit in the social structure. Farmers with these areas probably did not aim at profit maximisation. They aimed at providing family needs, and the demands of state, church and landlord. Once this target income had been gained, they balanced the rewards of extra labour against its irksomeness. Thus, to attain the target income the family might have to work beyond the point where marginal output falls below average output per head; thus population densities in peasant societies may be higher than in areas where farmers aim to maximise their profits.

Although many writers have emphasised the isolation of peasant communities, anthropologists have argued that peasant communities, in contrast to tribal societies, are always subordinate to some external force – landlord, state or church.[4] Not only does much of their income flow out of the village but the forces of change in peasant society have nearly always come from outside rather than being generated from within the community. Thus agricultural change comes from the rise of urban demand, the improvement of transport systems or the spread of new crops. Within the village community, from the fourteenth to the eighteenth or nineteenth century, farmers have been subject to the collective control of the village community, both in the choice of crops, and the stocking of the land. Not until the modern period has the individual been able to fully exploit the possibilities of his land untrammelled by village custom.

Not only does the peasant consume most of his own products, but most of his inputs are generated on the farm. Land and labour are the main inputs, capital plays a limited role, and additions to the capital stock are often the result of his own labour, in clearing new land, building barns and constructing farm implements. Common grazing inhibited selective breeding and prevented the import of stock from outside. The seed for the next crop came from his own harvest and was not purchased. Labour came mainly from the farm family. Fertilisers were unimportant, and livestock manure provided the bulk of the little used; only in a few areas, such as Flanders or Northern Italy, were urban wastes used, while the artificial fertiliser was unknown before the 1840s. Where the peasant was able to save and accumulate capital, he would often prefer to buy land to add to the family stock, rather than to purchase inputs which would help to increase output more efficiently than extending the area of the farm. This is because of the importance of land in family inheritance systems and the provision of dowries. All this contrasts with the modern capitalist farmer who hires labour, purchases seed, implements, feeds for livestock, artificial fertilisers and pesticides. In some Western economies today production costs take 60% of gross farm income.[5]

Peasant farmers have been and are reluctant to innovate because of the risks attached to innovation. Traditional farming was closely adjusted to local conditions; the farmer knew that in the absence of very bad weather, his combination of crops and methods would give a guaranteed return, if not the maximum possible. On the other hand new methods or new crops might fail; and failure was far more serious for the peasant with a handful of acres and a large family than for the modern capitalist farmer. Failure for the peasant could mean starvation; failure for the modern farmer only means a reduced income, at the worst bankruptcy. Thus, as Michael Lipton has put it, the peasant seeks survival algorithms, not maximising ones.[6]

Increasing agricultural output: expanding the cultivated area

We turn now to consider the ways in which the peasant of the pre-industrial age could increase agricultural output. It must be recalled that the capacity to increase productivity was limited compared with that of the modern farmer. In the last forty years cereal yields in England have nearly doubled due to the adoption of improved varieties, the increased application of artificial fertilisers and the use of herbicides and pesticides. Output per man has also increased as machinery has been substituted for man-power. Indeed in many Western countries productivity increase has been faster in agriculture than in industry in the last few decades.[7]

Such rapid increases in crop yields were not possible before the nineteenth century. When yield increases came, they were from the wider adoption of techniques often generally known but not used. Consequently the most obvious way to increase output was to bring new land into cultivation. Indeed this remains the most important way of increasing output in much of the world today. Estimates of the world's arable area are available from about 1870. Between 1870 and 1970 it doubled. Between 1870 and 1950 arable expansion kept up with population growth, with area per head remaining at about half a hectare, but since 1950 this has slowly declined.[8]

Before the nineteenth century there are few estimates of national arable area. But the literary and cartographic evidence suggests that in most parts of Western Europe the arable area expanded and contracted in step with movements in population and prices. From AD 1100 to 1300 the area slowly increased; after 1350 it declined as population fell, villages were abandoned, and only the better soils were cultivated. The sixteenth century saw a revival of arable cultivation; farmers returned to moorlands long abandoned to sheep, and marshes were drained and embanked. The final phase of expansion began in the middle of the eighteenth century, and reached its maximum in the late nineteenth century. In 1970 Europe's arable area was much the same as it had been in 1900.[9]

Two types of land reclamation can be distinguished. First was the encroachment of the village arable lands into the surrounding wood and waste; this was a slow process, as a plot was added here, a parcel there, sometimes by individual effort, sometimes by the collective efforts of all the villagers. The newly reclaimed land was then divided among those who had cleared the land, to add to the fragmentation of the village lands. Occasionally clearances were made deep in the forest, between two villages, and a daughter settlement established, a process recorded in the place-names of England, France and Germany. By 1300 the settlement of much of Western Europe had been achieved, although the process of slow expansion into heath, moor and woodland continued.

A second type of reclamation required the colonisation of land hitherto uncultivated or sparsely populated. The most dramatic of these was the movement of German-speaking farmers east of the Elbe in the eleventh and twelfth centuries, to settle in Slav-speaking lands. But large-scale reclamation of fen and marsh, often requiring large numbers of labourers, organisation and capital took place in coastal areas, particularly Holland and Flanders but also on the French and English coastlands.

It is sometimes suggested that the slow expansion of the arable area in Europe took farmers into progressively poorer lands, and reduced yields. This was not always so. The earliest farmers who established the primary rural settlements in the second half of the first millennium looked for places where they could easily clear the natural vegetation and also cultivate the soil with the ard. New technologies changed the farmer's assessment of land; the heavy, mouldboard plough made it possible to cultivate and drain, however imperfectly, heavy clays, with their high nutrient status. Several hundreds of years later the adoption of high farming gave the easily tilled but shallow limestone soils an advantage over the heavy clays. Some of the richest soils in Europe were not settled until, first the windmill, and then the steampump, made their drainage effective.

Although such large-scale schemes as the drainage of the English fenlands or the Dutch polders required organisation and capital, most of the additions to the European cultivated area were carried out by individuals or village communities, the clearance being undertaken in the slack season of winter. It was labour not capital that expanded the cultivated area. The progress of the arable area, seen in the long run, marched in time with the rise and fall in population. But at some times and in some places increases did not match population growth, nor were the new lands always going to those without land. And where these two deficiencies came together, the problems of overpopulation were most acute.

Increasing the frequency of cropping

If cereal crops are grown continuously upon the same piece of land without a break and without the use of fertilisers or manure, crop yields will decline as the initial soil fertility is exhausted. Plant diseases specific to the crop become endemic, and it is difficult to keep weeds down. In modern agriculture artificial fertilisers, herbicides and pesticides have made continuous cereal cultivation possible. But in the past it was impracticable, and a period of fallow, where the land carries no crop for a season or more, was found in every traditional agricultural system before the eighteenth century. This of course meant that part of the arable land was not in use. The elimination of the fallow in traditional agriculture was finally achieved by the adoption of rotations including a root crop and artificial grasses. Clover and other legumes helped to maintain soil nitrogen and provided extra grazing and thus more manure. Root crops, sown in rows, allowed weeding during cultivation, and, like the grasses, prevented the build up of cereal disease. Turnips and other roots such as mangolds provided winter fodder which helped to increase the supply of farmyard manure. Sugar-beet acted as a break and cleaning crop, a source of cash, and the remnants of the beet after sugar had been extracted could be fed to livestock. The potato provided human food as well as animal food, needed careful weeding and manuring, and helped to build up fertility for the following cereal crop.

But there were few parts of Europe where the fallow was not found before the eighteenth century. In the more sparsely populated areas and on poorer soils land was broken up, sown for a few years, and then abandoned. The re-establishment of the natural vegetation allowed soil fertility to recover. More common were the two- and three-field systems, where in the first case half the arable was fallow in each year, and one-third in the other. The two-field system persisted longer in southern Europe, for in areas of drought it was one of the few ways of building up soil moisture. But at the opening of the present millennium it was common in much of northern Europe. The introduction of the three-field system thus reduced the fallow and increased the area under cultivation.

The reduction of the fallow was a major way of increasing the area under crops in Western Europe. In the eighth century the two-field system predominated in both north and south; the first three-field system has been identified in the same century, but it was not until the twelfth and thirteenth centuries that the three-field began to replace the two-field system in the more densely populated areas, and not until the eighteenth and nineteenth centuries that the fallow began to be extinguished.[10] Ester Boserup has seen the reduction of fallow as the central theme in agricultural history.[11] She has argued that output per man-hour is highest in long-fallow systems, and it is only the stimulus of population growth that leads to the reduction of fallow. She envisaged a series of progressively more intensive land-use systems following in sequence as population density increases. When an area is sparsely populated and there is a forest cover, land is cleared, cropped for two or three years, and then left under natural fallow for twenty-five years or more before it is cleared again. The only tools needed are a dibbling stick and an axe, and the recolonisation by secondary forest restores soil fertility. Further increases in population require the reduction of the length of fallow. With *bush* fallowing the length of fallow is between six and ten years, and the forest cannot re-establish itself; bush and grasses require the use of the hoe, which was not necessary with the forest-fallow. When *short* fallowing, with only two or three years fallow, is forced upon the cultivator, Mrs Boserup argues that the plough has to be used. Eventually *annual* cropping, with no year-long fallow, has to be adopted, and finally *multiple* cropping, where more than one crop is grown in a year on the same land.

A shift to higher yielding crops

Food crops vary a great deal in their yield, in their calorific output, and in the loss of calorific content during preparation. Some indication of the range at present in West Africa can be seen in table 3. The root crops – with the exception of cocoyams – compensate for their low calorific value with very high yields; manioc yields over four times more calories per hectare than millet and sorghum, and this together with the rapid increase in population this century accounts for its rapid diffusion through Africa since its introduction from the Americas.[12]

Prior to the discovery of America there were no very great differences in the yields and calorific values of the food crops in Western Europe; wheat and rye provided flour for bread, barley provided malt for beer but also could

Table 3. *Staple crop yields and calorific output in Africa*

	Yield/ha (tonnes)	Calories per 100 grams	Index of calorific yield
Millet & sorghum	0.6	345	100
Rice	0.7	359	121
Maize	0.7	360	122
Cocoyams (Taro)	3.0	86	125
Sweet potatoes	4.0	97	187
Yams	6.0	90	261
Plantains	8.0	75	290
Manioc	8.0	109	421

SOURCE: B. F. Johnston, *The staple food economies of western tropical Africa* (Stanford, 1958), p. 93.

be used in gruel; oats formed the basis of porridge, oat-cakes and gruel, whilst buckwheat was grown as a food crop in some areas. Vegetables were only grown in small quantities, and peas and beans were the most common. Before 1492 there was little possibility of shifting to higher yielding crops. But both maize and potatoes give higher yields per hectare than the existing food crops. Under modern conditions potatoes yield twice the calorific value per hectare that wheat does, and a third more protein; maize a quarter more calories but one-sixth less protein. But as the yield of wheat has increased more than that of the potato since the eighteenth century, the advantage of the potato was probably greater in the past.[13]

The potato and maize were, until recently, climatically complementary, the potato being grown in northern and central Europe, maize being confined to the hotter regions of the south and south-east. But until the middle of the eighteenth century neither crop had been adopted on any scale in Western Europe except in Ireland, where the potato was already a significant but not a major part of the diet, and Aquitaine, where maize was grown for fodder and food. Thereafter both crops increased in importance in their particular regions, and by the mid-nineteenth century the potato had become a major food crop in all the countries of Western Europe. Unfortunately, the chronology of adoption is difficult to trace. Some believe that it was the rapid adoption of the potato and maize that increased the food supply and allowed the great increase in Europe's population after 1750.[14] Others, however, noting that most Europeans regarded the potato as a fodder crop, believe that it was only adopted as population growth outran the increase in the cereal area, and see its growing importance as a sign of impoverishment.[15]

Increasing labour inputs

Land and labour were the principal inputs in the pre-industrial agricultural economy, and the ownership of labour was almost as important as the ownership of land. Indeed some have seen the rise of serfdom in the later part of the first millennium as an attempt to gain control of a labour force in a sparsely populated society. Certainly output could be increased by greater application of labour to the land. Ploughing depended upon the number of oxen or horses available; but weeding, the use of mallets to break the clods formed by the plough, the movement of manure, the application of lime, marling, underdrainage and a variety of other tasks depended upon labour; and the greater application of labour would always produce some increase in output, just as more harvesters and gleaners could rescue more grain from the fields. Of course without any advance in technology there would come a point where diminishing returns to labour would set in. But as was noted earlier in this chapter, peasants who aim for a target output would not be unduly influenced by this.

Technological advance in the agriculture of pre-industrial Europe

In the last fifty years there have been quite remarkable changes in agricultural technology in the Western world, the result of the application of science to agronomy and plant breeding, and the adoption by farmers of inputs manufactured by industry. The beginnings of this transformation of traditional agriculture can be traced back to the 1840s.[16] Before that the pace of technological change was slow. But this is not to say that there was no progress. There are no reliable figures on crop yields for England before the 1880s, when the average yield of wheat for the country as a whole was 2020 kg/ha. In the 1820s a sample of yields in midland and southern England put the average yield at 1410 kg/ha.[17] Before this date the yield figures are fragmentary and often only come from the better farmed estates. One of the best existing series is that for the Winchester estates between 1209 and 1349; nearly half the yields recorded in this period fell between 540 and 810 kg/ha; data from other estates in the fourteenth century suggest average yields of 675–810 kg/ha.[18] The mean yield for the whole of the Winchester estate between 1209 and 1349 was 675 kg/ha. This suggests that between 1200 and the 1820s there was a sufficient flow of innovations in English agriculture to at least double output per hectare. Slicher van Bath's studies of seed–yield ratios suggest an increase of comparable magnitude: the average ratio in England in the first half of the thirteenth century was 1:3.7, but this had risen to 1:10.6 by 1750–1820. France had a ratio of 1:3.0 before 1200, but this did not rise above 1:10 until after 1820.[19]

In England in the 1820s traditional agriculture still prevailed. Seed drills were still uncommon, and the flail had not been replaced by the threshing machine except in a few areas in Scotland and eastern England. The harvest was still reaped with the sickle, although the scythe was gaining ground. Artificial fertilisers were not manufactured until the 1840s and guano was not yet imported. Animals were fed largely on crops grown on the farm; the age of imported oil-cakes and other feeds was yet to come. Thus a national yield of 1410 kg/ha probably represents the best that traditional agriculture could manage; yields would of course have been higher in eastern and southern England, where the climate was more suited to cereal growing, and doubtless higher yields would have been obtained on the better managed farms.

It would be out of place here to notice all the changes in agricultural technology that would have produced the slow increase of yields between 1200 and 1820. But they can be divided into two broad categories: those that improved the cultivation of the soil and the maintenance of a good tilth; and those that helped to maintain and increase soil fertility.

The main implement used by farmers was the plough, although in some parts of Western Europe the hoe was still used for breaking the soil as late as the eleventh century. At the beginning of this millennium the ard was still in general use in northern Europe. Light and wooden, the ard had been developed in the Mediterranean; it did little more than scratch the soil and was not very effective in the heavy wet soils of the north. It was improved by adding a coulter, which could cut the turf, an improved share, and a mouldboard which turned the sod. This all needed a large wooden frame, and wheels were sometimes added; it needed a larger team of oxen to pull this heavy implement. But it allowed much more thorough cultivation, and made possible the cultivation of intractable clays, and the formation of ridge and furrow which gave some drainage. This type of plough seems to have been widely adopted by the thirteenth century. Frost broke up the heavy clods left after ploughing, although mallets were sometimes used; harrows were primitive until the sixteenth century, and often no more was done than to drag a thorn brush over the soil. The use of the horse in ploughing and harrowing speeded up the process of preparing the seed bed, and allowed more frequent cultivations which would have increased yields. Until the adoption of the drill, for the most part delayed until the nineteenth century, seed was broadcast by hand or dibbled. Weeding was carried out with the hoe, and the frequency of weeding depended upon the labour available. As long as seed was broadcast, weeding during the later stages of growth was impossible. Once the mouldboard and coulter had been added to the ard, the only improvements made to the plough were the use of metal for the contact parts, and the design of innumerable local ploughs adapted to special conditions of slope and soil. The very slow progress in implement design allowed only equally slow increases in yield.

Once a seed bed had been prepared crop yields depended upon the weather, which could not be controlled, weeding, and the maintenance of soil fertility; the fallow played a limited role in this, for only a long fallow where the natural vegetation was restored could build up soil fertility. Hence the major element in maintaining soil fertility was livestock manure; this depended upon the number of animals which could be kept, which in turn depended upon the fodder resources available to the village community. This in turn relied upon the population density: the higher the density the greater the area under cereals, the less grazing available to the animals. But if livestock manure was the major element in maintaining soil fertility, it was supplemented by a wide range of other fertilisers. Near the coast seaweed and sand were used; crushed bones provided phosphorus, marl improved soil texture, lime reduced acidity. But until the fourteenth century no crops were known that could help restore soil fertility except beans, vetch and peas. The use of clover was thus of fundamental importance; it became widely used in the Low Countries and then in England after 1650. It added to grazing and helped to restore soil fertility, creating soil nitrogen; combined with turnips, which allowed weeding during growth, it gave rise to rotations which ended the fallow, checked plant disease, increased stocking densities and raised the supply of manure.

The dating of the adoption of these innovations and many others, such as the use of water-meadows, underdraining, ley farming and so forth, is extremely difficult; even in the modern period it has led to furious debates about the timing of the agricultural revolution in different parts of Europe. However, it would seem that progress after 1600 was greater than in the period before. Clover and turnips, for example, were little used before then in the Low Countries or England. It seems likely that yields increased more rapidly after 1600 than before.

The division of labour and regional specialisation

In the simplest peasant societies the household not only grows its own food and raises livestock, it also makes its own clothes and simple implements, and carries its produce to market. Thus there are few specialists, and the level of craftsmanship is low; furthermore, the peasant household may well find it cannot spend enough time upon its agricultural tasks. Efficiency may thus be greatly improved if the non-agricultural tasks are undertaken by specialists – blacksmiths, carpenters, cobblers, corn merchants, carriers and so forth. Unfortunately the history of rural specialisation is little known. The censuses of the nineteenth century reveal the remarkable diversity of occupations in rural England, and recent work has shown the growth of this specialisation in Holland in the sixteenth century. But it is difficult to mark where and when it first arose. Nonetheless it is one important way in which income per head could have been increased.[20]

So too was regional specialisation. As long as agriculture remained self-sufficient each household had to produce a range of goods to satisfy consumption needs; cereals were the main item, but livestock were kept for draught, manure, and perhaps milk. Once transport improved and a system for trading in corn was established, it was possible for each region to specialise in those products for which it had, in climate, soil or location, a comparative advantage. But such specialisation was slow to come in much of Europe before the nineteenth century. The earliest areas of specialisation were those near great cities and with easy contacts with waterways. The earliest signs of specialisation, in industrial crops such as flax, madder, woad, hops and in dairy products, came in Flanders and Holland, where there was a precocious growth of cities and easy import of Baltic grain. Until the arrival of the railway, however, it was only high-value products, such as wool, cheese and wine that entered into any but local trade.

Domestic industry and seasonal migration

The peasant economy, then, lacked any marked division of labour. Equally significant was the fact that industry was not concentrated in towns. It is true that in the heyday of the guild system the towns of western Europe had much of the manufacturing. But with the decline of the guilds industry in the fourteenth and fifteenth centuries it became increasingly located in rural areas. Rural households could supplement their incomes by working in these industries. Of most importance was the textile industry; much of the industry was organised by urban merchants who put out flax and wool for spinning and thread for weaving to farm households and labourers' cottages.

Seasonal and temporary migration was another way for the peasant to supplement his income. In parts of Europe labourers and small peasants could move to other areas to help with the harvest. This was well established in southern France, where the difference in height between the uplands of the Massif Central, the Alps and the lowlands of Languedoc gave a difference in the timing of the harvest. Longer periods of residence in the towns as labourers also helped supplement farm incomes, and often led to permanent migration.[21]

Thus the peasant community was not without means of increasing output and income in the face of rising populations. But they were rarely dramatic. There were no green revolutions in the pre-industrial world. In the event of failure to match population growth with output growth, the peasant community could however attempt to control its numbers. To these demographic adjustments to population growth we must now turn.

CHAPTER 5

DEMOGRAPHIC ADJUSTMENTS TO POPULATION GROWTH

The ways in which output can be increased have been discussed in chapter 4. Their application may well stave off the consequences of population growth; population grows, but so too does output, and average output per head may be maintained. If technological advance is inadequate then the community can also limit the rate of population growth, either by controlling the number of births or by emigrating. If technological advance, emigration and the limitation of births cannot prevent a fall in output per head then, as average income per head falls to the minimum level of subsistence, mortality will rise and eventually halt the rate of population increase. This, however, is hardly a strategy likely to be chosen by any community, nor is the relationship between rising mortality and living standards as simple as Malthusian theory suggests.

Fertility control

Older writers on the demography of pre-industrial societies often assumed that fertility was uncontrolled and that fertility was high and constant. Indeed some writers still maintain such a view. Such authorities believe that before the late nineteenth century marriage was universal and early, and that there was no birth control within marriage; the long-term decline in fertility which has taken place in Western Europe since 1880 is thus thought to have no precedent. At first sight this view has much to support it. Effective physical methods of birth control were not available until the second half of the nineteenth century; and before then public discussion of what means there were was restricted, so that comparatively few people, even in urbanised societies, could have known about these methods.

But this viewpoint has been greatly undermined in the last ten or twenty years by the work of historical demographers. They have shown that in pre-industrial Europe – or at least in Western Europe – marriage was comparatively late; that it was not universal; that fertility fell far short of the biological maximum; and that there were marked variations in fertility between regions.

All this suggests that pre-industrial societies attempted to control their numbers. Indeed modern studies of primitive societies show that they have methods of regulating their numbers, while the work of animal ecologists shows that both mammals and birds have social mechanisms to prevent numbers outrunning resources. Animal communities rarely allow their numbers to rise so as to outrun food resources; starvation is rare among wild animals. Two processes help to control numbers: hierarchy and territory. Animals low in the hierarchy are unable to get mates, while those unable to defend a territory cannot breed.[1]

Evidence on fertility levels before the nineteenth century is difficult to obtain. Births, deaths and marriages were registered by the clergy in Norway, Sweden and Denmark from the middle of the eighteenth century, and together with the census counts dating from the same period, can be used to calculate crude birth and death rates.[2] In England and France parish clergy recorded baptisms, burials and marriages for their parishes and these data can be analysed in two ways: by aggregating the numbers to show changes in the total numbers of births, deaths and marriages from year to year; and by the method of family reconstitution, which does not allow the calculation of crude rates, but permits the construction of more sophisticated measures for a closed group, such as age-specific fertility and mortality, and the average age of marriage. Such calculations are available for a number of parishes in France after 1670, and for one parish in England from the 1550s to the introduction of civil registration.[3]

In the absence of effective physical methods of birth control within marriage, how could fertility be controlled in pre-industrial societies? One determinant of fertility is the number remaining unmarried during the reproductive period. It has been observed that a higher proportion of the population of Western Europe remained unmarried in the seventeenth, eighteenth and ninetenth centuries than of the population of Eastern Europe, or indeed of much of the rest of the world, and that before the seventeenth century celibacy was less marked and marriage earlier.[4] Unfortunately reliable evidence on long-run trends in the proportion married are hard to come by. However, there is one good example of the influence of celibacy on fertility. In Ireland age-specific fertility rates remained largely unchanged from the 1880s to the 1950s. However, the proportion remaining unmarried rose, as did the age of marriage.[5]

Changes in the age at first marriage provide a second method of controlling numbers, for the higher the age of marriage the fewer the births possible within marriage. Studies of villages in England and France suggest that there have been long-term changes in the age of first marriage. Thus in Colyton in Devon the mean age of brides in the late sixteenth century and early seventeenth century was 27.0 years, rose to 29.6 in 1647–1719 and fell to 25.1 between 1770 and 1837.[6]

A third possible method of retarding population growth is to limit the number of births within marriage. This was the distinctive method throughout Western Europe after 1880, for fertility declined without any major changes in the proportion marrying or in the age of marriage. Some authors doubt that limitation of births within marriage occurred before the second half of the nineteenth century. However, some studies of the spacing of births within marriage in seventeenth-century England, eighteenth-century Sweden and early nineteenth-century France suggest that some form of limitation of numbers took place. Before the age of physical methods of contraception it must be assumed that *coitus interruptus* was the principal means, although changes in the length of suckling may have been significant.[7]

Although there is still much to be discovered about fertility and fertility controls in pre-industrial society, there is now sufficient evidence to suggest that peasant communities could exert some control over their numbers, and indeed may have reduced family size as population pressure increased. Such a reaction has been described as homeostatic, a fall in income being compensated for by a fall in the number of births.[8]

Migration as a form of control

Migration is sometimes thought of as a modern feature, a result of the Industrial Revolution and the transformation of the transport system in the nineteenth century. Yet there was a remarkable mobility in pre-industrial societies, as studies of English villages have shown, even though the distances moved may have been short.

Migrations may be classified in a number of ways; we need note here only three types: rural–rural, rural–urban and overseas migration. Rural–rural migration can be divided into two types, already noted in chapter 4. There was movement over very short distances from the primary rural settlements to found daughter settlements in the waste and woodland between villages; this had largely been completed by the fourteenth century. There was also the movement into more distant unoccupied areas to found new villages; this was at its height in the second half of the first millennium; it continued in the twelfth and thirteenth centuries as Germans moved east of the Elbe and the Spanish reoccupied southern Spain. Thereafter there were few opportunities for frontier settlement in Western Europe, although in the eighteenth century the Hungarians occupied the Aföld after the retirement of the Turks, and in the nineteenth century there was colonisation in northern Scandinavia.[9] But after the Middle Ages there was little space left for colonisation which could afford relief from population pressure. The main direction of migration was from the countryside to the towns.

Until the nineteenth century Western Europe was overwhelmingly rural. In 1800 the Netherlands, Belgium and Britain were the only countries with more than 10% of their population in towns of more than 10000 people.[10] In the nineteenth century there was a remarkable increase in both the urban population – urban growth – and also in the proportion of the population living in urban places – urbanisation. But this did not mean that there was no rural–urban migration before the nineteenth century. Indeed such little evidence as exists on differences between rural and urban fertility and mortality suggests that most towns could only maintain their numbers by immigration, for the death rate in the towns not only exceeded that in the countryside, but exceeded the birth rate in the towns. This was particularly true of the very large towns such as London, Paris and Amsterdam where overcrowding and poor sanitation encouraged epidemic disease.

Thus there was a constant movement from the countryside to the town; most migrants moved only very short distances, and only the great cities had migration fields extending much beyond 50 km. In Stratford upon Avon in the thirteenth century 90% of the immigrant burgesses came from within 26 km; in 1851 70% of the migrants into Preston came from within 48 km.[11]

It cannot be argued that this movement was simply a result of overpopulation in the countryside, for the attraction of the towns was equally important as a cause of movement. But whatever the cause, rural–urban migration did offer a partial safety-valve for many rural areas. But it could not afford a major outlet until the possibilities of urban employment grew rapidly, and this did not occur until the nineteenth century. With the rapid growth of manufacturing industry and secondary employments – particularly domestic service – the flow to the towns became so great that rural populations began a permanent decline in numbers and as a proportion of the total population. This decline in many ways marks the end of the peasant community. In most countries it coincided with the early stages of the Industrial Revolution, the spread of the railway and the beginnings of the industrialisation of agriculture. It began in Britain in the 1850s, in Belgium and France in the 1860s, and in Germany in the 1880s; in much of Eastern Europe it did not take place until after the Second World War, while throughout the underdeveloped world rural populations still continue to increase.[12]

For a short period overseas migration offered an opportunity to reduce the rate of population growth. From the sixteenth century there was movement from Western Europe to colonies in America, particularly by the Spanish and British. Yet numbers were small both in an absolute sense, and as a proportion of the home population; indeed it was not until the 1840s that it was possible to carry large numbers safely and cheaply across the Atlantic. But between 1845 and 1855 some two million left Ireland, and three-quarters of a million left Germany between 1850 and 1855. The flow from Europe increased throughout the rest of the century, reaching a peak in the period before the First World War. Until the 1860s the bulk of emigration was from the British Isles and Germany, but Scandinavia then played an important role, and at the beginning of the twentieth century southern and eastern Europe was providing three-quarters of all immigrants to the United States.[13] Emigration did not affect all parts of Europe equally; the rate from France, Switzerland, Belgium, and the Netherlands was remarkably low; that from Norway, Britain, Ireland and Italy very high. After the First World War the flow of emigration declined, and most of the countries in Europe went through the process of industrialisation and ceased to be largely agrarian. Overseas emigration then provided a release from overpopulation for only a very short period, from 1840 to 1914. As with rural–urban migration it cannot be seen only as a function of rural population pressure, for the attractions of the United States, and the other countries of new settlement were important factors in the timing of emigration.

Mortality as a control of population

In Malthus' system the major control over population growth was mortality. As population outran production, so output per head declined; this reduced family incomes, and so consumption per head not only of food but of clothing, housing, fuel and other necessities declined. As income per head and material well-being deteriorated, so mortality rose, until population growth came to a halt, with income per head at the minimum subsistence level. Thus death as well as the limitation of births and emigration can be a control of population growth. But this control only occurs after overpopulation – in terms of optimum theory – has become established; nor is it a strategy that any peasant community is likely to accept as a conscious choice. Indeed we have so far assumed that exceeding the optimum density will trigger off mechanisms that will increase output or reduce the rate of population increase. Rising mortality then is a sign of overpopulation; it is a control only in that it stabilises numbers at the very lowest standard of living.

Nor is the relationship between population pressure and rising mortality as simple as might be thought. Mortality was high in pre-industrial societies. Thus the crude death rate in Sweden averaged 27.4 per thousand between 1751 and 1800, but by 1951–70 it had fallen to 9.9 per thousand.[14] Although there are no comparable figures for other parts of Europe at this time, it is generally thought that Scandinavian mortality was lower than that in the rest of Western Europe; crude death rates of over 30 per thousand would probably have been more representative of the eighteenth century in France and England.

Pre-industrial mortality contained two elements: 'normal' mortality, and 'crisis' mortality; this is clearly demonstrated in the diocese of Akershus in Norway, where there were remarkable fluctuations in the death rate from year to year until 1815, after which the variability greatly diminished. Although the crude death rate was below 30 per thousand in most years between 1735 and 1815, it rose to over 60 per thousand in 1742, 1773 and 1809 and was over 30 per thousand in another eleven years.[15] Similar patterns can be shown to exist for villages in England and France. Unfortunately there are no entirely reliable data on the causes of death in any European country before the nineteenth century, although the Swedish clergy did record causes in the eighteenth century. But it would seem that crisis years were associated with

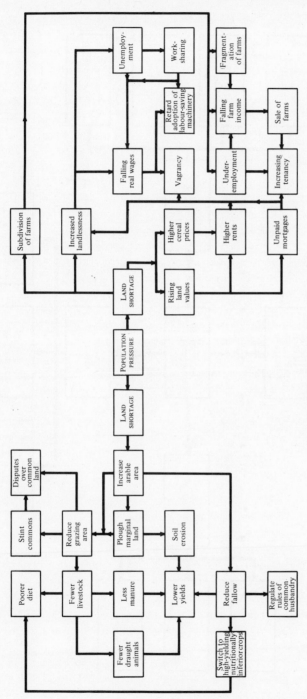

Fig. 6. Symptoms of overpopulation.

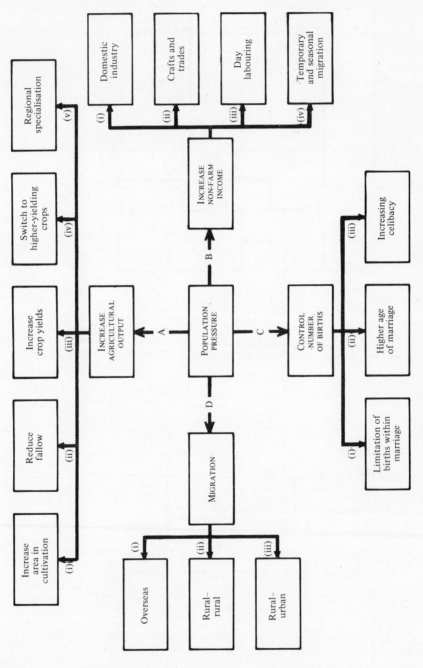

Fig. 7. Production and demographic responses to population pressure.

two types of event. In northern France very high death rates followed poor harvests, and the crisis mortality was due either to hunger, illness due to eating rotten food, or disease caught because of malnutrition. Other crises, and apparently more typical of Western Europe in general, were a result of outbreaks of infectious disease. Of these bubonic plague, which did not occur in Western Europe after 1721, was the most spectacular. In the eighteenth century, the most important of the identifiable causes of death were tuberculosis, pneumonia and smallpox.[16]

Crisis mortality was not for the most part related to population pressure. Harvest failure was generally a consequence of climatic accidents, of which excessive rain in summer and autumn was the most critical; such an occurrence fell upon the densely populated and the sparsely populated alike. Nor were epidemics of infectious disease a function of population pressure. Inadequate public and private hygiene, and a total lack of medical therapy made any population easy prey to outbreaks of disease. Thus if rising mortality did operate to control the rate of population increase as Malthus envisaged, it must have done so through the slow rise of 'normal' mortality, not by the greater frequency of 'crises'.

An approach to agrarian change

The previous chapters have outlined a possible approach to the study of agrarian change. Population growth in the absence of technological change leads to overpopulation, which is difficult to measure but can be recognised by the presence of a number of symptoms (chapter 3 and fig. 6). But few societies do not respond in some way to the challenges of population growth, although they may respond in very different ways (fig. 7). The production responses have been outlined in chapter 4, the demographic responses in this chapter. It is now time to turn and consider how different parts of Western Europe responded to periods of population growth.

PART TWO
MALTHUS JUSTIFIED

CHAPTER 6

EUROPEAN POPULATION IN THE LONG RUN

It was suggested above that European population since AD 1000 has gone through three periods of growth, separated by two periods of stagnation or decline. In this chapter an attempt will be made to substantiate this interpretation. It should be said straight away that there is little reliable evidence on the size of populations before the nineteenth century, and even less on their demographic characteristics. Censuses were not regularly taken until after the middle of the eighteenth century – in Sweden from 1749, in Britain from 1801, Ireland 1821, the Netherlands from 1830 and in France from 1800.[1] For the period before the eighteenth century, historians have had to rely on enquiries made for quite different purposes – usually for raising taxes – and to infer national totals from these often incomplete manuscripts. England is fortunate in having documents over a longer period than any other country, and there is some agreement on the order of magnitude of the population since 1086. But it needs only a brief account of the documents upon which these figures are based to see how difficult it is to derive reliable figures. The first document is the Domesday Book, which lists occupiers of land, but omits urban populations, the counties of Cumberland, Westmorland, Northumberland and Durham, and most of what is now Wales. Occupiers of land are assumed to be heads of households, and so a multiplier for the average size of household has to be estimated, a source of possible error.[2] The next document which has been used is the poll tax of 1377, apparently imposed on all those over 14, but omitting Cheshire and Lancashire; the clergy were not taxed, nor is there any means of estimating tax evasion.[3] No national figure is available again until the 1520s when the muster rolls purport to list all males of sixteen and over; Julian Cornwall has arrived at a figure for the population of England by assuming that the six counties for which the rolls survive contained the same proportion of the total population as they did in 1377 and 1689 – 11.3% and 10.85% respectively – and has estimated the proportion of the population who were under sixteen.[4] In 1603 lists of communicants to the Church of England give an opportunity to make another estimate of England's population, although examination of the diocesan returns indicates numerous mistakes.[5] At the end of the century Gregory King made an estimate of the population of England and Wales which demographers have accepted, although its source is far from clear.[6] There is no further documentary basis for a national figure until the first census in 1801.

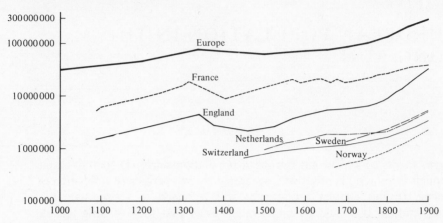

Fig. 8. The population of Europe, AD 1000–1900. Source: Colin Clark, *Population growth and land use* (London, 1967), p. 64; J. A. Faber *et al.*, 'Population changes and economic developments in the Netherlands: a historical survey', *A.A.G. Bijdragen* 12 (1965), 47–114; K. Helleiner, 'The population of Europe from the Black Death to the eve of the vital revolution', in E. E. Rich and C. H. Wilson (eds.), *The Cambridge economic history of Europe*, vol. 4, *The economy of expanding Europe in the sixteenth and seventeenth centuries* (Cambridge, 1967), pp. 20–7, 40; B. R. Mitchell, *European historical statistics, 1750–1970* (London, 1975), pp. 19–28; E. Le Roy Ladurie, *Histoire de la France rurale*, vol. 2, *L'Age classique des paysons, 1340–1789* (Paris, 1975), p. 576.

For the rest of Europe the basis for an estimate of population before the census era is much less reliable than for England. It follows that estimates for the continent as a whole can hardly be more than an inspired guess. Colin Clark's estimates (fig. 8) show that population doubled between AD 1000 and 1340; declined thereafter into the fifteenth century, revived again in the sixteenth century, and then grew at an accelerating rate from the later seventeenth century. The peak reached in 1340 was not passed again until the seventeenth century. The trends for France and England, for which estimates are imperfect but plausible, do indicate a rather different pattern (fig. 8). Population rose in both countries until the first half of the fourteenth century, then declined dramatically; revival began in the fifteenth century. The late fifteenth and the sixteenth centuries were a period of growth quite as rapid as the previous period of increase. This growth came to a halt in England in the mid-seventeenth century, and was followed by a century of slow increase; in France population reached about 20 million in the 1580s, and then oscillated between 20 million and 18 million until the mid-eighteenth century. In both countries there was then a decisive upturn which continued until the twentieth century, although England's increase was far more dramatic than that of France. We turn now to look in more detail at the three periods of growth.

1000–1347

Nearly all historians are agreed that population grew substantially in the first three centuries of this millennium, although there is doubt as to when the period of growth began and some believe that decline had set in before the Black Death in 1347. Nor is there any way of knowing if this period of three centuries had any marked internal variations in the rate of increase. Much of the evidence of population growth is based on indirect evidence of land clearance, of new settlements, of expanding towns and new cathedrals. The only documentary basis for estimating population growth rate is for England, where the figures from the Domesday Book can be compared with the poll tax of 1377. But all are agreed that the Black Death reduced the population by a substantial amount, and therefore the figure for 1377 must be raised to arrive at a pre-plague figure which represents the culmination of three centuries of growth. These uncertainties allow a variety of interpretations. The population of England and Wales in 1086 has been put as low as 1.2 million and as high as 2.6 million while estimates for 1340 have ranged between 3.7 million and 7 million. A consensus figure suggests an increase from 1.5 million to 4.5 million, which gives an average rate of increase of 0.43% p.a.[8] Evidence for increase in other parts of Western Europe is less reliable. In France, population is thought to have increased from 6.2 million in 1100 to 17.6 million in 1328, the latter figure having a firmer basis than the guess for 1100, which has been put as high as 10 million.[9] This gives a rate of increase of 0.49% p.a. Estimates for Italy give an increase from 5 million in AD 950 to 8 million in 1300; for Denmark, from 850000 in 1000 to 1.5 million in 1300; both yield an average rate of increase of less than 0.2% p.a. An estimate of the population increase in the Moselle valley suggests an increase of 0.46% p.a. between 1000 and 1237. Clark's figures for Europe as a whole give a rate of increase of 0.26% p.a. between 1000 and 1340.[10] Unfortunately it is not possible to trace any changes in the rate of increase during the first three centuries of the second millennium. J. C. Russell has suggested that population growth began to increase in Italy about 950, a little later in Western Europe, and that the period of most rapid increase was between 1150 and 1275. By the second half of the thirteenth century the rate of increase was falling, and between 1300 and 1340 the population was declining in parts of Europe.[11] We shall return to this point later (see pp. 79–80).

The period between AD 1000 and 1300 or 1340 is a period of comparatively rapid growth in Western Europe, between the slow recovery from the plagues of the sixth century and the drastic decline which followed the return of plague in 1347, and the subsequent outbreaks in the second half of the fourteenth century. Unfortunately little is known about the demographic characteristics of the population at this time; it is not possible to state whether the slow but steady increase in numbers was due to rising fertility or falling mortality, or a possible combination of these two trends. Historians have, however, offered a number of general explanations. First, Western Europe was free from the ravages of bubonic plague between the seventh century and its return in 1347.[12] Secondly, the latter part of the first millennium saw a series of attacks on Western Europe by outsiders; the Vikings in the coastal areas of the north-west, the Magyars on the inland fringes of the west, and the Saracens in the southern coastal areas. By AD 1000 these pillaging raids were fading away.[13] Thirdly, between the eighth and twelfth centuries the climate of north-west Europe was warmer and drier than it had been in the preceding centuries, and was to be in the following two centuries. Whether this improved the reliability of harvests and hence reduced mortality, it is difficult to say.[14] Fourthly, the decline of slavery may have increased the number of marriages and led to a rise in fertility. Fifthly, and most historians have emphasised this, advances in agricultural technology between the eighth and thirteenth centuries increased the area under cultivation and the yield of crops, and thus allowed a greater population. Most historians, then, believe that population growth was a result of increases in the food supply which was a result of what some have called an 'agricultural revolution'; only a few have speculated that population growth was independent of agricultural improvement, the result of a decline in mortality, and that it was population growth itself that compelled agrarian changes in this period.[15]

1347–1740

In late 1347 there were outbreaks of bubonic plague in southern Europe; by 1351 the pandemic had reached every part of Western Europe. There have been numerous attempts to calculate the effects of the plague on the population, relying mainly on surviving lists of deaths in monasteries or of city councillors; the population may have fallen by 25% or as much as 33%. But the disease returned in 1359–61, 1369–76 and 1382–4, and was semi-endemic in the towns of Western Europe until the middle of the fifteenth century.[16]

Historians are not agreed upon the date when population began to increase again. Thus some believe that in England growth occurred after 1400, others believe that the decline continued until the 1440s, whilst some argue that recovery was delayed until the 1470s and was not substantial until the 1520s.[17] But once recovery had got under way it affected every part of Europe (table 4), and was at a rate higher than that experienced in the earlier period of growth between 1000 and 1300. France, for example, doubled its population between 1450 and 1560; a sample of some 1400 villages and 676 towns in Germany have been estimated to have been increasing at 0.76% p.a. in the 1520s, at 0.6% p.a. in the 1550s and at 0.33% p.a. at the end of the century, while the province of Holland grew at 0.8% p.a. between 1514 and 1622.[18] There is some evidence that population growth began earlier in southern Europe, and that the rate of increase there was higher in the first half of the

Table 4. *Population changes in selected countries in Europe, c. 1450–c. 1600*

Region	Date	Population (1000s)	Average rate of increase (% p.a.)	Region	Date	Population (1000s)	Average rate of increase (% p.a.)
Rural Zürich	1467	27.8	1.1	Sicily	1501	600	0.74
	1529	53.5	0.67		1548	850	0.74
	1585	77.8			1570	1000	0.26
					1607	1100	
Switzerland	1450	600–650	0.26 to 0.36	Italy	1500	10000	0.2
	1530	800	0.32		1600	13270	
	1600	1000					
England	1460	2100	0.29	France	1440	8000–10000	0.58 to 0.77
	1520	2500	0.59		1560	20000	−0.12 to 0.0
	1603	4100			1600	19000–20000	
Norway	1520	246	0.54	Netherlands	1500	900–1000	0.44 to 0.47
	1590	359			1600	1400–1600	
Sardinia	1485	26.2[a]	0.79	Holland	1514	275	0.83
	1603	66.7[a]			1622	672	

[a] Hearths, not population.

SOURCES: F. Braudel, *The Mediterranean and the Mediterranean world in the Age of Philip II* (London, 1972) vol. 1, pp. 404, 410; W. Abel, *Crises agraires en Europe (XIIIe–XXe siècles)* (Paris, 1973), pp. 136, 139; K. Helleiner, 'The population of Europe from the Black Death to the eve of the vital revolution', in E. E. Rich & C. H. Wilson (eds.), *The Cambridge economic history of Europe*, vol. 4, *The economy of expanding Europe in the sixteenth and seventeenth centuries* (Cambridge, 1967), pp. 20–7, 40; J. A. Faber, H. K. Roessingh, B. H. Slicher van Bath, A. M. van der Woude and H. J. Van Xanten, 'Population changes and economic developments in the Netherlands: a historical survey', *A.A.G. Bijdragen*, 12 (1965), 47–114; F. Lütge, 'Economic change: agriculture', in G. R. Elton (ed.) *The new Cambridge modern history*, vol. 2, *The Reformation, 1520–1559* (Cambridge, 1958), p. 29.

sixteenth century than in the second half; this would seem to be true of France as well.

There is somewhat more demographic information for the sixteenth century than there is for the earlier centuries. Little is known about the fifteenth century, and it is difficult to trace trends in fertility and mortality in the fifteenth century and the early sixteenth century. However, the registration of baptisms, burials and marriages began in England in the second half of the sixteenth century, while in some parishes in the west of France baptisms were recorded in the fifteenth century, and in northern France for much of the sixteenth century.[19] Such evidence as exists suggests that fertility in the later sixteenth century was high, and certainly higher than in the seventeenth century. In the sixteenth century the median age of marriage of daughters of Florentine patrician families was 19; in four towns in Lorraine the average age of brides was 22, while in Normandy *c.* 1550 it was 21; among the Genevan bourgeoisie the average age of brides was 22 in the second half of the sixteenth century, and the daughters of the English peerage married at the same average age.[20] It is possible that marriage was not only early – much earlier than in the seventeenth or eighteenth centuries – but it may be that more married. In French villages in the eighteenth century 10–15% of the girls remained unmarried. In the Nantes region in the sixteenth century only 3.5% of women of 50 years and over were still unmarried when they died.[21]

Where baptisms have been recorded in French parishes, the absolute numbers increased in the sixteenth century until the 1580s, and a similar pattern is found in English parishes in the second half of the sixteenth century. The mean family size of English peers was 5.75 in the last quarter of the sixteenth century and at that time the average size of completed family of those women who married under 30 years in the village of Colyton in Devon was 6.4, higher than at any later time. Some workers have used the number of children mentioned in wills as a measure of family size. In Worcester it rose between 1510 and 1560, and then declined. In France the average number of children mentioned in a sample of wills in Lyons was 1 between 1350 and 1400, 3 by 1440, and 4 by 1480. At St Hilaire near Cambrai, in the north of France, the average size of family rose between 1470 and 1560.[22]

Thus while it seems certain that marriage was earlier in the sixteenth century than at later dates, while it is possible that more married, and while the few long-run series on fertility – for Colyton and British peers – show that it was higher in the sixteenth century than at any subsequent date, it is not possible to compare this with the fifteenth century, when growth began. There are however some reasons why we might expect fertility to rise and mortality to decline in England and France after about 1450. First, the impact of bubonic plague lessened, and there were few outbreaks after the 1440s.[23] Secondly, both England and France suffered from widespread internal warfare until the middle of the fifteenth century: the Hundred Years War in France and the Wars of the Roses in England were then over. Warfare promoted the spread of disease, and looting and pillaging reduced the peasant's livestock and stores of grain. While the numbers engaged in warfare were small it should be noted that one-fifth of the lay peers in England died from violent causes in the fifteenth century.[24] Thirdly, it is possible that there was a long-run improvement in the climate of north-west Europe. In France there were few harvest failures between 1439 and 1543 compared with the numbers before or after, while in England there were fewer poor harvests in the first half of the sixteenth century than in the second half.[25]

It is possible that 'crisis' mortality declined during the fifteenth century, and, this in itself might have promoted population growth. But the fifteenth century was also apparently favourable to increases in fertility. The catas-trophic deaths of the second half of the fourteenth century meant that there was more land available and farms were larger; grain was cheap, and real wages rose, and this shortage of labour allowed the peasantry of Western Europe to free themselves from some of the restrictions and impositions of

Table 5. *Population changes in selected countries in Europe, c. 1600–1750*

Region	Date	Population (1000s)	Average rate of increase (% p.a.)	Region	Date	Population (1000s)	Average rate of increase (% p.a.)
Italy	1600	13 270	−0.23	Netherlands	1600	1 400–1 600	0.34 to 0.55
	1658	11 545	0.28		1650	1 850–1 900	0.0 to 0.052
	1700	13 000			1700	1 900–1 950	0.0 to 0.053
					1750	1 900–1 950	
Belgium	1650	2 000	−0.2	France	1625	20 000	−0.13 to −0.27
	1714–15	1 750			1663	18 000–19 000	0.43 to 0.88
					1675	20 000	−0.12 to −0.25
					1717	18 000–19 000	
Spain	1600	8 500	−0.12	Sweden	1570	427–530	0.8 to 1.1
	1700	7 500			1630	850–900	0.24
					1720	1 119	
Switzerland	1600	1 000	0.18	Norway	1590	359	0.44
	1700	1 200			1665	500	0.1
					1701	520	0.5
					1735	616	
England	1603	4 100	0.6	Denmark	1650	580	−0.23
	1650	5 500	0.1		1660	458	0.5
	1700	5 800	0.13		1769	810	
	1750	6 200					

SOURCES: See Table 4 references; E. Le Roy Ladurie, 'De la crise ultime à la vraie croissance 1660–1789', in E. Le Roy Ladurie (ed.), *Histoire de la France rurale*, vol. 2, *L'âge classique des paysans 1340–1789* (Paris, 1975), p. 576; S. Dryvik, 'Historical demography in Norway 1660–1801; a short survey', *Scandinavian Economic History Review*, 20 (1972), 27; A. Lassen, 'The population of Denmark in 1660', *Scandinavian Economic History Review*, 13 (1965), 4, 29.

feudalism. All this would encourage early marriage; indeed it is easier to explain why population increased in the late fifteenth century than it is to explain why the increase did not come earlier.

By the mid-sixteenth century population was once again pressing upon resources. One French author has argued that during the late fourteenth and early fifteenth centuries plague and war led to very high mortality; marriage was early and universal, for there was abundant land. But because of high mortality there was little increase in the population; indeed decline continued into the fifteenth century. But as the plague waned, as harvest failures became fewer, and as internal wars became less common, so catastrophic or crisis mortality declined, and population began to increase. But marriage remained young and universal, so that population growth accelerated; a century after the end of the plague fertility remained high in Western Europe. In effect populations had developed the high fertility suited to an age of exceptionally high mortality, and retained this pattern into an age of lower mortality.[26]

Although population grew quite rapidly throughout Europe in the sixteenth century, there are some indications that the rate of increase was declining in the later sixteenth century, and particularly in the Mediterranean countries. By the seventeenth century the age of growth was over (table 5). Europe's population, as estimated by Roger Mols, rose from 89.2 million in 1600 to only 97.8 million in 1700; Colin Clark has put the increase at about 13 million, from 72.4 million in 1600 to 86.3 million in 1700.[27] But there were marked regional differences; in southern and central Europe population actually declined, and it did so in Spain and Portugal throughout the century. In Italy population declined in the first half, although there was some recovery in the later part of the century.[28] The most dramatic decline came in the German Empire; the decline in population during the Thirty Years War has been put as high as 40% in the rural areas and 33% in the towns. The population of France stagnated between 1580 and 1720, oscillating between 18 and 20 million, while in that part of the Low Countries which is modern Belgium, population fell in the second half of the seventeenth century.[29]

But in north-western Europe there was a different pattern. In England and Wales the population growth of the sixteenth century continued into the first half of the seventeenth century, but there was little increase between 1650 and 1750. The Netherlands followed a similar sequence, although there was virtually no increase between 1650 and 1800. In Sweden and Norway the vigorous growth of the late sixteenth and early seventeenth centuries was followed by slow increase in the second half of the seventeenth century. In contrast, Denmark after a catastrophic decline during the war with Sweden, grew rapidly in the late seventeenth and early eighteenth centuries.[30]

Thus although there was a marked contrast between central and southern Europe on the one hand, and north-west Europe and Scandinavia on the other, in both regions the boom of the sixteenth century had come to a halt by 1650, and for the following century there was at best a slow increase in population.

More is known about the demography of the seventeenth century than the sixteenth, for studies have been made of individual parishes in England and France using both the aggregate analysis of baptisms, burials and marriages, and the methods of family reconstitution. Both methods suggest that mortality rose in the seventeenth century, particularly after the 1630s. In a number of English villages baptisms exceeded burials in the first half of the seventeenth century, but burials began to exceed baptisms in an increasing number of years after 1640.[31] In Crûlai in north-western France in the late seventeenth century mortality was high; infant and child mortality was particularly so. Of those born in any one year 20–25% would not reach their first birthday; 50% would be dead before their twentieth birthday, and 75% before their forty-fifth birthday; only 10% would reach their sixties. The expectation of life at birth was only 32 years.[32] Even among British peers, a group presumably less susceptible to changing economic fortunes, the expectation of life at birth fell from 36.5 years in 1575–99 to 29.6 years in 1650–74.[33]

The causes of this increased mortality are not easy to establish. In France the period between 1560 and 1714 was one of much internal disorder; there were 45 years of war in this period. This was not so in England, although the death toll in the Civil War has been put as high as 100000.[34] In France there were frequent subsistence crises, when not only did the death rate soar well above the average, but the number of conceptions and marriages declined. In England, on the other hand, although crises undoubtedly occurred, they were perhaps not so frequent as in France; a study of fifty-four parishes between 1550 and 1800 showed that about half the parishes had less than 4 crisis years – years when the number of burials was twice the average; crisis years were more common before 1675 than after.[35] In both France and England the plague returned with greater vigour in the seventeenth century, but in England and northern France it disappeared after 1670, in southern France after 1720.

If mortality was higher in the seventeenth than the sixteenth century, it would also seem that fertility was lower. The mean family size of British peers fell from 5.75 in 1575–99 to 4.46 in 1675–99, and fertility fell in the village of Colyton in Devon during the seventeenth century.[36] One cause of this declining fertility was the rise in the age of marriage: in sixteenth-century France girls had married at an average age of 21 or 22; by the late seventeenth century this was 23 to 25. This would have reduced marital fertility, but it has also been argued that in England there was some limitation of births within marriage, presumably by the practice of *coitus interruptus*. In France less evidence of family limitation has been found, until the eighteenth century. Nonetheless the very marked differences in fertility between Brittany and Aquitaine suggests that it may have existed.[37]

We can conclude that the lower rate of natural increase during the seventeenth century was due both to a lower rate of fertility and to higher mortality.

1740–1970

In the first half of the eighteenth century, as in the second half of the seventeenth, the population of Europe increased slowly, but from the middle of the eighteenth century it has continuously increased, so that the population of the continent is now five times what it was at the beginning of the eighteenth century. Most countries in Western Europe experienced an increase in their populations after 1750 (table 7), and at a rate higher than that experienced in the preceding century. But until the middle of the nineteenth century the rates of increase were not dramatically above those experienced in the sixteenth century (table 4). Sweden for example increased at 0.67% p.a. between 1750 and 1850, Norway at 0.8%, France at 0.49% and the Netherlands at 0.76%; England and Ireland on the other hand experienced rates of increase of over 1% p.a. in this period. If the population of Western

Table 6. *Population in Europe, 1700–1970*

	Population (millions)	Average rate of increase (% p.a.)
1700	86.3	0.25
1750	101.8	0.54
1800	132	0.96
1850	213	0.57
1900	284	0.64
1950	392	0.82
1970	462	

SOURCE: C. Clark, *Population growth and land use* (London, 1967), p. 64; UNO, *Demographic yearbook 1973* (New York, 1974), p. 81.

Europe had stagnated after 1850, as it did in France, or declined as it did in Ireland, the century after 1750 would not have looked very different in demographic terms from the late fifteenth and sixteenth centuries or perhaps even the twelfth and thirteenth centuries. But in most countries population continued to increase after 1850, in some cases at an even higher rate than in the first half of the nineteenth century. Indeed between 1950 and 1970 the Netherlands and France grew at a rate above anything they achieved in the eighteenth and nineteenth centuries.

However, since the middle of the nineteenth century there has been a very important change in the composition of European populations. In the first two periods of increase the figures of total increase accurately reflect the rate of increase of the rural and agricultural populations, for they were at least three-quarters of the total population. But from the beginning of the nineteenth century the rural proportion has steadily diminished as towns have grown faster than the rural population throughout Western Europe. Thus although rural populations increased between 1750 and 1850, it was at a lower rate than the urban populations, and at various dates after 1851 the absolute numbers in rural areas and in agricultural occupations began to decline. This has no precedent in European history, except in the century after the Black Death, and has been of course for very different reasons.

Although increase was general throughout Western Europe, there were very marked differences in the rates of increase. Whereas the population of France doubled between 1450 and 1560, the 22 million in France in the 1750s did not reach 44 million until the 1950s; rates of increase were very low indeed after the 1850s. Ireland's population has had an even more dramatic history, doubling between 1780 and 1841, and thereafter falling continuously from census to census until after the Second World War.

Unfortunately it is no easier to explain the causes of the early stages of

Table 7. *Population change in Western Europe, 1700–1970*

Dates	Population (1000s)	Rates of increase: average per annum (%)	Dates	Population (1000s)	Rates of increase per annum (%)
England			**Ireland**		
1700	5800	—	1712	2751	—
1750	6500	0.23	1754	3191	0.32
1800	9200	0.69	1791	4753	1.08
1850	17900	1.34	1821	6802	1.2
1900	32500	1.2	1841	8175	0.92
1950	43700	0.59	1901	4457	−1.01
1970	48600	0.53	1950	4328	−0.06
1700–1800	—	0.46	1970	4470	0.17
1750–1850	—	1.01	1712–1751	—	0.67
1800–1900	—	1.27	1751–1841	—	1.09
			1841–1901	—	−1.01
Sweden			**France**		
1700	1369	—	1700	20000	—
1750	1781	0.52	1755	22000	0.17
1800	2347	0.55	1801	27500	0.49
1850	3484	0.79	1851	35800	0.53
1900	5136	0.78	1901	38900	0.17
1950	7041	0.63	1950	41600	0.13
1970	8043	0.67	1970	50768	0.99
1700–1800	—	0.54	1700–1800	—	0.32
1750–1850	—	0.67	1750–1850	—	0.49
1800–1900	—	0.79	1800–1900	—	0.35
Norway			**Netherlands**		
1701	504	—	1700	1950	—
1750	642	0.48	1750	1950	0.0
1800	883	0.64	1795	2078	0.14
1855	1490	0.97	1850	3057	0.7
1900	2000	0.65	1900	5104	1.03
1950	3278	0.99	1950	9600	1.27
1970	3877	0.84	1970	13028	1.54
1700–1800	—	0.56	1700–1800	—	0.06
1750–1850	—	0.8	1750–1850	—	0.76
1800–1900	—	0.79	1800–1900	—	0.86

SOURCES: B. R. Mitchell, *European historical statistics, 1750–1970* (London, 1975), pp. 19–28; N. L. Tranter, *Population since the Industrial Revolution* (London, 1973), pp. 41–2; D. S. Thomas, *Social and economic aspects of Sweden's population movements, 1750–1933* (New York, 1941), p. 32; Ø. Øyen, 'Norway's population', in N. R. Ramsøy (ed.), *Norwegian society* (Oslo, 1974), p. 11; J. C. Toutain, *La population de la France de 1700 à 1959* (Paris, 1963), p. 16; K. H. Connell, *The population of Ireland, 1750–1845* (Oxford, 1950), p. 25; B. H. Slicher van Bath, 'Historical demography and the social and economic development of the Netherlands', *Daedalus*, 97 (1968), 607.

growth in Western Europe after 1750 than it is in the sixteenth century. Although baptisms, burials and marriages were recorded by the parish clergy throughout the eighteenth century in England, the data are thought to have considerable defects; nor can they be related to parish totals until 1801. Civil registration did not start until 1837. In France civil data on births, deaths and marriage are available from 1801, but France's demographic history is acknowledged to be atypical. However in Norway, Denmark and Sweden the parish clergy recorded births, deaths and marriages from the middle of the eighteenth century. Although these records are not without defects, they do provide a series that encompasses the early stages of growth. In all three countries the major cause of the increase in population seems to have been a decline in the crude death rate, which began in the second half of the eighteenth century, but was more marked after 1815 and accelerated after the middle of the nineteenth century (fig. 17). In contrast the crude birth rate remained relatively unchanged from the 1750s to the 1880s and then declined. A noticeable feature of the Scandinavian data is the decline of the crisis year, which was still evident in the eighteenth century, but which disappeared after 1810. Similar demographic data are not available for other European countries – except for France – before the 1840s. Attempts to construct crude birth and death rates for England from aggregated parish data have produced contradictory results: more recent work on English parishes suggest that fertility increased in the second half of the eighteenth century and mortality declined.[38]

The trends in mortality and fertility are still unknown for much of Europe before the middle of the nineteenth century, and there is uncertainty about the underlying causes of such trends as are known. To some extent the issue has been confused by an undue concentration upon England. Here population growth, the agricultural revolution and the Industrial Revolution all apparently began in the second half of the eighteenth century. It used to be assumed that the Industrial Revolution caused the population revolution. But the increase took place at much the same time in Ireland, Norway and Sweden, all of which remained overwhelmingly agrarian societies until well into the nineteenth century.

It is beyond the scope of this chapter to review the possible causes of the decline of the death rate; or the relative importance of declining mortality and rising fertility in explaining the growth of population after 1750. Suffice it to say that most monocausal explanations have their critics: thus Talbot Griffith thought that in Britain the decline of the death rate was the prime factor and that this was due to improvements in medicine and public sanitation. Subsequent writers have argued that there was little advance in either of these fields until the second half of the nineteenth century, although it should be noted that more recently the view that smallpox vaccination before Jenner was ineffectual has been challenged, and there have been attempts to rehabilitate the reputation of the early hospitals. An alternative view is that agricultural changes improved diets, both in quality and quantity, and the population of Western Europe became more able to resist infectious diseases – the main cause of death at the time. But while the spread of the potato, the introduction of better methods and new crops may have raised yields, such little that is known about the consumption patterns of the population does not suggest any dramatic improvement before the middle of the nineteenth century. A third view stresses the disappearance of bubonic plague; it did not reach Western Europe again after 1720. A fourth explanation may lie in the disappearance of catastrophic mortality after the end of the Napoleonic Wars. No longer did harvest failure double death rates: this, it is argued, was due not only to improved farming methods but better transport and the improvement of famine relief.

The population expansion may, on the other hand, be due not to the decline of mortality, but to a rise in fertility: it has been argued that the spread of industrialisation encouraged early marriage and higher fertility. Some evidence exists to suggest that this occurred in England. But throughout much of rural Europe in the first half of the nineteenth century there was little industrialisation and rural underemployment was a major problem; industrial growth was not sufficient to absorb the rural surplus. Some of these problems will be turned to again in later chapters.

However, the upswing of population in the eighteenth century was not without precedent; it had occurred in the twelfth and thirteenth centuries, and in the fifteenth and sixteenth. Nor was the rate of increase strikingly above that of at least the sixteenth century; what is different is that high rates of increase continued much longer. It follows from this that it may not be necessary to seek new causes for population growth after 1750; what is needed is the reason why the growth was sustained after 1850.

WESTERN EUROPE IN THE THIRTEENTH AND EARLY FOURTEENTH CENTURIES: A CASE OF OVERPOPULATION?

We turn now to consider a number of possible cases of overpopulation in rural Europe. It will be recalled that between AD 1000 and 1300 there was an undoubted increase in the population of Western Europe, but following the Black Death in 1347–51 there was a decline; this decline was arrested in the fifteenth century, and from 1450 to as late as 1650 – sometimes called the 'long' sixteenth century – there was renewed growth, followed by stagnation from 1650 to 1750. *A priori* we might expect to find symptoms of overpopulation at the end of these long swings of increase. Now any investigation of the occurrence of overpopulation relies upon the existence of written records of agricultural and population change, and these are of course few in the Middle Ages; the best archives are those in England and France. But even these documents have their limitations, for they are often records kept for large ecclesiastical or lay estates, where conditions may not be representative of those on the small peasant farms whose workers made up the bulk of the population. Nor are there documents for all the country; in England most of the surviving documents describe conditions in the south and east, in France the north. From the late thirteenth century there survive texts on agricultural practice, but they are indebted perhaps too much to classical authors, and describe what should be done rather than what was done.

More is known of the sixteenth and seventeenth centuries both from documents and printed works. But the historian's task is still difficult. Documents which give information on farm size or landownership covering a long period are rare, and nothing can be said with confidence about national trends in land use, although rents and prices are better known.

But even where comprehensive statistics are available there is still the problem of interpretation. If England and France were overpopulated by 1300, why was it so? Was it simply that population had outrun the supply of land and the technical knowledge available? Or were institutions such as those embraced by the term 'feudalism' retarding the adoption of new techniques, and demanding an undue proportion of the peasant's income? Would the peasant have been less impoverished under a different system of landownership? Centuries later the case of Ireland exemplifies this problem: in 1840 there were few Englishmen who doubted that Ireland's miseries were due to excessive population growth, but there were few Irishmen who did not blame Ireland's woes on England's economic policies. These differing interpretations of the causes of rural poverty still appear prominently in modern discussions of the plight of the Third World.

We turn in this chapter to consider the case of Western Europe at the beginning of the fourteenth century; then in chapter 8 to consider England in the early seventeenth century, then France at the same time and finally Ireland in the nineteenth century.

Overpopulation in Western Europe *c.* 1300

Between 1100 and 1340 the population of England may have tripled, and that of Germany and France at least doubled. By 1300 some regions within Western Europe had population densities as high as those reached in the mid-nineteenth century (see p. 67). But then in 1315–17 major harvest failures due to prolonged wet weather led to a widespread European famine, and from then onwards crises came with increasing frequency; in 1347 bubonic plague reached France and by 1351 had reached west to Ireland and north to Sweden. Many historians see this as a culminating disaster due ultimately to the fact that population growth had outrun the means of subsistence; Carlo Cipolla has suggested that at the beginning of the fourteenth century several areas were overpopulated in relation to production and the prevailing technology.[1] Wilhelm Abel believed that there was a Malthusian situation in Germany by about 1300;[2] H. Dubled has argued that by the early fourteenth century there was a dangerous demographic tension in Alsace, and the impact of the plague was all the greater because the population was malnourished, a view with which B. H. Slicher van Bath agreed.[3] George Duby and others have also argued that Europe was overpopulated by 1300.[4] But perhaps the most persuasive advocate of this view has been M. Postan, who has long argued that England was overpopulated at the end of the thirteenth century.[5]

The argument of these writers may be briefly paraphrased.[6] After the plague in the sixth century, and the instability of the *Völkerwanderung*, European population slowly increased at the end of the millennium. Indeed by the ninth and tenth centuries some parts of Western Europe were already densely populated – Flanders and the Île de France, and northern Italy – but there were still great areas which were sparsely inhabited. By the eleventh century much of the good land – fertile and easily tilled – was in cultivation. But population growth continued, and indeed became more rapid. Marginal land had to be brought into cultivation, poorer soils, from which only very low yields could be obtained. Expansion into the surrounding waste land reduced the supply of grazing and hence of manure, and yields began to decline, even on the longer farmed, more fertile soils. Further signs of population pressure were the subdivision of holdings below the subsistence level, the growth of a landless population, the rising cost of land, and the fall in real wages. By the middle of the thirteenth century the supply of cultivable land had run out, and the agricultural techniques available to farmers did not permit of any further increase in yields. As population continued to grow so a malnourished population became more susceptible to disease and harvest failure; by the end of the thirteenth century death rates were rising and the rate of population increase was falling: between 1317 and 1348 the population was actually declining as crises became ever more frequent. The Black Death was thus a last – if gigantic – blow to a system where population had outrun both the supply of the land and technological capacity. Europe in the early fourteenth century was in a Malthusian situation in the sense that output per head had fallen to the subsistence level, and it was the positive checks of war, disease and starvation which were adjusting numbers to resources. Such an interpretation raises a number of questions. What were the symptoms of overpopulation? Were the harvest failures and the Black Death a result of overpopulation? How had population growth been sustained before 1250? Was it true that the techniques available to farmers were inadequate? And was rising mortality the only possible adjustment to population pressure?

The symptoms of overpopulation

The symptoms of overpopulation were outlined in chapter 3. Our task here is to see whether they appear in Western Europe at the end of the thirteenth century. We may begin, however, by considering a symptom not discussed earlier: population density. Few modern writers would accept crude population densities as a comparative measure of population pressure, even where rural populations are related to the agricultural area, as they were by Doreen Warriner (see above, p. 17), many reservations must be made. Such comparisons reflect differences in the quality of land, in technological and labour inputs, in the type of farming practised, in productivity and the degree of specialisation. On the other hand densities may be less misleading as a guide to comparative population pressure in simple, self-sufficient rural societies, where there are no fundamental differences in the type of farming or productivity. In such circumstances population densities will reflect differences in soil quality, but also in population pressure.

But population densities have been cited as a measure of population pressure in 1300 in a quite different way. In 1300 population densities in parts of rural Western Europe were as high as those reached in the same regions in the early nineteenth century, in the middle of the third great upward swing in rural populations. Yet by the early nineteenth century agricultural productivity was certainly higher than in 1300, crop yields per acre were higher and a smaller proportion of the harvest had to be retained as seed, the three-field system had replaced the two-field everywhere in Western Europe except the Mediterranean region and northern Scandinavia, while in the Low Countries and much of England the fallow had been abandoned so that more of the arable land was sown each year.

Two historians have argued that there was overpopulation. In Germany in 1300, according to Wilhelm Abel, the population was 13 million, the average yield of cereals, 750 kg/ha, and the minimum consumption needs of grain, 150–200 kg per head per year. To produce this amount would have required 4.3 million hectares in cereals, and a total arable area of 15 million hectares. He believes that the evidence suggests a much lower arable area and that Germany was thus in a Malthusian situation in 1300.[7] A similar line of argument was put forward by J. Thorold Rogers with reference to England. He estimated that the average yield of wheat in England in *c.* 1340 was 540 kg/ha, and assumed a minimum consumption need of 217 kg per head per year. If there had been the same area in cultivation in 1340 as there was in the 1860s when Rogers was writing – a very unlikely possibility – then sufficient grain would have been produced to support a population of $2\frac{1}{2}$ million. Yet as many writers put the population in 1340 at $4\frac{1}{2}$ million, the standard of living must have been very low. Rogers' assumptions were criticised by F. Seebohm, who believed the grain output could have been sufficient to support a population of between 5 and 7 million.[8]

Not all Western Europe was densely populated in 1340; there were still sparsely populated regions, but in some areas densities were very high. In England the highest densities were to be found in the east and south. In parts of the English Fenlands densities reached 114 per square kilometre in the thirteenth century; the same parishes had an average density in 1951 of only 80 per square kilometre. In parts of France densities in the early fourteenth century were equal to or higher than those reached in the nineteenth century at Laon, Beaumont le Roger, and the hilly lands near Bordeaux. Even in the infertile mountain region of Oisans, densities were as high as in the nineteenth century whilst Beauce in 1250 had a higher density than in 1850. Northern Italy, along with the Paris Basin and Flanders and Brabant were the most densely populated parts of Europe. Tuscany had about 1.2 million in 1250; it declined thereafter, and that figure was only reached again in the first half of the nineteenth century.[9] In 1340 the population of France was 18–20 million, a figure not reached again until the mid-sixteenth century, and not surpassed until the late eighteenth century, while the English total of $4\frac{1}{2}$ million was not reached again until the late seventeenth century.

These figures suggest that parts of England and France must have had a very low standard of living in the early fourteenth century. Such evidence as there is on the structure of land holding would support this view. In the early fourteenth century large parts of northern France and south-eastern England were still farmed in large farms, owned by seigneurs, clerical or lay and cultivated by peasants who owed labour dues or were paid in wages. But an increasing proportion of the total area was cultivated in peasant holdings. A minority of these were held by free owner-occupiers but most were held in return for labour obligations due to the lord, or, increasingly, for a cash payment that recognised the right of the seigneur or lord; only in parts of the two countries was contract rent in its modern form appearing. Most of these holdings were very small, although it must be remembered that with only family labour available there was an upper limit to the area which the peasant could work. The Carolingian manse was about 8–10 hectares; this was very soon subdivided.[10] On an ecclesiastical estate in the Paris region in the ninth century the modal holding was 9–11 hectares, but the range was from 3 hectares to 35 hectares of arable land. But by 1300 the great bulk of peasant holdings in France were less than this mode.[11] In 1305 70% of the tenants on an estate of the Abbey of St Bertin at Beauvrequem had less than 4 hectares, 43% less than 2 hectares. In three villages in the Namur region in 1289, 72%, 54% and 38% of the villagers had less than 4 hectares; in the Gantoise region most peasants had only 2 to 3 hectares, while in the Bordelais this was the average.[12] At Ivwy in Hainault in 1313, 80% of the holdings were less than 2.75 hectares; in the Île de France 50% of the peasant population had no more than 2–3 hectares; one historian has argued that in the Paris Basin as a whole 66% of the holdings were less than 5–6 hectares.[13]

In England peasant holdings were small, and were being subdivided as population grew in the thirteenth century. On the Bishop of Worcester's estate in 1250 33% of the tenants held a yardland – 10 to 12 hectares or more – but by 1300 only 25% did; at Kempsey the number of smallholders tripled between 1182 and 1299. On a manor at Taunton each peasant had an average of 1.3 hectares in 1248 but this had fallen to 1 hectare in 1311. By the end of the thirteenth century on a sample of estates owned by the Abbots of Glastonbury and Bury St Edmunds, the Bishop of Winchester, the Prior of Christ Church, Canterbury and the Abbot of Ramsey, 33% of the population had less than 1 hectare. Across the Channel there is also evidence of subdivision. Holdings in Alsace in the early fourteenth century were one-fourth what they had been in Carolingian times; in northern Picardy the average size of farm was halved in the thirteenth century.[14]

Not only were farms becoming smaller, but they were dropping below the minimum size needed to provide subsistence. J. Z. Titow has calculated that the average peasant household in England of 4.5 people would need a minimum of 5.5 hectares if it followed a two-field system, 4 hectares with the three-field system; H. E. Hallam has put the minimum as 4.5–5 hectares. N. J. G. Pounds has calculated that in France, with a three-field system, 4.5–6.5 hectares was the minimum needed; Guy Fourquin has argued that the minimum needed in France was 4–5 hectares.[15] What is clear is that a majority of peasants in England, France and Flanders had less than this, and many could not survive without some alternative source of income. They were particularly vulnerable to harvest failures, when they had to buy grain, and even those with 5 hectares or so would suffer desperately in bad years.

As the number of very small farms increased, so too did the class of landless, or quasi-landless, who depended on another occupation to provide a livelihood for their families. Whether there emerged a totally landless class, with only a cottage and a garden, it is difficult to say, for they would have been omitted from so many of the surviving documents.[16] However, it is apparent that by the end of the thirteenth century a majority of peasant holdings in England were both too small to provide a subsistence living for a family without alternative earnings, and too small to provide full-time employment to an average peasant family. West European agriculture was thus characterised by *underemployment*. A. R. Bridbury has observed that the Black Death had relatively little effect upon the working of farms in England, and from this infers massive underemployment on the eve of the Black Death.[17] It was only later, after the return of the plague, and as the greatly depleted cohorts thinned by the plague reached maturity that land was abandoned and there was a trend to pastoralism.

One way in which the near-landless could supplement their earnings was by day labouring on the large farms. Hired labour was probably necessary on holdings with more than 12 hectares;[18] but there were comparatively few peasant holdings of this size, and so it was the seigneurial demesne and the large ecclesiastical estates that provided employment. These had formerly been worked by serfs who had labour obligations to work the land in return for subsistence holdings, or by farm servants who received a cottage, food and some cash. The demesne had been slowly rented out in peasant holdings. But in England in the thirteenth century the demesne was increasingly brought back under direct control. There appear to have been two reasons for this: first in a period of rising prices and fixed dues, the lord did not gain from price inflation; secondly, it was only by direct control that the standard of farming and hence income, could be raised.[19] Whatever the cause it meant that it was increasingly possible for the landless to find employment.

But in most parts of England and France population growth was such as to provide an abundant supply of labour. Cereal prices rose throughout the thirteenth century, but on the other hand money wages did not, and so real wages fell. It has been estimated that the purchasing power of the wages paid on the estates of the Bishop of Winchester, the Abbot of Westminster and the Abbot of Glastonbury fell by 25% between 1208 and 1225 and by at least another 25% between 1225 and 1248.[20]

The growing shortage of land in the twelfth and thirteenth centuries led to a steady increase in the price of food and the price of land. The only continuous prices series are for England: there was a leap in cereal prices between 1180 and 1220, and then between 1250 and 1310. This would seem to reflect the growing shortage of land, although inflation has been attributed to debasement, and changes in the stock and circulation of the currency.[21]

The dues paid by peasants to feudal landowners in England were not competitive contract rents but were fixed by custom; during the inflation of the late twelfth and thirteenth centuries lords overcame this by raising entry fines, paid at the change of tenancy. A peasant land market also appeared in the thirteenth century. There are examples of rising land values in other parts of Western Europe – in parts of France and the Moselle valley – where prices doubled in the thirteenth century; in Tuscany rents, paid in cash, rose steadily until 1275, and then stabilised as population stagnated.[22]

The growth of population led to an expansion of the area in crops, but this had adverse consequences, which have already been noted (pp. 27–8 above). The reduction of grazing land in England in the thirteenth century seems to have led to a fall in livestock numbers, and on one estate the fall in manure supplies led to a decline in cereal yields.[23]

The advance into forest and waste led to a growing conflict between the lord of the manor and the peasant, between the peasants themselves, and between the village communities and outsiders. In France and England destruction of woodland threatened hunting rights of kings and seigneurs. As the waste was held in common, its diminution led to conflict between individual peasants as to the number of cattle that could be run on it. It led to conflict between lord and peasant as the former tried to enclose a part of the common grazing. It led to conflict between neighbouring parishes over the intercommoning of shared commons, and parish boundaries were more carefully demarcated. Lastly, villagers were no longer prepared to accept squatters on their commons.[24]

The shortage of arable land and the decline of common grazing had more far-reaching consequences for the village community. It was once thought by historians that the common-field system was brought fully developed from Germany to England by the Anglo-Saxons. But recent research in Germany suggests that the earliest farming was in severalty, with little fragmentation of individual holdings, little collective control of cropping, and without common grazing of the stubble or fallow. These features appear late in the Middle Ages, and it has been argued that they were a result of the shortage of land that resulted from population growth between 1000 and 1300. Joan Thirsk has argued that the distinctive features of the English common fields – the division of holdings into scattered strips, common pasturing, cropping regulations – do not appear *together* in English village communities until the twelfth and thirteenth centuries, and were a consequence of the population growth of this period.[25]

There is then some evidence of overpopulation in some parts of Western Europe by the end of the thirteenth century. Before considering why this had occurred it is necessary to look at agricultural change in the preceding three centuries. How was the doubling of population supported? There are three views on this. Some believe that between the sixth and tenth centuries there were great improvements in agricultural technology. The diffusion of these new techniques allowed the rapid growth of population in the twelfth and thirteenth centuries; others believe that the new technology had spread to only a few parts of the continent by the thirteenth century, and the increase of the preceding period was sustained largely by the reclamation of arable land. A third view is that population growth was independent of any advances in farming methods; it was, rather, population growth that forced farmers to adopt techniques that were long known. Whichever of these views is correct, there is no doubt that the period from AD 1000 to 1300 was one of considerable arable expansion.

An age of expansion

There is abundant manuscript evidence describing the expansion of the cultivated area in Western Europe, but it is too scattered in time and space to allow any estimate of the area under cultivation or to give any quantitative expression to its progress. It occurred on a variety of soils and at very different scales. Probably the most important way in which reclamation took place was by assarts in the waste and woodland around established villages: a field here, a field there, sometimes by one individual's efforts, at other times by collective effort of the village community. This was one way in which peasant holdings could become fragmented, for each area collectively reclaimed would be divided among those who took part in the reclamation. A second method of adding to the arable area was by establishing new settlements in the forest between two existing villages; here isolated farmhouses or hamlets appeared on the map of Europe for the first time. Before the ninth century most of the population of France lived in villages, but from the ninth century cottages and farmsteads in cleared patches of the forest became more common, and by the thirteenth century they were numerous. Monastic orders, particularly the Cistercians, also established estates in remote areas. A third means of increasing the arable area was by the colonisation of unoccupied or sparsely populated areas, often requiring large-scale organisation. The movement of Germans east of the Elbe, especially after 1150, is the best-known example of this. Further south the advance of the Spanish into Islamic Iberia was a process of settlement as well as military reconquest. Within the heartland of Western Europe such projects were rarer, if only because the frontier had gone. But in the tenth and eleventh centuries the colonisation of the uninhabited maritime areas of Flanders was organised by the Counts of Flanders.[26]

The expansion of the cultivated area was not confined to any one type of environment. The major advance was into the forest, which in AD 1000 still covered much of Western Europe, and this reached its peak in the twelfth century. By then the continuous forest cover in France had gone; for the first time the surviving areas of woodlands were receiving individual names. Nor was this advance into the woodland without opposition, for the forest gave a livelihood to charcoal-burners and iron-workers, vagrants and hunters. In England the Royal Forest covered a third of the realm; in Germany the steady encroachment into forest land gave rise to repressive game laws.[27]

There was much reclamation in the coastal areas, by building embankments to keep out the sea, and cutting dykes to drain the marshes. This was most marked in the maritime areas of Flanders. Until the tenth century this area had been sparsely inhabited, but the fall in sea level which began in the ninth century made their reclamation feasible. However, to attract colonists the Counts of Flanders had to offer tenancies free from seigneurial dues and obligations. Further north Dutch reclamation from the sea and from the great inlet of the Zuider Zee began in the eleventh century and continued well into the thirteenth century. The coastal areas between the Zuider Zee and the Elbe saw reclamation, particularly at the mouths of the major rivers; this continued to the middle of the thirteenth century. Across the North Sea marshland was reclaimed in parts of Sussex and Essex, but most strikingly on the Lincolnshire and Norfolk coasts. It is doubtful if attempts to reclaim the poorly drained lowlands of the English fenland were very successful, but much further south, in the flatlands of the Po valley in northern Italy, large areas of arable were reclaimed successfully.[28] In France there was successful embankment of marshland in the estuaries of a number of rivers on the Channel and Atlantic coasts, and parts of the Loire valley were embanked to protect the rich soils from floods.[29]

In the eleventh and twelfth centuries the major advance was into the lowland forest in France and England, but by the end of the twelfth century continued population growth forced settlement into upland areas; in France the poor soils of the upland areas of Brittany were occupied, the hills above the Moselle in Lorraine, the Vosges, and south in the Alps and Pyrenees. In England new settlements appeared on Dartmoor at over 300 metres, while the lower chalk downs, which had been sparsely populated when the Domesday survey was compiled, were well settled by the thirteenth century.[30] The reclamation of new land seems to have continued vigorously until the middle of the thirteenth century. But by the end of the thirteenth century and particularly between 1300 and 1340 there were signs of land being abandoned, not only in England but in parts of France and Germany. Some would argue that this was because by then, long before the Black Death, population was falling, and the poorer soils were being deserted.[31]

There seems little doubt that there was a substantial increase in the arable area in Western Europe between the middle of the eleventh century and the end of the thirteenth century, but it is not clear whether this alone was sufficient to support the approximate doubling of the population. It has been argued by some that the area under arable in 1086 in England was little short of that in the late nineteenth century; it was therefore impossible for the area under cultivation to have doubled, let alone tripled, as did population, between 1086 and 1300. Thus arable land per head must have declined sharply during the thirteenth century. Unfortunately, although the Domesday Book records both ploughlands and ploughteams, there is little reliable indication of the area the ploughlands occupied. Nor are there any figures for changes in the arable area of other parts of Europe.[32]

We must turn now to see if there were other means of increasing output. A second way of increasing the area under crops was to reduce the fallow; prior to the eighth century crops were sown in northern and southern Europe in a two-field system; of the available arable, one half was sown with winter crops, the other left fallow. This system had its origins in the Mediterranean region where rainfall was low and concentrated in winter. It was found that one cereal crop needed two winters rainfall to give a good yield. The system has less climatic rationale in northern Europe, where there was rain in spring and summer; on the other hand the fallow rested the soil and allowed cultivation to eliminate weeds. But in northern Europe it was possible to sow crops in spring and get a good crop. Thus the three-field system grew up. One-third of the arable was sown in autumn with wheat or rye, one-third in spring with barley, oats or legumes, and the remaining third was left fallow. Not only did this add to the range of crops which could be grown but it increased the area of arable under crops in any one year. The first evidence of a three-field system comes from northern France in the eighth century. But it seems to have spread very slowly. In southern France the summer drought and the unreliability of rainfall in spring made the sowing of a spring crop difficult. But even in the north the three-field system was slow to replace the two-field. Thus by 1250 it was only well established in parts of the Paris Basin; in England there are references to the system in the twelfth century, but it seems to have spread rapidly only after 1250, and as it has been suggested that the supply of new land had run out by then, it may be that it was the continued population growth that compelled the reduction of the fallow. The three- and two-field systems certainly co-existed in the thirteenth and fourteenth centuries; some have argued that their distribution was a function of soil fertility rather than population pressure, the three-field system being found on fertile soils, the two-field on less fertile. In the late thirteenth and early fourteenth centuries there were the first signs of the complete suppression of the fallow, for in parts of Flanders legumes and forage crops were grown on the fallow. But this was only a sign of things to come.[33]

Improvements in agricultural methods

There is much dispute about the progress of agricultural methods during the Middle Ages. This is not surprising for there is little documentary evidence on methods, little is known of the design of implements, and such material as exists from which inferences can be made generally refers to the better farmed demesne of lay or ecclesiastical estates. The problem could be resolved if there existed long-run series of crop yields for a nation, a region or an estate. But, with the exception of the Bishop of Winchester's estates in southern England, for which reliable figures exist for the period 1209 to 1349, references to crop yields exist only for scattered farms and generally for only one harvest, and are rare indeed before the thirteenth century.[34] But even in the thirteenth century there seem to have been marked regional differences in crop yields. In the very north of France, which was densely populated and intensively cultivated, and where in places the fallow had been entirely abandoned, seed–yield ratios as high as 1:8 were obtained, and in some isolated cases reached yields as high as the average yield in modern France. Further south, the better soils of the Île de France gave 1:6 or 1:7, but in southern France 1:4 was the average.[35] In England wheat gave an average yield of 675–810 kg/ha on a number of estates in Sussex: the mean yield of wheat in 1209–1349 on thirty-nine manors on the Winchester estates was 645 kg/ha.[36] Yields on peasant farms in the north and west of England were probably lower. Such a low yield in the thirteenth century does not encourage the belief that there could have been a dramatic increase in yields between AD 1000 and 1300. George Duby, however, has argued that yields in Carolingian times were very low; he believes the seed–yield ratio in the ninth century to have been only 1:2.5 and that this rose to 1:3 in the twelfth century and 1:4 in the thirteenth century. If allowance is made for the seed deducted for the next crop, the surplus available to the farmer would have doubled between the ninth and thirteenth centuries. Duby's figures have been disputed by Slicher van Bath, who has made the most comprehensive collection of seed–yield ratios for Europe. He believes that Duby underestimated ninth-century yields, and, while admitting that there was progress, doubts if it merits the term agricultural revolution.[37]

In the absence of any reliable series of yield figures for the Middle Ages one is forced to consider the improvements that *could* have been made, and try to trace their diffusion. This is difficult in an age with so little documentary evidence. However, most historians believe that improvements to the plough were responsible for an increase in yields. These improvements have already been noted (see above, p. 37). In addition an improved yoke raised the traction of oxen teams, and the spread of the horse-shoe and horse collar allowed the use of the horse, whose greater speed made harrowing after spring ploughing possible.[38] The plough was improved by the use of iron for contact parts, although this was not common until the thirteenth century, and in the early fourteenth century the harrow was still made entirely from wood. Where the horse did replace oxen, and in the thirteenth century it seems that this had only occurred in parts of the Paris Basin, and not at all in England except for harrowing, the frequency of cultivation could be increased.[39]

Although the preparation of the seed bed was improved by the spread of the heavy plough and the harrow, weeding still depended on the use of the hoe and the hand; the increase in population increased the supply of labour for this important task, and would have helped to raise yields. But of paramount importance in increasing crop yields was the maintenance and building up of soil fertility; the short fallow of the two- and three-field systems had no value here. Of greatest importance was the supply of livestock manure. Much of the livestock manure was wasted on the common grazing land, the stalling of cattle and the use of farmyard manure seems to have been confined to the great estates, and folding of sheep was only found on the chalk uplands of England. Further, it seems that livestock numbers fell in the arable areas of France and England during the thirteenth century. It was this, together with the encroachment onto marginal land, which has led some to argue that crop yields fell in the later thirteenth century. Farmyard manure was not the only manure in use: marling and liming were practised in the thirteenth century in northern France and south-east England, but not, it would seem, on any great scale.[40]

This left only one other possible way of increasing yields: the growth of leguminous plants. These – including clover, vetch, peas and beans – have nodules on their roots that help bacteria to fix nitrogen in the soil, and if grown in rotation with cereals, help to maintain soil fertility. Clover was not known in Western Europe before the fourteenth century. Vetch, peas and beans were all known, and peas and beans formed an important part of the peasant's diet. But it was only in the thirteenth century that they appear as a field crop: in part of Artois legumes formed 20% of the spring-sown crops, and on the estates of the Bishop of Winchester the proportion of the sown area under legumes rose from 0.97% in 1206 to 8.26% in 1345, although most of this increase came in the fourteenth century.[41]

It is difficult to come to any firm conclusions about the diffusion of these new techniques in England and France between 1000 and 1340. But it would seem that the advance of the three-field system, the growth of legumes and the wider diffusion of the heavy plough accelerated in the thirteenth century, when easily cultivable land was in short supply and intensification was the only possible way of increasing output. But to set against this, livestock numbers, and hence the supply of manure, were declining, while it seems unlikely that the advances in methods were widely adopted outside the demesne land. Whatever the long-term trend in crop yields, it could well have been difficult for yield increases to keep up with population growth in the thirteenth century; indeed there is no need to postulate a *decline* in crop yields to sustain the argument that parts of England and France suffered from population pressure in the thirteenth century.

So far we have noted ways in which agricultural output could be increased: by extending the area under arable, by reducing the fallow, by technological changes, and by greater labour inputs in cultivation, weeding and the use of marl. In the Middle Ages it was not possible to replace the cereals with higher yielding food crops; none were known. A further possibility was regional specialisation, and this depended on the spread of markets, the wider use of money and an efficient transport system. The twelfth and thirteenth centuries saw considerable advances in all three conditions; in England 2500 market charters were granted in the twelfth and thirteenth centuries. But much of the trade in agricultural produce was in the hands of the great landlords; the sale of grain came largely from demesne land, and the wool trade was very much in the control of lords and monasteries. In France the peasant with a much subdivided holding could turn to the production of wine, and areas of specialisation appeared near navigable rivers to serve not only the French urban population, but demand from England, Flanders and the Rhineland. Northern France was the most important for it was near the areas which could not grow vines: Soissons and Laon served the Scheldt market, Moselle wines went down the Rhine to the Low Countries and England; the Middle Seine served Paris and the overseas market, the Loire exported wine, and Bordeaux had a long established market in England. By the thirteenth century vines occupied as much as 20% of the agricultural area in some of the parishes in the regions of viticulture. Vines required constant attention throughout the year, and they allowed a living to be made on a very small holding.[42]

Migration and urbanisation as alternatives

So far it has been concluded that changes in agricultural technique, the expansion of cultivation and regional specialisation may have been insufficient to maintain rural incomes per head in the later thirteenth century as population continued to grow. As we have already seen, peasants could find other employment in the countryside, could migrate to the towns, or could attempt to control their numbers; if all these failed and income per head fell even further, then we might expect mortality to rise and end population growth.

Within the countryside the peasant with a holding less than the subsistence minimum of 5–6 hectares had to find some supplementary form of income. Probably the most important source was labouring on the farms of those peasants who had holdings of 15 hectares or more or, more important, on the increasing number of demesnes worked directly by the lord with the aid of day-labourers. There were some other opportunities; in a few areas it was possible to spin and weave at home but this was rare, as until the late thirteenth century the textile industry, by far the most important manufacturing industry in the Middle Ages, was concentrated in the towns, and the guilds prevented its dispersal into the countryside. The spread of the water-driven fulling mill accelerated the dispersal from the towns which became more marked in the fourteenth and fifteenth centuries. On the other hand the twelfth and thirteenth centuries saw an increase in the number of craftsmen and artisans working in villages and small towns. The spread of a monetary economy made it possible to have division of labour; in some sparsely populated areas it was only population increase that made this possible. Village blacksmiths grew in numbers in the twelfth century, and in the towns specialisation in food-processing emerged: butchers, bakers and millers proliferated. The forests still provided subsidiary employment for charcoal-burners, wood-cutters and carpenters, while the tanning of leather was largely a rural activity; glass-making too required the fuel that only the forest areas could provide.[43]

But it was rural–urban migration that many historians believe provided a partial safety-valve for the overcrowded countryside. Before AD 1000 there was little industry or trade in Western Europe, and towns were few and small; the twelfth and thirteenth centuries were thus a period of remarkable economic development. Unfortunately, there are few reliable statistics on the population of towns, particularly for the eleventh century. But there is no doubt there was remarkable urban growth between the eleventh and the fourteen centuries. N. J. G. Pounds has written that there were only a hundred places that could be called towns in Europe in AD 1000, and nearly half of these were in Italy; by 1300 there were between four and five thousand.[44] Some were large cities; in the early fourteenth century the populations of Florence and Venice were not far short of 100000, of Paris about 80000, of London and Ghent about 50000. North of the Alps and the Danube, Europe's urban population had probably reached 2 million. In England Domesday Book and the poll tax allow estimates of the population of England's ten largest towns: the total was 67000 in 1086, 163400 in 1340.[45]

But while there is no doubt about the vigour of urban growth between 1000 and 1340, it is less clear that there was a dramatic increase in the proportion of the population living in towns. The 2 million living in towns in Europe in 1300 made up only 4% of the population. In England the population of the ten largest towns was 4.5–6% of the total in 1086, 3.5–4.5% in 1340. This, based admittedly on very fragile information, nonetheless does not suggest a dramatic urbanisation of the population. It was only in the southern Low Countries and Northern Italy that the urban population increased much more rapidly than the rural population. The urban population of Lombardy and Tuscany has been put at no more than 10% in the eleventh century; by 1300 26% of the population of Tuscany was living in places with more than 3000, and the urban population of the southern Low Countries has been put as high as 30%.[46]

It would seem from this that the migration to the towns did not offer a solution to overpopulation in rural Europe, except in two regions, and in the hinterland of isolated cities such as Paris, London or Cologne. But the fact that urban populations did not grow more rapidly than rural in much of Western Europe does not mean that there was no migration from rural to urban areas. Evidence on demographic differentials between town and country in the Middle Ages is limited and contentious, but such as it is, it suggests that death rates in the towns were higher than in the country and that rural birth rates exceeded urban birth rates. In late medieval Italy marriage was later in the towns than in rural areas, and family size smaller. Most historians are agreed that medieval towns grew not by natural increase but by immigration from surrounding rural areas, and while this did not solve the problems of rural overpopulation, it did relieve them. Medieval society was far more mobile than has sometimes been thought. The major movements to colonise new areas are well known but there was also a constant movement from country to town. Although in the eleventh and twelfth centuries the serf was supposedly tied to the manor, he could obtain release by the payment of a comparatively small fine.[47]

Most of this movement was over very short distances. Lists of burgesses and freeholders in medieval towns give some indication of the distance that migrants travelled. Thus in Stratford upon Avon in the middle of the thirteenth century only 10% of the immigrant burgesses had been born more than 26 km away; in medieval Amiens virtually all the burgesses had been born within 32 km of the town. A study of migrants to Toulouse in the twelfth century shows that 55% had been born within 50 km; the figure for Beauvais, a much smaller town, in the early fourteenth century, was 89%. But as towns grew larger, so their migration field extended. Thus in Montbrison, in the Forez, 78% of all migrants came from within 20 km before 1260, and none from more than 60 km; by the first half of the fourteenth century less than 50% came from within 20 km, and 20% from more than 60 km. The larger the town, the larger the area from which it attracted migrants; nonetheless the bigger towns still recruited most of their populations from within a comparatively short distance. London, which possibly reached 50000 by the 1340s, attracted migrants from every county in England in the Middle Ages but the bulk came from south-east of an arc drawn from the Wash to Chesil Beach.[48]

The towns offered a variety of occupations to migrants from the countryside and generally at higher wage rates than were obtained in rural areas; migrants were thus attracted to the towns as well as simply pushed from the countryside. But the growth of towns was not sufficient to absorb the surplus labour in the countryside, and while migration to the towns helped to relieve conditions there, it was no solution to the problem.

Demographic adjustments

If by the late thirteenth century the populations of Western Europe had passed their optimums for the technology, resources and institutions of the time, it is reasonable to suppose that they would have attempted to adjust their numbers either by migration or by reducing the number of births. If this, together with attempts to increase output were insufficient, then income per head would have fallen towards the minimum subsistence level, mortality would have risen, and population declined or stagnated. The Black Death would seem to fit this case. Although there is little agreement on the exact decline of Western Europe's population as a result of the plague pandemic of 1347–51, none have denied that the population fell substantially, and continued to do so until at least the early fifteenth century. To many historians then, the Black Death is seen as retribution for expansion of numbers beyond the resources of the age. But two points have to be made here. First, the spread of bubonic plague was independent of population pressure; it killed rich and poor, young and old, in densely populated areas and in sparsely populated regions. Its impact can only be related to overpopulation if it can be shown that it killed so many because in 1347 the population of Europe was malnourished from a long period of falling income per head. Secondly, it has been argued that the population growth of the thirteenth century did not continue unchecked to the eve of the Black Death, instead population increase slowed in the last quarter of the thirteenth century, and declined – or at least stagnated – from 1300 or possibly 1320, to 1347. This view has been put forward by M. Postan who has argued that increasing poverty led to a rising death rate in the later thirteenth century; indeed mortality rose so high that population ceased to increase and fell away until it was further reduced by the Black Death. This then would be a true Malthusian crisis: population had risen so much above the optimum that average output per head fell towards the subsistence minimum until mortality rose and consistently exceeded fertility. This standpoint can be partially substantiated. In some areas of Western Europe population did decline: in parts of Provence population increased from 1250 to 1315 but declined between 1315 and 1328, in eastern and southern England there is evidence of decline between 1300 and 1340, in rural Tuscany population declined from the middle of the thirteenth century, in Flanders between 1315 and 1347, in the Île de France and Normandy and in parts of the Massif Central after 1300. There are, however, other parts of Western Europe where the population continued to increase until the eve of the Black Death: in parts of southern and midland England, in Bas Languedoc, Sweden and Scotland.[49]

It is less clear that the decline – if decline there was – was due simply to rising mortality. J. C. Russell has used the *Inquisitiones Post Mortem* to calculate expectation of life for landowners born before 1276 until the middle of the fifteenth century; in the earlier period the expectation of life at birth was 35 years but it fell to 31 in the following quarter century, to 29 in 1301–25 and 30 in 1324–48. After a nadir of 17 for the plague years of 1348–75, it rose to 32 in 1420–50. M. M. Postan and J. Z. Titow have used lists of heriots – death duties paid on the death of tenant of a customary holding – to show that mortality was rising in the later thirteenth century and particularly after 1290. But these calculations have been severely criticised.[50] However, there are other – although indirect – indications that population was declining after 1300 or 1320. In many parts of England land was abandoned, real wages rose in England and France suggesting a scarcity of labourers, and land values declined, suggesting less competition for land. The increasing frequency of crises suggests that mortality would have been high in the first half of the fourteenth century, and particularly during the great crisis of 1315–17 which led to famine conditions in many parts of Western Europe.[51]

Not all historians are satisfied with this interpretation, and have pointed out that there were areas where land continued to be reclaimed, and where land values did not decline.[52] In addition it is difficult to see the essentially climatic crisis of 1315–17 as in any way connected with population pressure, for it was a result of very poor harvests – yields in England were half the normal level – due to two very wet summers. Locally, famine was a result of speculative hoarding and poor transport conditions. The presumed decline of population in the early fourteenth century need not of course be due to rising mortality. It could have been due to a decline in fertility. But as with mortality, there are few reliable materials from which to reconstruct indicators of fertility. It is often supposed that the Middle Ages were a period of early and nearly universal marriage and consequent high fertility, in contrast to the modern pattern of late marriage and small families that emerged in Western Europe in the seventeenth century. But there is little evidence for this: calculations of the size of the families of socmen in a number of English villages suggest an average of 3.35 living children in the tenth century, 4.85 in the eleventh. The average family size of English kings was 5 and in Picardy the average number of sons in aristocratic families in 1075–1200 was 2.4; this excludes childless couples.[53] None of this material suggests very large families. It may be then that marriage was late, or that some form of birth control was practised within marriage. Unfortunately there is no means, either direct or indirect, of knowing whether fertility declined, whether by later marriage, by increased celibacy or by limitation of births within marriage, between 1275 and 1348.

Conclusions

We must now turn to answer some of the questions posed at the beginning of this chapter. Had the population of Western Europe, given its agricultural techniques and resources, exceeded the optimum density? It is of course impossible to determine the optimum density, but as some parts of Western Europe had by 1300 densities as great as those they reached in the nineteenth century, when farming technology was superior to that possessed in the Middle Ages, it seems reasonable to suppose that the optimum density had been exceeded. Certainly by the late thirteenth century symptoms of overpopulation were appearing: prices and land values were rising, in many regions there was little left to bring into cultivation, holdings were small, and a majority of peasants probably had too small a holding to support a family without some alternative employment, which in most cases would be labouring on the larger farms. The other possibilities open to the peasant were limited: there was no chance of overseas emigration, the frontier movement into the empty areas east of the Elbe and south of the Pyrenees was open to a very small minority of the population, and while urban growth was considerable it did not provide enough employment opportunities for the surplus population of the countryside. Nonetheless there was a steady movement from country to town which must have prevented rural conditions getting even worse. As for alternative employments within the countryside, the guilds limited the dispersal of industry from the towns until the end of the thirteenth century. While the growth of craftsmen and artisans in the countryside was noticeable in the twelfth and thirteenth centuries, this could hardly have provided an adequate income for the half of the population without enough land (pp. 68–9). Indeed as Wilhelm Abel has noted, at times of overpopulation there is frequently an oversupply of craftsmen, artisans and petty traders, and it is characteristic of rural and urban society in the Third World today.[54]

Had then Western Europe in 1300 reached a Malthusian situation? Was further population growth being checked by rising mortality which was a result of output per head falling to the minimum subsistence level? There is evidence of population declining or stagnating in some areas before the Black Death; but because of the lack of adequate evidence on the demography of these populations we cannot be sure that there was a long term rise in 'normal' mortality levels. But it does seem likely that there was a rise in 'crisis' mortality: the terrible famines of 1315–17 are well attested. Yet crisis mortality, whether due to famine, war or epidemic disease is not necessarily a function of population pressure. Harvest failures are a result of poor weather conditions and are independent of population pressure, except in that deaths increase because of the malnourished state of the population before the crisis.

By no means all writers believe that populations had grown beyond the technology and resources of the period; J. C. Russell believes that in the early fourteenth century England was a prosperous country, perfectly capable of feeding its admittedly large population.[55] This view is difficult to reconcile with contemporary events. It is more plausible, however, to attribute the failure of medieval society to imperfections in economic organisation. The manorial system or the feudal mode of production had defects that inhibited technological change.

First, the feudal nobility and clergy took some 50% of the peasants gross output in the form of taxes, tithe and rent; where demesnes were worked by peasants in return for land it took his time, often at critical moments of harvesting and sowing. Without the extraction of this surplus – which left the peasant little beyond his subsistence needs – the standard of living of the peasant population would have been higher.

Secondly, the feudal nobility and clergy did not invest the income they derived from the peasant's labour in a productive manner: much of their income went in conspicuous consumption such as the maintenance of a large retinue, or in the construction of castles and monasteries, or the purchase of luxury goods. Studies of a number of ecclesiastical estates in England and France show that no more than 5% of gross income was spent on the estate, and much of this was for maintenance and repairs. Few peasants, with small holdings and carrying the burden of feudal rent, were able to invest in their farms.[56]

Lastly we must ask whether farmers in the thirteenth century had the technological capacity to increase output. Even on estates which were well farmed average wheat yields did not exceed 675–810 kg/ha, and on these estates legumes were grown, marling and liming practised, and livestock manure applied. Yields must have been much lower on peasant holdings, where less land could be spared for legumes, marl and lime would be too expensive, and livestock too few to provide adequate supplies of manure. Nor can there have been much land left in the more densely populated areas such as eastern England, Flanders, and northern France, to bring into cultivation.

We can conclude then that by 1300 population densities in *some parts* of Western Europe had exceeded the optimum density for the technology, resources and institutions of the time, that there may in some regions have been a Malthusian crisis: that is to say, population growth was arrested by rising mortality, a result of a long term decline in income per head. But neither the great famine of 1315–17 nor the Black Death in 1347–51 were connected with the growth of population. For perhaps two centuries the expansion of the cultivated area and the adoption of new techniques was sufficient to keep production up with population growth. But by the middle of the thirteenth century the supply of agricultural land was running out; it was in this century that there are most signs of attempts to intensify production by growing legumes and reducing the fallow but they seem to have been insufficient. The primary blockage to improving yields was the lack of livestock manure, and in the densely populated arable areas of south-eastern England and northern France this reflected the lack of grazing, as population growth led to the ploughing of grazing land.

CHAPTER 8

ENGLAND IN THE SIXTEENTH AND SEVENTEENTH CENTURIES

Whether or not the Black Death was the last blow to a system impoverished by the growth of population beyond resources, or a chance happening, it greatly reduced the population of Europe. Some believe that population decline continued until the 1380s, and then, in the early fifteenth century, recovery began; others, a majority, see revival occurring only in the second half of the fifteenth century. But from 1450 to 1650 there was continuous population growth in north-western Europe, at a rate above that experienced in the twelfth and thirteenth centuries, and in the sixteenth century comparable with that experienced in the later eighteenth century. By the late sixteenth century densities in many parts of Western Europe were not far short of what they had been in 1300, and the familiar symptoms of overpopulation were appearing again. With the spread of printing it is possible to know what contemporaries thought about the relationship between their numbers and their resources: many believed that their numbers were too great. Some expressed themselves in picturesque terms. Brantôme, courtier to Charles IX of France, thought that his country was as crammed full as an egg. 'The whole of Germany', wrote Sebastian Franck in 1538, 'is teeming with children', and Ulrich von Hutten had urged, twenty years earlier, a war against the Turks as a cure for Germany's excess population.[1] English writers in the later sixteenth century believed that England was overpopulated, although they did not use that term. 'Our multitudes', wrote Robert Gray in 1609 in *A God Speed to Virginia*, 'like too much blood in the body do infect our country with plague and poverty...' Sir Humphrey Gilbert was more succinct; 'England', he wrote, 'is pestered with people'.[2] Thus the Germans looked to the east as they did in the Middle Ages, and were to do so again; the English for the first time looked across the Atlantic as a way of overcoming problems at home.

Population growth in England

No historian denies that the population of England was greatly reduced in the Black Death and the later fourteenth-century outbreaks of the disease: between 1347 and 1377 the population may have fallen from 4.5 million to 2.2 million. Whether or not there was further decline is debatable; some see

Table 8. *The population of England, 1377–1695*

	Population (millions)	Rate of growth (% p.a.)
1377	2.2	
		−0.1
1430	2.1	
		0.1
1522–5	2.3	
		0.9
1545	2.8	
		0.5(0.8)
1603	3.75(4.5)	
		0.6(0.3)
1650	5.1	
		−0.04
1695	5.0	

SOURCES: J. Cornwall, 'The English population in the early sixteenth century', *Economic History Review*, 23 (1970), 32–44; D. V. Glass, 'Gregory King's estimate of the population of England and Wales, 1965', in D. V. Glass and D. E. C. Eversley (eds.), *Population in history* (London, 1965), pp. 183–220; W. K. Jordan, *Philanthropy in England, 1480–1660; a study of the changing pattern of English social aspirations* (London, 1959), pp. 26–7.

the nadir in the very early fifteenth century, others in the middle of the century, yet other authorities believe renewed growth was delayed until the beginning of the sixteenth century. None would dispute that there was no strong revival before the middle of the fifteenth century. Thereafter there was rapid growth for over a century. Non-demographic evidence such as trends in prices and real wages suggests that the rate of increase may have fallen in the 1620s, and by the middle of the seventeenth century increase had come to an end. Indeed the population at the opening of the eighteenth century may have been lower than it was in 1650 (table 8). Some earlier authorities believe that there was a slow increase in population between 1650 and 1700 (see table 5 and fig. 8). The figure of 3.75 million is thought by some to be an underestimate; 4.5 million has been preferred; such a version would give a higher rate of increase in the sixteenth century and a considerably lower rate of increase between 1603 and 1651.[3]

Contemporary views reflect these changing rates of increase. In the early part of the sixteenth century some believed the country was underpopulated. Concern at the depopulation thought to be caused by enclosure was combined with a fear that England could not muster enough men to withstand an invasion. By the end of the century such fears had gone, and were replaced by a belief that only colonisation overseas could relieve the poverty at home: 'the people do swarme in the land as young bees in a hive in June; insomuch that there is hardly roome for one man to live by another...' But from the middle of the seventeenth century quite different views were being expressed: emigration was thought to be damaging the economy.[4]

Modern historians have been chary of suggesting that Elizabethan or Stuart England was overpopulated. Early historians neglected population growth, and much subsequent work has been concerned with the relationship between enclosure and sheep grazing, and the changing fortunes of different classes of landowners.[5] Less has been done on the more mundane matters of land use and technology, although it has been increasingly recognised that by the early seventeenth century English agriculture was having difficulty in matching population growth with increased output.[6] This view has been put most emphatically by W. K. Jordan who wrote

> the most important of all causes for rural poverty in our era was the steady and relatively steep increase in population . . . the rural population of the realm was growing more rapidly than a tightening and somewhat harassed agrarian system could possibly absorb . . . Even the most casual examination of parish records . . . suggests all too clearly that rural parishes were seriously and heavily overpopulated from about 1550 onwards.[7]

Symptoms of overpopulation

It was seen in chapter 7 that one of the symptoms of population pressure in the thirteenth century was the steep rise in cereal prices as output failed to keep up with demand for food products. And so dramatic was the rise of prices in the sixteenth century, after the stability of the fifteenth century, that the change is often referred to as the 'price revolution'; it was once thought that the inflation of prices – all prices and not simply agricultural prices – was due to the debasement of coinage and the flooding of Europe with American silver. Recently such interpretations have been criticised and more stress has been put on the growth of population, the consequent land hunger and the inability of agricultural output to keep up with demand.[8] Throughout Western Europe agricultural prices rose more than non-agricultural prices, and cereal prices more than livestock prices. In England agricultural prices showed little change in the second half of the fifteenth century, but the trend was steadily upward from 1500, sharply upward from the 1540s and then less rapidly from the 1620s. Prices of industrial goods rose slowly until the 1540s, sharply until the 1590s and then at a rate comparable to that of the early sixteenth century. It has been assumed that this slow increase was due to the adoption of cost-reducing innovations in industry; there was little such advance in agriculture.[9] Of the individual agricultural products wool and dairy products rose least, the cereal crops most (table 9). The failure of wool prices to rise as rapidly as cereals, particularly after the 1560s (fig. 9) was of significance, for in much of the fifteenth century wool and cereal prices had shown the same trend. By the end of the seventeenth century wool gave lower returns to the farmer than most other enterprises.[10]

The pressure of population growth was also seen in the rising value of land: during the late fourteenth century and for much of the fifteenth century there had been an abundance of land and relatively little competition for it, demesne farming had declined, and land was now let out in a variety of ways. Apart

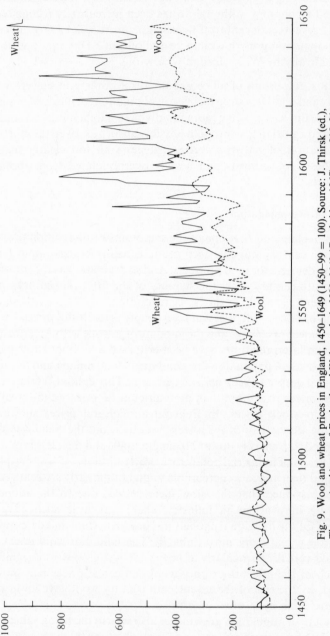

Fig. 9. Wool and wheat prices in England, 1450–1649 (1450–99 = 100). Source: J. Thirsk (ed.), *The agrarian history of England and Wales*, vol. 4, *1500–1640* (Cambridge, 1967), pp. 815–21, 839-45.

Table 9. *Price indices, 1450–1649 (1450–99 = 100)*

	1625–49		1625–49
Wheat	709	All cattle	633
Barley	800	All sheep	652
Oats	783	Dairy products	403
Rye	812	Wool	401
All grains	721	All agricultural	621
Other crops	605	products	

SOURCE: P. J. Bowden, 'Agricultural prices, farm profits, and rents', in Joan Thirsk (ed.), *The agrarian history of England and Wales*, vol. 4, *1500–1640* (Cambridge, 1967), pp. 815–50.

from freeholders, there were copyholders, who only paid entry fines at the change of tenancy; leaseholders, on a fixed rent for a long period; and tenants at will, who had only an annual lease. It was once argued that landowners benefited less from the price inflation of the sixteenth century than tenants, but studies of a number of estates suggests that rent increases did keep up with prices. In parts of Devon and Cornwall rents rose tenfold in the sixteenth century, on some Yorkshire manors rents were raised eightfold between 1558 and 1642, and in the seventeenth century rose more than prices; on most aristocratic estates rents were doubled between 1590 and 1640, but prices rose by only one-third. In East Anglia landlords did not fail to raise rents: on a group of manors in west Suffolk leasehold income increased ninefold between 1530 and 1656; on the Bures estate rents were raised fourfold between 1530 and 1586. In Wiltshire rent per acre on new tenanacies rose ninefold between 1520 and 1630.[11]

In the long run the traditional methods of holding land did not prevent rents adjusting to higher prices: very long leases were common only on estates leased from the Crown and the Church, and the land held by them diminished during the century. Leases were shortened throughout the century and copyholders found themselves having to pay greatly increased entry fines, especially towards the end of the sixteenth century.

The growing shortage of land was reflected in the steep rise in the cost of land and the cost of agricultural products, but it does not seem to have led to the subdivision of holdings. In the fifteenth century demesne land ceased to be worked by its owners, clerical and lay, and was let out to peasants and to more prosperous tenants who had large holdings and considerable capital: at the beginning of the sixteenth century there was already a substantial class of capitalist farmers, and a marked inequality of farm size in most villages, although the completely landless were few.[12] During the ensuing century and a half there was no overall decline in the average size of farms, and it is the opinion of most historians that the average size of farm increased. Unfortunately this view is not based upon any reliable statistics; there were no national figures, and few series of estate records have been examined to check the assumption.[13] Historians have concentrated instead on the changing fortunes of different classes of landowner in the sixteenth century. This period saw the decline of the Crown and the Church as landowners, due to the sale of royal land and the dissolution of the monasteries. There was also, it has been argued, much forced sale of land by the aristocracy, who failed to adjust to the new age of commercial farming. On the other hand a new competitive, capitalist group of landowners appeared, the gentry, who brought to agriculture the hard economic policies they had learned in trade or the professions. Such a view has been much debated.[14] But it throws little light upon changes in the size of operational units, farms, as distinct from the size of ownership units, or estates.

Such evidence that there is on farm size in the sixteenth century suggests there were regional contrasts in farm-size trends. In parts of the North Riding population growth in an area where partible inheritance was practised led to the creation of many very small holdings. In Cumberland and Northumberland, where there was still much common waste, there was considerable squatting on the commons, as there was in much of the remaining forest land in England. In six parishes in the Forest of Arden the average size of farm between 1530–69 was 13 hectares, but in 1570–1609 it fell to 11.2 hectares; there was no sign of engrossing until after 1670. On the other hand in the parish of Tonbridge the average size of farm grew larger in 1621–64. Two parishes in Cambridgeshire show what may have been a more general trend; in the thirteenth century the modal farm was the half-virgate of 5–6 hectares, and there were few large and few small holdings. But in the sixteenth century these holdings disappeared and there appeared instead a large number of very small holdings and a few large farms.[15]

The assumption that farms became larger in the sixteenth century is based on contemporary complaints of engrossing, particularly in the late fifteenth century and early sixteenth century, when many landlords evicted tenants and converted arable holdings to sheep farms. Subsequent work suggests that this process was largely over by the 1520s, save for a brief revival in the 1590s. But it seems that through much of the sixteenth century landlords amalgamated holdings when tenancies became vacant, preferring to let to large capitalist farmers rather than to numerous peasants. The growth of commercialism in agriculture made this profitable, and the fact that the landowning class retained and exercised control over land meant that the simple connection between population growth and subdivision was broken. Certainly by the mid-seventeenth century the typical farm in England was larger than that in France or the Low Countries: in Leicestershire it was 20 hectares, in the Lincolnshire Wolds 32–40 hectares, in Essex and Oxfordshire 20–24 hectares. In Durham in the late sixteenth century most parishes had one or two gentleman farmers who leased large farms from the Bishop; yeoman farmers had 40–60 hectares, the average farmer 20 hectares; but they were outnumbered by cottagers with an acre or so.[16]

Amalgamation of holdings and enclosure was one cause of the growth of landlessness in sixteenth-century England; another was the rapid growth of the rural population. At the beginning of the sixteenth century comparatively few people were without any land, and many of these were peasants' sons waiting to inherit their fathers' land. But as population grew, peasant holdings were subdivided, squatting on common land increased, and the trend to amalgamation further limited the chances of gaining a tenancy. Thus the landless increased absolutely and proportionally; two village studies exemplify this. In Myddle in Shropshire, only 7% of the population was without land in 1541–70, 23.4% in 1571–1600, and by 1631–60, 31.2%. A study of six villages in Arden shows an increase in landlessness throughout the sixteenth and seventeenth centuries: the 1663–74 hearth tax returns show that 40% of the houses had no land. One contemporary estimate put the labouring population of England at 25% of the total in 1641, while at the end of the century Gregory King estimated it at 47%. It would seem that it was this period that saw the growth of a large landless population in England. But the national estimates should not perhaps be accepted without reservations, for the labouring population included those living in towns as well as the country. A reasonably accurate account of the occupations of rural Gloucestershire in 1609 shows there were at least two farmers, possibly five, for every one agricultural labourer.[17]

The growing number of men without land, or with an insufficient amount of land to support a family, had an adverse effect upon the real wages of the agricultural labourer: although money wages rose in the second half of the sixteenth century, they rose less than the prices of agricultural products; real wages fell steadily. The nadir was reached in the 1620s when the daily wage of an agricultural labourer bought half what it would have done in the late fifteenth century. It was not until population growth slowed and prices stabilised that real wages began to recover, in the second half of the seventeenth century. This decline may exaggerate the fall in the living standard of the labourer, for many had some land and grazing rights on the common, and, while agricultural prices rose steeply, industrial products did not. Nonetheless there is no doubt that the standard of living of the landless and the quasi-landless did fall. This was in sharp contrast to conditions in the late fourteenth and fifteenth centuries, when real wages were rising for much of the period.[18]

Not all the landless could find employment on the land or in the towns, and vagrancy became a problem as the century wore on. Doubtless contemporaries exaggerated the number of vagrants – one recent authority believes that they never exceeded 80000. Nonetheless their presence was sufficient to promote Acts which allowed their whipping or branding. Most of the vagrants were young and either labourers or weavers; they drifted southwards in an attempt to find work, from the northern pastoral regions to the arable areas of the south and east.[19]

One response to the growth of population was the expansion of arable farming into areas of grassland, particularly after the 1550s; this led to conflict. In the first place squatters on the common lands became the enemies of both lords who wished to enclose commom lands for their own purposes, and of villagers who needed the grazing land. Secondly, the expansion of the arable area reduced the land available for grazing, and compelled the introduction of stinting, whereby the numbers of cattle and sheep that could be grazed by each individual was limited. Thirdly, the increase in landlessness and the subdivision of peasant farms made common grazing, the use of woodland for fuel and timber, and the grazing of the arable stubble all the more valuable, and so the more jealously protected. Fourthly, the increasing numbers farming the arable fields and the growth of landlessness made regulations for the operations of the system all the more necessary; not only were rules drawn up, but litigation – over intercommoning in Yorkshire for example, or the fold-course in East Anglia – became ever more common in the sixteenth and seventeenth centuries.[20] Thus by the early seventeenth century the English agrarian economy was showing signs of strain as the population continued to grow. But in fundamental contrast to the thirteenth century, there is little sign of subdivision forming a multitude of small peasant holdings. The main burden fell upon the landless, who increased in number and lost in wages as the century wore on. The bigger farmers and rentier landlords did well, as the farmhouses and manor houses of Elizabethan times attest; with rising prices and more slowly rising wages they had every opportunity to increase profits. It is time now to turn to the responses made to population growth in the sixteenth and seventeenth centuries.

Agricultural change, 1500–1650

Until the 1580s there were few innovations in English agriculture, and the most important way of increasing output was to expand the area under crops. Reclamation was probably slow in the first half of the sixteenth century, for wool prices still favoured sheep grazing. But as wheat prices rose faster than wool prices in the second half of the century, crops began to encroach on grass. One of the more striking trends in the south of England was 'disparking', the conversion of parkland used for grazing to arable land. More dramatic were the attempts to drain poorly drained land, both inland – the 'mosses' of Lancashire and the Bedford Level in the southern Fens – and on the coast where marshland was embanked and dyked on the Sussex coast, around the Wash, on the north Norfolk coast, in Essex, both north and south of the Thames estuary, and on the lower Medway. Inland, cultivation began to encroach on upland areas long abandoned to grazing, and some possibly not previously cultivated, even in the fourteenth century. In the Cumbrian hills plots of grazing land were brought under crops, in Durham warrants allowing intakes of moor are numerous in the sixteenth century, and further south in the Yorkshire Pennines large areas of waste were enclosed. The dwindling forest area was also attacked, particularly in the Weald. In the south-west cultivation once again moved into the inhospitable moorlands of Dartmoor and Exmoor in the later sixteenth century, and there was much building of new farms at considerable heights above sea level.[21]

There is no way of measuring the increase in the area under cultivation in the sixteenth century, but without doubt much of it was on poor soils. In the lowland areas much of the new cropland came from areas of common grazing, provoking the conflict referred to earlier. Nor was it simply the farmer who put pressure on the woodlands: English forests still provided timber for the construction of houses, carts and ships, and fuel for domestic and industrial purposes, and the iron industry still relied on charcoal. The shortage of fuel enforced the growing use of coal for domestic purposes, while timber had to be imported from the Baltic.[22]

It was seen earlier that in the thirteenth century some parts of England may have changed from a two-field system to a three-field system, and thus reduced the area under fallow, and increased the area in crops in any one year. But as early as the thirteenth century it did not follow that a two-field system had a crop–fallow rotation, nor a three-field system a three-course rotation. By the late sixteenth century, where common fields still predominated – which was in nearly all England except the south-west, Kent and the area to the north-east of London, the Welsh marches, Cheshire and Lancashire – there was a diversity of field systems and rotations.[23] Thus in Holderness in the late sixteenth century there was a two-field system and a rotation of crop and fallow, but on much of the fertile land in the East Midlands there was a four-field system. Throughout the sixteenth century land was enclosed, not only for grazing but to improve arable husbandry, and there seems little doubt that the proportion of the land under crops was increased and the fallow reduced.[24]

Thus the area sown to crops increased in the sixteenth and early seventeenth centuries both by the reclamation of land formerly in grazing, and by sowing the arable more frequently. But it is less than clear that there was any advance in farming methods and thus of crop yields before the seventeenth century. In the fifteenth century poorer land had been abandoned and cropping was concentrated on the more fertile soils, but as the area under cultivation began to expand again in the sixteenth century poor soils and upland areas were brought into cultivation, with low yields. Before the 1580s there is little sign of any innovation which could have significantly increased yields. Unfortunately there is little reliable evidence on crop yields in this period. M. K. Bennett argued that the average yield of wheat in England rose from 570 kg/ha in 1450 to 740 kg/ha in 1650, but his figure for 1450, based on a smaller sample of manors on the Bishop of Winchester's estate than that of J. Z. Titow, probably underestimates the average. His figure for 1650 is a speculative guess, based on some figures contained in Gregory King's work in 1696. G. E. Fussell's estimate of 1345 kg/ha in 1700, although probably an overestimate, suggests a substantial increase between 1450 and 1700, and this is borne out by a recent study of grain yields in East Anglia based on probate inventories, which shows that wheat yields doubled between 1580 and 1740. But much of the increase came after 1650.[25]

There are isolated instances of quite high yields in the sixteenth and seventeenth centuries: William Harrison recorded cases of wheat yields between 1075 and 1410 kg/ha in the second half of the sixteenth century, and seed–yield ratios of 1:8 – about 1075–1345 kg/ha – in Cuxham in Oxfordshire in the 1570s; on Robert Loder's farm the average yield of wheat between 1612 and 1620 was 1680 kg/ha and in two years reached 2355 kg/ha; but yields as high as this were recorded in the thirteenth century, and they are thus no indication of a trend in the sixteenth century.[26] Thus, it seems reasonable to suppose that there was an increase in yields between the mid-fifteenth century and the end of the seventeenth century; but there is no means of determining whether this increase was evenly spaced within this period, or concentrated in an earlier or later part. But the absence of an important innovation before the 1580s, and the slow diffusion of those adopted after 1580, suggests that yield increase came mainly in the seventeenth century.

In the late sixteenth century farming practices were much the same as they had been in the thirteenth century. Marling and liming were practised; on the lighter soils sheep were folded and the fold-course was an important method of maintaining soil fertility in East Anglia and in some of the southern chalk upland areas; in coastal regions seaweed and silt were applied; in a few areas cattle were stall-fed and the manure applied to the arable fields, but for the most part manure was still wasted on the common grazing lands; their extent was reduced by the expansion of the cultivated area. By the end of the sixteenth century there were no new leguminous crops: vetch, peas and beans, as in the thirteenth century, were the only plants used to maintain soil nitrogen; clover, first grown in the Low Countries in the late fourteenth century, was still unknown in Britain. Seed was still broadcast, and the flail used for threshing; improvements to the plough consisted mainly in adapting the details of its construction to local conditions.[27] Thus there had been no fundamental advance since the Middle Ages. Any improvements that took place in the sixteenth century could only have come from two sources. First, the existing methods might have been more widely adopted, that is to say, more farmers might have applied more lime or marl, or devoted more arable to leguminous crops. Secondly, agriculture may have become more labour-intensive, and the land more thoroughly cultivated and weeded. All this is perfectly plausible, but difficult to substantiate. Historians have, on the whole, assumed that there was little progress in productivity in the sixteenth century. 'All that sixteenth-century agriculture seems to have achieved', David Crossley has written, 'was the avoidance of a spiral of exhaustion and falling yields which could have led to a catastrophic decline in lower-class living standards comparable with the late thirteenth century.'[28]

But in the late sixteenth century there were signs of new techniques appearing in English agriculture. The first of these was ley farming or convertible husbandry. In traditional agriculture there was a sharp distinction between arable land always in crops or fallow, and grassland, which was the common land, never ploughed, and meadow, which was limited in extent, and again, never ploughed. But as early as the late fifteenth century some farmers had sown arable plots to grass and left it down for a year or more; by the end of the sixteenth century the practice of alternating crops and grass had grown more common, particularly in the Midland counties, and it has been claimed that the spread of this 'up and down' husbandry led to considerable increases in crop yields. This is perhaps dubious; arable land under grass was rested, and the roots helped to improve soil structure. It also gave extra grazing, but it was not until the introduction into England of pasture legumes – clover, trefoil and sainfoin – whose nodules helped bacteria to fix soil nitrogen, that ley farming could have contributed much to increased yields of following cereal crops. These, together with turnips, were not adopted until the second half of the seventeenth century.[29]

A second improvement, which increased the fodder supply and hence the supply of manure, as well as improving the feeding of cattle, was the watering of meadows. Although recorded as early as 1589 in Hereford it only became common much later in other parts of England – after 1629 in Dorset for example – and by its very nature was confined to a small proportion of the agricultural land.[30]

It seems possible then that the application of new methods and the wider adoption of traditional practices led to some increase in cereal yields at the end of the sixteenth and in the early seventeenth centuries. The behaviour of agricultural prices would support this, for although grain prices continued to rise after 1600, it was at a lower rate than in the sixteenth century. This was the time too when there was little land left which could be reclaimed with existing techniques, and only by intensification – by reducing the fallow and by increasing yields – could output be maintained.

There was however one way in which the efficiency of English agriculture could be improved in the later sixteenth century, and that was by greater regional specialisation. As long as farming was predominantly self-sufficient and transport was poor, cereals were the major crop in every part of the country; but with growing commercialisation, and particularly the growth of urban demand, it was possible for some farmers to produce specialised products. The role of London was paramount in this. In 1500 the town had no more than 40000 people, but by 1600 it had 250000, and by 1650 it may have reached 400000; the city thus had to rely on an ever expanding hinterland to provide its food supplies. In the sixteenth century its grain came from the immediately adjacent counties, and particularly Kent, but by the seventeenth century East Anglia and other counties on the east coast were providing an increasing proportion of London's grain. The London market also stimulated the growth of a market gardening industry on the southern side, begun by Flemish immigrants in the 1560s. In Kent hops – introduced into England in the 1530s – and fruit became local specialities, although there were no extensive areas devoted to the crops until the 1660s. As London grew, it had to attract livestock from the west and north of the country; these were driven towards the south-east on the hoof, and fattened on good pastures near the city before being sold for meat in the metropolis. A few areas appeared as specialist dairying regions; southern Cheshire was largely given over to grass and dairying.[31]

Industrial demand became increasingly important to farmers. Wool was the principal product, and it was increasingly grown, not on large grass farms, as it had been in the first half of the sixteenth century, but as part of a mixed farming system on limestone uplands, where sheep manured the thin soils for barley. On a more local scale dyes were important: there were 5000 acres under woad in 1586. Flax and hemp also provided a cash income for farmers in many parts of the country.[32]

There were thus a number of ways in which the rural population managed to match population growth with increased output in the sixteenth and seventeenth centuries. First, by increasing area under cultivation; secondly, by reducing the fallow by pursuing more intensive rotations; thirdly, by increasing yields – although this was probably confined to the seventeenth century, when reclaimable land had run out; and fourthly, by regional specialisation. Nonetheless many historians believe that output per head was declining at the end of the sixteenth century. Certainly the plight of the small farmer and the landless was grievous, although yeomen and landlords did well; but the plight would have been greater had there not been alternative employment in this period in industry and in the towns.

Rural industrialisation and urbanisation

The sixteenth and seventeenth centuries saw a considerable growth of the urban population of England and Wales, and of those employed in non-agricultural occupations. This provided an important outlet for the rural populations threatened with overpopulation. Not only were industrial jobs created in the countryside, but there was a steady movement from the countryside to the towns.

At the beginning of the sixteenth century no more than 155000 lived in towns of more than 5000 people; England was one of the least urbanised countries in Western Europe, and probably no more urbanised than it had been in the early fourteenth century. The urban population doubled however in the sixteenth century and more than doubled in the seventeenth century. The urban population rose more quickly than the total population, from

Table 10. *The urban population*[a] *of England and Wales, 1520–1851*

Year	Total urban population (1000s)	Urban population without London (1000s)	London (1000s)	England and Wales (1000s)	Urban population as a proportion of total (%)
c. 1520	155	95	60	2500	6.2
c. 1600	343	93	250	4100	8.4
c. 1700	812	282	530	5200–5500	14.8 to 15.6
c. 1750	1200	525	675	6140	19.5
1801	2314	1354	960	8892	26.0
1851	8028	5665	2363	17927	44.8

[a] Living in places of more than 5000.

sources: W. G. Hoskins, *The age of plunder: the England of Henry VIII, 1500–47* (London, 1976), p. 89; F. V. Emery, 'England circa 1600', in H. C. Darby (ed.), *A new historical geography of England* (Cambridge, 1973), pp. 293–301; C. W. Chalklin, *The provincial towns of Georgian England, 1740–1820* (London, 1974), pp. 3–14; A. F. Weber, *The growth of cities in the nineteenth century* (New York, 1963), p. 43.

6.2% in the 1520s to 8.3% in 1603 and to 15% in 1696. A considerable proportion of this growth was accounted for by the remarkable rise of London, from some 60000 in the 1520s to 250000 in 1603; by 1650 it may have reached 400000 and overtaken Paris as Western Europe's largest city. Indeed, the towns other than London seem to have grown very little in the sixteenth century, although urban growth was more widespread in the seventeenth century.

Comparatively little is known of urban–rural demographic differentials in the sixteenth and seventeenth centuries, but it would seem that mortality was higher in the towns than the country, and that rural fertility exceeded that in the towns. Thus a comparison of Worcester with some nearby rural areas shows that the size of families of those that left wills was greater in the country than in the town throughout the period from 1540 to 1630; mortality has been assumed to be higher in towns than rural areas, largely because of overcrowding and the ease with which epidemic diseases could be transmitted to large numbers in a small area. The assumption however is based on mortality rates in London at the end of the seventeenth century.[33]

It is thus likely that most towns grew mainly by immigration from surrounding rural areas; periods of growth due largely to natural increase were rare. Though Barnstaple had a considerable surplus of births over deaths in the century after 1540, and Gloucester, Stafford and Exeter all owed some of their growth to natural increase, a more common experience was that of Colchester which lost population in a series of plagues in 1579, 1586, 1597, 1603, 1626, 1631, 1644, and most disastrously in 1665–6, when half the

Table 11. *Place of birth of apprentices in London* (*excluding those born in London*)

	1540–1640 (%)	1690 (%)
Home counties	14.6	24.8
Rest of south-east	36.8	37.9
Total south-east	(51.4)	(62.7)
Midlands	28.5	20.6
North	12.5	7.1
South West	5.3	7.3
Wales	2.2	2.2
Others	0.1	0.1
	100.0	100.0

SOURCES: D. F. McKenzie, 'Apprenticeship in the Stationers Company 1550–1640', *The Library*, 13 (1958), 292–8; D. V. Glass, 'Socio-economic status and occupations in the City of London at the end of the seventeenth century', in A. E. J. Hollaender and W. Kellaway (eds.), *Studies in London History* (London, 1969), pp. 373–85.

population died; but the population of the towns grew over this period. In contrast many local villages did not increase their population in the sixteenth and seventeenth centuries. Their natural increase was lost to the town.[34] English rural society was remarkably mobile; a study of the list of names in Nottinghamshire villages showed a remarkable turnover in the late Tudor and early Stuart period, a mobility also to be found in Restoration England. But if there was much toing and froing in rural areas, it was mainly over very short distances. Studies of the place of birth of brides and grooms indicate how limited were these movements. In some villages in Northamptonshire 80% of the grooms came from villages within 8 km of the place of marriage, in East Sussex a sample of middle-class witnesses at archdeaconry courts was little more active and of the changes in residence they had made in their lifetimes, 59% were of less than 16 km.[35] Nor was movement to towns over any great distance: although Norwich was the nation's second town at the beginning of the seventeenth century, the great majority of its immigrants came from within 32 km; Canterbury was perhaps one-third the size of Norwich, and 75% of a sample of its immigrant population were born within 24 km, while in the north 66% of all apprentices in Sheffield came from within 34 km of the town. London, so much larger than any provincial town, drew more of its immigrants from farther afield. Two studies of the origins of apprentices illustrate this: over the period 1540–1640 half the apprentices to the Stationers Company came from the south-east – south of a line from the Wash to the Severn – but half came from the rest of England. A smaller sample of apprentices in 1690 shows that nearly 63% came from the south-east – but 40% came from more than approximately 120 km away. No other town in Britain could exert such an attraction.[36]

One must conclude from this that by the seventeenth century, if not before, rural–urban migration offered a significant outlet for those parts of the countryside suffering from overpopulation. Although the total population of England and Wales increased by 108% between 1520 and 1696, the rural population increased by rather less – by 88%.

Nor, by the seventeenth century, was agriculture the only form of employment in rural England. From the fifteenth century industry was progressively less concentrated in the towns. Rural areas attracted industry because it enabled an escape from the restrictions of the urban guilds and wages were, for the most part, lower than in the towns. The emergence of the 'putting out', or domestic system, whereby the merchant capitalist provided raw materials and simple equipment which the small peasant worked in his home, allowed a remarkable growth of rural industry. Much of the industry of the sixteenth and seventeenth centuries was based on the processing of agricultural raw materials and of these the textile industries were by far the most important. The spinning and weaving of wool, hemp and flax were widely spread in the sixteenth and early seventeenth centuries, but were particularly important in the villages around Norwich, in central Suffolk, in the Pennines, and in the Cotswolds and other parts of the south-west.[37] Much of this was carried on by landless labourers or small peasants in their homes; a sample of labourer's probate inventories in the period 1540–1640 suggests that 60% of all labourers had some by-employment, and possibly a quarter of the cottagers in England were employed in the woollen textile industry.[38] The tanning and dressing of leather was also an important source of employment – it was probably the second or third industry in the country in terms of employment, providing saddles, harnesses, buckets, gloves, shoes and bellows.[39] Areas of forest provided full-time and part-time employment in cutting timber, making charcoal and the various carpentry trades that relied upon wood. Mining and metal working required capital to be concentrated at a point, and were not appropriate to the domestic system; even so tin-mining in Cornwall or lead-mining in Derbyshire was often undertaken by men who also worked in agriculture. Indeed until the middle of the seventeenth century the distinction between agricultural and non-agricultural occupations was blurred, as it is today in many countries of Africa and Asia. Not only did many small peasants and cottagers work in trade and industries but yeomen farmers often had other activities – in woollen textiles, iron-smelting and coal-mining.[40] It is thus difficult to distinguish the proportions of the population engaged in agricultural and non-agricultural pursuits; but the proportion dependent solely upon agriculture must have fallen significantly in the period under discussion, although the absolute numbers continued to increase. By the end of the seventeenth century mining and manufacturing may have employed between 25% and 33% of adult males.[41] In some areas the proportion in agriculture was comparatively low at an even earlier date. A muster roll for Gloucestershire in 1608 gave the occupations of all men between 20 and 60 years. If the three towns are excluded, only 49.5% of men worked in agriculture; textiles and the making of clothes employed 22.6%, mining and quarrying 1.2%, leather-working less than 1%, wood-working and construction 5.8%.[42] This was already a remarkably diversified economy, and suggests that population pressure in many parts of rural England in the sixteenth and seventeenth centuries had been much ameliorated by migration to the towns and by the rise of alternative employments in the countryside.

Demographic adjustments

So far it can be argued as follows: population growth at a comparatively rapid rate went on for a century after 1520. By the end of the sixteenth century most of the easily cultivated land was in crops, but the means of increasing yields were little better than those available to the medieval farmer. Thus by the 1620s there was rural overpopulation. The impact of this fell mainly on the peasant with a smallholding, and the growing number of cottagers without land; one historian has argued that the 1620s were the lowest point in English agricultural history.[43] But bad as the condition of the labourer was, it was not as bad as that of his ancestor in the early fourteenth century. First, the towns offered a possible opportunity for migration, and secondly, the rise of rural industry provided a means by which many of the rural population could supplement their meagre income from day-labouring on large farms or working a smallholding. Nonetheless, the circumstances of the late sixteenth century suggest that there might have been some attempt to limit further population increase.

One possibility that was open to the men of Tudor and Stuart England, but not to their predecessors, was emigration, and many writers were arguing in the late sixteenth century that colonisation would solve England's problems. Unfortunately there is very little reliable evidence on the numbers emigrating, and less on their reasons for going. It has been estimated that some 80 000 people left England between 1620 and 1640 to settle in Ireland, North America and the West Indies.[44] This represents about 15% of natural increase in this period, and was thus of some considerable importance. But by no means all were pushed out by chronic poverty at home. Some went for religious reasons; others, to Ireland, to seize land and establish English control. Of those who went to North America, few were landless labourers or even poor. Thus, of those who sailed on two ships from Sandwich and Great Yarmouth in 1637 only one-fifth were farmers, the rest mainly urban artisans; few were poor, and most travelled as families. Of emigrants from Bristol between 1654 and 1685 a majority were urban artisans, although one-third were farmers; there were few labourers. It was, perhaps, only farmers who could raise the capital to cross the Atlantic and to provide themselves with the means of a livelihood at the other end; those who suffered most from population pressure – the landless – could not afford to leave.[45]

Mortality

It was seen earlier that population growth in England ceased about the middle of the seventeenth century. The population stagnated for half a century and then increased very slowly from 1700 to 1750. Revised figures for England and Wales, together with material on real wages and agricultural prices, suggest that the rate of increase slowed in the first half of the seventeenth century, particularly from the 1620s. Is there here then, some indication of a Malthusian crisis? Was further increase halted by increasing poverty and thus higher mortality?

Aggregate studies of baptisms and burials do show that the surplus of births over deaths narrowed in the second half of the seventeenth century; mortality increased from the 1640s. In a number of parishes baptisms consistently exceeded burials in the sixteenth century, and down to 1650; thereafter burials outnumbered baptisms. Such a pattern can be seen in Colyton in Devon, and Landbeach in Cambridgeshire; elsewhere the surplus of births was greatly reduced, but not completely eroded, as at Audley in Staffordshire or in the city of Worcester. But there were different trends in two Cambridgeshire villages, Willingham and Orwell: baptisms exceeded burials until 1650, from then to 1680 burials exceeded baptisms, then the surplus of baptisms reasserted itself.[46] A similar pattern occurs for a sample of 400 parishes: there was a surplus of births over baptisms from 1540 to 1650, with the exception of the 1550s, when there were influenza epidemics, 1598, the last of three poor harvests, and 1625, a year of plague. From 1650 to 1682 the surplus of baptisms disappears, only to reappear after 1685.[47] Now while this evidence is illuminating, it cannot be said with assurance that mortality was rising. However, a study of the British peerage does show a continuous increase in mortality from 1550–74, when the average expectation of life of males at birth was 36.5 years, to 1650–7, when it was 29.6 years.[48]

The reasons for this steady increase in mortality from the end of the sixteenth century are far from clear. There does not seem to have been any great increase in subsistence crises, indeed they were diminishing in frequency after 1650. The frequency of epidemic disease – particularly bubonic plague – may have increased in the late sixteenth century, on the other hand there were no further outbreaks in England after 1667. In the absence of any convincing evidence on the climate and its effect on harvests, or on the chance effects of bubonic plague,[49] it may be that the long-term fall in the expectation of life from the late sixteenth century was due to increasing poverty resulting from population pressure.[50] But this is not sufficient to account for the stagnation in population after 1650.

Table 12. *Mean family size of British peers, 1550–1799*

Date	Family size	Date	Family size
1550–74	4.92	1675–99	4.46
1575–99	5.75	1700–24	3.83
1600–24	5.04	1725–49	4.51
1625–45	4.48	1750–74	4.91
1650–74	4.54	1775–99	4.98

SOURCE: T. H. Hollingsworth, 'The demography of the British peerage', *Population Studies*, 18 (1965), Supplement.

A decline in fertility?

The rise in mortality after the late sixteenth century was slow. It is also probable that there was a decline in fertility. Two substantial pieces of evidence suggest that this occurred. The trends in fertility which can be reconstructed from the accurate data on the British peerage show that mean family size was an average of 5.75 in the last quarter of the sixteenth century, and that this fell almost continuously until the first quarter of the eighteenth century, and then rose again until the beginning of the nineteenth century (table 12).[51] But it may be reasonably argued that the families of British peers were unlikely to be affected by population pressure and increasing poverty. However, there is evidence from more representative samples. E. A. Wrigley's study of Colyton in Devon shows evidence of falling fertility, for not only did the average size of completed family fall between the first and second halves of the seventeenth century, but so too did age-specific fertility.[52] It is possible then that there was a conscious attempt to limit family size, beginning in the second half of the sixteenth century.

There were two ways in which the number of births could be controlled. If marriage was deferred, the reproductory period was reduced; in addition the number of births within marriage could be limited, presumably by the practice of *coitus interruptus*, by longer lactation periods, infanticide or abortion. Evidence on the average age at the first marriage of women is available for the wives of British peers and for the women of Colyton: the mean age for the former was 22 between 1550 and 1624, 23.1 in 1625–49, 23.0 in 1650–74, and 23.7 in 1675–99. In Colyton the average age was high in 1560–1646 – just under 27 – but rose dramatically to 30 in 1647–59, and remained high until the 1720s, after which it declined slowly until the 1820s.[53] By no means all writers are agreed that this change in marriage ages occurred generally in England and Wales: a study of the mean age of marriage of spinsters based on marriage licences drawn from eight counties produced a variation between only 23.7 and 24.5 between 1615 and 1841. Some would argue that even the wider range demonstrated for wives in Colyton and of peers was insufficient to significantly change fertility. It may be, then, that there was effective limitation of births within marriage.[54]

Conclusions

What then can we conclude about the relationship between population growth and agricultural change in England in the sixteenth and seventeenth centuries? In the first place there are some of the signs of population pressure in the later sixteenth century: prices rose, as did rents, the landless population grew proportionally and absolutely, and there was a steady fall in the real wages of agricultural labourers and urban artisans. On the other hand the great landlords prospered as did the yeomen. Thus the consequences of population pressure bore hardest upon the peasant and the landless. Their lot was, however, ameliorated in two ways: the growth of towns, and particularly London, provided the possibility of migration, and the rise of rural industry provided the opportunity of supplementing income at home.

Of fundamental importance was the fact that there was no widespread subdivision of farms. While small peasant buildings were subdivided, and squatting created many new *minifundia*, most of England remained farmed in medium sized holdings. This was because much of England's agricultural land remained in the control of substantial landlords or yeomen, who preferred to work their land – or rent it – in comparatively large units. In this England was in great contrast with much of Europe.

But there was little technical advance in the period before 1600, and the new technologies of ley farming and water-meadows had only a localised impact on crop yields before the 1620s. Thus until then agricultural output had great difficulty in keeping up with population growth. It is possible then that the real income of a substantial proportion of the population was falling from the 1580s; this may have led to a long term rise in 'normal' mortality, as increasing poverty reduced food intake, the standard of housing, clothing and other necessities. This may well have borne hardest upon the very young. It is also possible that there was a long-run limitation of births in an attempt to control population increase. Thus both the Malthusian adjustments to population growth occurred in the seventeenth century: mortality rose, and fertility declined. But these were adjustments, there was no Malthusian crisis.

CHAPTER 9

FRANCE IN THE SIXTEENTH AND SEVENTEENTH CENTURIES

Discussions of the economic history of France and England are apt to emphasise the contrasts between the two countries; yet in the sixteenth and early seventeenth centuries their demographic and agricultural histories have much in common. In France, as in England, the Black Death led to a great fall in numbers. In 1328 the population of France was 17, or possibly 20, million, but in 1440 it was less than 10 million.[1] Recovery began at different times in different places, but between 1450 and 1560 the national population doubled. The increase was less in the extreme north, for there the effects of the Black Death were less disastrous than elsewhere, and the region was still densely populated in the early fifteenth century; between 1450 and 1560 the population rose by only 50%. In contrast, in Provence, the number of households – as estimated from the hearth taxes – tripled between 1480 and 1560.[2] In the century after 1450 the population of the country as a whole was increasing at an average of 0.7% p.a., and by the mid-sixteenth century densities in many parts had reached those attained in the 1330s; indeed in some regions – the Loire valley and the Toulouse region – densities were higher than those found in the same areas in the seventeenth and early eighteenth centuries.[3] Many historians believe then, that by the later sixteenth century many parts of France were suffering from relative overpopulation.[4]

The subsequent course of French population change is not easy to follow; there are no bases for an estimate of the national population between the hearth tax figures of the Paris Basin in 1328 and the estimates of Vauban in 1700–04. This means 'that all the figures which have been put forward in various works on the population of France in 1500, 1600 or 1660, are pure inventions or at best bold extrapolations'.[5] But it would seem that there was little advance after 1570: the Wars of Religion *may* have actually reduced numbers; between 1600 and 1630 population began to increase again, but much more slowly than in the first half of the sixteenth century. In Languedoc, for example, population increased by 11.5% in each decade between 1500 and 1560, but after 1600 by only 2–3% per decade.[6] By 1630 or 1640 population is thought to have been back to the level of 1570 – some would put this as high as 20 million – but the 1640s and 1650s were a period of decline; recovery occurred however between 1662 and 1690, when there were few harvest failures and little internal warfare. But famine in the 1690s and a series of epidemics between 1706 and 1709 halted growth; in 1717 the population is thought to have been 18 to 19 million, but by 1737 it had recovered to 21 million.[7]

The survival of tithe figures for many parts of France has made it possible to construct approximate indices of agricultural production. These suggest that total output reached a maximum in 1560–70, as did population; it declined during the Wars of Religion, but then rose from 1600 to 1625, fell in many parts of the north in the middle of the century, rose between 1662 and 1692, and finally fell between 1699 and 1718; thereafter there was uninterrupted growth. The essential point is that population and production followed much the same course and there was, until the eighteenth century, little if any increase in output per head.[8] It has thus been argued that between the middle of the sixteenth century and the middle of the eighteenth century France was trapped in a Malthusian situation. There were no advances in agricultural methods and most of the cultivable land was already in arable by 1570; thus population was reduced in 1570–1600 by war, famine and disease. This reduction allowed a subsequent recovery in numbers between 1600 and 1630, but once again population reached the maximum that could be supported with the resources and technology available. A similar sequence of decline and recovery occurred in 1640–60 and 1660–90, but the decline of 1690–1720 was followed by continuous increase in output and population as the adoption of new farming methods allowed continued increase in numbers, if not in output per head. Thus France was relatively prosperous in the late fifteenth century; enjoyed an increase in population and output between 1450 and 1560, reaching a peak in output and population in 1560–70. Thereafter, until the middle of the eighteenth century, periods of growth alternated with periods of stagnation or decline. Each time population advanced towards the maximum numbers that the country's resources and static technology could sustain, the surplus was lopped off by war, famine and disease. Thus between 1560 and 1740 the population oscillated between a maximum of 20 million and a minimum of 17 or 18 million.[9]

Signs of stress

By the middle of the sixteenth century densities in France were returning to the level they had reached in the 1330s, and if there had been no fundamental changes in agricultural technology, signs of overpopulation might have been expected to reappear, as indeed they did. In France population recovered earlier than in England, and this was reflected by the steeper rise of prices in the first half of the sixteenth century: wheat prices in Paris increased by 50% in the period between 1500–09 and 1540–9. Over the century as a whole cereals prices rose six and a half times, a far greater increase than in any other part of Western Europe.[10] A peak was reached in 1590, and thereafter prices declined, stagnated from 1600 to 1620, rose slowly from 1620 to 1650, fell after 1660 and remained low until the famines of the 1690s.[11]

The pressure of population was reflected in the price of land as well as in the price of products. In the fifteenth century the shortage of labour had allowed the French peasant to throw off serfdom, and gain control of his land. The peasant in most parts of France could sell his land or bequeath it to whom he wished; rents were often fixed on long leases or were very low. On the other hand the French peasant did not free himself from the petty burdens of feudalism. If rents were low or fixed, he still carried a heavy weight of dues: the *cens*, a small sum paid annually, the *lods*, a fee payable to the seigneur on the sale or inheritance of land, and the *champart*, a seigneurial tithe; he was also still subject to the *banalitiés* – having to grind his corn at the lord's mill and press his grapes in the lord's wine press. Thus at the beginning of the fifteenth century the French peasant had greater control over the land than his English counterpart, but was more burdened by feudal dues, which together with the clerical tithe and the taxes due to the crown, took – even in the seventeenth century – some half of his gross output.[12]

Thus there was perhaps less opportunity for rents to rise in France than in England, where the landlord had emerged from the Middle Ages with much firmer control over the land. Nonetheless where cases of rents or sales occurred, they do show striking increases in the sixteenth century. At Poitiers for example, the sale price of land rose fivefold between 1531 and 1590; in the region around Paris rents began to increase in the late fifteenth century and rose by 20–40% between 1520 and 1560; in the south, in Languedoc, rents doubled between 1550 and 1650. The rise in rents continued, if more slowly, in the first half of the seventeenth century, although the rate of increase of prices had by then slowed down.[13]

In the second half of the sixteenth century landlords began to feel the effect of rising prices; their inability to increase rents led them to attempts to raise their income by re-imposing long forgotten dues and obligations. It also led to the spread of *métayage*, where the landlord took a fixed proportion of the peasant's produce; this was a clear attempt to share in the prosperity which the larger peasants enjoyed in the price inflation of the sixteenth century.[14] In much of France the large tenant farmers prospered. Those who suffered – the seigneurial impoverishment was only relative – were the growing number of landless or quasi-landless.

As in England, there is little firm evidence on trends in farm size in the sixteenth and seventeenth centuries; and French historians, like English historians, have been more concerned with landownership than the size of operational units, for in the sixteenth and seventeenth centuries peasants seem to have lost land to the Church in the north, to the urban bourgeoisie near the cities, and to the larger nobles everywhere. What in England would be called the smaller gentry also suffered.[15]

The rapid growth of population in the sixteenth century led to the subdivision of peasant holdings. As early as 1550 many of the farms in the Paris Basin were extraordinarily small, in seven parishes near Hurepoix 94% of all the holdings were less than 5 hectares, in an area south of Poitu in the mid-sixteenth century 88% of all holdings were less than 2.5 hectares, while in Beauvais 80% of the peasant population had less than 12 hectares. In Languedoc the number of smallholdings multiplied in the sixteenth century but the number of large holdings also increased; it was the medium sized farms that disappeared. By the middle of the sixteenth century the bulk of peasant holdings were small, too small indeed to provide a livelihood for a family. Large farms were few, although they occupied a large proportion of the cultivated area: the main region of large farms was north of Paris where holdings of 80–130 hectares were common, often farmed by tenants with capital who drew their labour from those peasants whose subdivided holdings could not provide them with a living.[16]

The growth of population and the subdivision of farms did not create a totally landless population, but it did, however, create a rural population that had to find a supplementary source of income to survive. In northern France the large farms provided day-labouring, but the growth of the rural population ensured that real wages fell in the sixteenth century, in contrast with the fifteenth century. In Poitu the wages of farm labourers in 1578 bought only 52% of what they had in 1470, and in Languedoc wages in 1600 purchased only 54% the amount of goods they had in 1500, while in the Paris Basin real wages of agricultural workers fell by 50% between 1450–60 and 1550–60. This was reflected in the declining quality of the peasant's diet. In the fifteenth century there had been a shift to wheaten bread in many parts of France. In the sixteenth century poverty led to a return to oats and rye, and in the west to a new crop, buckwheat, while meat played a diminishing role in the diet.[17]

The growth of landlessness led, as it did in other parts of Europe, to vagrancy, and as early as the 1530s there were attempts to control vagrants' movements. As the arable areas encroached on the waste and reduced the forest area, so there were growing demands to control the grazing of common lands, and stinting was introduced. In the Midi the cultivation of poor upland soils led to soil erosion, and this in turn caused silting and the flooding of rivers in their lower reaches. In much of the south there was growing opposition to the transhumants where flocks crossed the arable land of the lowlands, and there was growing hostility to graziers in the rest of France.[18]

Thus in the second half of the sixteenth century there appeared in France many of the symptoms of population pressure that had characterised the thirteenth century, and which were very similar to those appearing in England in Elizabeth's reign. But in the preceding century there had been a remarkable growth of population. How had this been sustained?

Agrarian response to population growth

The decline in population after the Black Death was compounded by the devastation of the Hundred Years War. These two disasters had two effects on settlement. First, the Wars led to the abandonment of a number of good agricultural areas; secondly, many isolated farmhouses and hamlets were abandoned as the population moved to larger villages, often for protection; in addition, many living on poor land moved to occupy good land that had been abandoned. Some 213 villages were abandoned in Alsace in the fourteenth and fifteenth centuries. Deforestation in the mountains of Haute Provence led to a retreat to the lowlands.[19] As a consequence there was no shortage of agricultural land for the diminished population, and when population began to grow again in the middle of the fifteenth century, there were migrations from the more densely settled areas to the devasted areas now freed from the terror of war. In some cases seigneurs offered less onerous obligations and dues to attract peasants to their empty domains; this was noticeable in the Bordelais, which was resettled by peasants from Brittany between 1470 and 1530, while the Paris Basin drew settlers from Picardy and Normandy, in the south Provence attracted Italians.[20] But by the 1530s much of this abandoned land was resettled and the growing population had to look elsewhere for new land. In places meadows were ploughed for crops, and even vineyards were turned over to cereals. Later in the sixteenth century there were attempts to drain coastal marshlands, especially in the north, where Dutchmen were imported to carry out drainage in the early seventeenth century, and in the malarial coastlands of Provence and Languedoc. But from the middle of the sixteenth century new cropland could only come from marginal soils, such as the heathlands of Poitu, and at the expense of grazing land.[21]

An alternative way to increase the area under crops was to reduce the area under fallow, but this does not seem to have occurred in France on any scale before the middle of the seventeenth century: in the south the two-field system, with cereals alternating with fallow, persisted until the spread of maize in the eighteenth century, and in the north the three-field system, with one year in fallow, remained until well into the eighteenth century. Enclosure was uncommon, except in Normandy, where land was enclosed for livestock production.

Farming methods

There were few advances in farming methods in the sixteenth and seventeenth centuries. In the sixteenth century there was a revival of interest in agronomy, but the only three books on husbandry published by French authors relied heavily on classical texts, and there was no work published between 1603 and the middle of the eighteenth century, although there was much written on gardens and landscaping. Peasants of course would not – indeed could not – have read such works, but the absence of such a literature reflects the lack of interest of French landowners in agriculture: land was a source of rent, but it occurred to few to improve their land in order to increase their incomes.[22]

In the north in the Paris Basin the open-field system persisted, and during the sixteenth and seventeenth centuries arable land increased at the expense of the commons; the reduction of grazing reduced the number of livestock and thus the supply of manure, and so crop yields. In some places crisis conditions had been reached: in a number of parishes in Beauvais in the seventeenth century the open fields occupied 85% of the total area, houses and gardens 8%, woodland 5% and common grazing land a mere 1%. Everywhere in the north of France there was an inadequate supply of manure, and there is little evidence of lime and marl being used in significant quantities at this time, although marling was practised in Picardy and other parts of the north in the sixteenth century.[23] In parts of the north good crop yields were obtained, especially on the borders of France and Belgium, where the intensive methods of Flanders were practised. In Beauvais and Brie seed–yield ratios of 1:5 and 1:7 were common, but these were not matched elsewhere. In much of Brittany 1:3 was usual, in northern Burgundy 1:3.5, while throughout much of the Midi 1:4 was the norm, 675–810 kg/ha; in the Auvergne, as late as the eighteenth century, yields of 1:3 were common, with 1:4 only on the better soils. Not only is there little evidence of any increase in yields between 1500 and 1700 but in much of the south yields actually declined in the later seventeenth century, from 1:4.5 to less than 1:4. On one estate near Arles the seed–yield ratio for wheat was 1:6.84 in 1621–52, less than 1:6 in 1661–1740, and 1:5.22 in 1751–89.[24]

The low yields were due principally to the limited amount of manure applied, and this in turn reflected the limited and diminishing supply of grazing land as grassland was converted to cereals. But little arable land was devoted to vetch, beans and peas, which would have helped maintain soil nitrogen. Nor were artificial grasses grown. There is evidence of sainfoin being grown in Normandy, Brie and areas near to Paris in the 1620s, but it was not widely adopted, and fodder roots were rare until the nineteenth century. Convertible husbandry, as practised in midland England, seems to have been unknown, and it was only in French Flanders that urban waste was purchased to manure the fields. The small size of holdings meant that in parts of northern France only half the peasants owned any cattle, and only one-quarter a plough; this meant that cultivation was too late and too little; in addition, except in the far north, weeding was neglected. Although sheep were by far the most numerous animals, they were rarely folded and their dung was wasted on the small area of common grazing land.[25]

Nor did new crops revitalise French agriculture: the artificial grasses which were to play such an important role in English and Dutch agriculture in the seventeenth century were known but not widely adopted; in the west buckwheat was new and spread widely in the seventeenth century, but its value was in its ability to yield on poor soils rather than in higher yields. The adoption of the potato was delayed until the late eighteenth century. The major innovation was of maize. It was being grown in the foothills of the

Pyrenees in the middle of the sixteenth century and spread slowly through the south-west in the following century, used both as a fodder and a food crop. But it was only in the eighteenth century that it was generally adopted, and was grown in rotation with wheat and barley, thus reducing but not eliminating the fallow in the Midi. Implements showed few changes, with one exception: in many parts of the south the mouldboard was added to the *araire*, or ard.[26]

There were however important advances in regional specialisation, if only on a local scale. The first half of the sixteenth century saw a growth in the urban consumption of wine – the number of taverns in Lyons quintupled between 1515 and 1545 – and the remarkable growth of Paris encouraged the spread of viticulture in its vicinity, as it did the beginnings of market gardening. Foreign demand for wine was also buoyant in much of the sixteenth and seventeenth centuries. The Low Countries were a major market for the wines of northern France and Alsace: a third of the Low Countries' imports from France were made up of wine. The English connection with Bordeaux and the Loire was renewed in the late fifteenth century, while towards the end of the sixteenth century French wines gained a footing in the Baltic. In Languedoc viticulture, curiously enough, did not expand. Local consumption was already high in town and country, and the quality was low. The region lacked the water transport to connect it with the towns of the north. On the other hand olives did expand into the upland *garrigues*, and north up the Rhône valley, while the silk industry of Lyons encouraged the growth of mulberry. In the west, particularly in Brittany, the vine retreated from marginal areas as transport improved, and was replaced by cider orchards. Many small farmers could just manage, by devoting their land to these crops and others – flax, hemp and the dye plants. A farmer gained as good an income from 2 or 3 hectares in vines as he did from 10 or 12 hectares in cereals. But important as these tree and shrub crops were, they occupied a small proportion of the cultivated area, which during the sixteenth century was devoted more and more to cereals, mainly at the expense of livestock, which flourished chiefly in those regions unsuited to cereals.[27]

Thus by 1570 the growth of population had once again brought the French rural population to a precarious situation. There seems to have been little advance in agricultural technique in either the sixteenth or the seventeenth century, nor was there any reduction of fallowing in the south and little in the north. The consolidation and enclosure of fields was rare except in Normandy. Thus the population relied largely on the growth of the arable area to maintain food output, and by the 1560s this growth was increasingly onto very poor soils. The conditions of the bulk of population, living on subdivided holdings, was only locally ameliorated by specialisation in cash crops.

Urbanisation and rural industrialisation

By the late sixteenth and seventeenth centuries the lot of the rural population of France was poor – more so than in England[28] – and would have been worse had it not been for the growth of industries in the countryside and the possibility of emigrating to the towns.

There seems little doubt that there was a greater rate of natural increase in the French countryside than in the towns. Infant mortality, for example, was between 300 and 400 per thousand in the poorer districts of the towns, 250 and 300 per thousand in market towns, and 200 and 250 per thousand in rural areas, although in unhealthy rural areas – where, for example, malaria was endemic – the infant mortality rates matched those in the working-class districts in the towns. Less is known about the comparative levels of fertility in town and country; but in Europe as a whole in the seventeenth century there were 4 to 5.5 baptisms for every marriage in the country but only 3 to 4.5 baptisms to every marriage in the towns.[29] There seems little doubt then that French towns grew mainly by rural–urban migration. At Lyons, for example, in the sixteenth and seventeenth centuries, some 54% to 60% of the patients in the local hospital had been born outside the city. Towns drew their recruits mainly from local areas, and this often reduced the rate of rural population increase. In the Nantes region for example, both the town and the surrounding rural parishes increased their population between 1500 and 1570; thereafter Nantes continued to increase, but many of the surrounding parishes declined as emigration to the city grew.[30] Paris, with a much larger population than any other French town, drew its immigrants from much further afield: at Crûlai, some 130 km from Paris, the average rate of natural increase was 0.5% p.a., yet the population remained constant at about 1000 from 1600 to 1740, for the young habitually emigrated to Paris. There were also regions suffering particularly from overpopulation whose migrants were especially numerous; thus the Limousin uplands and the Pyrenees contributed a disproportionate number of migrants to Bordeaux, and the Massif Central to Paris.[31]

There is no doubt that there was a marked urban growth in France in the sixteenth and seventeenth centuries, and much of this was due to rural–urban migration, thus providing an important safety-valve for the overcrowded rural regions. In the century of rapid population growth between 1450 and 1550 many of the larger towns doubled their population. Lyons quadrupled its population between 1450 and 1550; Rouen tripled and Toulouse doubled its population between 1500 and 1550. Bordeaux rose from 20000 in 1500 to 50000 in 1550, and Marseilles from 15000 in 1520 to 40000 in 1590.[32] The same century saw the foundation of entirely new towns – Le Havre in 1517–20, Nancy in 1587 and Charleville, somewhat later, in 1603. But whether this dramatic urban growth also led to rapid urbanisation is a moot point. Data on French urban populations are no more reliable than those for England.

However, a synthesis of contemporary estimates of urban populations suggests that there was very little increase in the numbers living in places of more than 20000 in the sixteenth century, but a substantial increase in the seventeenth century.[33]

As in England much of the urban growth was accounted for by the capital city. Paris had reached 200000 before the Black Death, and was then by far the largest city in Western Europe. In the middle of the sixteenth century its population was somewhere between 200000 and 500000. It declined in the last two decades of the sixteenth century – some 30000 died from a typhus epidemic in 1580 – and one estimate puts it as low as 250000 in 1600, but by 1700 it had reached 500000.[34] While it is difficult to compare the progress of urbanisation in France with that of England in the sixteenth century it seems likely, first, that Paris accounted for less of France's urban growth than did London of England's; but that the rate of urbanisation in England was more rapid in the sixteenth and seventeenth centuries. This comparatively slow urbanisation in France continued in the following century. At the end of the seventeenth century approximately 10% lived in towns of more than 10000, at the end of the eighteenth century 20% and in 1851 still only 25%.[35]

Within the countryside there was an increasing number of employment opportunities: local craftsmen, who in the Middle Ages had worked only for their immediate localities, now produced goods that could be marketed in more distant regions; this was made more posssible by improvements in transport, which itself provided employment.[36] But it was the growth of rural industry, attracted by the cheap labour available – a function of population growth – which provided much of the opportunity for employment. Indeed by the middle of the seventeenth century half those employed in 'manufactures' in France were to be found in the countryside; there were no more than 100000 genuine urban industrial workers and only Amiens, Tours and Lyons could be properly described as industrial towns.[37]

The textiles were the leading rural industry in France, as they were in the rest of Western Europe; in the west, hemp and flax provided employment for cottagers and peasants, in the north, wool, and in Lyons and its region, silk. The metal-working industry became more important in the countryside as running water was increasingly used as a source of power: it was found in Normandy, Bourgogne and Champagne, in Poitu and Perigord, and particularly in the Forez and Dauphiné.[38]

Thus the opportunities for migration or 'by-employment' were greater in the sixteenth and seventeenth centuries than they had been in the Middle Ages, and at least partly improved the lot of the small peasant. But his condition was still unenviable. Burdened by tax and feudal dues, with rents rising and wages falling, his condition declined after 1540 and provided a marked contrast with the fifteenth century. As the decline in numbers had then improved his position vis-à-vis the seigneur, so it was weakened in the sixteenth century as numbers grew beyond the opportunities of employment, and made possible the 'seigneurial reaction' of the late sixteenth century. After 1570 there were few possibilities left of expanding the area under cultivation and little progress was made in farming methods. Under these circumstances it might be expected that the French peasant would have attempted to control his numbers.

Demographic adjustments

Although rural–urban migration and the growth of industrial employment in the countryside may have ameliorated the lot of the peasant, they do not, of course, help to explain the course of population change after 1570. Migration out of France cannot have had much influence on numbers: comparatively few Frenchmen settled in the Americas in the seventeenth century, though rather more moved to other parts of Europe. There was a considerable migration to Catalonia in the sixteenth century, declining after 1620; there were some 200 000 Frenchmen living in Spain in 1669.[39]

In the long run French population change from AD 1000 to 1740 appears to follow a Malthusian course. Between AD 1000 and 1340 population probably doubled from 7–10 million to approximately 17–20 million; it was then reduced by a third by the Black Death and continued to decline until 1440 when it numbered less than 10 million. The following century saw a return to about 17–20 million; but in the absence of any significant advance in agricultural technology, the population stabilised at this peak in 1560–70. The following century and a half saw alternating periods of decline and growth, each of about thirty years. From 1570 to 1600 population fell, or at least stagnated; from 1600 to 1630–40 it increased; from 1640 to 1660 it declined; from 1660 to 1690 it increased; from 1690 to 1710 it declined; and thereafter it increased without any further decline until the mid-nineteenth century, when it stagnated.

Several modern French historians have interpreted this sequence in Malthusian terms, arguing that population tended to grow to the maximum possible with the existing technology; as most of the population were then living at a precariously low standard of living, war, disease and famine thinned numbers once a generation. This reduction allowed a temporary growth, until once again all available land had been occupied, and the population was at risk when harvests failed or epidemics broke out.[40]

Unfortunately there is little reliable evidence to confirm this interpretation; even the national totals are in doubt in the sixteenth and seventeenth centuries, and there is little reliable evidence on demographic trends; that which exists is based on family reconstitution of a number of parishes, and it is only after the 1660s that French parochial records are accurate and comprehensive enough to allow this method to be used. Mortality was certainly high in the late seventeenth century. Out of every thousand children born 200–250 died before their first birthday: half died before they reached

20, three-quarters before they were 45, while only 10% of any cohort survived into their 60s. The expectation of life at birth was low: at Crûlai it was only 32 in the late seventeenth century, and the crude death rate averaged 31 per thousand.[41]

The distinctive feature of mortality trends in France in the late seventeenth and early eighteenth centuries was the occurrence of crisis years, or groups of years, when the death rate was well above the average, and when the number of conceptions, births and marriages declined, only to recover rapidly when the demographic crisis had passed. In France there were two causes of these high death rates; in northern France the principal cause was harvest failure, due particularly to prolonged summer rainfall. This led to deaths from starvation, to intestinal diseases, a result of eating decaying or rotten foods, or a lower immunity to infectious disease. In the south and in the coastal regions of the west and north 'subsistence' crises were less common, as grain could be more easily imported than in the inland regions. In these regions demographic crises were due more to epidemic disease, of which plague, malaria, typhus, typhoid and smallpox all took a terrible toll.[42] The occurrence of wars, and particularly internal wars, also influenced the death rate, but more by the spreading of disease as armies moved around than by direct loss on the battlefields; there was certainly more warfare after 1560 than before. Between 1453 – the end of the Hundred Years War with England – and 1560, France was largely free from internal wars but between 1560 and 1715 there were 45 years of warfare, beginning with the religious wars of the late sixteenth century, then the battles of the Fronde in the mid-seventeenth century, and the adventures of Louis XIV at the end. It is possible that bubonic plague was less common in the period 1450–1550, and then more frequent until its final disappearance in the north in 1670 and in the Midi in 1720. It is also possible that harvest failures became more frequent after 1580 as Western Europe experienced colder winters and wetter summers.[43]

It may be then that mortality was higher in the seventeenth than the sixteenth century, although there are no reliable demographic data to prove this. But even if this were so it is not possible to show that mortality rose in the periods of presumed population decline in 1570–1600, 1640-60 and 1690-1715. Further, even if this were so, it is difficult to connect the causes of death with the long-run decline in income per head that resulted from rising population in the sixteenth century. Harvest failures were the result of climatic accidents, and the frequency and virulence of infectious diseases were independent of poverty or prosperity in the rural population. Even less connection can be shown to exist between population growth and the frequency of warfare. Thus the slower rate of population growth after 1570 may have been due to rising mortality, and this may have been because the century of rapid growth between 1450 and 1550 brought French population to the limit it could support without some fundamental advance in agricultural technology. As this did not take place, the population oscillated around this equilibrium position, which in Malthusian theory would be at the point where output per head was at the minimum subsistence level, but of course well beyond the optimum point where output per head would be maximised with existing technology and resources.

There is also of course the possibility that the slower rate of growth was due to some adjustment in fertility rates. There is rather more evidence on fertility than mortality in the sixteenth and seventeenth centuries, but it is still fragmentary. Thus studies of the aggregate number of baptisms in a number of parishes – in Rouen, Nantes, Beauvais and in Seine and Marne – show an increasing number of births until the 1570s and then a decline; only after 1600 did the absolute number of births begin to increase again, and then only until the 1630s. It may be that this reflects a fall in fertility, although this of course cannot be inferred simply from the absolute number of baptisms.[44]

Equally limited evidence suggests that the age of marriage rose in the seventeenth century. Thus in Normandy the average age of brides was 21 in the sixteenth century, a century later 24 or 25. In four towns in Lorraine in the sixteenth century the modal age of brides was 18; in Crûlai in the late seventeenth century it was 22 and the average age of women at first marriage in France seems to have been between 23 and 25. This suggests – but hardly confirms – that there was a rise in the age of marriage after 1570. This could have had a considerable influence on fertility. In Crûlai in the later seventeenth century girls who married at 20 had an average of eight children, those who married at 25, six children, and those who married at 30 had but four children. When combined with a strict observance of chastity outside marriage the deferment of marriage could have limited the number of births in the seventeenth century. French demographers have as yet been unable to detect any sign of the limitation of births within marriage before the 1720s or 1730s. Yet as at that time there were very marked differences in marital fertility between different regions in France – between Aquitaine and Brittany for example – it is certainly possible that there was some attempt to limit the number of births, either by *coitus interruptus*, or by lengthening the period of suckling. It is equally possible that not only was marriage deferred after 1570, but that a rising proportion never married. In Nantes in the sixteenth century only 3–5% of those buried were unmarried. In Crûlai in the later eighteenth century of the women who died at 50, 2–12% were unmarried, while in Beauvais in the seventeenth century 10–15% remained unmarried. Again, this suggests the possibility of rising celibacy in the seventeenth century, but it is no more than a suggestion.[45]

By the end of the seventeenth century then France was characterised by comparatively late marriage; comparatively small families – an average size of 4 in Crûlai; strict chastity outside marriage – illegitimate births were only 1% of all births in rural areas, 4% in towns, and there were few pre-nuptial conceptions. Marriage may have been less universal than it was in the sixteenth century, and about 10% remained unmarried. Thus the seventeenth century may have seen the emergence of the West European model of marriage, and it may have been an adjustment to the declining incomes of the late sixteenth century, an attempt to limit family size to diminishing family incomes. But this, sadly, is little more than surmise.

Conclusions

There seems little doubt that the growth of population in the late fifteenth and earlier sixteenth centuries eroded the standard of living of the French peasant; farms became smaller, real wages fell, prices rose and the land became increasingly expensive. To some extent the progressive impoverishment of the rural population was ameliorated by the growth of industrial employment, and the towns provided a safety-valve, although the rate of urbanisation was slow between 1500 and 1700, however great the urban growth. What was critical was the slow rate of change in agricultural methods; here lies the difference between France on the one hand, and England and Holland on the other. In England improvement in methods was slow until the 1620s and 1630s, but there were fundamental improvements thereafter; in France this was not so. Whether in consequence mortality rose in the seventeenth century, or fertility fell, in an effort to stabilise numbers around the 20 million that France could support, is sadly little more than speculation.

CHAPTER 10

IRELAND: THE GREAT TRAGEDY

In nearly every country in Western Europe the population increased between the middle of the eighteenth century and the middle of the nineteenth century; in most it doubled, a rate somewhat higher – but not greatly so – than that experienced in the sixteenth century. As in that earlier population cycle the period of growth had been preceded by a century of stagnation; but quite unlike the periods of the early fourteenth and early seventeenth centuries, the period of rapid growth between 1750 and 1850 was not followed by stagnation or decline, but by continued rapid growth, that did not begin to falter until the 1920s. The two exceptions to this were France and Ireland.

The population of Ireland grew rapidly from 1780 to 1845, rising from about 4 million to just over 8 million (table 13). In 1845 the potato crop, on which a large proportion of the population depended, was attacked by a blight, *Phytophthora infestans*, and much of it destroyed. In the following year the crop was an almost total failure; in 1847, although the blight was less virulent, much of the seed potato had been eaten, and there was little left to sow; 1848 saw a further harvest failure. In 1849 the blight was less severe, and in 1850 only a few counties were affected.[1] When the 1851 census was published, the population totalled only 6552392. Between 1845 and 1851 some 800000–1000000 died, mainly from infectious diseases, although 21770 were recorded as having died from starvation, and over a million emigrated.[2] This was the last great demographic catastrophe in Western Europe. Although proportionally no more of the population died than had done in the crisis of 1740–1 in Ireland itself, in Finland in the 1690s or in Denmark in the 1650s,[3] whereas these earlier catastrophes were followed by a rapid recovery in numbers, the population of Ireland continued to fall, from 6552392 in 1851 to 4390219 in 1911 and then more slowly to 4243803 in 1961; this was a result of declining fertility as marriage was postponed, and a continuing rate of emigration.

The Famine was once seen as a great divide in Irish history, precipitating changes not only in population, but also in land use and land tenure. Nor were contemporary Irish writers in doubt as to what caused Ireland's poverty before the Famine, what caused the Famine itself, or what caused the comparatively slow economic progress after the Famine. They believed that the land tenure system, in which the bulk of the land was owned by a

116   *Malthus justified*

Table 13. *The population of Ireland, 1687–1971*

1687	2167000	1781	4048000	1871	5412377
1712	2791000	1785	4019000	1881	5174836
1718	2894000	1788	4389000	1891	4704750
1725	3042000	1790	4591000	1901	4458775
1726	3031000	1791	4753000	1911	4390219
1732	3018000	1821	6802000	1926	4228553
1754	3191000	1831	7767000	1936–7	4204476
1767	3480000	1841	8175000	1946–7	4289275
1772	3584000	1851	6552392	1951	4329587
1777	3740000	1861	5798564	1971	4514313

SOURCES: T. W. Freeman, *Ireland: a general and regional geography* (London, 1969), p. 120; K. H. Connell, *The population of Ireland, 1750–1845* (Oxford, 1950), p. 25.

largely absentee Protestant population but farmed by mainly Catholic tenants, was the cause of agricultural backwardness in the early nineteenth century; that British restrictions on Ireland's manufacturing industries and agricultural exports before the Union in 1801 had prevented the fullest exploitation of resources; and that after the Union the introduction of free trade between Britain and Ireland destroyed all but the most efficient Irish industries. And although the potato blight itself could not be blamed upon Britain, the ineptness of government policy was thought to have been responsible for the magnitude of the disaster. '...the Almighty sent the potato blight, but the English created the Famine', wrote John Mitchel.[4]

More recently the historiography of modern Ireland has been much revised. The Famine is no longer seen as a great turning-point, for emigration was already substantial before 1846, while in parts of Ireland the attempt to control numbers by postponing marriage was established by the 1820s, if not before. The decline in tillage and the swing to pastoralism, once thought to be a result of the Famine and the subsequent decline of population, is now believed to have begun in the period of low cereal prices after 1815. Even the Protestant landlord, once thought the source of all Ireland's woes, has been treated more kindly, if not rehabilitated. Fortunately it is not necessary here to judge these contentious matters, except in as far as they influence the relationship between population and agriculture. The first question to be answered is why Irish population grew so rapidly between the middle of the eighteenth century and 1841.

The growth of population in Ireland

The first census of Ireland was taken in 1821 – an earlier attempt in 1813 was never published – and is thought to underestimate the population, while that of 1831 is almost certainly an overestimate, so that the census of 1841 is the first reliable account of the population of the country.[5] The only sources

Table 14. *The rate of population increase in Ireland, 1712–1851 (% per annum)*

1712–54	0.32	1821–31	1.3
1754–81	1.0	1831–41	0.5
1781–91	1.6	1841–51	−2.2
1791–1821	1.2		

SOURCE: Connell, *The population of Ireland, 1750–1845*, p. 25.

for estimating the population before 1821 are the hearth taxes, revised at regular intervals from 1687. These data are liable to two principal sources of error. The average size of household is not known, and there were considerable but unknown omissions of households from the lists. The traditional estimates of population based on the hearth taxes have been revised by K. H. Connell (table 13), but his estimate of the average size of household and of the number missing was rather arbitrary, and may overstate the rate of increase (table 14).

Ireland's population increased slowly in the first half of the eighteenth century. In 1740–1 a failure of both the grain and the potato crops led to a terrible loss of life, and between 200000 and 400000 may have died, one tenth of the total population.[6] Thereafter population grew steadily (table 14) by 27% between 1754 and 1781, by 68% between 1781 and 1821, and by 20% between 1821 and 1841. Between 1780 and 1841 the population doubled; in view of the fact that the figure for 1781 is thought to be an underestimate, the rate of increase over this sixty years was not greatly different from that in England and Wales, while between 1754 and 1841 the rate of increase in the two countries was almost identical. Thus although the rate of increase in Ireland may have been greater than in England and Wales, it was not dramatically so; the discrepancy is not as great as Talbot Griffith, the first writer to compare the two countries, believed. He estimated that the population of England and Wales increased by 88% between 1750 and 1841, and that of Ireland by 172%.[7] But it must be remembered that in this period about 1750000 Irish emigrated to Britain and North America and therefore the rate of *natural* increase may have been higher than that in Britain.

The causes of growth

When Talbot Griffith made his classic investigation into the causes of population growth in the British Isles in the eighteenth century, he concluded that in England the major cause was a decline in the death rate, and this was due to improvements in medicine and public sanitation. In Ireland, however, he was unable to find any evidence of a decline in the death rate, and contemporary writers believed that the great increase in population after 1780 was due to rising fertility. The adoption of the potato allowed a man to support a family on a hectare of land; this released the prudential check, and made it possible for most of the Irish to marry, and to marry young.[8] Early marriage was made possible not only by the spread of the potato, but by the subdivision of holdings. 'The subdivision of the land and the increase of the population form a vicious circle; as the population increases so does the subdivision of land, for in the system on which that increase is built, it is necessary for each family to have its own potato patch; as the subdivision of land increases so does the population...'[9]

Substantially the same view was taken by K. H. Connell twenty-five years later. He could find little evidence for an improvement in public health or for advances in medical treatment. Smallpox inoculation may have reduced mortality in the towns, but not in the remoter rural areas, while the growth of hospitals and dispensaries had little effect on the death rate. He concluded therefore that the great increase in population after 1780 was due to a rise in fertility, and this in turn was due to earlier marriage. He believed, however, that by the 1830s marriage rates were falling.[10]

Unfortunately there is little statistical evidence on the age of marriage, the proportion marrying or the rates of marital fertility before the second half of the nineteenth century. Connell used data in the 1841 Census of Ireland to calculate the crude birth rate in the 1830s – which he thought was only a little higher than in England – and the child–woman ratio, which was somewhat higher. A subsequent revision of both these figures suggests that the crude birth rate in Ireland in the 1830s was over 35 per thousand compared with 33 per thousand in England between 1841 and 1850, and that marital fertility rates were 11% above those in England. Connell assumed that fertility had risen from the 1770s, and was falling by the 1830s, and that the major determinant of these changes was the fall in the age of marriage in the eighteenth century, and its rise from the 1820s.[11] Unfortunately evidence on the age of marriage before 1841 is purely literary. Such statistics as exist on the age of marriage and the proportions marrying suggest that the differences between England and Ireland were not as great as might be expected. In 1841 only 21% of women in urban areas in Ireland aged between 17 and 25 were married, a figure little different from that for England, while in the late 1830s the average age of women at marriage in both countries was 24.5 years. Nor was the proportion unmarried greatly different: in 1851 only 11% of women in Ireland between 45 and 54 were unmarried, in England, 12%.[12]

Such comparisons at mid-century do not of course preclude the possibility that fertility had arisen in the second half of the eighteenth century and declined to rates comparable with England in the 1820s and 1830s. But the reasons for such an increase are less clear; in England it has been argued that the growth of the factory system, with its opportunities for the employment of man, wife – and later, children – encouraged earlier marriage. In Ireland there was no growth of industrial employment; instead, it is argued, the rapid diffusion of the potato made early marriage possible and hence greater fertility. The potato gave calorific yields per hectare two or possibly three times that of wheat, and thus, according to Arthur Young and other English visitors, made it possible for a man to support a wife and family on 0.8 hectares (but see p. 122). About 4.5–7.0 kg of potatoes a day, together with half a litre of milk provided an adequate if dreary diet, and thus the country could support a much higher density than when cereals were the basis of subsistence. The wider adoption of the potato could have had other consequences. Between 1741 and 1807 there were fewer failures of the potato harvest, and thus the catastrophic mortality typical of the period before 1741, and later between 1807 and 1845, was much reduced, not only cutting the death rate, but extending the duration of marital unions. It has even been suggested that a potato and milk diet was superior to that based on cereals and animals products that prevailed before 1740, and thus made the population less susceptible and more resistant to infectious diseases.[13] The diffusion of the potato is thus central to the argument that increased fertility was the cause of the increase in population between 1750 and 1845. But there is little reliable evidence on the chronology of the adoption of the crop or on the proportion of the population who were solely or mainly dependent upon it. On the eve of the Famine there were just under one million hectares under potatoes, between 30% and 40% of the total area under crops, and this was the sole food of 40% of the Irish population. When the potato became the staple diet of the Irish is impossible to tell in the absence of reliable agricultural returns: it has been variously put at 1680, 1730, between 1740 and 1780, and after 1780. If the potato was so central to the growth of population then it is likely to have become the staple only after 1750, for population increase was slow before then. K. H. Connell has argued that the swing from pastoral to arable farming in the second half of the eighteenth century encouraged landlords to allow the subdivision of what were once pastoral holdings. On these families grew wheat to pay the rent and potatoes for subsistence. Thus the change in prices, the rapid adoption of the potato, and the tolerance of subdivision allowed early marriage, which gave rise to greater fertility and faster population growth.[14]

But in the absence of any reliable statistical evidence it is perfectly plausible to argue that the growth of population was not a consequence of the rapid adoption of the potato, but a cause of it. If the death rate in Ireland had begun to decline in the middle of the eighteenth century this would have led to an increase in the rate of growth; this in turn would have led to the subdivision of holdings and later a shift from the low yielding cereal diet to an inferior but higher yielding crop, the potato. As has been noted before, there is little evidence on the course of mortality before the 1860s but there seems to have been little advance in public health, medical practices or private hygiene. However, one possible cause of a decline in mortality was the spread of smallpox vaccination. In the early eighteenth century smallpox accounted for

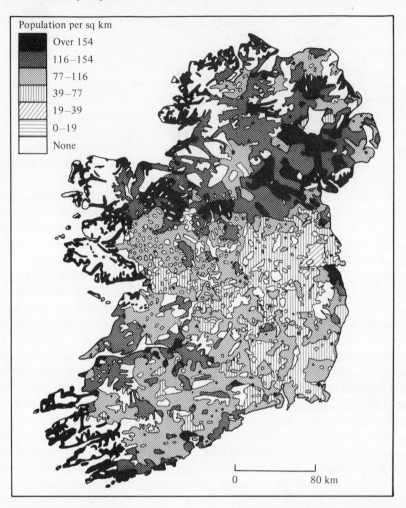

Fig. 10. Population density in Ireland, 1841. Source: T. W. Freeman, *Pre-Famine Ireland* (Manchester, 1957), p. 18.

20% of deaths in Dublin: inoculation was introduced into Ireland in 1725 and the improved Suttonian method in 1768; inoculation was universal by the early nineteenth century. This may have been sufficient to reduce the death rate and release the rapid rate of increase that took place after 1750 and more especially after the 1770s.[15]

Thus the causes of population growth in Ireland after 1750 are far from clear; their consequences, however, are much more certain. In the first half of the nineteenth century there was much poverty in Ireland, and contemporaries – or English contemporaries at any rate – had little doubt that this was a result of overpopulation. We turn now to consider the symptoms of overpopulation.

Table 15. *Agricultural population densities*, c. *1841*

	Arable area (1000 ha)	Agricultural population (1000s)	Agricultural population per 100 ha of arable
Ireland	2630[a]	5600[b]	213
England and Wales	5382[c]	3500[d]	65
France	25001[e]	20000[f]	80

[a] G. O'Tuathaigh, *Ireland before the Famine 1798–1848* (Dublin, 1972), p. 136.
[b] The agricultural population is assumed to be 70% of the total population.
[c] L. Drescher, 'The development of agricultural production in Great Britain and Ireland from the early nineteenth century', *The Manchester School*, 23 (1955), 167.
[d] The agricultural population is assumed to be 22% of the total population.
[e] J. C. Toutain, *Le produit de l'agriculture française de 1700 à 1958* (Paris, 1961), p. 48.
[f] J. C. Toutain, *La population de la France de 1700 à 1959* (Paris, 1963), p. 54.

The symptoms of overpopulation

The rapid growth of population in the late eighteenth and early nineteenth centuries had made Ireland one of the most densely populated countries in Europe. The average density of population was 98 per square kilometre, rather less than that for England and Wales, where it was 106 per square kilometre. But whereas in England only 20% of the labour force was engaged in agriculture and 38% of the population lived in towns of 10000 or more, in Ireland 70% of adult males were employed in agriculture, and 92.3% of the total population lived in hamlets, villages and towns of less than 10000. The population was not evenly distributed: the south-eastern quarter of the island had densities well below the national average (fig. 10): densities above the national average were to be found in the north, in the north-west and in the south-west. Some of the highest densities were in the coastal fringes of the west in Mayo, Galway, Donegal, Sligo, Kerry and Cork, although only short distances inland were virtually uninhabited upland areas. The agricultural population densities in Ireland were remarkably high: for the country as a whole just over three times that of England and Wales and two and a half that of France (table 15).[16]

One of the most marked consequences of the growing population was the subdivision of farms. This was not the result simply of population growth, for in much of Ireland, particularly in the west, it was the practice for farmers to divide their holdings among all their sons. In the later eighteenth century many landlords let land not directly to the peasant but to 'middlemen', at fixed rents over long periods. They did not work the land, but let again to sub-tenants; as neither the primary landlords or the middlemen provided buildings in a lease, it was to the middleman's advantage to subdivide his lease

Table 16. *Farm size in Ireland, 1845–1911*

Area (hectares)	1845 (Number)	(%)	1847 (Number)	(%)	1851 (Number)	(%)	1911 (%)
0.4–2	181950	23.6	139041	19.04	88053	15.3	11.1
2–6	311133	40.4	269534	36.8	191854	33.4	22.8
6 and over	276618	35.9	321434	44.0	290401	50.6	62.1
Total	769701	100.0	730009	100.0	570338	100.0	100.0

SOURCE: P. M. A. Bourke, 'The agricultural statistics of the 1841 census of Ireland: a critical review', *Economic History Review*, 18 (1965), 380.

on annual rents. The swing from pastoralism to wheat in the later eighteenth century also encouraged the subdivision of holdings, for more labour was needed.[17]

There is no statistical evidence of the subdivision of holdings in Ireland in the century before the Famine, although contemporaries had no doubt it was going on, particularly outside the commercialised farming areas of the south-east. The census of 1841 published figures on farm size, but they are thought to be defective. Those collected by the Poor Law Commission are more reliable (table 16); in 1845 Ireland was a country of predominantly small farms. Excluding holdings of less than 0.4 hectares nearly two-thirds of all holdings were less than 8 hectares and less than one-tenth had more than 20 hectares. The predominance of small farms was most marked in the west, and least so in the south-east where commercial farming of both wheat and cattle was to be found. Not only were the farms small but many were less than the area contemporaries believed necessary to provide a minimum livelihood; this minimum, the Devon Commission thought, was 4.2 hectares if badly farmed, 2.6 hectares if well farmed. As about 35% of all holdings of more than 0.4 hectares were less than 3 hectares, and 48% less than 4 hectares, a large proportion of the farmers were on the brink of subsistence; to this must be added the very large number who had less than 0.4 hectares, or no land at all, and rented the use of land for potatoes from nearby farmers for part of the year. According to P. M. A. Bourke there were 650000 men who had no access to land other than this 'conacre' land in 1845.[18] But in the eighteenth century Arthur Young and others thought that a family could exist on a much smaller area than 4.2 hectares (see p. 119 above).

In the middle of the eighteenth century the landless were a small proportion of the rural population and the cottier, was not, as many visitors believed, typical of Ireland. But the rapid growth of population between 1770 and 1841, and the practice of partible inheritance, had led to the rise of a large landless population by the eve of the Famine. In 1845 there were 935448 occupiers of land, however small the amount, and 650921 labourers without any land.

Thus over a third of rural households were completely landless: this number had grown by 90000 since 1831, an increase of 14%. This was not due, as it was at least partly in England, to expropriation at enclosure, for in Ireland the enclosure of common field in eastern Ireland was complete by 1750, while in the west the rundale system was largely extinguished by 1845 except in Mayo.[19]

The great growth in the landless had an adverse effect on the wages of agricultural labourers, and this was compounded by the post-war agricultural depression and the swing to pastoralism, with its lesser demand for labour. There were few large farms on which day-labouring could be obtained, and on the bulk of peasant holdings family labour provided the necessary work force. Thus from the 1770s wages failed to keep up with prices; the fall in incomes was particularly striking after 1815. In 1811 the average income per annum of the Catholic population of Ireland – the overwhelming majority – was £4–£6 a head; by 1821 it had fallen to £3.3. An increasing proportion of the labouring population found it impossible to find employment in the country or in the towns. In 1823 one-quarter of the working population of Westmeath had been destitute for five years. In the 1830s between one-third and one-half of the labourers in County Cork could find only occasional employment; indeed one contemporary argued that only one-third of the labourers in the country as a whole had permanent employment. There is little doubt that the standard of living of a substantial proportion of the rural population was declining in the 1820s and 1830s, and this was reflected in the diet. Not only did an increasing proportion of the population become solely dependent on the potato, but milk consumption diminished as fewer smallholders could afford to keep a cow, and the growing number of pigs were not eaten, but fed upon potatoes and sold to pay the rent. There was even a shift to inferior potatoes. From 1808 the 'lumper', a higher yielding but less palatable variety spread rapidly. Housing standards were appalling. Much of the growth of population, especially in the west, was made possible by squatting on waste in quickly erected cabins. By 1841 40% of the 'houses' in Ireland were one-roomed cabins.[20]

The consequences of rapid population growth bore hardest upon the landless, but the smallholders also suffered. By the 1840s there was not only unemployment in Irish agriculture, but *underemployment*, for many of the small farms could not provide work for the family throughout the year. The Famine led to a fall of over one-fifth in the agricultural labour force, yet output fell very little between 1846 and 1851; R. D. Crotty has concluded from this that 20% of the labour force had a marginal productivity of zero.[21]

The rapid growth of population led to fierce competition for land, and a rise in rents and land prices. It has been frequently stated that while agricultural prices doubled between 1760 and 1815, rents were quadrupled; thus agricultural profits were transferred from the tenant to the landlord. But where actual cases are cited, increases seem more moderate. Thus on the

Fitzwilliam estates in Wicklow, Wexford and Kildare rents rose 86% between 1746 and 1783, and by a further 89% between 1783 and 1815. On the Earl of Upper Ossory's estate in Queen's County rents were raised 49% between 1758 and 1776, and by 60% between 1776 and 1812; a higher rate of increase was found on an estate in Enniskillen, where rents were raised by 288% between 1738 and 1780. But in England rents rose by 50% between 1750 and 1790, and by a further 90% between 1790 and 1815. The competition for land did not affect only the farmer. Labourers who sought the use of 'conacre' land were having to pay £25–£30 per hectare in the neighbourhood of towns in the 1830s.[22]

Few have denied the poverty of Ireland in the first half of the nineteenth century. By the 1840s many of Ireland's farms were too small to provide a livelihood and the growing numbers of landless were in a precarious condition. But not all were agreed that this was simply due to the growth of population. Before considering the alternative explanations of Ireland's plight, we turn to consider the various responses made to population growth in the late eighteenth and early nineteenth centuries.

The agricultural response to population growth

In the middle of the eighteenth century Ireland still had a pastoral economy, in which cattle were the dominant livestock, sheep being unimportant. Beef cattle and stores were exported to Great Britain, and dairy exports were growing rapidly. Wheat production, on the other hand, was not sufficient to meet home demand, and it was imported between 1733 and 1776. The arable acreage, however, began to expand, under two pressures: first was the increase of population. The demand for food was met, especially in the west, by expanding the area under potatoes. The second pressure was the growing demand for wheat in Britain, and the area under wheat began to increase from the 1760s, especially on the south-eastern part of the island which was dry, near the ports, and already integrated into a commercial economy. The expansion of wheat was often combined with the growth of potatoes: landlords subdivided larger pastoral holdings and tenants grew wheat in rotation with potatoes, the wheat being sold for cash for the rent, the potatoes grown for subsistence. The expansion of the wheat area accelerated after 1784, when the Corn Act provided bounties on wheat exports. Between 1784 and 1806, one contemporary estimated that 40 500 hectares were added to the arable area. During the Napoleonic Wars Ireland provided one-third of Britain's cereal imports. Nor did the fall of grain prices after the Wars halt the increase in cereal output. In the 1830s 406 000 tonnes were being exported a year, enough to feed 2 million people.[23]

By the 1820s the fall in grain prices had prompted a swing to grass and livestock in some parts of the country, but the continuing rapid increase in population in the west prompted a further increase in arable land, mainly reclaimed from poor soils for the cultivation of potatoes. By the 1830s the limits of arable cultivation were being approached. Many contemporaries believed the further reclamation of bog and moor was one way of solving Ireland's population problem. Richard Griffith thought that there were 1 520 000 hectares of waste that would be brought into cultivation in the 1840s, 577 000 of which could be used for crops, the rest for grass. But although there was certainly reclamation after 1845, the greater part was for grass: on the eve of the Famine the arable area – between 2.6 and 3.2 million hectares – was probably very near the maximum that could be cultivated with contemporary technology. It has not been exceeded since.[24]

Thus the reclamation of land hitherto uncultivated was an important way of increasing output in the century before the Famine. In England at the same period the elimination of the fallow was a major way of increasing the area sown to crops. Whether this was a major source of increased cropland in Ireland is not clear. Certainly by the middle of the nineteenth century fallow was an insignificant proportion of the arable: in 1851 only 3.3% of the cropland was in fallow. Whether this indicates a massive reduction of the fallow acreage after 1750 is not certain. At that time most of the open field was enclosed in eastern Ireland, and only grazing land remained to be enclosed; but in the 1770s much of this enclosed arable was still farmed with the traditional three-course rotation, including a year in fallow. In the west the rundale system survived until the early nineteenth century: here land was held in joint tenancy and farmed in scattered strips, while grazing land was held in common; but fallowing was not an indispensable part of the system. Thus it is probable that there was a decline in the area under fallow after 1750, even though turnips and artificial grasses were little grown before the Famine.[25]

Prior to the eighteenth century agricultural communities in Western Europe did not have the opportunity to shift to higher yielding crops as a means of increasing output in response to population growth; the potato, introduced in the sixteenth century from the Americas, was little more than a curiosity until varieties appropriate to the day-lengths of Western Europe had been bred, and even then it was for long widely regarded solely as a fodder crop. However, it was grown as a field crop for human consumption in Ireland in the seventeenth century, and had become the dominant food crop before the Famine, possibly reaching a peak in area in the 1830s. In 1845 there were a million hectares under potatoes, in an arable area which has been put as high as 3.2 million hectares, but may not have been more than 2.6 million hectares. The crop thus occupied between 31% and 38% of the total cropland, and on the eve of the Famine provided the sole food of 40% of the population and a substantial proportion of the diet of the remainder. It was also fed to livestock, particularly to pigs; indeed one-third of the crop was consumed in this way. One-third of all the pigs in Ireland were kept on holdings of 0.4 hectares or less.[26]

The supreme virtue of the potato was that its calorific yield per hectare was between two and three times that of wheat, allowing the support of more people on one hectare of land. But it had other values: not only did it provide fodder for pigs and, to a lesser extent, cattle, but it could be grown on fallow land. The crop required careful cultivation and weeding, and the abundant use of manure; this benefited following crops of wheat, and thus potatoes filled the role in Ireland that the turnip did in England. In addition, it would grow on acid soils and in high rainfall areas.[27]

There is no doubting the significance of the potato in Ireland, although perhaps its relative importance in other countries has been neglected, and thus its comparative importance in Ireland may have been overstated; there were dramatic increases in the potato area in nearly all the countries of Western Europe in the first half of the nineteenth century. In Norway for example the crop increased remarkably in the first three decades of the nineteenth century and by the 1830s its output could feed one-fifth of the population.[28]

But the relationship between population growth and the growth of the potato area in Ireland is, as we have seen, a matter of dispute. According to one view the potato was already an important food crop in the mid-eighteenth century; its wider adoption allowed earlier marriage, and the crop, combined with milk was an improvement in the diet, which in turn reduced the death rate and extended the length of marital unions. In this view, the adoption of the potato caused population growth. An opposed view argues that the potato in the mid-eighteenth century was the staple of only a minority; that the diet of cereals and animal products enjoyed by the majority was superior; and that it was the rapidity of population growth that led to subdivision and the wider adoption of the potato. Thus the spread of the potato was an indication of impoverishment, and it was forced upon the population as rapid growth subdivided farms below the minimum necessary for subsistence on a cereal diet.[29]

So much attention has been paid to the potato by historians that the rest of Irish agriculture has been neglected. The consensus is – or was – that Irish farming methods were backward compared with those in Britain, and that this was largely due to the indifference of Irish landlords and the poverty of Irish tenants, who were reluctant to improve in case their rents were raised. Arthur Young was unimpressed by agriculture in the east on his visit in the 1770s, and much subsequent description is a catalogue of defects. Turnips and artificial grasses were uncommon until the 1840s, and implements were few, not surprisingly when so many of the farms were so small. Rollers, harrows or good ploughs were rare in County Cork in 1815. Seed was broadcast, and the sickle was still used for harvesting cereals until the 1830s. Little weeding was done, there was insufficient manure and unselected seed was used.

Some improvements were noted. An improved plough was introduced from Scotland in 1810 and spread slowly, although the spade remained the main implement on the small farms. By the 1830s the scythe began to replace the sickle, and in Meath in the 1830s theshing machines were coming into use. The potato was better cultivated between 1815 and 1845; more manure was used, and towards the end of the period, underdrainage and the drill were being adopted.[30]

Nonetheless the usual picture of Irish farming on the eve of the Famine is unflattering: yet the evidence on crop yield implies that Irish agriculture must have been more efficient than the literary evidence suggests. Potato crops averaged 15 tonnes/ha, a figure not only higher than that found in many other parts of Europe at that time, but higher than that obtained in Ireland after the Famine. A recent estimate of Irish wheat yields – the crop was grown mainly in the east – puts them at 1550 kg/ha, almost identical with that in England in the 1830s.[31]

Criticisms of Irish agriculture may have been too harsh, and too prone to compare the farming systems of the country with that of south-east England. Sheep were comparatively unimportant in Ireland – much of the country was too wet – and therefore there was little demand or need for turnips. While there were few machines, there was little need for them except in the south-east, for everywhere else farms were too small to make their use economic, and there was in any case an over-supply of labour. The introduction of the potato into rotations may have helped to increase yields in the preceding century. Although it would be unwise, on the present evidence, to argue that crop yields had risen dramatically in the century before the Famine, there seems no doubt that the traditional picture of backwardness must be modified.

It is impossible to quantify the relative importance of the different ways of increasing agricultural output before the Famine. But it would seem that by the 1830s there was little easily reclaimable land left; to what extent the reduction of fallow had increased the area under crops it is difficult to say; and as to increases in yields, all that can be suggested is that if potato and wheat yields were as high on the eve of the Famine as recent estimates suggest, then there must have been some improvement in farming methods in the preceding century. But clearly by the 1820s a large proportion of the Irish population was becoming increasingly impoverished. Had there been any demographic adjustments made in response to increasing population pressure?

Industrialisation and urbanisation

We have seen in preceding chapters that rural industry provided an important source of extra income for smallholders and the landless in seventeenth-century England and France, while in the late eighteenth and the nineteenth centuries population pressure in the English countryside was relieved by large scale rural–urban migration (see below, pp. 183–5). Neither of these opportunities was open to the Irish in the first half of the nineteenth century.

At the beginning of the eighteenth century Dublin was the only town in

Table 17. *The urban population of Ireland, 1841–1926 (people in places of 1500 or more, %)*

1840–1	15	1890–1	25
1850–1	20	1900–1	28
1860–1	20	1910–11	29
1870–1	22	1920–6	32
1880–1	23		

SOURCE: R. E. Kennedy, Jr., *The Irish: emigration, marriage and fertility* (Berkeley, 1973), p. 82.

Ireland of any size, with about 75 000 people; there were few other large towns and the numbers living in places of 5000 or more were no more than 155 000, about 6% of the total population.[32] In the eighteenth century Dublin grew rapidly, and with about 200 000 people was the second city in the British Isles in 1800. In the first half of the nineteenth century Belfast and Cork grew rapidly; the former had reached 75 308 in 1841 and the latter 80 720. Dublin had, by then, nearly a quarter of a million but while the total urban population – those in places of more than 5000 – had reached three-quarters of a million by 1841, it was only one-tenth of the total population. Indeed between 1821 and 1841 the rural population had grown more rapidly than the urban, and the proportion of people in non-agricultural occupations actually declined.[33]

Nor did urbanisation greatly increase after the Famine. In 1841 15% of the population lived in places of more than 1500, at the end of the century, 28% (table 17); but in 1907 the urban population of Ireland was less in absolute numbers than it had been on the eve of the Famine.[34]

The growth of towns before 1845 was due mainly to rural–urban migration, for mortality was higher in the towns – particularly child mortality – than in the country, while rural fertility exceeded urban fertility.[35] But the volume of rural–urban migration within Ireland was low: Dublin drew most of its migrants from its immediate hinterland, and in the 1840s there were few from the west, which was the most densely populated and the most rapidly growing area.[36] There were two reasons for the slow rate of urbanisation, one following from the other. First was the failure to develop an urban, industrial economy, except in the enclaves of Belfast and, to a lesser extent, Dublin; second was the diversion of rural–urban migration overseas, for the great bulk of the rural Irish who left Ireland before and after the Famine went to the cities of the United States and Britain, not to the countryside in those nations.

The failure of Ireland to industrialise is a controversial issue. Many Irish historians believe that the main cause was British policy. In the early eighteenth century Irish linen was excluded from Britain, although this did not prevent the development of a substantial domestic industry spinning and weaving flax in cottages in Ulster; bleaching was more centralised. In the later part of the eighteenth century factories to spin and weave cotton and flax were established in and near Belfast. In 1710 the Irish brewing industry was compelled to import hops from Britain, and this delayed its growth for part of the eighteenth century but did not prevent the emergence of a powerful brewing industry in Dublin. In 1746 Irish exports of glass to Britain were prohibited. More serious, it is thought, were the economic consequences of the Union of Great Britain and Ireland, for the tariffs which had been raised against British goods were reduced and finally abandoned in 1824. This allowed the free entry of British goods, and the infant Irish factory industries found it impossible to compete with cheaper British products. The cotton and woollen industries failed; fortunately some cotton spinners turned to linen. Power spinning concentrated in Belfast, but this too had adverse effects. The greater prosperity of Ulster, although its farms were as small and its population density as high as the west, was due to the widespread domestic spinning of flax; but by the 1830s home-spinning could no longer compete with the Belfast factories.[37]

There was little industrial growth elsewhere before the Famine; ship-building in Belfast only became important in the second half of the nineteenth century, and the brewing and distilling industries suffered a set-back as a result of successful temperance campaigns in the 1840s. Nor was there much further development after the Famine; there was a boom in railway building in the 1840s, and by 1853 there were 1600 kilometres of line. But Ireland suffered from a severe lack of resources and capital. There was little exploitable coal, ferrous or non-ferrous metals; most of Ireland's woodland had gone by the nineteenth century, so there was no possibilty of exporting timber or pulp, as did the Swedes, nor were there fisheries to supplement agricultural income as there were off the Norwegian coasts.[38]

In the first half of the nineteenth century contemporary British economists believed that Ireland's difficulties stemmed from the fact that population growth had outrun the capital available, and Irish writers believed this was due to the loss of income in Ireland as rent flowed to absentee landlords resident in England. This flow certainly existed, but was probably exaggerated, and modern writers have argued that there was not a shortage of capital in Ireland, but a shortage of *risk* capital. Capital was put not into new enterprises, nor profits ploughed back, but put into land, British government stocks and the Catholic Church.[39]

Whatever the causes of Ireland's lack of industrialisation rural–urban migration within Ireland could not solve the difficulties of Ireland's rural population. On the eve of the Famine the urban poor were also becoming a considerable problem. But if there was no industrial development in Ireland, there was of course rapid industrialisation in Britain and the United States in the nineteenth century, and it was to these regions that the Irish rural population went.

Demographic adjustments

In the 1820s and 1830s the Irish rural population was in great poverty. In earlier periods and in other countries rural populations had ameliorated their condition by producing domestic manufactured goods, by specialising in crafts and trades, and by migrating to towns. These opportunities were greatly restricted in Ireland. The growth of factory industries in England and in Belfast undercut the domestic spinning and weaving of flax and wool. In much of western Ireland there was still a self-sufficient, subsistence economy, and without the existence of a fully monetarised economy the rise of trades and services was inhibited. Nor did the towns provide a safety-valve. While there was undoubtedly movement from country to town, the lack of industrialisation meant the towns were quite unable to absorb the rural surplus.

What then were the demographic adjustments which could be made? It used to be argued that the Famine was the great divide in Irish history. The Famine itself, with a terrifying mortality, could be seen as a Malthusian check. In addition the Famine was thought to have begun the age of mass migration, while the fear of a repetition of the Famine led the Irish to adopt new marital habits. Marriage was postponed until an adequate holding was available and few were prepared to marry on the tenuous security of a potato patch. No doubt the traumatic memories of the Famine encouraged these trends in the second half of the nineteenth century. But emigration was already well established before the Famine, and the postponement of marriage already common in the east in the 1820s.

Although permanent migration and the postponement of marriage were the most important ways in which the Irish attempted to control their numbers both before and after the Famine, there was one further way in which some could add to their incomes, and that was by seasonal migration.

Migrant Irish labourers were recorded helping with the harvest in parts of England in the middle of the eighteenth century, and reports became more common in the later part of the century, particularly in the 1790s when there was a shortage of labour in some parts of England at harvest time. The demand for seasonal labour had grown in England between 1750 and 1850, with the spread of the Norfolk four course, which had two peaks of demand in spring and late summer. Although the English rural population continued to grow in this period, and in the 1820s and 1830s there was a surplus permanent labour force, there was still the need for extra hands at harvest, while the construction of railways in the 1830s and 1840s needed a vast labour force. These demands were partly filled by the seasonal flow of labour from Ireland across the Irish Sea to Glasgow and Liverpool and from there to much of the rest of Britain. This was made easier by the establishment of the first regular steamboat service between Dublin and Liverpool in 1816, and in 1821 Belfast was connected with Greenock and Liverpool. By the 1830s it was estimated that some 40000 a year left for the harvests in eastern England and lowland Scotland. The only data collected on the numbers were in 1841 when 57651 were recorded as leaving for Britain.[40]

Most of the seasonal migrants came from the north and north-west, which experienced a rapid growth of population between 1821 and 1841. Migrants as a proportion of the total population were most numerous from Donegal, Leitrim, Sligo, Mayo and Roscommon, where rapid population growth and subdivision and squatting went hand in hand. The seasonal labour requirements of the potato made it possible to sow the crop and then make the trip to England for the harvest, returning before the potato crop was lifted in autumn. But in the south-west counties of Kerry and Cork, which were as densely populated and as impoverished as those of the north-west, there was little movement over the Irish Sea; from this region there was instead a seasonal movement to the large grain farms of south-east Ireland. The seasonal migration to Britain came to a halt in the Famine, and no records were kept of sailings until 1880, but records kept by railway companies and the police suggest that the movement returned to its old level in the 1860s. In 1880, when records were kept again, there were 38000 involved, still predominantly from the north-west; there were now few from Ulster, for industrial growth in Belfast was providing employment. In the south-west there was still a summer movement to the south-east of Ireland, and to Dublin. In the 1890s the number greatly declined, although the movement, now on a much smaller scale, has persisted until the present.[41]

Emigration overseas

Seasonal migration affected a small minority of the population of the west, both before and after the Famine, and could only ameliorate conditions; it was often, for example, possible to earn enough in England to pay the rent of a potato patch. Permanent migration, on the other hand, could apparently reduce population pressure in Ireland, although the early classical economists such as Malthus and Ricardo were sceptical of this; they believed that the land left empty by migrants allowed others to marry, and nothing was thus done to reduce the rate of population growth. But by the 1820s the British government thought emigration, preferably to British colonies, was a solution not only for Ireland but for the surplus rural population of England, and some tentative attempts to assist migrants were made, although with little success. When the English system of Poor Relief was introduced into Ireland in the late 1830s, union districts were allowed to levy a migration rate.[42]

Emigration from Ireland, and particularly from the north, was established before the period of rapid population growth, but it was more a result of the dissatisfaction of Presbyterians with the Church of Ireland, or hostility to the land tenure system, than population pressure. One estimate puts the rate of emigration from Ulster in the mid-eighteenth century at 12000 a year, and

Table 18. *Emigration from Ireland, 1821–1920*

	A Population of Ireland (1000s)	B Emigrants from Ireland (1000s)	C B as % of A	D Irish migrants into the USA (1000s)	E D as % of A
1821–30	6802	—	—	50	0.7
1831–40	7767	—	—	207	2.6
1841–50	8175	1195	14.6	780	9.5
1851–60	6552	1011	15.4	914	13.9
1861–70	5798	849	14.6	435	7.5
1871–80	5412	623	11.5	436	8.0
1881–90	5174	770	14.8	655	12.6
1891–1900	4704	433	9.2	388	8.2
1901–10	4458	316	7.1	339	7.6
1911–20	4390	150	3.4	146	3.3

SOURCES: K. H. Connell, *The population of Ireland, 1750–1845* (Oxford, 1950); D. A. Harkness, 'Irish emigration', in W. F. Willcox (ed.), *International migrations: interpretations* (2 vols., New York, 1931), vol. 2, p. 265; W. F. Willcox (ed.), *International migrations: statistics* (2 vols., New York, 1929), vol. 1, p. 730; U.S. Bureau of the Census, *Historical statistics of the United States: colonial times to 1957* (Washington, D.C., 1960), pp. 56–7.

at the time of the American revolution a sixth of the population of the colonies was Irish and mainly from Ulster. But large-scale migration was delayed until after the end of the Napoleonic Wars when the growing population, the post-war depression, and in Ulster the decay of the domestic linen industry, prompted a surge in migration both to Britain and North America.[43] No figures of Irish emigration are available before 1841, although US immigrant figures date from 1820; it has been estimated, however, that between 1780 and 1845 1 140 000 Irish left for the United States and Canada, and some 630 000 settled in Britain. Irish immigration into the United States steadily mounted between 1820 and the Famine; between 1840 and 1845 nearly a quarter of a million entered that country. This was more than twice the number entering the United States from Germany, and three times the number from Britain.[44]

It was of course the Famine that transformed this rising tide into a torrent. In the years of the Famine one and a quarter million Irish left the ports of the United Kingdom. Nor did the end of the Famine see the end of the flood: a further 639 000 left in 1852–5. Thereafter the rate of emigration and the absolute numbers declined, with two periods of resurgence, both following harvest failures, in 1860–2 and 1879 (fig. 11, table 18).[45]

Although the rate of emigration fell away after the end of the Famine, a substantial emigration continued, so that between 1852 and 1911 nearly 5 million Irish left their country, of whom between a fifth and a quarter went to Britain, and the bulk of the remainder to the United States.[46] But neither before nor after the Famine was emigration related simply to population pressure; before the Famine a majority of the emigrants came from Ulster,

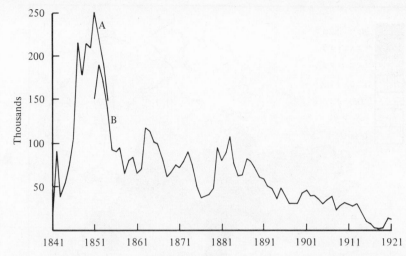

Fig. 11. Emigration from Ireland, 1841–1921. Source: W. F. Willcox (ed.), *International migrations*, vol. 1, *Statistics* (New York, 1929), pp. 730–1. A, Irish-born leaving UK ports 1841–54. B, Persons leaving Ireland for Britain and overseas 1851–1921.

which was no more densely populated than the west coast. But in Ulster the decline of the domestic linen industry cut the incomes which had supplemented those from agriculture, while the Ulster custom of tenant right allowed a tenant to sell the right of occupancy to the incoming tenant; thus small farmers could raise enough capital to pay for the still expensive crossings of the Atlantic. Religious differences between members of the Presbyterian population in Ulster and both the Roman Catholic population and the Church of Ireland, the established Protestant church, was also a cause of emigration.[47] In the west, in contrast, there was still wasteland available for squatters, although it supported a deplorably low level of living, and it was here that many still spoke only Irish, and were thus less familiar with the prospects in Britain or the United States. During the Famine the emigration rate from all parts of the country was high, but again, it was not directly related to population density; if it had been, emigration rates would have been highest in the west and in Ulster. Yet rates were low in much of the north, and the southern half of the west coast. The highest rates were to be found in the east centre, and the northern central districts, particularly along an axis running from Sligo to Wicklow (fig. 12). The relatively low rates in Ulster were due to a combination of factors: the famine had less effect here, and so the Poor Rates did not mount to overwhelm the small farmer as they did in much of the west, and the landlord class provided aid and employment. In contrast in the western counties there was extreme poverty and little help from the landlords, who were mortgaged and overburdened by Poor Rates. In many parts of the west coast a high proportion of the rural population

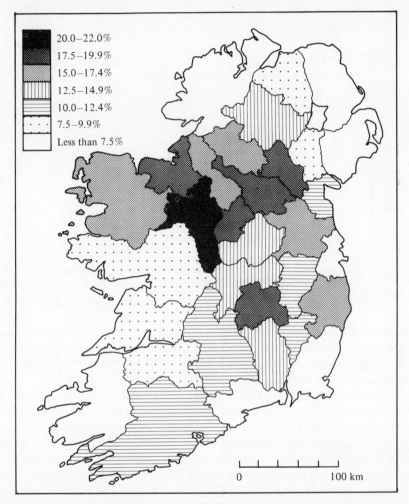

Fig. 12. Regional rates of emigration from Ireland during the Famine: emigration 1846–51 as a percentage of the population of 1841. Source: S. H. Cousens, 'The regional pattern of emigration during the Great Irish Famine, 1846–51', *Transactions of the Institute of British Geographers*, 28 (1960), 121.

were quite without land, except rented 'conacre', and thus could not find the money to pay to go to either Britain or the United States. This changed after the Famine, when destitution diminished and remittances from relations and friends allowed landless labourers to form a large part of the migration from the south-west in the 1850s.[48]

The thirty years after the Famine were years of comparative prosperity for rural Ireland; death and emigration in the Famine years had greatly reduced the number of very small holdings and the numbers of the landless, and continued emigration further reduced the landless after the Famine, although there was only slow progress to further amalgamation after 1851. But the differences between the west and the remainder of the country were not removed. Here were still to be found the highest population densities and large proportions of the arable land were still devoted to potatoes which, in the country as a whole, were far less extensively grown.[49] And although the population of Ireland fell between 1851 and 1881, the smallest decreases were all found in the west, and in some districts there were increases. In spite of this there was little difference between the emigration rates of east and west until the 1880s, following the failure of the potato harvest in 1879. However, by the 1900s when national emigration had fallen to a pre-Famine level, emigration rates in the west were well above those in the east and south.[50]

But in spite of the lack of correlation between emigration rates and population pressure within Ireland, there is no doubt that migration before the Famine was an attempt to adjust numbers to the potential of the land, albeit to a supra-optimal density. During the famine destitution, eviction and despair drove hundreds of thousands from the land, and in the early 1850s a brief improvement in living standards allowed many more to leave. Thereafter it is less easy to relate the continuing high rate of emigration simply to population pressure. The attractions of Britain and the United States, with which most of the Irish were increasingly familiar, and in the 1880s rising expectations even in the once isolated west, must have played as great a role as the stark forces of expulsion that had operated before 1851.

Changes in fertility

In every decade between 1851 and 1946–51 emigrants exceeded natural increase; thus emigration was a major cause in the decline of Ireland's population after the Famine. But there were also changes in fertility. The absolute number of births declined in every decade from the 1870s to the 1960s as did the natural increase. The crude birth rate in Ireland fell from the 1860s, as indeed it did in nearly every West European country, although the decline in Ireland has been slow. General fertility also fell between the 1870s and the 1880s, and thereafter showed little change to the 1920s; marital fertility on the other hand did not show a decline between 1870 and 1920, and the average size of family showed little change in this period (table 19).

Unfortunately there is little reliable evidence on fertility before the 1870s; the registration of births, deaths and marriages was not required before 1863. The data on births in the 1841 census have been used to construct indices of fertility but these do not show that Irish fertility was unequivocally above that of England at that time. The crude birth rate in Ireland before the Famine has been put at 33 or 35 per thousand and possibly higher; in England the crude birth rate in the 1840s was 33.1 per thousand. In the 1870s, when data for both countries are available, the English crude birth rate was well above

Table 19. *Trends in Irish and English fertility, 1870–1920*

	Crude birth rate (per thousand)		Live births per 1000 women aged 15–44			Legitimate live births per 1000 married women aged 15–44		
	Ireland	England	Ireland	England		Ireland		England
1871–80	26.3	34.4	118.9	153.6	1870–72	307	1871–80	295.5
1881–90	23.3	32.3	102.6	138.7	1880–82	284	1881–90	274.6
1891–1900	23.1	29.1	99.6	122.7	1890–92	287	1891–1900	250.3
1901–10	23.3	26.25	100.5	109.0	1900–02	292	1901–10	221.6
1911–20	21.6	21.8	98.7	87.7	1910–12	305	1911–20	173.5

SOURCES: E. A. Wrigley, *Population and history* (London, 1969), p. 195; Kennedy, *The Irish: emigration marriage and fertility*, p. 176; M. S. Teitelbaum, 'Birth under-registration in the constituent counties o England and Wales: 1841–1910', *Population Studies*, 28 (1974), 335; B. R. Mitchell and P. Deane, *Abstrac of British historical statistics* (Cambridge, 1962).

that in Ireland and remained above until the 1920s, as did general fertility (table 19).[51]

If the crude birth rate was as high in the 1840s as 35 per thousand, then there must have been a profound decline in fertility during the Famine and in the decade after the end of the Famine; and this has often been so argued. It has been suggested that before the Famine the Irish married young and most of them married. During the Famine the number of baptisms declined, which would be consistent with what is thought to have happened in subsistence crises in traditional societies. The Famine, however, is thought to have delivered a traumatic shock to marital habits. The Irish were determined never again to be dependent upon the potato, and instead of marrying young, and all marrying, they attempted to prevent subdivision of holdings by passing the farm to the eldest son, and not dividing it between all the children. The eldest son inherited the farm, but at a relatively advanced age; the eldest daughter received a dowry; the others were left to fend for themselves and traditionally emigrated.[52]

Thus fertility declined in Ireland for two reasons: because sons had to wait for their fathers to die before getting the farm, the average age of marriage rose; and an increasing proportion remained unmarried. There is evidence that is consistent with this interpretation: in 1861 the median age of Irish brides was 23.5 years, by 1926–7 it was 29.1; in County Cork in 1841 only 11.2% of women aged 45–54 were unmarried, in 1901, 18.6%, while for County Derry the figures were 16.8% and 30.1%; for the country as a whole the proportion of females between 15 and 45 who were ever married fell from 43.1% in 1871 to 36.5% in 1911.[53]

But a different interpretation can be put on these facts if the regional aspects of demography are considered: in 1841 the child–woman ratio in Ireland was highest in the western counties, lowest in the east and south-east; on the other hand marital fertility did not vary greatly from region to region, but the proportion of women marrying did, and it was this, rather than the age of marriage, which seems to have accounted for the differences in fertility between the west coast and the rest of the country. Between 1821 and 1841 there was a pronounced difference in the rate of population increase between east and west. In the north-east emigration was a factor in causing this lower rate of increase, in the east and south-east it was the postponement of marriage, in the west marriage was much more common and earlier than in the east. This was partly accounted for by the differences in land use and land tenure. In the east there were larger farms, little unreclaimed land, and landlords were partly successful in preventing further subdivision. In the west there was still wasteland available on which cabins could be erected and potatoes grown. Thus in the east the shortage of land prevented early marriage, and there were already signs of the *match* where farmers tried to ensure that the family holding descended undivided to one son.[54]

The Famine did not lead to an immediate change in marital habits or fertility in the west. Mortality was highest in the west, and although there was less emigration than in other parts of Ireland, there were vacant holdings, and a pattern of early marriage and high fertility was re-established; it was not, in fact, until the 1870s that a pattern of celibacy and late marriage became established. In County Cork in 1841 11.2% of women aged 45–54 were unmarried, and in 1871 it was still only 12.0% but by 1901 had risen to 18.6%.[55] In 1871 the proportion of women ever married was already low in Leinster and Ulster, but still high in the western provinces of Munster and Connaught; but by the end of the century the differences between the two regions had largely disappeared (table 20).

It is thus plausible to see the deferment of marriage as an adjustment to rapid population growth, first appearing in the east where land first came in short supply; in the Famine there was an increase in the deferment of marriage in both east and west, and then in the west old habits reasserted themselves until the 1870s, when the customs long established in the east spread into the region.

The decline in the crude birth rate and general fertility that took place in Ireland as a whole in the second half of the nineteenth century owed more to increasing celibacy than any major decline in marital fertility. However, after the 1870s there was some sign of a decline in marital fertility in the south-east, although not in other regions.[56] Thus the Irish chose to limit their numbers in a quite different way to the English or the French; in neither of these two countries were there *major* changes in the proportions of the population marrying in the second half of the nineteenth century. On the other hand there was a significant decline in the number of births within marriage, beginning in England in the 1870s, and in France at a much earlier date. The Irish however combined emigration, the deferment of marriage, and celibacy

Table 20. *Ever-married as a percentage of all females, 15–45, in Ireland*

	1871	1881	1891	1901	1911
Ireland	43.1	40.5	36.6	35.1	36.5
Leinster	40.7	40.5	37.4	35.8	37.0
Ulster	40.1	38.5	35.9	35.8	37.9
Munster	47.4	41.8	35.9	33.5	34.6
Connaught	48.6	43.8	38.0	34.7	34.1
England and Wales	52.8	52.2	49.7	49.1	49.6

SOURCE: B. M. Walsh, 'Marriage rates and population pressure: Ireland 1871 and 1911', *Economic History Review*, 23 (1970), 148–62.

as means of curtailing their numbers; before the Famine the postponement of marriage was most marked in the south-east, emigration rates were highest in the north, while in most of the west marriage rates were high and emigration rates low. In the first twenty years after the Famine there was little change in the west in marriage rates, and emigration rates were no higher than those in the east, where marriage rates was lower. Thereafter the west changed markedly: marriage rates declined and emigration rates rose; in the east the continuing decline in marriage rates after 1871 was much slower than in the west, but there was a beginning of the limitation of births within marriage.

Mortality

In Malthus' system unlimited population growth led eventually to a rise in death rates which ended the period of population growth; it would seem that the Famine played such a role in Irish history. Indeed some contemporaries believed that the Famine was not only inevitable but necessary. But the catastrophic mortality of 1845–51 had been preceded by an increasing number of crises. Between the great crisis of 1740–1 and 1807 there were few failures of the potato or cereal harvests – only 1765, 1770, 1795 and 1800 were poor years; but thereafter, the harvest failed or partially failed in 1811, 1816, 1817, 1821, 1825, 1829, 1830 and 1832–3, 1834, 1836, and 1839, 1841, 1842 and 1844. These failures did not lead to starvation, but they were followed by outbreaks of 'famine fevers' – of which typhus was the most important – which were spread throughout the isle by beggars and vagrants seeking charity or employment. Typhus together with dysentery, scurvy, and 'relapsing fever', took a terrible toll of a population ill fed, badly housed and cold: in the typhus outbreak of 1817–19 50000 died, and 46175 died from cholera in 1832–4.[57]

The period between 1810 and 1845 was then one in which living standards fell as numbers continued to increase, and the impoverished population was susceptible to infectious disease. There are no figures, but it seems likely that 'catastrophic' mortality was rising in the thirty years before the Famine. Yet the 'normal' death rate in Ireland before the Famine has been estimated to have been 22 per thousand, below that found in England and Wales; this was probably due to the greater numbers living in towns in England and Wales.[58] But the catastrophic mortality of 1845–51 cannot really be seen as a Malthusian crisis. The arrival of the blight was a chance event; much of the mortality can be attributed to the incompetence of the British government – rather than its malevolence, which many Irish believed, and still do – and of course to the fact that such large numbers of the population were at such a low standard of living before the blight.

But as has been seen, population pressure was already causing adjustments in Ireland's demographic behaviour before the Famine. Unable to migrate to the towns, with little reclaimable land left, and with little prospect of industrial development, emigration and the postponement of marriage were already being used as solutions to overpopulation. Many modern historians have argued that even without the Famine, Irish population would have ceased to grow in the second half of the nineteenth century, by continuing emigration to the industrial towns of Britain and the United States and possibly by an earlier and wider extension of the postponement of marriage. If the marital habits of Ireland before the Famine had continued and if there had been no migration, the population of Ireland would have reached 50 million by the 1960s.[59]

Conclusions

Ireland would seem to be one of the clearest cases of overpopulation so far considered; and its special interest is in the way in which numbers were subsequently reduced. Some see Ireland as a special case of the Western European method of controlling numbers, but the maintenance of a high rate of marital fertility with steadily increasing celibacy has no parallel in the rest of Europe. But not all historians would agree that sheer numbers were the root of Ireland's problem. To many – both English and Irish – it was British government policies and in particular the land-tenure system that was the cause of Irish poverty.

In the 1770s 95% of Ireland was owned by Protestant landlords; land had been confiscated under Cromwell and again at the Williamite succession, while the few remaining Catholic landlords were harried by the penal laws in the eighteenth century. Not all, or even a majority of these landlords were absentees: the only figures, for 1876, show that only 21% were never or rarely resident in Ireland.[60]

Nonetheless much of the rental income flowed across the Irish Sea. Irish landlords invested little in their estates. Land was let, but buildings were not provided; improvements, such as drainage or reclamation were rare. There was no compensation for tenant improvements except in Ulster, and tenants who did improve were apt to have their rents raised. The combination of unenterprising landlords and an insecure tenantry was not likely to create a spirit of improvement, nor the combination of alien landlords and indigenous tenantry with memories of expropriation likely to foster good will. Yet when Catholics again were allowed to buy land they did not behave any better than their Protestant predecessors. Nor were many landlords in a position to provide buildings or improvements for such a multiplicity of smallholdings. In England the tenant–landlord relationship worked not only because of mutual trust, but because farms were large. It is difficult to see how any system of land tenure would have improved the situation in 1845, when 5.6 million people worked between 2.6 and 3.2 million hectares, with between 0.4 and 0.6 hectares a head. The terrible losses of the Famine and the continuing emigration after 1851 allowed a system of somewhat larger farms to emerge (table 16), while between 1881 and Independence the country became one of peasant proprietors. But this would have all been in vain if the demographic habits of before the Famine had continued.[61]

CHAPTER 11

INTERIM CONCLUSIONS

Four cases of presumed overpopulation in pre-industrial Europe have now been considered. It is appropriate to ask here whether in fact these countries can be said to have been overpopulated. This is of course difficult to do. If overpopulation is to be defined in terms of optimum theory, then we have already seen how difficult it is to define an optimum population and from that derive a surplus population as a measure of overpopulation. Nor is it easy, even at present, to measure the two special cases of overpopulation: the point where the marginal productivity of labour falls to zero; and the point where average output per head falls below the subsistence level so that mortality rises and ends population growth.

In fact, there is no alternative but to take the symptoms outlined in chapter 3 as diagnostic of overpopulation. It would seem then that in the thirteenth century, the sixteenth century and in early nineteenth-century Ireland the demand for food outran the supply and this was expressed in rising grain prices in all three periods. Further, the demand for land exceeded the supply and this was reflected in rising rents and land values. But both these statements must be qualified. In the first place, some writers would argue that the trend in agricultural prices reflected the general trend in prices, and that this in turn was a function of the circulation and stock of money. Secondly, the shortage of land was a function not only of the amount, but also of the ownership, of land. In the thirteenth century much land was held in great estates operated by wage labourers; had land been more equitably divided, it can be argued, there would have been less of a shortage. This applies with equal force to the sixteenth and seventeenth centuries, when the system of landholding in England and France had shifted from a feudal mode to one based on contract rent.

In all three periods there appears to have been subdivision of farms as population grew, and in the cases of thirteenth-century France and England, sixteenth-century France and nineteenth-century Ireland a large proportion of the holdings were too small to sustain a family and so peasants had to have some other source of income. But in sixteenth- and seventeenth-century England there is less evidence of subdivision and it seems that if there was a discernible trend in farm size it was towards larger farms.

Where land is in short supply and there is a growing rural population there is likely to be the formation of a landless class. This seems best illustrated in England where at the beginning of the sixteenth century the landless were a small proportion of the rural population and were for the most part sons waiting to inherit their father's land. But by the end of the century the landless were much more numerous and remained landless all their lives. Doubtless the amalgamation of holdings that followed enclosure accounted for some of this, but enclosure affected only limited parts of the country and only in the early part of the century. Nor can the growth of a large landless class in nineteenth-century Ireland be attributed to enclosure.

The growing numbers of landless seeking labouring jobs on farms – and elsewhere – ensured that money wages did not keep up with food prices in the thirteenth, sixteenth and early nineteenth centuries, and so real wages fell drastically in all the cases studied. Even on family farms which relied little on hired labour there was underemployment, and it has been argued that the decline in population after the Black Death and the Irish famine had only a little effect on output, showing that much of the labour employed before had a marginal productivity close to zero. All three periods saw a deterioration in the incomes and diets of the majority of the rural population. In sixteenth-century France wheat began to be replaced by inferior grains, and in Ireland not only did potatoes progressively replace wheat for much of the population, but by the 1820s inferior varieties of potato were ousting nutritionally superior varieties, while milk intake was diminishing. In all three periods vagrancy was a problem. Lastly, periods of rapid population growth generally see an expansion of arable into land which has other uses. The cultivation of common grazing land may have reduced livestock numbers, the supply of manure and hence caused a reduction in crop yields. It certainly caused conflict between landlords and tenants, between farmers and cottagers, and between villagers and squatters.

The symptoms appeared in all four cases studied, and in this sense it is justifiable to argue that there was overpopulation, although less can be said about the degree of overpopulation; it has been argued that in early fourteenth-century England and nineteenth-century pre-Famine Ireland the point where the marginal return to labour had become zero had been reached. What of the extreme Malthusian cases, where average output falls below the subsistence level? Both the Black Death and the Irish famine appear at first sight to fit this case, but both can be shown to be due to causes independent of falling income. There is however some evidence of rising mortality in late-thirteenth-century England, and again in late-sixteenth-century England and France. But the evidence is not sufficiently reliable to assert that these were both cases of Malthusian overpopulation.

Responses to population growth

It was argued in chapter 5 that when population exceeds the optimum and as income per head falls rural societies can take a number of courses of action to arrest the decline. Agricultural change was not the only response, but before the nineteenth century was the most important. Of the four agricultural responses, the extension of the area under crops was the most important, if only because the possibilities of increasing crop yields were limited. There was a continuous expansion of the cultivated area in France and England until the middle of the thirteenth century; after the Black Death much land was abandoned, so that when population growth began again in the fifteenth century, this could be brought beneath the plough. By the middle of the sixteenth century arable was encroaching on pasture in England, and in France on vineyards as well as grass. In Ireland wasteland continued to be brought into cultivation in the west until the 1830s.

A second possible response was to reduce the part of the arable in fallow. By the middle of the thirteenth century, when suitable uncultivated land was running short, there was a switch from the two-field to the three-field system in both France and England, and in the sixteenth-century England there were further reductions in the fallow. In Ireland fallow was a very small proportion of the arable area in the 1840s, and it must be supposed that fallowing had been much reduced in the preceding period of population growth. These two methods of increasing output must have been of great importance because before the eighteenth century there were no higher yielding crops for farmers to switch to, although of course in Ireland the adoption of the potato was the major response to the rapid population growth after 1750. Nor was there much possibility of rapidly increasing crop yields in the medieval and early modern period. The main means of increasing yields was by more frequent cultivation and by applying more manure; the latter was in short supply as long as livestock relied on common grazing land for their fodder. Labour was not in short supply, but farmers constantly came up against diminishing returns in the absence of any significant technological advance.

But agricultural change was not the only possible response to population pressure. Some attempt could be made to control numbers. This was less easy in the medieval period. There was no possibility of emigration at this time. There was on the other hand the opportunity of migrating to the towns, and the urban growth of this time suggests that there was a considerable movement out of the countryside, for the higher death rates in urban areas meant migration was essential for urban growth. But there seems to have been little urbanisation at this time, and so urban growth can only have ameliorated rural problems, not solved them. Little is known of medieval demography. There is of course the possibility that attempts were made to check fertility by deferring marriage or limiting births within marriage, but there is little reliable evidence to confirm this. The problems of the countryside were compounded by the fact that the guild system kept industries within the towns.

By the late sixteenth century there were more strategies open to the rural population, particularly in England. Emigrants to North America were few but locally significant, and in the sixteenth and seventeenth centuries there was a marked growth of rural industry throughout Western Europe. Further, urban growth was rapid, and a number of great cities emerged in this period – London, Paris and Amsterdam. In England and in the Netherlands (see chapter 12) there was marked urbanisation, suggesting a greater rural–urban flow than had occurred in the past. There is also some evidence that there was a change in marital patterns between the late sixteenth and the mid-seventeenth centuries; later marriage in England and France may be seen as an adjustment to falling incomes.

In the nineteenth century the strategies adopted in Ireland differed greatly from those of the early modern period. In eastern Ireland there seems to have been deferment of marriage well before the Famine, but in the West fundamental changes did not come until well after the Famine. Rural industry could not provide a solution, and indeed industry in Ireland was finding it difficult to survive in the face of imports from England. Within Ireland there was urban growth, but little urbanisation – indeed the rural population grew faster than the urban between 1820 and 1840. It was thus emigration to Britain and North America which was the main response to population pressure before the Famine.

It would seem then that the poverty brought by population growth was far greater in 1300 than in 1600, not so much because agriculture was more efficient, but because the alternatives open to the rural population were more numerous. More significant, in all the cases studied the responses to population growth all came very late in the cycle. Thus population grew over three centuries in the medieval period, but it was not until the middle of the thirteenth century that there was a change from the two-field to the three-field system, or any adoption of the mouldboard plough, and the growth of legumes came even later. In the later cycle the changes in farming methods began in the 1580s but were not properly underway until the middle of the seventeenth century, yet English rural society was under pressure from the middle of the sixteenth century. This suggests that peasant societies prefer to adjust to a lower standard of living rather than make fundamental changes in their way of life. Indeed it would seem that it was only when average output was falling towards the subsistence level that changes were made.

PART THREE
MALTHUS REFUTED

CHAPTER 12

HOLLAND IN THE SIXTEENTH AND SEVENTEENTH CENTURIES*

In the preceding chapters it has been shown how by 1300 the population of much of Western Europe had reached the maximum that could be sustained with the existing technology and resources. Landlessness, falling real wages and smaller farms all gave rise to a low standard of living. The Black Death resolved this problem. In England and France in the sixteenth century population grew again towards the maximum it had reached in the early fourteenth century, but by the late sixteenth century the familiar symptoms of overpopulation were occurring again. Real incomes were falling, and by the middle of the seventeenth century a combination of reduced fertility and rising mortality led to a long period of stagnant population. In little of the period from AD 1000 to 1650 was there any sustained increase in income per head, except possibly in the fifteenth century.

Thus two great cycles of population growth saw the failure of technology and institutions to increase output at a more rapid rate than population could grow. This adverse relationship is usually thought to have ended in the nineteenth century when, although population was growing rapidly, national incomes grew more rapidly; this was due largely to a shift of population from agricultural activities into manufacturing industries; so great was this shift, that in the second half of the nineteenth century the absolute numbers employed in agriculture were falling in most countries in Western Europe. The process of industrialisation began in England, but spread rapidly to Belgium, France and Germany, and later in the century to parts of Scandinavia.

But there had been one area where a partial break-through had already occurred: that was in the Low Countries and particularly in the Netherlands; and within the Netherlands, the province of Holland was most transformed in the sixteenth and seventeenth centuries. In 1514 the Low Countries, South and North, became part of the Spanish Empire; at that time the southern Low Countries was the most urbanised and industrialised part of Europe, had Europe's leading port (Antwerp) and an intensive agricultural system. The Netherlands was less urbanised, had little industry, was primarily pastoral

---

* In this chapter the Low Countries is used to describe the area occupied by the modern states of Belgium and the Netherlands; the Netherlands refers to the modern Netherlands; Holland to the provinces of South and North Holland.

and fewer agricultural innovations were practised than in the South. When the revolt against the Spanish ended in the South, the Northern provinces, united in opposition to Spain, continued the war and had *de facto* independence by 1609, although it was not recognised by treaty until 1648. By then the United Provinces, or the Netherlands, had become Europe's leading trading nation, was the most urbanised part of the continent and had a greatly admired agricultural system. When, in 1696, Gregory King made the first estimate of national incomes for some European nations, the Dutch were the richest people in Europe. Yet this was all in spite of a rate of population growth between 1500 and 1650 quite as fast as anywhere else in Europe. This supremacy, however, was not maintained. In the eighteenth century the Dutch were outpaced by France and England, and in the nineteenth century the Southern Low Countries, or Belgium, industrialised long before the Netherlands.

Population growth and population pressure

The Netherlands shared the rapid population growth experienced in Western Europe in the sixteenth and early seventeenth centuries (table 21), increasing from about one million in 1500 to just short of two million in 1650. The population then stagnated for a century, and even in the second half of the eighteenth century there was only a slow rate of increase. The most rapid rate came in the first half of the sixteenth century, 0.5% p.a., falling to 0.4% p.a. in the second half and to 0.3% p.a. between 1600 and 1650. Of the provinces for which estimates are available, Holland had the most rapid rate of growth, increasing at 0.83% p.a. between 1514 and 1622, and at 0.5% p.a. between 1622 and 1680. Thus the province, which had only one quarter of the Netherlands population in 1500, had two-fifths in 1650 and provided 58% of the federal revenue. After 1650 the population of the Netherlands stagnated for a century, although the experience of the separate provinces varied. Holland increased slowly to 1680 and then declined; Friesland declined after 1650, and still had not recovered in the mid-eighteenth century; Veluwe and Overijssel however, continued to increase after 1650.[1]

The reason for the increase in population in the sixteenth and early seventeenth centuries is unknown, and, as there are few extant records of baptisms and burials, is unlikely to be known; but in the absence of any evidence of a decline in mortality it was probably due to rising fertility.[2] It might be expected that by the second half of the sixteenth century there would be evidence of population pressure, and indeed there are some such signs.

Grain prices increased in the Netherlands as they did in the rest of Europe, but somewhat less rapidly. Cereal prices tripled in the Low Countries but quadrupled in England and rose nearly seven times in France between 1500 and 1600; this lower rate of increase may have been due to the import and efficient distribution of cheap grain from the Baltic areas of Prussia and

Table 21. *The population of the Netherlands and some of its provinces,*
1475–1815 (1000s)

	Netherlands	Holland		Overijssel	
1500	900–1000	1514	275	1475	53
1550	1200–1300	1622	672	1675	71
1600	1400–1600	1680	887	1750	122
1650	1850–1900	1795	793		
1700	1850–1950				
1750	1900–1950	Veluwe		Friesland	
1795	2078	1526	36	1511	75–80
		1650	40	1650	145–50
		1750	54	1689	129
		1795	65	1744	135
				1815	173

SOURCES: J. A. Faber, H. K. Roessingh, B. H. Slicher van Bath, A. N. Van der Woude and R. J. Xanten, 'Economic developments and population changes in the Netherlands; a historical survey', *A.A.G. Bijdragen*, 12 (1965), 47–114; J. L. Price, *Culture and society in the Dutch Republic during the seventeenth century* (London, 1974), pp. 48–51.

Estonia. In contrast to England or France the prices of dairy products rose as rapidly as cereals. Real wages fell, but much less so than in other parts of Europe; indeed the purchasing power of building workers wages in Antwerp actually increased in the sixteenth century. In the Netherlands real wages fell until the 1620s but comparatively slowly, and then rose between 1625 and 1700 by 50%. By the middle of the seventeenth century Dutch labourers and artisans were the best paid in Europe, with wages some 20% above those in England. This does not mean that the labourer was affluent, but there were no subsistence crises in the seventeenth century, and few of the food riots that characterised rural and urban life in the rest of Western Europe.[3]

Although, as we shall see, there was a great increase in the area under cultivation in the sixteenth and seventeenth centuries, there was great competition for land and this led to very considerable increases in rents, which continued from 1500 to 1650; only after then did rents fall as population stagnated, and declined in some areas. In some parts of Holland rents may have risen as much as tenfold between 1500 and 1650.[4] There were regions in the Netherlands where population growth led to the subdivision of farms; this happened in Overijssel in the seventeenth century, for example. But in Holland farms do not seem to have grown smaller, partly because the area under cultivation was greatly extended; the result was, that a landless population grew up, but for the most part they did not sink into the depths of poverty as did the landless in France and England.[5]

That there was stress in the rural Netherlands in the seventeenth century cannot be doubted, but in the first half of the seventeenth century there was not the poverty that could be found in many parts of England in the 1620s or in much of France. For example, farmers in Friesland in the 1650s were better off than they had been in the 1550s: inventories show an increase in farm equipment and bigger farm buildings, furniture was better, and tin bowls and dishes replaced wooden plates, while Delft porcelain and clocks appear in some lists. In the towns the most conspicuous feature was the growth of a substantial middle class, with a considerable demand for luxury goods. Holland was the envy of Europe, and it occurred to few that the country was overpopulated, even if by the mid-seventeenth century it was one of the most densely populated parts of Europe. Indeed Sir William Petty, one of the many English observers of Dutch prosperity attributed it to the very density of the population, which permitted a number of economies of scale.[6]

The agricultural response to population growth

Holland's wealth in the seventeenth century was due primarily to its commanding position in European trade, but the growth of population prompted – indeed necessitated – considerable changes in its agriculture. Although in the seventeenth century the province was known for its dairy products and intensive arable agriculture, the great achievement of the sixteenth and seventeenth centuries was the reclamation of new farmland from sea and lake. Two types of land were reclaimed. First were the low lying lands behind the coast, which had to be protected from the sea by dykes. These embankments began to be made in the coastal areas in about AD 1000, from Friesland in the north to Zeeland in the south; their reclamation was aided by the end of a long period of rising sea level. There was much reclamation both on the coasts of the Netherlands and also further south, in Flanders. In the middle of the twelfth century the sea level began to rise again, but neither this nor the Black Death, which had less effect in the Netherlands than in much of Europe, halted the progress of reclamation, particularly in the southern islands. But the period of most rapid expansion came from the late fifteenth century onward (fig. 13) as population grew and cereal prices increased. Between 1540 and 1665, 125 000 hectares of polder were dyked; one half of this was in Zeeland and North Brabant, one third in Holland, the remaining sixth in Friesland and Groningen (fig. 14).[7]

In the seventeenth century a new type of reclamation got under way. In Holland and Friesland there were considerable areas of shallow lakes, formed by peat diggings; these were pumped dry by windmills. This type of reclamation was particularly active between 1600 and 1650 in a number of lakes north of Amsterdam; between 1540 and 1665 some 31 600 hectares of internal lakes were reclaimed. In the coastal areas the embankment of polders was undertaken by local drainage boards; but much of the pumping of the lakes was financed by merchants living in Amsterdam and other towns, who from the 1580s found this a profitable investment. In the second half of the

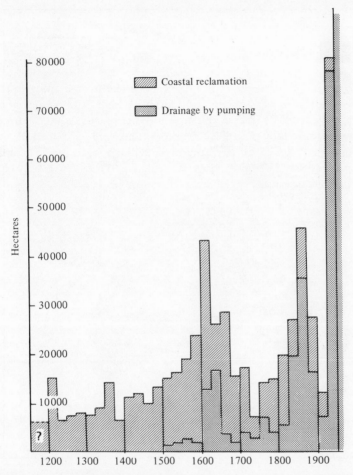

Fig. 13. The changing rate of land reclamation in the Netherlands, 1200–1950. Source: Paul Wagret, *Polderlands* (London, 1968), p. 76.

seventeenth century the rate of reclamation fell away as prices declined, and did not revive until population and prices began to rise again after 1750. The great area of reclamation then was not the coast, but the internal lakes south of Amsterdam, of which Harlemmermeer was the most important. The area brought into cultivation was remarkable: between 1550 and 1650 the population of the Netherlands increased by some 600000 but the area reclaimed was some 162000 hectares.[8]

This increase in the area under cultivation was not however enough to make Holland self-sufficient in cereals; indeed since the fifteenth century the Low Countries had been importing grain, mainly from England, France and the Rhine. In the sixteenth century the Dutch had to turn to Prussia and

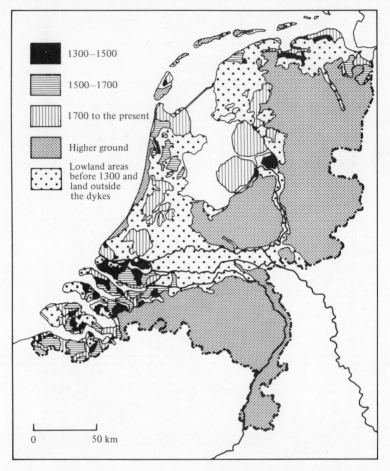

Fig. 14. The chronological pattern of land reclamation in the Netherlands. Source: *Atlas of the Netherlands* (The Hague, 1963–77), Plate VIII–4.

Estonia, for population growth in the former regions meant there was little surplus grain left for export. Imports from the Baltic, mainly of rye, increased steadily, reaching a peak in 1650, but as early as the 1560s Baltic grain was providing 13% of the Low Countries' cereal consumption.[9]

Although reclamation greatly added to the area under cultivation in the Netherlands, by no means all of it was devoted to cereals. In the newly drained lakes the clay soils were used for crops, often vegetables, but the peat soils were more commonly used for pasture. What of the arable lands that had existed before the era of reclamation? One way of increasing the area under crops was to reduce the fallow of the three-course rotation, and in the southern Low Countries and particularly in Flanders, means of doing this had been developed in the fourteenth and fifteenth centuries. The open-field system had already been extinguished in much of the Netherlands at the beginning of the sixteenth century; this did not however mean that the fallow had been abandoned. In the fourteenth and fifteenth centuries a number of crops were introduced in the southern Low Countries, particularly in Flanders and Artois, which could be grown on the fallow. In the sixteenth century they were more generally adopted in the southern Low Countries, and spread into the Netherlands.[10]

Although a great many new crops were adopted in the Low Countries between the fourteenth and the seventeenth centuries, there was no new high-yielding food crop: maize, which had some importance in southern France at this time, could not be grown so far north, and the potato was not adopted until after 1650. It was first grown as a field crop in West Flanders in the 1670s and was found in west Zeeland in the 1690s, in South Holland in the 1730s and in Overijssel by the 1740s; it was widely grown in the United Provinces by 1780, but mainly as a fodder crop.[11]

Thus although this important means of increasing food output was not available to the Dutch in the sixteenth and seventeenth centuries there were important ways in which agriculture could be improved; many of these methods were first established in Flanders in the fourteenth and fifteenth centuries, and spread later into the Netherlands.

First was the system of convertible husbandry. In the open fields there was a permanent distinction made between grassland and arable. The latter was sown to crops and periodically left fallow; the grazing land was rarely ploughed, except in those regions where the infield–outfield system was practised. However it was possible to grow cereals, have a year in fallow, and then lay the land to grass for three or more years before cultivating the land again. This allowed more livestock to be kept, and increased the amount of manure, to the benefit of the cereal crops. Such a system was practised in parts of Flanders in the fourteenth century, but its full value was not reached until pastures including clover were grown; this seems to have first been practised in the Netherlands in the late sixteenth century. By the 1620s the Netherlands was exporting clover seed to England.[12]

A second way of reducing the fallow and increasing yields was to grow peas, beans or vetch – all leguminous crops and capable of maintaining soil nitrogen – as catch crops on the fallow; this practice has been identified in Flanders in the fourteenth century but was not unique to the Low Countries for it was practised in southern England and northern France in the thirteenth century (see above, p. 75).[13]

A third improvement was the growth of turnips; these of course provided fodder as well as acting as a cleaning crop, and reduced the fallow. In the early seventeenth century, rotations including turnips, clover and grain were being practised in Flanders, and were subsequently imitated in East Anglia to form the basis of the Norfolk system.[14]

A fourth, and perhaps critical feature of Dutch and Flemish agriculture was the application of very large amounts of manure. Cattle dung was the most important constituent, but night-soil, marl, residual clays from brick-making, lime and peat ash were all applied; the amounts used could not have been obtained solely from the small farms, and from an early date fertilisers were purchased from off the farm. In Holland the intricate canal network made the movement of manures feasible. One unusual source of manure was cole-seed, which was first grown in the Netherlands in the mid-fourteenth century, and during the sixteenth century largely replaced rape. Both crops were grown for their oil, but when this had been extracted, to be used for lighting and cooling, the residue formed a valuable cattle feed which in turn increased the supply of manure. Heavy manuring was probably the major reason for the high yields obtained in the Low Countries in the late sixteenth century. In both north and south seed–yield ratios averaged 1:10, compared with only 1:6.7 in England.[15]

But by no means all of the Netherlands was devoted to arable farming. The most important area of cropping was in Zeeland and South Holland where the embankment of polders was most active in the sixteenth and seventeenth centuries, and which was close to the intensive arable areas of Flanders. Much of Holland was unsuited to arable farming, and the land was predominantly under grass for dairying. But the sixteenth, and especially the seventeenth, centuries saw the emergence of specialised arable farming in parts of the Netherlands. First was the growth of crops for industrial purposes. The use of hops to flavour beer was probably invented in Holland in the early fourteenth century. By the late fifteenth century it was an important crop in North Brabant and South Holland, and there were major brewing industries in Gouda, Delft, Breda and Haarlem. Industrial development encouraged other crops: rape and cole-seed have already been noted, but the shipbuilding industry and the textile trade encouraged the growth of flax and hemp, grown mainly on small farms. The Dutch woollen industry concentrated on the bleaching and dyeing of white cloth imported from England and so the growth of woad and madder for dyes was locally important; madder was grown in Zeeland as early as 1325. In the seventeenth century a small area of tobacco growing became established around Amersfoort in Veluwe to supplement the imported tobaccos.[16]

Flemish agriculture was carried out on very small farms. The spade was much used, or on larger farms the light Brabant plough, pulled by horses rather than oxen. Labour inputs were considerable; commercial crops were grown in rows, although the drill was not yet known, and weeding was frequent. Such methods were easily applied to vegetable crops, and the sixteenth and seventeenth centuries saw the rise of horticulture on the outskirts of Amsterdam, Hoorn and Alkmaar. By the middle of the seventeenth century this had ceased to be merely a suburban activity and there had emerged specialised regions of horticulture, particularly on the light soils inland from the coastal dunes in Holland and also in Friesland. This was made possible by the growing affluence of the Dutch urban population. Turnips, cabbages and carrots had been grown in market gardens in the sixteenth century. In the seventeenth century lettuce, cauliflower, beans, cucumbers and strawberries were also being produced, while the beginnings had been made in the cultivation of tulip and hyacinth bulbs.[17]

At the beginning of the sixteenth century Holland had mainly a pastoral economy; grain was grown, but cereals predominated only in the eastern, upland provinces. In the sixteenth and seventeenth centuries specialisation in dairying on farms increased, as many farmers abandoned cereal production. This was only possible because of the import of Baltic grain, but it was prompted by the rise in dairy prices; the price of butter, cheese and meat all rose more than grain prices in Holland in the sixteenth and early seventeenth centuries. Nor surprisingly much of the reclaimed internal lake area was put down to grass in the seventeenth century. Dairy farming in Holland saw a number of improvements in the sixteenth and seventeenth centuries. The average size of herd increased on farms that did not greatly increase in size. This was made possible by the improvement of grassland, particularly the adoption of clover in ley farming in the seventeenth century; the same period saw the use of manure on grass, and improved drainage. Although this increased the output of summer grazing and hay, it was still not sufficient to feed the cows throughout the winter. The canal system allowed the movement of hay from surplus to deficit areas, but more important was the use of rape- and cole-seed residues to feed the cattle. Together with some improvements in breeding, this better feed increased milk output. The output of dairy products in Holland steadily mounted until the middle of the seventeenth century; some of this growth was absorbed by the affluent towns, but much was exported, in the form of cheese.[18]

It will be apparent that farmers in Holland responded to the growing population and rising prices of the sixteenth and seventeenth centuries in quite a different way to farmers in France, or in England before the 1620s. Instead of turning increasingly to grain production they specialised in dairying, industrial crops and horticulture, and relied on grain imports to provide their basic foods. This was only made possible by the internal growth of urban demand, and the expansion of the bulk trade in grain. But even these changes left a considerable increase in the population to be absorbed. How was this achieved?

Demographic adjustments: rural–urban migration

By far the most impressive demographic change in Holland – as distinct from the Netherlands as a whole – in the sixteenth and seventeenth centuries was the massive growth of the urban population. Holland was already highly urbanised in 1514, when one-fifth of the population lived in towns of 10000

Table 22. *The urban and rural populations of Holland, 1514 and 1622*

| | 1514 population | | 1622 population | |
	(1000s)	(as a % of total)	(1000s)	(as a % of total)
Rural[a]	217.4	79.2	342.9	51.1
Amsterdam	13.5	(4.9)	104.9	(15.6)
Other urban[b]	43.5	(15.9)	222.7	(33.3)
Total urban[c]	57.0	20.8	327.6	48.9
Total	274.4	100.0	670.5	100.0

[a] Population living in places of less than 10000.
[b] Population living in places of more than 10000 but excluding Amsterdam.
[c] Population living in all places of more than 10000.

SOURCE: J. De Vries, *The Dutch rural economy in the Golden Age 1500–1700* (New Haven, 1974), p. 87.

or more (table 22); at the same time only 6–7% of the population of England and Wales lived in towns of over *5000*, while as late as 1700 only 10% of the population of France lived in places of more than 10000 inhabitants.[19] Yet in the next century there was a remarkable growth in the urban population. Between 1514 and 1622 the total population of Holland increased by 144%; the rural population rose by only 58% but the urban population grew by 471%. Admittedly the phenomenal growth of Amsterdam was important in this, but the other towns of more than 10000 increased from 43500 to 222746, an increase of 412%; in 1622 almost half the population of Holland lived in places of more than 10000.

Thus between 1514 and 1622 the total population of Holland increased at an average rate of 0.83% p.a., the urban population by 1.6%, and the rural by only 0.4%. Such a high urban rate of growth could not have been due to natural increase alone for it would have required either death rates much lower than those found in the rest of Western Europe at this time, or a remarkably high level of fertility. The limited evidence on urban death rates suggest they were high, and higher than the birth rates: in the second half of the seventeenth century the death rate averaged 43.5 per thousand in Amsterdam, but the birth rate was well under 40 per thousand. It is probable then that the Dutch cities grew, as did those of France and England at this time, mainly by immigration.[20]

One source of migrants was the southern Low Countries, for the conflict with Spain led to a dramatic fall in the population there; in many parts of Flanders and Brabant it fell by one-half to two-thirds between 1572 and 1609, and in Antwerp it fell from 84000 in 1582 to 42000 in 1589; as many as 80000 may have settled in the Netherlands between 1570 and 1600. In the first decade of the seventeenth century one-third of Amsterdam's population and one-fifth of Rotterdam's came from the southern Low Countries.[21] But although these immigrants from the south were important in the rapid growth of urban population in Holland most of the migrants came from the rural areas of the Netherlands, and from within Holland itself, for although the rural population was mobile the bulk of urban immigrants came from comparatively short distances away.[22]

The rapid growth of Holland's cities came mainly after 1570; this was the time when the flight from the south began. But it was also the time when signs of population pressure appeared in the Dutch countryside, and when the cities began to provide a safety valve for the countryside.[23] But unlike France, or England before 1650, industrial and commercial development in Holland's towns was sufficient to absorb much of the rural exodus. Dutch prosperity was based on trade, which owed its beginnings to fishing. In the fifteenth century the shoals of herring in the Baltic migrated through the sounds into the North Sea. It was discovered that the herring could be preserved by pickling in salt, and this led the Dutch south to France, Spain and even the Canary Islands in search of salt supplies; an important market for herrings grew up in the Baltic states, so that trade from Dutch ports extended along the whole of Europe's western and northern coastline. The fishing industry continued to grow in importance. By 1636 the Dutch had 2000 *buis*, or fishing boats, in the North Sea, and in the mid-seventeenth century the industry was thought to employ at least as many men as agriculture.[24]

The fishing industry had much wider repercussions; the *buis* were only engaged in herring fishing for a short part of the year, and were available for trade in the rest. The long established import of grain from the Baltic lands now began to expand. The Dutch carried herrings, salt, cheese, butter, beer and cloth eastwards, and brought back grain, timber, iron, copper and tar. Grain was the most important of these commodities, for not only did it supply Holland's grain deficit but it was re-exported. The failure of grain harvests in the Mediterranean in 1589–90 gave the Dutch an opportunity they were quick to seize. In 1590s a new bulk carrier, the *fluyt*, was designed and introduced; it substantially reduced the cost of transporting bulk goods and the Dutch could undercut most other merchant vessels. An increasing proportion of the trade of other countries – including England and France – began to be carried in Dutch ships.[25]

The Dutch also entered into the trade with the Americas and the East Indies, the Dutch East India Company being founded in 1602, and the West India Company in 1621; the vessels involved in this trade were only 0.2% of the total Dutch merchant tonnage but they brought back spices, tobacco, tea, coffee, dyes, sugar and cocoa. Amsterdam thus usurped Venice's position, and as the major market set the price for much of Europe's commodity trade.[26]

This remarkable trade expansion prompted industrial growth within Holland, based, with the exception of agricultural produce, on imported raw materials. Much of this industrial development was based in the towns; an edict of 1531 prohibited the growth of industry in rural areas, in contrast to the southern Low Countries, where the power of the urban guilds had been broken, and indeed with England and France, where in the fifteenth and sixteenth centuries there was a rapid growth of rural industry. There was already some industrial development in the towns in the early sixteenth century. Coarse woollen cloths were made in Leiden in the fourteenth century, and to a lesser extent in Utrecht and Deventer. In the late sixteenth century immigrants from the south brought with them the skills needed for the new lighter textiles. But much of the Dutch textile industry was based on the bleaching and dyeing of unfinished woollen cloths imported from England. Leiden remained a centre for woollen cloths, but linen was spun and woven in Haarlem, and silk in Amsterdam.[27]

The fishery industry, and later the grain trade, encouraged the rise of a substantial shipbuilding industry, particularly in villages on the river Zaan north of Amsterdam: grain and tar were imported from the Baltic, but the allied manufacture of ropes, nets and sails encouraged the growth of hemp. Brewing was a long established industry, relying upon local hops and barley, and beer was exported to the Baltic. By the seventeenth century a variety of specialised trades were growing up: the flight from the south meant that Amsterdam replaced Antwerp as the major European diamond centre, and from the 1570s a printing industry flourished, in many cases started by immigrants, but encouraged by the demand for maps. The preparation of imported raw materials became important – sugar-refining, tea, cocoa and tobacco all gave rise to industries that re-exported much of their produce.[28]

The rise of industry within Holland then provided employment for the rapidly growing towns, as did the merchant navy and the fisheries. By the middle of the seventeenth century it is possible that agriculture did not employ more than one-third of the working population of Holland; some fragmentary data on the rural and urban populations of the other provinces at the same time suggests that the agricultural population of the Netherlands as a whole could not have exceeded half of the total.[29] Between 1514 and 1622 the rural population of Holland increased by 57%, yet there seems to have been little change in the average size of farm. This was partly because there was a considerable area of new land reclaimed, and this absorbed some of the increase. But whereas at the beginning of the century there had been few landless people, the growth of population created a landless class, and rural society became increasingly stratified. It has been argued that this had beneficial consequences for agricultural productivity. In the early sixteenth century farms had been primarily subsistence orientated, and peasant families carried out many non-agricultural activities such as fishing, fowling, peat-digging, spinning and weaving, transporting goods to market, and making and repairing buildings, carts and farm implements. As the number of landless grew, they began to undertake these jobs; specialisation made them more efficient and the services were more cheaply provided. Similarly the farm family could now spend more time on strictly agricultural activities, and carried them out more efficiently, so that the division of labour forced upon rural society by population growth increased productivity in the rural sector, and increased the beneficial interaction between town and country. Agriculture became more commercialised, selling produce in the town and buying some inputs from there. Thus although there were certainly landless labourers who relied upon day-labouring for their income, they were a relatively small proportion of the rural population.[30]

In short then, the rural population of Holland found outlets in the towns, the fishing industry and the merchant navy; those who remained on the farms became more efficient, and the non-landowning population were effectively employed. This is not to suggest that there was not poverty or chronic stratification of rural society in seventeenth-century Holland. But clearly rapid population growth had a less adverse effect on Holland than on France or England at the same time.

Demographic adjustments: fertility and mortality

The population of the Netherlands followed much the same course as the rest of Western Europe between 1500 and 1650. Growth was most rapid in the first half of the sixteenth century, and then the rate of increase fell slightly in both the following half centuries; from 1650 the population stagnated, until late in the eighteenth century. It is possible that the population was increasing in the late fifteenth century, but there are no estimates for the population at that time.

The roles of fertility and mortality in causing this characteristic pattern – rapid growth, deaccelerating growth and then stagnation – were far from clear. There is some evidence that fertility declined in the seventeenth century, but the evidence relates to very small numbers and restricted classes. The average age of girls who married town councillors in Zierikzee was 20 years in the first half of the sixteenth century, 24 in 1550–74, 26.5 in 1600–24, 21 in 1650–74 and 25.4 in 1675–99. In Amsterdam the average age of brides in 1626–7 was 24.6, by 1676–7 26.6, and in 1726–7 it was 27.2. This suggests that fertility was falling in these towns in the seventeenth century, but it is hardly conclusive; little is known of rural regions, although a special census of the village of Twisk in 1715 showed a disproportionate number of bachelors and spinsters, and the probate inventories of farmers show a marked decline in the number of beds per household in 1650–75.[31] But these are only straws in the wind; they suggest the possibility that later marriage may have reduced fertility and this may have been partly responsible for the slowing rate of growth in the first half of the seventeenth century and the stagnation of the second half. The pattern is similar to that found in England at this time. But it is not clear that the Dutch necessarily limited their families to adjust to a falling standard of living. Bearing in mind the relative affluence of the urban middle class and the improved condition of farmers between 1550 and 1650 (see above, p. 150) it is possible that this was adjustment due to rising expectations rather than falling incomes.

It is likely that mortality rose in most parts of Western Europe in the seventeenth century although the causes are far from clear. Some would attribute it to the economic dislocation that began in the 1620s – the general crisis of the seventeenth century.[32] In some cases it is plausible to argue that the first half of the seventeenth century saw a decline in living standards, and that rising mortality was a function of economic decline. Yet another view is that it was the consequence of the multiplication of disease and war. There is little evidence on mortality levels in Holland in the first half of the seventeenth century. It is true that outbreaks of plague were unknown between 1486 and 1557–8, the period of fastest growth; thereafter outbreaks became more common, particularly between 1615 and 1670, after which the disease disappeared. Amsterdam, for example, had nine attacks of plague between 1617 and 1664; in some cases the death toll was huge. Leiden, which had a population of 44 745, lost 9897 people in 1624. But plague was a random event, largely unrelated to economic conditions.[33]

Nor is it possible to show that there was a major decline in income per head, either on the national scale, or for large proportions of the population, in the first half of the seventeenth century; it was only after 1650 that the economy and the population stagnated. However, there is one possible way in which the national death rate may have risen. In pre-industrial Europe mortality was higher in towns than in the countryside: and the larger the town, the higher the death rate. Thus growing urbanisation could raise general levels of mortality, as an increasing proportion of the total population was exposed to the greater risks of the cities. Such a process could hardly have affected the national death rates of most European states until the nineteenth century, for the rate of urbanisation was so low. But this was not so in Holland. At the beginning of the sixteenth century one-fifth of the population lived in cities of over 10 000 people, by 1650 one-half. This was a shift important enough to influence overall mortality without any upward trend in rural or urban death rates.[34]

Conclusions

It is beyond the scope of this book to explain why there was not a pronounced decline in income per head in Holland as population rose in the sixteenth and seventeenth centuries. But some remarks can be made. In the first place the prosperity of the country as a whole was due not to any great advance in the agricultural sector, but to the growth of trade and industry. This, together with the expansion of the fishing industry, allowed the relatively successful absorption of those who left the countryside for the towns.

Although the rural population did increase between 1500 and 1650 it did so at a much lower rate than urban population. While possibly three-quarters of the working population was engaged in agriculture in Holland in 1514, this must have fallen considerably by 1650, when half the population was living in towns over 10000. As some of the residue was certainly engaged in urban functions, and as some of the true rural population was engaged in activities servicing the agricultural population, the proportion directly engaged in farming may have fallen as low as one-third.

In many ways the outstanding feature of the sixteenth century was the rapid commercialisation of agriculture; this made possible the growth of specialisation in dairying, horticulture and industrial crops, a feature found in south-east England and parts of France at this time, but on a smaller scale. Interaction between town and country increased, labour and produce moved to the towns, capital and inputs such as fertilisers flowed from town to country, while within the countryside the greater division of labour made the rural economy more efficient and delayed the onset of diminishing returns to labour. Specialisation was of course made possible by the import of grain, but it should be recalled that this was also occurring before 1500. Thus the relative success of the rural economy in overcoming the challenge of population growth came as a result of forces external to that economy – international trade and the growth of an affluent urban demand for high-value products. But within agriculture there was one major advance and that was the reclamation of large areas of new land.

But when this has been said, it should be recalled that even in 1500 the Dutch agrarian economy had a number of special characteristics which made such a response possible. First, Holland already had a relatively large urban population and an intricate system of waterways which allowed not only the cheap movement of food, but of inputs such as hay and fertiliser. Nor were Dutch farmers hampered by any seigneurial burden. In early medieval times the Netherlands had been an unattractive area, and the manorial system had not taken root, except in part of the eastern provinces. The fact that so much of the country had to be reclaimed from the sea by local co-operation had fostered a spirit of democracy. There was thus a very small noble class, and nowhere in Holland were there the large estates typical of France and England. Serfdom and the burdens of feudalism had disappeared in Holland, although they lingered in parts of the eastern Netherlands into the nineteenth century. Nor did the church own much land, although tithe was imposed.[35]

This did not mean that all Dutch farmers were freeholders, although in Holland farmers did own 42% of the land they worked. But even tenants had some security; by the beginning of the seventeenth century the custom of compensating tenants for improvements had become established. If farmers were relatively free from the heavy burdens of 'feudal rent' – although drainage rates were heavy – they were also untrammelled by much of the custom which village communities imposed upon themselves elsewhere in

Europe. The common fields had gone from much of Holland by 1500 and, thus, many of the difficulties of common husbandry and grazing.[36]

Thus Dutch farmers were not inhibited by many of the restrictions which impeded the progress of English and French farmers. The advances were made, it should be noted, without any growth of a new landowning class – although urban merchants bought land – nor were there any signs of amalgamation into very large farms, long thought a necessary feature of English agricultural advance.

Thus the essential points to be made are that, first, the rural communities of Holland avoided the worst features of population pressure because of forces external to their economy – the growth of trade enriched the towns, increased demand for products other than cereals, and provided employment for the rural surplus – and secondly, the absence of both feudal institutions and the restrictions of the traditional village communities made easier the adjustments which occurred within agriculture.

CHAPTER 13

BREAKING OUT: ENGLAND IN THE EIGHTEENTH AND NINETEENTH CENTURIES

Although the Dutch in the early seventeenth century had given some evidence that output could rise faster than population, and that Malthusian crises or adjustments were not necessary, it might nevertheless be argued that their case was unique. Holland was, after all, a very small country, and its firm grip on European trade could not be repeated. Yet in the century afterwards England went through a very similar series of changes. Agricultural methods were borrowed from the Low Countries, and adapted to English conditions; England also seized much of the growing volume of international trade, particularly with the American colonies and the West Indies, and at the same time emulated many of the financial methods the Dutch had developed. But it was after 1750 that England made the great leap forward that finally broke the connection between population and subsistence. Total real output doubled between 1750 and 1800, and tripled between 1801 and 1851. This rate of growth was above that of population increase, so that between 1801 and 1851 national product per head of the population doubled.[1] Since 1851 output per head has continued to increase. On the other hand while national income has advanced more rapidly than population since the early eighteenth century, the benefits of this advance have not been equally distributed throughout the population; nor has the pace of change been the same in each sector of the economy. It is a matter of continued controversy whether the standard of living of the ordinary Englishman was much changed in the early stages of the Industrial Revolution. Much of the increased output was swallowed up by investment, particularly in the construction of houses, and in the provision of industrial equipment; the cost of the Napoleonic Wars took much that could have been used to raise living standards, and food imports also had to be paid for.[2] This reduced the proportion of the national income left to raise the standard of living of the mass of the population; it was only after the 1840s that living standards can be shown unequivocally to be rising, and have, with periodic lapses, continued to do so to the present.

This breakthrough was not achieved by any prodigious advances in agriculture, for agricultural output increased far less rapidly than industrial output. In the eighteenth century industrial output rose at three times the rate of agricultural output and between 1811–21 and 1841–51 industrial output grew at 3.7% p.a., agricultural output at only 1.5%, little more than the rate of population growth.³ Throughout this period the agricultural population of England and Wales continued to increase, but at a much lower rate than the urban population. In 1851 the rural and agricultural populations of England and Wales reached the highest point they had ever reached – unless we accept some of the more inflated estimates for 1340. But from then onward the rural population declined slowly to the end of the century, and the primary and secondary rural populations – those directly involved in agriculture and those servicing those in agriculture – declined more sharply both in absolute numbers and as a proportion of the total population. At the same time England began to rely on food imports, to a greater extent than Holland had done in the seventeenth century. In the 1840s British grain provided all but 10% of the country's requirements, and only 5% of the total calorific requirements of the United Kingdom were imported. But by 1909–13 the country was importing 79% of the grain and flour needed for human consumption, 40% of its meat, and 72% of its dairy produce.⁴ Thus the relationship between population growth and food supply was not overcome, but sidestepped. Britain's industrial supremacy made it possible to exchange manufactured goods for raw materials and food. In the countryside the pressure of population was eased as men moved in increasing numbers from country to town, and a not inconsiderable number left the rural districts for North America and Australasia.

In a sense then, the problem of population pressure in the English countryside was never resolved; instead the rules of the game were changed completely. Although many writers have emphasised the role of increases in the productivity of English agriculture in promoting the Industrial Revolution, modern research suggests that the achievement of English agriculture in coping with population growth after 1750 was less impressive than was once thought. Indeed in the period between 1750 and 1850, the English countryside was under severe stress, much of this a result of the difficulty of absorbing the increasing rural populations. 'The mid-century can indeed be seen as a period when population growth started to erode the rate of growth of per capita income. Maybe the mid-eighteenth century should be envisaged as a time when the "Malthusian" threat of a "low level" equilibrium trap was still important.'⁵

The course of population growth

More has been written on the growth of population in England in the eighteenth century than any other topic in demographic history, yet there is still no agreement on the nature and causes of this growth. This is largely because of the absence of reliable data. The first census was taken in 1801, but births, marriages and deaths were not required to be registered until 1837. The ecclesiastical recording of marriages, baptisms and burials is thought to have grown increasingly unreliable in the eighteenth century as the number

Table 23. *The population of England and Wales, 1695–1939*

Date	Population (millions)	Rate of growth (% p.a.)	Date	Population (millions)	Rate of growth (% p.a.)
1695	5.2		1821	12.0	
		1.2			1.6
1701	5.8		1831	13.9	
		0.3			1.4
1711	6.0		1841	15.9	
		0.1			1.3
1721	6.0		1851	17.9	
		0.1			1.2
1731	6.1		1861	20.1	
		0.2			1.3
1741	6.2		1871	22.7	
		0.4			1.4
1751	6.5		1881	26.0	
		0.4			1.2
1761	6.7		1891	29.0	
		0.6			1.2
1771	7.2		1901	32.5	
		0.5			1.1
1781	7.5		1911	36.1	
		1.0			0.5
1791	8.3		1921	37.9	
		1.1			0.6
1801	9.2		1931	40.0	
		1.1			0.4
1811	10.2		1939	41.5	
		1.8			

SOURCE: N. L. Tranter, *Population since the Industrial Revolution; the case of England and Wales* (London, 1973), pp. 41–2.

of dissenters rose and the urban populations grew beyond the capacities of one parish priest.[6] At the first census John Rickman required the parish clergy to provide him with details of the number of baptisms and burials for each year between 1780 and 1801, and for every tenth year before then. These data, listed in the Parish Register Abstract, have formed the basis of nearly all calculations of birth and death rates in the eighteenth century, and for national totals. Yet they are doubtless faulty. 'The root cause of misunderstanding of the historical demography of England between 1700 and 1850', wrote T. H. Hollingsworth in 1969, 'seems to be the very collection and publication of the copious parish register abstracts by Rickman in the early censuses. If we ignored the baptism and burial data completely in the first instance, we should make fewer mistakes.'[7]

Although the bases for the estimates of national totals are unreliable, historians agree that there was little increase in population between the middle of the seventeenth century and the time of Gregory King's estimate of the national population in 1692; some would argue that there was renewed growth between 1690 and 1720, but the rate of increase was slow in the first half of the eighteenth century. There was an upturn in the 1740s (table 23), but a more significant increase in the 1780s; from then until the First World War the average annual rate of increase per annum did not fall below 1% in any decade, although the highest rates were recorded in the first half of the nineteenth century.

Although the mid-eighteenth century is often seen as a fundamental turning-point in English demographic history, the rate of increase in the late eighteenth century was not particularly high, and it took eighty years for

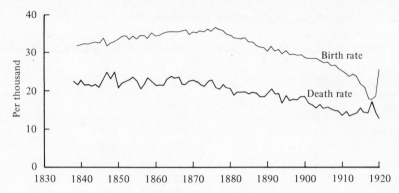

Fig. 15. Crude birth and death rates in England and Wales, 1838–1920. Source: B. R. Mitchell, *Abstract of British historical statistics* (Cambridge, 1962), pp. 29–30, 34–35.

the population to double, from 1750 to 1831. Such a rate of increase was paralleled elsewhere in Europe at this time – in Ireland for example – and was not greatly above the rates of increase found in some parts of Western Europe in the sixteenth century. But whereas in the seventeenth century a century of increase was followed by stagnation, population growth in England continued at a high rate of increase for another eighty or ninety years. This was not so in all parts of Western Europe. In Ireland the population fell from mid-century, and in France the rate of increase fell dramatically. Thus in many ways the great problem is not why English population began to grow again in the 1740s, but why it continued to grow so rapidly after the 1840s. Civil registration of births and deaths began in 1837. In 1841–51 the crude death rate averaged 22.4 per thousand and the crude birth rate 35.0 per thousand. Neither changed profoundly until the 1870s when both began to fall (fig. 15).[8] Much ingenuity has been expended on trying to reconstruct the course of birth and death rates before 1837, mainly by re-working the figures in the Parish Register Abstract; but quite contradictory results have been obtained. G. T. Griffith thought the birth rate rose before 1740 and thereafter remained constant, and most of the increase he attributed to a decline in the death rate, beginning in the 1760s but accelerating after 1780. J. T. Krause however has argued that there was very little change in the death rate between 1700 and 1820; he attributes the increase to rising fertility, as did many writers in the nineteenth century.[9]

The belief that mortality declined in the eighteenth century is supported by some evidence other than that of the P.R.A. material. The life expectation at birth of British peers, for example, rose from 32.9 years in 1675–99 to 49.2 in 1800–25 and that of county families in Hertfordshire and Northamptonshire from an average of 37 years for 1681–1730 to 50 years in 1781–1830. In London there was a substantial fall in child mortality between 1730–49 and 1810, while in three English villages infant mortality declined from the first half of the eighteenth century.[10]

There is rather less evidence – other than the fertility rates calculated from the Parish Register Abstract – to support the belief that fertility rose in the eighteenth century. Study of some 200 rural parishes suggests that the baptism–burial index rose after 1750, while the average family size of British peers rose from 3.83 in 1710–24 to 3.98 in 1775–99. A possible cause of this was a fall in the age of marriage. In Colyton in Devon the mean age of marriage for women fell from 30.7 years in 1700–19 to 26.4 in 1775–1800, while in Shepshed in Leicestershire it fell from 28.1 in the late seventeenth century to 22.6 in 1825–50.[11]

A recent attempt to reconstruct demographic rates in the eighteenth century, using a method of backward projection from data in the early censuses suggests that the gross reproduction rate showed little change in the first half of the eighteenth century, and then rose till the early nineteenth century; the same method suggests that the life expectancy was rising from the mid-eighteenth century. It seems reasonable to suggest that both falling mortality and some increase in fertility were responsible for the growth of population after 1740.[12] What caused these trends has been the subject of as much debate as the attempts to reconstruct the trends themselves, and with as little agreement. The decline in mortality has been attributed to a variety of factors. It has been argued that improved agricultural methods raised the standard of nutrition; this is plausible before 1750, less so in the late eighteenth and early nineteenth centuries. Talbot Griffith and later writers believed that the growth in the number of hospitals may have been important, as may the spread of midwives and the adoption of inoculation against smallpox. There were improvements in public sanitation – particularly in the provision of water supplies – in the early eighteenth century, but public health in the growing industrial cities saw little improvement before 1840. Private hygiene may have improved in the early nineteenth century when cheap cotton cloths and cheap soap became more widely available. Medical therapy, it is agreed, had little impact before the end of the nineteenth century, save in the control of smallpox. In the mid-nineteenth century, when the causes of death are known, infectious disease was still by far the most important cause of death. One major killer had, however, disappeared. Bubonic plague was unknown in epidemic form after 1670.[13]

There is no certainty about the causes of falling mortality before 1850 and there is even less about the underlying reasons for rising fertility, if in fact this did occur. It has been argued that the growth of industry provided increased opportunities for employment of both man and wife, and, later, children; marriage was thus earlier and families larger. There is some evidence to support this view: in Nottinghamshire in the eighteenth century the industrial villages of the west grew more rapidly than the purely agricultural villages of the east, but there is little evidence on rural and urban demographic differentials in the eighteenth century.[14]

There are as yet no completely convincing explanations for the growth of English population after 1740; it would seem that both rising fertility and declining mortality had some part to play in the growth. But growth there undoubtedly was; it is the purpose of this chapter to see whether this had any impact on agricultural society, and how that society adjusted to growth.

The symptoms of overpopulation

Between 1750 and 1851 the population of England nearly tripled. It might be expected that rural society would have been under considerable stress by then, but of course the rural population did not increase at anywhere near the rate of the urban population (table 24). In 1751 the rural population of England and Wales – those living in places of less than 2500 – was between $4\frac{1}{2}$ and 5 million, by 1851 just over 8 million, an increase of 68–84%. In contrast the total population increased by 175–204% and the urban population by a staggering 555%, thus rural–urban migration greatly reduced the numbers that rural society had to absorb. If the rural population had increased at the same rate as national population, it would have numbered $13\frac{1}{2}$ million by 1851, and the density of the rural population to the arable area would have been little short of that in Ireland in 1841.

After 1861 the rural and agricultural populations began to decline – indeed they had stagnated since 1841 – but between 1751 and 1851 English rural society had difficulty in absorbing the comparatively modest increase of some three-quarters in numbers. This was felt most between 1815 and 1845, for not only were grain prices depressed after 1815, but during the Napoleonic Wars some of the surplus population found its way into the fighting services. But not only did rural society creak under the stress of rising numbers, but English agriculture had great difficulty in providing food for the rapidly increasing total population. As late as the 1840s only 10% of grain consumption was being imported although this had reached nearly 20% in isolated years in the Napoleonic Wars. However, grain imports may have indeed been higher, for it is thought that food imports from Ireland were understated in the records.[15]

Between 1815 and 1845 then, there was much poverty in rural England; indeed A. J. Peacock has stated that 'it was the most dreadful time of the English agricultural labourer's existence'.[16] It was upon the labourer that the problems of population pressure bore hardest, although small farmers suffered as well. What then were the symptoms of population pressure?

First was the rise in prices. Between 1650 and 1750 wheat prices were stable and low, and this undoubtedly reflected the growing efficiency of cereal producers and their ability to reduce the cost of production. But as population grew after 1740 there was no comparable increase in output and wheat prices rose, slowly at first, more rapidly after 1780, and astronomically during the Napoleonic Wars, when a series of bad harvests and the difficulty of importing grain pushed up prices. After the comparative stability of prices in the early eighteenth century, wheat prices doubled between 1750 and 1800, and in 1810–15 averaged more than three times the level of 1748–52. This increase

Table 24. *The rural and urban populations of England and Wales, 1751–1911 (1000s)*[a]

	Total	Rural	Urban	Rural as a % of total
1751[b]	5895	4417	1478	74.9
1751[c]	6500	5022	1478	77.3
1775	7349	5474	1875	74.5
1801	8829	5820	3009	65.9
1811	10164	6442	3722	63.4
1821	11999	7195	4804	60.0
1831	13896	7743	6153	55.7
1841	15914	8221	7693	51.7
1851	17926	8239	9687	46.0
1861	20066	8282	11784	41.3
1871	22712	7910	14802	34.8
1881	25924	7744	18180	30.0
1891	29002	7401	21601	25.5
1901	32526	7155	25371	22.0
1911	36070	7603	28467	21.1

[a] Urban is defined as places with a population over 2500; rural is the residue.

[b] P. E. Razell, 'Population change in eighteenth century England: a re-appraisal', in M. Drake (ed.), *Population in industrialization* (London, 1969), p. 131.

[c] N. L. Tranter, *Population since the Industrial Revolution: the case of England and Wales* (London, 1973), p. 41.

SOURCES: C. M. Law, 'Some notes on the urban population of England and Wales in the eighteenth century', *Local Historian*, 10 (1972), 13–26; 'The growth of urban population in England and Wales, 1801–1911', *Transactions of the Institute of British Geographers*, 41 (1967), 125–44.

in prices was at least partly due to the difficulty English agriculture had in meeting demand.[17] Much of the increase in output was obtained by bringing poor soils into cultivation, and this may have reduced the national average yield. Meat and wool prices also rose, particularly after the 1780s, but less dramatically than those of wheat.[18]

A second symptom was the price of land which rose as it became increasingly short in supply, but land shortage was not the only cause of rising rents. While tenants may have competed for the limited number of farms, and helped to push up prices, there were also a great many rental increases after land had been enclosed, and landlords asked more for the new consolidated farms. There are no rental series for the nation for this period but individual estates give some indication of the increase. In Lancashire the rent of nine manors belonging to the Earl of Derby rose from £1617 in 1760 to £15364 in 1800 and £19201 in 1815; in some areas rents were rising in the first half of the eighteenth century, even though prices were low and tenants on some estates were in difficulties; on the Holkham estate of the Coke family in Norfolk, rent per hectare increased 44% between 1710 and 1759. In the second half of the eighteenth century rents increased moderately – perhaps by 50% – but were often dramatically increased between 1790 and 1813. The Board of Agriculture believed rents rose by 80% in this period.[19]

Farm size and fragmentation

The rising population of the eighteenth century was accompanied by increasing rents and prices, as had happened in the thirteenth and sixteenth centuries, but there was no subdivision of farms and little fragmentation. This was in marked contrast to other parts of Europe, where farms were subdivided and holdings became more scattered. However, tracing changes in farm size at this time is difficult. There are no national *series* of figures on the size of farms before 1887, although data were obtained at the 1851 census. Also, changes in the size of farms have been assumed to be associated with Parliamentary enclosure. It used to be thought that Parliamentary enclosure forced small landowners to sell their holding, which were then amalgamated into large farms; the small landowners, together with cottagers who lost rights of common, formed the landless proletariat who worked the large tenanted farms and also provided the labour force for the growing industrial cities.[20] Such a view is no longer tenable: the small landowners were already a small proportion of English farmers before the era of Parliamentary enclosure, and the period of their greatest decline was probably in the late seventeenth and early eighteenth centuries, and again in the agricultural depression of the post-Napoleonic period.[21] Nor did enclosure or economic depression completely destroy the small farmer – whether tenant or owner-occupier. It is certainly true that by the mid-nineteenth century an unusually high proportion of English farmland was farmed in big units; half the farmland was held in farms of more than 80 hectares, only a fifth in farms of less than 40 hectares. On the other hand the small farmer was still an important part of rural social structure. In 1831 47% of all the farms in Great Britain were worked by farmers who hired no regular labour, and in 1851 42% of all farms in England and Wales were less than 20 hectares.[22] But, compared with Ireland or most other parts of Western Europe, England was a country of large farms. Less than one-third of all farms in Ireland were over 6 hectares, compared with four-fifths of those in England (see table 25).

Such evidence as there is on farm size before 1851 – drawn largely from estate records – suggests that farm size was increasing slowly, and that this occurred as rapidly in the first half of the eighteenth century as in the later eighteenth century or the first half of the nineteenth century. A recent analysis of the Leveson-Gower estates – over 12000 hectares – shows an interesting trend that may have been more general. The area occupied by large farms – over 81 hectares – rose dramatically between 1714 and 1832, and farms of less than 8.1 hectares also increased, but medium sized farms – between 8.1 and 81 hectares – which had occupied over 70% of the estate in 1714, occupied only 30% by 1832 (table 26).

Table 25. *Farm size in Ireland (1845) and in England and Wales (1851)*

Hectares	Ireland		England and Wales	
	(Number)	(%)	(Number)	(%)
0–2	316950	35.03	7656	3.43
2–6.1	311133	34.4	29316	13.13
6.1 and over	276618	30.57	186299	83.44
Total	904701	100.0	223271	100.00

SOURCES: P. M. A. Bourke, 'The agricultural statistics of the 1841 census of Ireland: a critical review', *Economic History Review*, 18 (1965), 38; *Census of Great Britain, 1851, Accounts and Papers*, 1852–3, vol. LXXXVIII, part 1, p. lxxx.

Table 26. *Farm size on the Leveson-Gower estate (% of the total area in each size class)*

	0–8.1 ha	8.1–40.5 ha	40.5–81 ha	Over 81 ha
1714–20	6.3	46.1	28.8	18.8
1759–79	6.2	26.6	35.0	32.2
1807–13	6.5	16.7	25.1	51.7
1829–33	9.6	14.9	16.2	59.3

SOURCE: J. R. Wordie, 'Social change on the Leveson-Gower estates, 1714–1832', *Economic History Review*, 27 (1974), 595.

The growth of the large farm may be explained in two ways. In the first place there were some economies of scale to be obtained even before the adoption of labour-saving machinery in the early nineteenth century; it allowed the more economic use of ploughs and wagons, for even the small farmer had to have these. The large farmer had better bargaining powers, especially with corn merchants and also with banks, which were playing an important role in financing agriculture by the late eighteenth century, and the farmer could specialise in managing, rather than carrying out farm work himself. Small and medium sized farms had few of these advantages. But the small farmer, with less than 8 or 10 hectares often had some other occupation as craftsman or trader, while the very small holdings of less than 2 hectares often belonged to farm labourers. Although much stress has been put on the losses of the small holder during enclosure, there was in many parts of England an attempt to provide the labourer with an allotment of some land to supplement his wages. Thus the number of very small holdings did not decline; it was the farmers with medium sized farms, especially those with 8–40 hectares, who felt the pinch at times of crisis and decided they could get a better living in the towns.[23]

The growth of large farms also had advantages for the landlord. It was easier to manage an estate divided into a few large farms than one with a multitude of small holders. It was customary in England for the landlord to provide the buildings, and this was costly if there were many small farms. Tenants provided the working capital, and those who took large farms generally had more capital than those on small farms, were more enterprising and more likely to undertake improvements.

The pattern of English landownership was largely determined by the beginning of the eighteenth century. Once over half of the land was held in estates which were divided into farms rented to tenants, there was no possibility of a growing agricultural population subdividing farms; it was the landlord, not the farmer, who made decisions about farm size. In the eighteenth century it was *believed* that large farms had economic advantages, and by the nineteenth century they certainly had. Thus the trend to large farms was not a function of Parliamentary enclosure – the Leveson-Gower estates, for example, were all enclosed before 1714 – but of the slow grouping of adjacent farms into larger units as tenants died or gave up the lease.

If there was little subdivision in the eighteenth century there was certainly no tendency for fragmentation to increase. On the contrary the principal consequence of Parliamentary enclosure was the consolidation of scattered strips into compact blocks of land. Some 1.8 million hectares of common field were enclosed in the eighteenth and nineteenth centuries, and the degree of fragmentation must have been greatly reduced.[24]

The growth of landlessness

In the absence of any subdivision of farms it was inevitable that the number of landless should increase between 1751 and 1851. Unfortunately there are no reliable statistics on occupations in the census until 1831; it is possible that the number employed in agriculture increased by 17% between 1831 and 1851.[25] Before then estimates of the rural population indicate the growth of those likely to be seeking employment in agriculture. In 1751 the number of those living in towns of more than 2500 was 1 478 000 (table 24). The size of the rural population – the residue – depends upon the estimate of the total population which is preferred, but was between $4\frac{1}{2}$ and 5 million. By 1801 this had reached 5 883 000 – this figure is reliable – and by 1851 8 239 100. The rural population thus increased by between 3.2 and 3.8 million, or by between 64% and 86%. The rate of increase was much greater in the period 1801–51 than in the preceding half century, and it was this former period, particularly the thirty years after the end of the Napoleonic Wars, that saw much rural poverty. Although poverty in the countryside was exacerbated by the Poor Law, enclosure and the fall in grain prices after 1815, the fundamental problem was the growth of a surplus population which in the east and south of the country could not be absorbed in agriculture or its ancillary industries; the consequence was a growth in unemployment, underemployment, work-sharing, low real wages, a retardation of technological advance and widespread rural discontent, expressed in a rising rate of crime. There were some signs of rural discontent before the outbreak of the Napoleonic Wars: in the first half of the eighteenth century the rural population, including the labourer, had been reasonably prosperous but after 1750 rising food prices began to erode the real wages of the farm labourer and riots became common in years of high grain prices.[26] On the other hand there was little difficulty in obtaining employment; the rural population increased comparatively slowly between 1750 and 1801, by between 18% and 33%, compared with a doubling of the urban population. This extra population could be absorbed, for this period saw new employment being created in the countryside. Parliamentary enclosure provided much labouring in the construction of roads, ditches and hedges. The reclamation of new land also required extra labour, and, where the new farming practices of the Norfolk system were adopted, there was a need for more labour to prepare the seedbed, weed turnips and carry manure. It has been calculated that labour needs on a farm practising the Norfolk four-course were 45% greater than on the same farm following a traditional rotation. The rising rate of population increase after 1781 was masked by the needs of the fighting services, but in 1815 at the end of the war some 400000 men returned to seek employment. From then until the 1840s there were more men seeking work in the English countryside than there were jobs.[27]

Rural poverty was not found in all parts of the country: it was greatest in the east and the south. This was the part of England that most relied on wheat production, had large farms worked by day-labourers, and was, except for the neighbourhood of London, remotest from the industrial towns with their higher wages. In England and Wales in 1851 there were 249000 farmers and 1 268000 labourers and farm servants – almost exactly 5 hired labourers to every farm; but the bulk of these were in the east and south; elsewhere the family farm was more important. It was this region that saw the most acute problems after 1815. It is notoriously difficult to calculate real wages in agriculture, but it would seem that these were high in the first half of the eighteenth century and that there was little difference between north and south. But after the 1770s wages in the north began to rise more than those in the south, due to the growth of factory employment. In the north and the midlands farmers had to offer higher wages to farm workers, in the south and east there was no such competition and the gap between agricultural wages in the corn areas and the north and midlands widened until the 1850s.[28] The money wages of agricultural labourers rose in the eighteenth century, and more so during the Napoleonic Wars, but it is doubtful if they kept up with food prices after the 1750s. The only study of the real wages of agricultural labourers – in part of Kent – shows that they fell from 1795 to 1825. The diet of labourers in East Anglia in the 1840s suggests impoverishment. Potatoes, which had formed an insignificant part of the diet in the 1790s, were with bread the staple, and meat was rare; indeed by the 1830s it was estimated that 2 million relied on potatoes in the country as a whole.[29]

In the eighteenth century a considerable proportion of the labouring population was hired on yearly contract and lived with the farmer's family, but by the turn of the nineteenth century this practice declined, for giving wages in kind was unprofitable for the farmer, and the growing surplus labour pool allowed him to hire and fire labour on a day-to-day basis. Living-in survived only in the pastoral areas, where livestock required constant attention, or where it was necessary to stop the flow of labour to the towns. In Lancashire as late as 1861 one-sixth of the labour force was living in.[30] Thus the problem in the post-war period was not merely of falling real wages – or at best stagnant real wages – but of getting employment at all. Increasingly a significant proportion of the labouring population was without work for much of the year.

Until the end of the eighteenth century there were few innovations in agricultural machinery that were overtly labour-saving in intent. But in 1786 the threshing machine was invented in Scotland, and in 1812 John Common patented a reaping machine. Yet as late as the 1840s more of the corn harvest in England was threshed with the flail than the threshing machine, and virtually none of the grain harvest was reaped by machine. The next thirty years, however, saw the virtual end of the flail, and the rapid spread of McCormick's reaper, which although imported from the United States was closely based on Common's design. There were probably several factors that retarded the adoption of these innovations – the early threshing machines did not always work satisfactorily, for example, and they were uneconomic on the smaller farms – but doubtless a major factor was the availability of large supplies of labour at low wage rates. In the case of the threshing machine there were more direct reasons. Threshing with the flail occupied some quarter of the total hours worked on a large arable farm, and was the only form of employment available for much of the period between October and March. It is not surprising that, when farmers in the south-east began to adopt machines in the 1820s, there was a violent outbreak of rioting in the Captain Swing riots of 1830–1, when machines were smashed and ricks burnt. When the agricultural labour force began to decline, as it did after 1851, and money and real wages rose, there was far more incentive for farmers to adopt both the threshing machine and the reaper, which they did.[31]

There seems no denying that much of the population of southern and eastern England lived in poverty after 1815. Many contemporaries thought – and some later historians did too – that the operation of the Poor Law was partly responsible for this. In 1786 Gilbert's Act had allowed the parish to offer relief to the poor without them having to enter a workhouse; in 1795 the magistrates at Speenhamland in Berkshire decided to supplement wages in accordance with movements in the price of grain and the size of a man's family. This was supposed to have led to a variety of abuses. Malthus believed that it removed the prudential check, encouraged early marriage and thus increased the rate of population growth, although there is little evidence for this.[32] Others argued that these supplementary payments allowed farmers to cut wages to below the subsistence level, and allowed them a pool of cheap labour that could be called on when needed, and left for the parish to support when they were not needed on the land. But as the poor rate was paid by the occupiers of land, and increased with the numbers requiring supplementation this was counterproductive. Indeed in some areas farmers took turns to employ the unemployed, at a low wage, whether they needed them or not, a parallel with the work-sharing found in many parts of Asia today. Certainly the arable farming system of eastern England at this time was prodigal with labour. But even so it is to be doubted that they could have fully employed all those available. In the 1830s the Select Committee on the Poor Law supposed that arable and mixed farming used one man to every 10–12 hectares, and pasture one man to every 20–24 hectares. As there were approximately 5 million hectares under arable at this time and about the same amount in grass, this would have afforded, at the most, employment for 750 000. Yet at the time of the 1831 census there were 961 000 families dependent on agriculture for a livelihood, 275 000 the families of farmers and 686 000 labourers' families; as the latter are thought to have been understated, there was clearly a surplus labour force. In 1851 there was theoretically employment available for 830 000, as the area under arable was greater than in the 1830s, but there were by then 249 000 farmers and 1 268 000 labourers; it is tempting to move from these figures to argue that, as in Ireland, a significant proportion of the agricultural labour force had a marginal productivity of zero; but neither the reliability of the figure on land use nor the accuracy of the estimates of labour requirements is great enough to bear such a statement.[33]

Nonetheless it seems reasonable to argue that the problems of rural poverty in southern and eastern England after 1815 ultimately stemmed from a surplus labour force; too few left for the towns, massive though the exodus must have been, and remote from the industrial areas there were few alternative employments. Not surprisingly rural poverty in this period led to a rising rate of crime, quite apart from the outbursts against threshing machines in 1830–1; sheep stealing, cattle maiming, poaching and incendiarism increased and were still common in the 1840s.[34]

The agrarian response to population change

The traditional view of the English agricultural revolution made it contemporaneous with population growth and the Industrial Revolution. It was argued that the widespread occurrence of open fields inhibited progress, but the rising prices of the second half of the eighteenth century spurred Parliamentary enclosure. The example of a few great innovators, notably in Norfolk, encouraged tenant farmers to change their farming practices: turnips and clover were grown in rotation with wheat and barley. This used the fallow and increased the supply of fodder, which in turn produced better quality livestock and a greater supply of manure, which raised cereal yields. The fencing of fields and the end of communal grazing allowed the improvement of livestock breeding following the methods of Robert Bakewell. The consolidation of scattered strips into larger, square fields and compact farms reduced the time needed to move around the farm, and the end of the intermixing of strips made the control of weeds, and plant and livestock disease easier. The drill, popularised by Jethro Tull, was more economical than broadcasting in the use of seed, and sowing in lines allowed inter-row cultivation. The Rotherham plough, the first all-metal plough, allowed more thorough cultivation. These and other innovations spread through England, so that by 1850 English agriculture fed a population three times that of 1750 with hardly any increase in imports.[35]

Such a view has increasingly been under attack. On the one hand some argue that the innovations thought to have spread after 1750 in fact were diffused between 1650 and 1750; in one case it has been argued that the English agricultural revolution began in the late sixteenth century and was complete by 1767, when there were no more improvements left to be made.[36] Another critique, however, points out that the rising grain prices of the late eighteenth century suggest that English agriculture failed to meet demand, and that there were no major advances in crop yields until the first half of the nineteenth century, when quite new techniques were being adopted – the use of artificial fertilisers, the purchase of oilcake for cattle food, and the wider use of new farm implements. Nor is Parliamentary enclosure given quite the central role it once possessed, for it has been shown that some new methods could be adopted without enclosure, and that much of England was enclosed before the 1740s.[37]

Any discussion of the progress of English farming before 1850 is inhibited by the absence of any national figures on total output, labour force, land use or crop and livestock yields. Before turning to these complex problems it should be noted that there was a considerable increase in the area under cultivation between 1650 and 1850, a new food crop – the potato – was adopted, and the area under fallow was much reduced.

The expansion of the cultivated area

There seems little doubt that there was a substantial increase in the area under cultivation in the eighteenth and early nineteenth centuries and that the land in waste much reduced. Unenclosed waste land made up approximately 25% of the total area of England and Wales in 1696, 21% in 1800 and only 6% in 1873.[38] But although doubtless some of this was put beneath the plough, by no means all could be cultivated, and became, at the best, improved pasture. Contemporary descriptions, however, make it clear that the later eighteenth and early nineteenth centuries saw a great increase in the area under crops. In the Yorkshire and Lincolnshire Wolds, for example, sheepwalk

Table 27. *Major land uses in England and Wales, 1696–1866 (1000 hectares)*

	1696	1801	1808	1812	1827	1846	1854	1866
Arable	4450	4585	4676	4545	4582	5373	5638	5763
Pasture and meadow	4050	6785	7068	—	7112	—	5533	4147
Total cultivated	8500	11370	11744	—	11694	—	11171	9910
Uncultivated	7280	3683	3809	—	3573	—	—	—
Grand total	15780	15053	15553	—	15267	—	—	—

SOURCES: 1696: G. E. Barnett, *Two tracts by Gregory King* (Baltimore, 1936), p. 35; 1801: B. P. Capper, quoted in H. C. Prince, 'England *circa* 1800', in H. C. Darby (ed.), *A new historical geography of England* (Cambridge, 1973), p. 403; 1808: W. T. Comber, in Prince, 'England *circa* 1800', p. 403; 1812, 1846 and 1854: from L. Drescher, 'The development of agricultural production in Great Britain and Ireland from the early nineteenth century', *Manchester School*, 23 (1955), 167; 1827: W. Couling quoted in P. G. Craigie, 'Statistics of agricultural production', *Statistical Journal*, 46 (1883), 6; 1866: Ministry of Agriculture, *A century of agricultural statistics: Great Britain 1866–1966* (London, 1968), p. 94.

was ploughed; in the Fenlands improved drainage, particularly after the introduction of steam pumping in the 1820s, allowed large areas once used only for summer grazing, to be sown to crops.[39] The fact of increase is not in doubt; what is not clear is the order of magnitude of this increase. Figures for land use before 1866, when the Board of Agriculture began to collect and publish statistics, have considerable defects (table 27). Even today the distinction between rough grazing, or waste, and grassland, is not always easily made; the estimates for 1801 and 1808 do not include temporary grasses, although an estimate made in 1812 recorded 459600 hectares under clover, nor are potatoes included in the early nineteenth-century estimates although R. N. Salaman believed there were 64000 hectares under the crop by 1814.[40]

The least reliable figure is that for 1696, estimated by Gregory King; indeed Charles Davenant reduced King's figure for arable from 4.45 to 3.64 million hectares.[41] If this is taken as the area under arable at the beginning of the eighteenth century then there would seem to have been an increase of about 905000 hectares by the end of the Napoleonic Wars.

Although it is often suggested that the fall in grain prices after 1815 resulted in a conversion of arable to grass, this seems to have been localised. In spite of falling grain prices, the arable area had increased by a further 800000 hectares by the late 1840s. Thus between 1700 and 1850, the population of England increased by 220% but the arable area by only 48%. However it is likely that the area sown to crops increased more, for 'arable' included fallow land. Fallow land was only slowly eliminated, for although fodder roots and later potatoes began to be grown on the fallow, there were still 800000 hectares in the 1800s, 600000 hectares in 1846 and 362000 hectares in 1854.[42]

Table 28. *Area and consumption of potatoes in England and Wales*
(*excluding gardens*)

	Hectares (1000s)	Daily consumption (kilograms per head)
1775	20	0.11
1795	40	0.18
1815	65	0.21
1838	113	0.28
1851	142	0.32
1866	172	0.36
1891	187	0.29
1901	209	0.26
1914	216	0.24

SOURCE: R. N. Salaman, *The history and social influence of the potato* (Cambridge, 1949), p. 613.

The sown area in 1812 was thus about 3.7 million hectares, some 4 770 000 hectares in 1846 and nearly 5 280 000 hectares in 1854. Unfortunately there is no way of knowing the area under fallow in 1696. But if one-third of the 3.2 million hectares Davenant believed to be in cereals was in fallow then the sown area would have been 2.12 million hectares. However, it is unlikely that in 1696 all the cereal acreage was grown in rotations which had one year in three fallow. The sown area was then more likely to be 2.8 to 3.0 million hectares. Thus the maximum possible increase in the sown area from 1696–1854 was 88% compared with a 220% increase in population.

If the expansion of the cultivated area had been the only means of increasing output then there would have been a drastic fall in consumption levels after 1750. However, output of food crops could also be increased by raising yields and by substituting higher yielding crops.

The potato

Although the potato was grown in parts of England in the seventeenth century, it was not important except in Lancashire; at the end of the eighteenth century it still occupied a small area although it had increased rapidly since the 1770s, when disputes about whether it should be tithed indicate that it was becoming a significant crop. It was only of importance as a field crop in Lancashire and to a lesser extent in the Lincolnshire fenland, but even in these areas it was grown mainly as a fodder crop. It was only during harvest failures in the Napoleonic Wars that it began to be grown as a food crop. The national area, as estimated by R. N. Salaman, rose from 40 000 hectares in 1795 to 142 000 in 1851 and consumption per head nearly doubled (table 28). But this was not entirely a gain; Salaman has suggested that wheat

Table 29. *Wheat yields in England in the nineteenth century* (*kg/ha*)

(a) Liverpool corn merchants		(b) Rothamsted		(c) Board of agriculture	
1821–29	1430	1852–59	1885	1885–89	1700
1830–39	1600	1860–67	1915	1890–97	2070
1840–49	2245	1868–75	1795	1900–09	2165
1850–59	2320	1876–78	1820	1910–19	2110

SOURCES: (a) M. J. R. Healey and E. L. Jones, 'Wheat yields in England, 1815–59', *Journal of the Royal Statistical Society*, Series A, 125 (1962), 108–9; (b) J. B. Lawes and J. H. Gilbert, 'On the home produce, imports, consumption and price of wheat over twenty eight (or twenty seven) harvest years, 1852–3 to 1879–80', *Statistical Journal*, 53 (1880), 330; Ministry of Agriculture, *A century of agricultural statistics, 1866–1966* (1968).

consumption fell in the first half of the nineteenth century. Indeed the growth of potato consumption must be seen as a sign of impoverishment. In 1836 it was argued that 2 million people depended on potatoes who, twenty years before, had eaten wheaten flour.[43]

Changes in farming methods

It was observed earlier that it was once thought that radical changes in farming methods only came after 1750; there is now some agreement that turnips and clover were introduced into rotations in parts of East Anglia after the 1640s, and were widely known, if not widely grown, by the beginning of the eighteenth century. Although the first references to the growth of clover, sainfoin and perennial rye grass come from the Weald, the Cotswolds and East Anglia in the 1640s and 1650s, they were well established in Worcester in the 1670s and all known in Wales by the 1690s.[44] In Midland England, especially on the heavier clay soils, which were unsuitable for turnips, a quite different system, convertible husbandry, was established. Three to four years under crops were followed by six to seven years under grass. Other changes were made in the later seventeenth century; there was much enclosure by agreement, an increase in farm size, the growth of large estates, the spread of water meadows and the possible use of more fertiliser.[45] Thus the agricultural revolution must be stretched to cover two centuries, not one; it was underway long before the rise of population and prices after 1750.

What is difficult is to establish the increase in productivity over this period. National figures on crop yields do not begin until 1885, and even these have been subject to criticism.[46] Before the nineteenth century figures on yields often refer to only a few farms, may be in climatically unrepresentative years, and are drawn mainly from the south and east of England. The first attempt at a national enquiry was made by the Royal Society in the 1660s; although they gathered much information on farming methods, there was little evidence on yields. However, in the south-west of England good wheat yields were thought to be between 1345 and 1680 kg/ha, average yields between 540 and 1000 kg/ha, and in a poor year they ranged from 336 to 672 kg/ha.[47] G. E. Fussell, after a survey of contemporary estimates of yields, put the national figure at 1345 kg/ha in 1700.[48] M. K. Bennett on the basis of some rather dubious sources has attempted to estimate the national wheat yield over a much longer period. He believed the average was 740 kg/ha in 1650, 960 kg/ha in 1685, and 1075 kg/ha in the 1750s. He obtained a figure of 1280 kg/ha for 1800 and 1815 kg/ha for 1850 by regression from the Board of Agriculture's more reliable figures that start in 1885. His figures before 1800 seem highly speculative.[49]

During the Napoleonic Wars the fear of food shortage prompted numerous reports on the state of agriculture and several partial enquiries into the area under crops and some evidence on crop yields. J. A. Yelling has reviewed yields in the open fields that survived at that date and believes the average yield was about 1345 kg/ha and McCulloch in 1816 put the national average yield of wheat at 1410 kg/ha. A reasonably accurate account of the area and produce of wheat in Kesteven in 1792–5 gives a yield of only 1075 kg/ha, while in the Lincolnshire Wolds yields ranged between 1345 and 1615 kg/ha in the 1790s.[50] A comparison of these figures with Fussell's estimate of 1345 kg/ha in 1700 suggests that there was surprisingly little increase in the *national* average in the eighteenth century although this does not preclude the possibility of advance in some regions (see above, p. 92).

The first half of the nineteenth century does show some evidence of yield increases. Between 1821 and 1859 Liverpool corn merchants annually took a sample of wheat yields on a circuit from Liverpool to London. M. J. Healey and E. L. Jones who have collated and published this data, believe that these figures overestimate actual yields and suggest a reduction in the ratio of 50:72 would give a more realistic series. This correction has been applied to their data and the results can be seen in table 29. This suggests there was a considerable increase in yield between the 1820s and 1850s. This is confirmed by other regional estimates. Wheat yields in Kesteven rose from 1075 kg/ha in the 1790s to 2020 kg/ha in the 1840s, and in the Lincolnshire Wolds from 1345–1615 kg/ha in the 1790s to 1885–2150 kg/ha in the 1830s. Between the 1840s and 1885 there are no national figures, although yields collected at Rothamstead on a field following normal farm practice show no upward trend and averaged just over 1800 kg/ha from 1852 to 1878 (table 29). In 1885 the Board of Agriculture began to collect and publish cereal yields. By the turn of the century national wheat yields were averaging over 2000 kg/ha.[51]

It is hard to derive any reliable figures from these estimates save that there was a substantial increase 1800–1900, and much of this increase came in the first half of the nineteenth century. If Fussell's figure for 1700 is accepted then there was little increase in the eighteenth century; on the other hand if

Bennett's figures for 1650 and 1700 are taken there must have been some increase in yields 1650–1750. However, there is some reason to suppose that output *per head* increased most rapidly between 1650 and 1750; indeed after 1750 output *per head* may have been falling. There now seems little doubt that there was considerable progress in agriculture in some parts of England in the seventeenth and early eighteenth centuries.[52] Turnips were first grown as a fodder crop in Suffolk in the 1640s, references to clover, sainfoin and perennial rye grass occur at the same time in East Anglia, the Weald and the Cotswolds. When combined with wheat and barley in rotation this not only increased soil fertility and yields, but increased the number of livestock that could be supported, as well as improving their quality. Thus not only were crop yields increased but there was a trend from simple corn production to mixed farming; livestock formed a growing proportion of total output. But this system was not appropriate to all regions. The turnip was suited to the lighter soils, particularly the limestone areas. These soils were easily cultivated compared with the heavier clays, and so the light soils began to grow an increasing proportion of England's cereals; the more advanced clay regions, particularly in the Midland Plain, turned to convertible husbandary, with its emphasis on higher livestock densities. Farmers everywhere had the incentive to reduce costs and diversify, for grain prices were low and livestock prices fell less than grain. Farmers seem to have believed, in the face of rising wages and falling prices, that the adoption of better farming methods would reduce the cost of unit output. Certainly there seems to have been a substantial increase in cereal output. By the 1690s there was a sizeable export trade in wheat and barley, which doubled between 1700 and 1750, and at its peak formed 10% of total output.[53] This seems to have been an era of prosperity both for farmer and labourer: the latter's consumption level was higher than in the early nineteenth century, and farmers had a surplus to buy consumer goods. As population was stagnant, some have argued that the first half of the eighteenth century saw home demand create early industrial expansion.[54]

The second half of the eighteenth century saw different circumstances. The new farming systems reached the remoter parts of the country – the first turnips were grown in the Yorkshire Wolds in 1745[55] – but the rise in grain prices suggests that supply could not match demand. Exports of grain – which had been England's third most valuable export, after wool and metal – dwindled, and in the late eighteenth century imports, admittedly small, were necessary.[56] After the 1780s the methods established in East Anglia in the early eighteenth century became more generally adopted in other areas but there were still problems in matching supply and demand. After 1815, when there was a fall in grain prices, farmers again sought to reduce production costs; they found it difficult to shed labour due to the workings of the Poor Law, but turned instead to intensive methods that raised yields. The 1820s saw the beginnings of what F. M. L. Thompson has called the Second Agricultural Revolution.[57] Oilcake was fed to cattle, and stall-feeding was widely adopted, heavy manuring became common, marl, crushed bones, guano and later artificial fertilisers were used. Labour was used prodigally to weed and collect stones from fields. This influenced yields. Grain yields rose, at the most optimistic assumption, by one-third between 1700 and 1800; they probably rose by the same proportion in the next half century. It is thus reasonable to argue that after the stagnant population and rising productivity of 1650 and 1750 English agriculture had difficulty in maintaining food output per head between 1760 and the 1830s. Ironically crop yields rose at the very time when the repeal of the Corn Laws would end the need for English agriculture to support its home population.

Demographic responses to population growth

The argument so far is that rural England, and particularly the arable areas of the east and the south were subject to population pressure in the first half of the nineteenth century. A surplus rural population could not find full-time employment in agriculture, and the agricultural system could only just match population growth; there is little evidence of any marked rise in the consumption levels of the mass of the urban and rural populations before the 1840s. But the 1840s were a critical turning-point. In the first place the agricultural population began to decline after 1851 as there was a massive exodus from the country to the town, where wage rates were higher and employment opportunities greater. Secondly, the repeal of the Corn Laws opened England to the cheaper grains and meats of Russia, the New World and later Australasia. English agriculture no longer had to provide the 'means of subsistence'; indeed it is doubtful if it could have. Free trade was therefore critical, as Sir John Clapham observed. 'Those who had followed Peel with open eyes, like Sir James Graham, had done so because population was growing at the rate of 300000 per annum. It had been a question of time, a race between life and food. To such men free trade was a need to be faced, not a treasure to be won.'[58]

Thus the first half of the nineteenth century was a critical period for the English rural population. As might well be expected there was some demographic response to population growth. The most important demographic adjustment was rural–urban migration. The rise of manufacturing industry was sufficiently rapid to absorb the rural surplus after 1851 and to cause the decline of the rural population. It was industrialisation, not any great changes in rural life itself, that relieved the acute poverty of the agricultural labourer and the small farmer. But this was not the only adjustment. A not inconsiderable number emigrated while there is some inconclusive evidence that fertility may have fallen in the 1820s, long before the well-testified decline that began in the 1870s.

Employment in the countryside

In previous periods trade and crafts offered some alternative form of employment in the countryside. It might be thought that the Industrial Revolution, with its use of machinery and steampower, and concentration in factories in towns, would have destroyed the pre-industrial pattern of rural industry. This happened in the late nineteenth century. But in the mid-nineteenth century there was still a surprising number of rural industries. First were those tied to their raw materials, such as quarrying and brick-making. Secondly, certain industries, such as leather-working, wood-working, brewing, corn-milling and baking, were still distributed uniformly throughout the population, and remained so until mass-production and cheap transport destroyed them later in the century. Thirdly, there were rural industries that produced goods that went to consumers outside their area: although the Norfolk and Gloucester woollen industries suffered from the West Riding factory products, there were still domestic lace and silk industries; there were 20000 female lace workers in Buckinghamshire and Bedfordshire in 1851, and the domestic out-working of shoes in Northamptonshire survived until the end of the century; in Bedfordshire and Hertfordshire straw was plaited in cottages for the hat industry.[59]

But these industries, locally important as they may have been, could hardly provide a livelihood, or even a supplementary income for all the burgeoning rural population of the early nineteenth century. But as long as the rural population grew, most villages could sustain a surprising number of tradesmen and craftsmen who provided services for farms and the farm population. Indeed in some villages they were so numerous as to suggest they were oversupplied; tailors, cobblers and carpenters were particularly numerous in rural England. Tradesmen, and some craftsmen, were often occupiers of smallholdings as well. But towards the end of the nineteenth century factory products began to undercut the local craftsmen. Ploughs were made in factories, not in the village; factory-made shoes and suits replaced those of the cobbler and tailor; and the absolute decline of the rural population further reduced the number of tradesmen and craftsmen needed in the villages.[60]

Rural–urban migration

In France the main response to rural population pressure was the limitation of births within marriage; in Norway and Ireland it was emigration. In England it was migration from the countryside to the towns, where the increasing complexity of urban life was creating many possible employments, not simply in manufacturing industries, but in domestic service and in a variety of comparatively new jobs.

The census did not distinguish between rural and urban population until 1851, when the population was equally divided, nor is there information on urban–rural demographic differentials before 1837; much of the mass of material upon this subject remains to be analysed. However C. M. Law has calculated the urban population for each census year (table 24), taking as urban parishes of over 2500 and with a density of more than 2.5 per hectare;[61] he has also listed the places with populations of more than 2500 in 1750 and 1775, and this gives the most reliable measure of urban and rural growth in our period. Between 1751 and 1851 the rural and urban populations increased at an average of 0.5–0.6% p.a. and 1.9% p.a. respectively. The urban rate of increase could not possibly have been sustained by natural increase alone. There must therefore have been a considerable out-migration from rural areas between 1750 and 1850. Immigration from Ireland and Scotland was admittedly important at this time, but it was not sufficient to explain this extraordinary rate of urban growth.

In the absence of any reliable information on urban and rural birth and death rates before 1837, the places of birth of residents in English cities in 1851 illustrate the great importance of migration in the generation before that date. The 1851 census included data on the place of birth for 62 towns in Britain: of the 3 336 000 of over 20 years in these towns only 40% had been born there, suggesting a considerable rural–emigration over the preceding generation. In London in 1851 only 46% of the adults were born there, in Norwich and Sheffield one half, and in Manchester, Bradford and Glasgow little more than a quarter were natives.[62]

Industry in the first half of the nineteenth century grew up mainly on the coalfields, in the ports such as Liverpool, and in London. It might be reasonably supposed that there would be a movement from the overpopulated east and south to the growing industrial cities of the Midlands and the north; this was not so. The population of these towns was recruited from relatively short distances away.[63] Half Liverpool's immigrant population in 1851 came from within Lancashire, and a substantial part of the rest from Ireland, which in terms of travel cost, was nearer than the south-east of England. Half the immigrants in Nottingham in 1861 came from the rest of the county, while in Bradford in 1841, 90% of the immigrants were Yorkshire-born. In the 1860s 70% of the migrants into Glamorganshire came from the adjacent Welsh counties. Thus most towns gained their migrants from the immediate neighbourhood; in 1851 70% of Preston's adult population had been born outside the town but of these 42% were born within 16 km, 70% within 48 km.[64] Only London drew many migrants from very long distances but even there a majority came from south of a line from the Wash to Hampshire. It was London then, that provided an outlet, if an insufficient one, for the surplus rural population of the arable south and east, not the industrial towns of the north. As the author of the 1851 census report put it: 'The tendency of the South Saxon population to emigrate into the North is excessively small.'[65]

Unfortunately it is not possible to measure migration from the countryside before 1841, but it must have been substantial. Where studies have been made of the comparative importance of migration and natural increase in accounting for urban growth, using aggregate figures of baptisms and burials, they show the great importance of migration. Leeds, for example, increased from 17117 in 1775 to 30669 in 1801; 64% of this was attributable to migration. In all the British cities whose growth has been studied migration was a more important component of intercensal increase until the second half of the nineteenth century, when natural increase became the most important. Such figures, however, to some extent understate the role of migration; immigrants from the countryside were predominantly young men and women between 15 and 35 years old. They married in the cities and their children form part of the natural increase.[66]

After 1841 it is possible to give some measure of the outflow from the rural districts (table 30). The absolute outflow increased steadily from the rural registration districts with a set-back only in the 1860s. It then fell away sharply in the decade before the First World War. Thus, whereas from 1750 to 1850 the rural exodus was insufficient to halt the increase in the population, by the 1850s rural outmigration and natural increase were much the same. The rural population, as defined by C. M. Law, fell from 8282000 in 1851 to 7155000 in 1901, recovering somewhat in the first decade of this century. The principal feature of this decline was the fall in the number of farm labourers, the number of farmers showed only a very small decline (table 31).

The reasons for this exodus are numerous: before 1851 the lack of employment in the countryside, and the widespread poverty must have created the desire to leave, as it had done in the past. But in contrast to the past the rapid growth of manufacturing industries, and trade and commerce created employment opportunities in the towns. Although there were periods of unemployment in industry, as the business cycle ran its course, in the long run employment did grow rapidly enough to absorb the rural surplus. Further, as the average wage in the towns was nearly twice that in agriculture from 1841 until after the First World War, the towns exercised a considerable pull.[67]

Emigration

Although there was a longstanding tradition of emigration from Britain, and although Britain, as distinct from Ireland, provided in absolute terms many of those leaving Europe in the nineteenth century, emigration did not play as great a role in relieving population pressure as it did in Ireland or Norway. Emigration statistics are notoriously difficult to interpret. Figures of those leaving England and Wales were kept only from 1852, but include passengers as well as emigrants; before 1852 the United States kept records of immigrants by national origin. As Canada was as important a destination for the English and Welsh at this time, the earlier figures doubtless understate the volume

Table 30. *Migrational gain and loss in England and Wales, 1841–1911*

	All towns	Rural residue	Net migration
1841–51	+742300	−443170	+299130
1851–61	+620256	−742573	−122317
1861–71	+623475	−683031	−59556
1871–81	+689154	−837452	−148298
1881–91	+228063	−845444	−617381
1891–1901	+605980	−660440	−54460
1901–11	−207096	−294902	−501998
Total	3302132	−4507012	−1204880

SOURCE: A. K. Cairncross, *Home and foreign investment 1870–1913; studies in capital accumulation* (Cambridge, 1953), p. 76.

Table 31. *Numbers employed in agriculture, England and Wales, 1851 and 1911 (1000s)*

	Farmers	Farmers' relatives	Hired labour	Others	Total
1851	249	112	1268	79	1708
1911	229	115	688	155	1187

SOURCE: J. R. Bellerby, 'The distribution of manpower in agriculture and in industry, 1851–1951', *The Farm Economist*, 9 (1958), 1–11.

Table 32. *Emigration from England and Wales, 1825–1909*

1825–29	23753	1870–79	967013
1830–39	125950	1880–89	1520831
1840–49	278741	1890–99	1133422
1850–59	677686	1900–09	1722393
1860–69	526293		

SOURCE: N. H. Carrier and J. R. Jeffery, *External migration: a study of the available statistics, 1815–1950* (London, 1953), pp. 92–3.

of emigration before 1852. But there seems no doubt that the volume was greater in the second half of the nineteenth century than in the first.[68]

There is unfortunately little evidence on where emigrants came from within England and Wales: however, the 1841 census did publish information on emigrants in the first half of that year. Half the emigrants came from south of the Trent, and the agricultural counties provided the majority of those who left. Both labourers and small farmers emigrated; the latter went not so much because of poverty, but resentment at high rents, taxes and tithe, and the

Table 33. *Rate of loss by migration, 1851–1939 (annual rate per 1000 mean population)*

	Wales	England	Scotland	Ireland North	Ireland South	Sweden
1851–61	−28	−16	−101	−194		−7
1861–71	−47	−7	−44	−169		−37
1871–81	−35	−5	−28	−119	−127	−32
1881–91	−11	−23	−58	−108	−163	−74
1891–1901	−5	−2	−13	−55	−118	−37
1901–11	+45	−19	−57	−52	−82	−36
1911–21	−21	−16	−50	−47	−88	−11
1921–31	−102	+3	−80	−82	−56	−15
1931–39	−72	+24	−8	−5	−63	+9

SOURCE: B. Thomas, *The Welsh economy: studies in expansion* (Cardiff, 1962), p. 7.

expectation of getting free land in Canada and the USA. In the first half of the nineteenth century then, at a time when England still had the majority of its population living in the countryside, the majority of emigrants came from the rural areas and probably intended to go to the rural areas of North America.[69] After the 1850s this changed; the absolute numbers leaving greatly increased, reaching a peak in the decade before the First World War, but the number of farmers and labourers leaving seems to have been proportionally less numerous, even though the British now went to South Africa and Australasia as well as North America. Between 1852 and 1911 farmers and labourers constituted between one-tenth and one-fifth of all emigrants from the United Kingdom, but as these figures include emigrants from Ireland, the importance of the emigration of the agricultural population from England and Wales was probably much less. From the 1850s and 1860s it was urban artisans who figure most prominently. In the later nineteenth century those who left the English countryside went to English towns, not American prairies.[70]

Thus emigration from England was greatest after 1851, when conditions in town and country were improving, and proportionally the outflow was unimportant compared with emigration from other countries or, above all, compared with the move to the towns within England. Within the British Isles the emigration rate from Ireland exceeded that elsewhere except for some isolated decades; and within Britain the emigration rate from England was generally less than that from Wales, and especially less than that from Scotland (table 33).

The comparison of the importance of internal migration to the towns from the rural registration districts of England and Wales with emigration overseas (table 30) shows that internal migration greatly exceeded emigration except

Table 34. *Crude birth and death rates in England and Wales, 1801–40 (per thousand)*

	Birth rate	Death rate
1801–10	41.4	30.1
1811–20	42.0	27.7
1821–30	40.1	26.1
1831–40	35.9	23.1

SOURCE: P. E. Razell, 'The evaluation of baptism as a form of birth registration through cross-matching census and parish register data: a study in methodology', *Population Studies*, 26 (1972), 128, 142.

in the 1880s, and in 1901–11, when net emigration actually exceeded migration loss to the towns from rural areas. Thus the main safety-valve for rural England and Wales was English cities rather than overseas farms.

The control of fertility

In France the comparatively rapid population growth of the second half of the eighteenth century was followed by the spread of the limitation of births within marriage, in contrast to Ireland where the postponement of marriage and emigration were practised. In England and Wales, it is thought the crude birth rate did not begin to decline until the 1870s. Most authorities would argue that this was a response to rising expectations rather than a homeostatic adjustment to population pressure. Indeed if there had been such an adjustment, it should have occurred in the 1820s, when living standards were at best stagnant, rather than in the 1870s when there had been two decades of undisputed improvement.

Unfortunately it is difficult to calculate directly the trends in fertility before 1837; however there is some evidence that fertility did fall after 1815, and then remained largely unchanged until the 1870s. T. H. Hollingsworth, for example, has used the tables on age and sex distribution in the 1821 census to calculate the crude birth and death rates between 1781 and 1821. He believes the death rate averaged 32.25 per thousand, and the birth rate 44 per thousand. As the same figures in the 1840s were 22 and 33 per thousand there must have been a pronounced decline in fertility after 1821. J. T. Krause and J. P. Huzel have also both argued that there was a fall in fertility between 1821 and the 1840s. The most recent attempt to produce national birth and death rates from baptisms and burials also suggests a decline in fertility and mortality in the early nineteenth century[71] (table 34). All this suggests the possibility of a decline in fertility after the end of the Napoleonic Wars. As prosperity returned in the 1850s, the decline was halted, and fertility remained relatively unchanging until the 1870s.

Conclusions

After the 1840s, Sydney Pollard has written, 'the population of Great Britain (though not of Ireland) was lifted for the first time in human history, by a clear margin above a subsistence standard...'[72] This was undoubtedly so. But it was 'a damn close-run thing'. The remarkable achievements of the century after 1750 have concealed the fact that English agriculture had great difficulty in keeping up with the demand for food within the country, and was probably not capable of producing the increase needed for a better fed population. Seen in this light the repeal of the Corn Laws was inevitable. The great achievement of this revolutionary century was the growth of urban employment opportunities. It is true that this was not sufficient to halt the growth of the rural population until after 1851, but the possibilities of migration to the towns did prevent the disaster that would have occurred if rural population growth had been as fast as national growth and there had been no rural–urban migration. In England therefore, there was no flight across the Atlantic as great as there was from Ireland and Norway, nor was fertility limited so early or so effectively as it was in France. The problems of rural population pressure were not relieved by changes within English agriculture, but by migration to the towns, where the Industrial Revolution was creating new jobs, and also products whose sale abroad allowed England to import the food that could not be produced at home.

CHAPTER 14

FRANCE IN THE EIGHTEENTH AND NINETEENTH CENTURIES

At the beginning of the eighteenth century the most likely places for industrial growth to take place were France, the Low Countries and England. In the event, the Industrial Revolution got underway first in England, and historians have made much of the differences between France and England at this time. More recently French industrial growth has been reappraised, and it may be that its achievement has been underestimated. Nonetheless the relationships between population growth and rural society in France were very different from those in England. French population growth was much slower than in England; it rose from nearly 22 million in 1755 to 35 million in 1851, an increase of 59%; it then stagnated for the rest of the century. France in 1750 had nearly four times the population of England and Wales, but on the eve of the First World War, France with 39 million, was only 3 million larger than England.

The growth of population 1700–1914

The early revolutionary governments made attempts to count the population of France in the 1790s, but the first census was not taken until 1801; the first reliable census, some think, was that of 1821. The changes in political boundaries influenced the rate of growth. Between 1701 and 1789 1 million of the increase of 7 million was a result of annexation; there were corresponding declines after 1815, and 1½ million were lost with the ceding of Alsace-Lorraine in 1874.[1] The first half of the eighteenth century saw little increase; indeed there may have been a decline in the first two decades (table 35). But between 1750 and 1780 there was rapid increase.[2] France increased its population by about one-third in the eighteenth century, mainly after 1750. Between 1801 and 1851 population increased by about 30%, but between 1851 and 1901 by only 3 million or 8.7%. Such a low rate of increase was not found anywhere else in Europe at this time, save in Ireland.

The growth of French population from the 1740s was of course paralleled elsewhere in Europe, and indeed down to the Revolution. Although population growth was less in France than in England or Ireland, the rate was not greatly different from that in other parts of Western Europe (table 36); between 1800 and 1850 the rate of increase was certainly lower than in some other countries

Table 35. *The population of France, 1700–1911*

	Number (1000s)	Rate of increase (% p.a.)		Number (1000s)	Rate of increase (% p.a.)
					0.44
1700	19000–19500		1851	35780	
		0.22–0.23			0.44
1755	21500–22000		1861	37300	
		0.72–0.84			−0.32
1776	25600		1872	36100	
		0.29			0.47
1801	27500		1881	37670	
		0.64			0.18
1811	29300		1891	38340	
		0.39			0.14
1821	30460		1901	38910	
		0.67			0.18
1831	32570		1911	39610	
		0.49			
1841	34230				

SOURCE: J. C. Toutain, *La population de la France de 1700 à 1959* (Paris, 1963), pp. 16, 19.

Table 36. *The rate of population increase in Western Europe, 1700–1910* (% p.a.)

	1700–50	1750–1800	1800–50	1850–1910
England and Wales	0.2	0.7	1.8	1.6
France	0.1	0.6	0.7	0.2
Holland	0.7	0.8	0.8	1.5
Belgium	0.8	0.7	0.9	1.2
Sweden	—	0.6	1.0	1.0
Ireland	0.6	1.1	0.6	−0.6
Norway	0.4	1.0	1.3	1.0

SOURCE: N. L. Tranter, *Population since the Industrial Revolution: the case of England and Wales* (London, 1973), p. 43.

but not dramatically so. It was, for example, little different from Holland and Belgium. It was in the second half of the nineteenth century that France's demographic experience was unique.

The causes of the increase from the 1740s are by no means clear: prior to 1792 there was no civil registration of births, deaths and marriages, and knowledge of trends in fertility and mortality depends on village studies made by the methods of family reconstitution, and estimates based on the age and sex distributions in the early censuses. Using the latter method

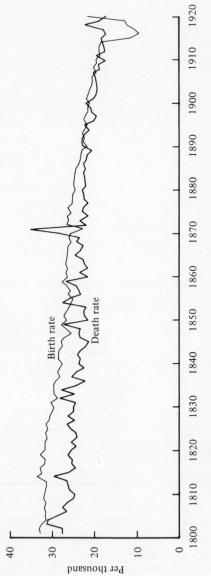

Fig. 16. Crude birth and death rates in France in the nineteenth century. Source: B. R. Mitchell, *European historical statistics, 1750–1970* (London, 1975), pp. 106, 109, 115.

J. Bourgeois-Pichat estimated that both fertility and mortality were falling from the 1770s.[3] Village studies have since confirmed that fertility was falling before the Revolution;[4] this suggests that rising fertility is unlikely to have been a major cause of the growth of population before 1801, and certainly not after 1792 when civil registration of births and deaths was established and more reliable data are available. The crude birth rate remained above 30 per thousand until 1830 and then fell away, until on the eve of the First World War it was below 20 per thousand. The crude death rate also fell slowly after 1801 (fig. 16).[5]

If mortality declined in the eighteenth century, it declined slowly. It has been argued that the infant mortality rate fell consistently throughout the second half of the eighteenth century, but adult mortality showed no similar trend. There was, however, an important difference between the two halves of the eighteenth century. In the first half demographic crises were common, in the second half they were rare until the few years before the Revolution. There was no outbreak of bubonic plague after 1720, and the subsistence crises became fewer. As in England, however, there seem to have been few advances in public hygiene or in medical therapy until well into the nineteenth century; inoculation against smallpox was uncommon until late in the eighteenth century. It has therefore been argued that the fall in the death rate can be attributed to an increase in agricultural production and the improvement of transport, which meant there were fewer isolated communities which were at risk at times of harvest failure. But there is no reliable evidence to show that agricultural output increased much faster than population in the eighteenth century. J. C. Toutain's estimate of an increase in the volume of agricultural output of 60% is generally held to be an overestimate, and there is little evidence of any great increase in agricultural productivity before the 1820s.[6]

The symptoms of overpopulation

Although the total population of France increased far less than that of England between 1750 and 1850, the rural population increased nearly as rapidly as that of England, particularly between 1760 and 1780. In the period immediately before the French Revolution there were many symptoms of population pressure in the French countryside, and some historians believe this was a contributory factor in the rural uprisings. In the 1820s liberal economists followed Malthus in arguing that poverty was a result of excessive population growth; others however, thought, like Godwin, that social organisation was the cause, and had little time for Malthus' views. 'There is only one man too many on this earth', wrote Proudhon, 'and that is Mr. Malthus.'[7]

Population growth continued until the 1840s. Many modern historians believe that France by then was overpopulated. A recent historian of the

French countryside has written 'l'accroissement des densités rurales se poursuit jusque vers le milieu au XIXe siècle, ou des signes caractéristiques de surpeuplement se manifestent', a view shared by other French historians. An English historian has recently written that by 1848 'the French countryside was overpopulated, to a degree which meant that any short-falling in the products of agriculture was likely to cause a social crisis'.[8]

What evidence is there to support this belief? Certainly land hunger can be detected as one cause of the rising trend in prices, land values and rents. Cereal prices rose by 65% between 1769 and 1789 and continued to increase during the Revolutionary and Napoleonic period, although they did not reach the extraordinary heights found in England at that time. At the end of the Wars cereal prices fell, but from the late 1820s they were rising, and continued to do so until the 1870s. Throughout the eighteenth century cereal prices rose more rapidly than those of livestock produce.[9] It has been estimated that rental income rose 98% between 1726-41 and 1785-9.

Nor did the short post-war depression halt the continued rise in rents; the Revolution had not converted France into a nation of peasant proprietors. Fully half the farmland was still tilled by tenants even in the late nineteenth century. Rents around Rouen rose by some 35% between 1815 and 1851, by 25% in the Calvados countryside; in single instances in Seine-et-Marne and Seine-et-Oise, rents rose by over 50% in the same period.[10]

The subdivision of farms

It is commonly asserted that farms in France were subdivided in the eighteenth and nineteenth centuries, but there were no national figures on farm size until 1862. Further, more attention has been paid to landownership than to farm size and indeed the two seem in some circumstances to have been confused.

In the second half of the eighteenth century peasant ownership of land was increasing. On the eve of the Revolution a number of regional studies suggest that peasants owned about one-third of the farmland, the nobility and the urban bourgeoisie one-quarter each and the clergy less than one-tenth. During the Revolution clerical land and that of some emigré nobles was confiscated and sold but only one-tenth of the total land changed hands. Nor did peasants buy all the land thus available, and few of the landless – already a numerous class in 1789 – could afford to buy. It was the bourgeoisie and the richer peasants who gained from the sale of expropriated land. In 1815 peasants still owned less than 40% of the total; by the end of the century – peasant ownership increased especially after 1850 – between 45% and 50%.[11]

It is often stated that population growth led to the subdivision of farms in the eighteenth century[12] and there are some local examples to support this belief. Thus in a study of four villages in the Auvergne there were 490 holdings

Table 37. *Farm size in France, 1892*

Size (ha)	Number	%	% excluding farms of less than 1 ha	Area	% of total area	% excluding farms of less than 1 ha
Less than 1	2235405	39.2	—	1327253	2.7	—
1–5	1829259	32.1	52.8	5489200	11.1	11.4
5–10	788299	13.8	22.7	5755500	11.7	12.0
10–40	711118	12.5	20.5	14313417	29.0	29.8
40 and over	138671	2.4	4.0	22493383	45.5	46.8
Total	5702752	100	100	49378753	100	100

SOURCE: P. Barral, *Les agrariens français de Meline à Pisani* (Paris, 1968), p. 27.

of less than 1 hectare in 1720, 870 in 1782–1800, and more instances of subdivision have been noted in Bourgogne, Vexon, Gascony and near Clermont-Ferrand.[13] Certainly by the eve of the Revolution the very small farm was an important feature of farm structure in many regions; in Limousin 58% of all holdings were less than 2 hectares, 76% in Laon, and in the department of the Nord 75% were less than 1 hectare, in Cambrésis 65% were less than 1 hectare, while in Lourmarin, in Provence, half the holdings were less than 4 hectares.[14] The subdivision of holdings seems to have continued in the first half of the nineteenth century, as rural population further increased. By the end of the nineteenth century, the small farm dominated rural social structure (table 37). Some 71% of all holdings were less than 5 hectares in size and only 2.4% exceeded 40 hectares. But this did not mean that French land was farmed exclusively in *minifundia*. Nearly half the farmland was in holdings of more than 40 hectares, and a further 29% in holdings of 10–40 hectares. The large farms were particularly numerous in the Paris Basin, as they had been since the Middle Ages.

Throughout the nineteenth century, the number of smallholdings increased, and in some areas the larger farms were subdivided. The average size of holding fell from 4.48 hectares in 1851 to 3.5 in 1881.[15] For a large proportion of the population holdings were too small to provide even the minimum subsistence. E. Labrousse has calculated that this was 5 hectares in 1789, but with increases in productivity, 2–3 hectares in the 1860s; then half the holdings were smaller than this.[16]

In England the period 1750–1850 was not only one of increasing farm size but of the consolidation of scattered fields. In France enclosure was a slow process and was confined to the extinction of collective husbandry rules and of common grazing rights. There was little consolidation; indeed it is only in the last thirty years that there has been a concerted campaign to consolidate. In the nineteenth century the fragmentation of holdings increased. This was encouraged not only by population growth but by the imposition of partible inheritance under the Napoleonic Civil Code; the passion for land also led many peasants to buy plots at some distance from their farmstead. By 1882 the French agricultural area was divided into 125 million separate parcels, an average of 22 per farm; and each parcel averaged only 39 ares in size.[17]

The growth of landlessness

Although there was subdivision of farms in the eighteenth century, this was not sufficient to provide all the growing rural population with land. By the 1780s the landless were a significant proportion of the rural population: in Flanders, three-quarters of the heads of families were without land, and in Lower Normandy they numbered a third of the population. In Lorraine, four-fifths of the population depended on labouring, two-thirds of the population of Troyes.[18] To these must be added the large numbers with some land but insufficient to provide a living. Their situation had deteriorated in those places where commons, which provided grazing for animals, had been enclosed; and the Revolutionary land settlement did little for them, for while the Revolutionary governments were happy to abolish feudal dues and obligations, they sold off expropriated land to the highest bidder. Few labourers could compete with the bourgeoisie or the richer peasants. The French rural population continued to increase in the first half of the nineteenth century, and the landless probably continued to increase in numbers and as a proportion of the social structure, although there are no accurate figures before 1851. In that year the male agricultural population numbered 7.8 million of whom 4.3 million were farmers, 3.5 million, or 45%, farm servants and day-labourers. The latter were most important in the northern half of the country, where in most départements they formed at least 40% of the male agricultural population. South of a line from Vendée to Geneva they were far less important except in Aude and Hérault. Although the second half of the nineteenth century saw an exodus of labourers from the countryside, they still formed 40% of the male agricultural population in 1882.[19]

The growth of landlessness meant that a substantial proportion of the population had to seek an income either working in rural industry or labouring on other farms, and their numbers kept wages low. In the second half of the eighteenth century the price of food and other necessaries rose by 65%, but money wages by only 22%, and in parts of the Bordelais money wages were unchanged between 1750 and 1789; in the Revolutionary and Napoleonic period wages did not keep up with prices. Between 1815 and 1851 there was no increase in the real wages of agricultural labourers and there was considerable unemployment in the countryside.[20]

It was thus not until after 1856, when the number of agricultural labourers began to decline, that their wages began to rise: the average weekly wage rose by 60% between 1850 and 1882.[21] As prices rose somewhat less the real income and diet of the labourer and the peasant with a smallholding began to show some improvement. But rural consumption lagged behind urban. Although consumption per head of meat in France rose from 19.9 kg per year in 1840 to 35.8 kg in 1892, *rural* consumption in 1882 was only one-third of urban, and much the same as the national average in 1840. Peasants drank little wine until the 1860s, and before then meat was rare; bread and potatoes were the staples; in the Cevennes chestnuts provided much of the food even as late as the 1870s.[22]

In the 1840s, then, the lot of the labourer and the smallholder, who together were a majority of the French rural population, was hard. The symptoms of population pressure were clear: real wages had fallen, unemployment had risen, farms were progressively subdivided and fragmented. The peasant sold his produce for cash, and ate the inferior part of his output. Vagrancy, begging and seasonal migration had all increased since the 1770s. And although French population growth between 1750 and 1850 was at only a modest rate compared with other West European countries, France was still one of the most densely populated countries in Europe. Within the country, the highest rural densities were to be found in the north-west from Brittany to the Belgian border, in the east in Alsace and Lorraine, in the south-west in the Landes and the Gironde, and in the south-east in the mountains. But the problems of population pressure were not confined to these regions.[23]

The agrarian response to population growth

In England the period between 1750 and 1850 was one of great economic change. Indeed the beginnings of industrialisation and the advance in agricultural productivity can be dated to the preceding century. In France, however, there was no such dramatic alteration in the way of life. Although towns grew, the nation remained overwhelmingly rural until the middle of the nineteenth century, and the growth of modern industry was delayed. There seems little evidence of substantial advance in agricultural methods in the eighteenth century, and indeed some French historians believe that crop yields did not begin to increase until after 1840. How then did French agriculture sustain the increase of some 15 million between 1700 and 1850 – for there is some agreement that the volume of output at least matched population growth, even though this population increase affected much of the rural population adversely. J. C. Toutain has argued that French agricultural output grew by 60% in the eighteenth century, but most now agree that this is an overestimate. E. LeRoy Ladurie puts it at 40%, slightly ahead of population growth; in the first half of the nineteenth century however, output outran population increase. How was this achieved?[24]

Table 38. *The arable area of France, 1701–1913 (million hectares; crops, fallow, market gardening and vines)*

Year	Area	Year	Area
1701–10	23.1	1852	26.1
1750–60	19.0	1862	26.6
1771–80	20.4	1882	25.6
1781–90	23.9	1892	25.2
1803–12	23.7	1913	23.6
1840	25.5		

SOURCE: J. C. Toutain, *Le produit de l'agriculture française de 1700 à 1958* (Paris, 1961), p. 48.

Table 39. *Area in fallow in France, 1701–1892*

	Million hectares	% of arable
1701–10	7.7	33
1781–90	8.1	34
1840	6.9	27
1852	5.7	22
1892	3.3	13

SOURCE: Toutain, *Le produit de l'agriculture française*, pp. 48, 62.

The extension of the cultivated area

There was no doubt an increase in the area under cultivation in the second half of the eighteenth century and the first half of the nineteenth century; thereafter there was little addition. Unfortunately there are no reliable national figures before the agricultural census published in 1840, but J. C. Toutain's estimates suggest an increase between 1750 and 1850 of about one-third (table 38).

Equally important, especially in the first half of the nineteenth century, was the decline in the land under fallow. In 1800 there were very few areas of France where the fallow had been completely extinguished: these included the extreme north, Flanders, on the borders of Belgium, where industrial and forage crops were grown, and a few limited regions where the four-course rotation had been adopted – in Lower Normandy, in parts of Savoy, around Poitiers and in some parts of Champagne. But these regions together occupied no more than 1% of the total area of France; elsewhere the three-field system north of a line from Bordeaux to Burgundy and the two-field to the south of this line still prevailed.[25] Thus in the early nineteenth century approximately one-third of French arable lay fallow each year; this had fallen to one-fifth by 1850, a substantial increase in the area under crops.[26] But this clearly lagged behind the English achievement. At the beginning of the nineteenth century no more than one-seventh of English arable was still fallow. Nor was the reduction in fallow of the same order in every part of France: in 1852 fallow was less than 15% of the arable in the north-west, in the east and north-east, but over much of the rest of France it was still more than one-fifth and in the Massif Central, the mountains of the south and the south-east, and on the Mediterranean it still exceeded one-third.[27]

More intensive crops

Although the potato was grown in parts of France in the seventeenth century, it was not a major crop until the nineteenth century; it was only reluctantly used for human food in the eighteenth century and then only by the very poor. By 1800 it was known in most parts of France, but was only important in a few limited areas: in Flanders in the north, in parts of Alsace and Lorraine, and in some of the mountainous areas of the Massif Central and the Alps. The harvest failures of 1811–12 seem to have accelerated its adoption. In the second decade of the nineteenth century, there were more than half a million hectares under the crop, and this had nearly doubled by the 1850s. By 1852 the potato occupied 3.1% of French arable, and it continued to increase in importance, both absolutely and proportionally.[28]

The growth of maize increased considerably in the eighteenth century, but was limited climatically to the southern parts of the country where, however, it played an important role in reducing the area under fallow. In the very north of France sugar-beet began to be grown in the early part of the nineteenth century and expanded rapidly between 1820 and 1833. The crop produced both sugar and cattle feed, and could be grown on the fallow. It was, however, little grown outside the four most northerly départements.[29]

Changes in agricultural methods

The agricultural revolution in France has attracted almost as much attention as that in England, and its discussion is equally hampered by the absence of any reliable figures on crop yields before 1840. However, although some advanced practices – such as the growth of artificial grasses – were known in the seventeenth century, nearly all historians think that there was little or no change in farming methods before the middle of the eighteenth century; indeed a majority believe there was little change before the Restoration, and others argue that there was no fundamental change before the second half of the nineteenth century.[30]

Certainly the first national yield figures from 1840 suggest there could have been relatively little advance in the preceding century. The average yield of wheat was only 940 kg/ha, about half that in England. Yet there was a very profound regional difference in yields: in the départements north from Orléans

to the Belgian border the average was 1480 kg/ha or more, high yields
were also found in the north-east, but in the south, half the départements
had averages of less than 810 kg/ha.[31] Rye and oats also showed this regional
difference, although rather more southern départements had high yields of
these crops than was the case with wheat; with potatoes the north–south
difference was much diminished.[32] The national average yield of wheat has
been put at 780 kg/ha in 1815, and in 1880, when national statistics were
available, at 1125 kg/ha.[33] This suggests some increase between 1815 and
1840, and as the yield was so low in 1815, precludes any radical change
before 1815. Indeed Michel Morineau has argued that wheat yields were as
high in the early eighteenth century in the northern départements, as they
were in 1840, and thus discounts the view that there was any agricultural
revolution before that year. Other writers believe there was change before
1840 – in the 1820s – but few still argue that there was any significant
advance in the eighteenth century.[34]

Even if there was no agricultural revolution in the 1760s, this period did
see a revival of interest in agriculture in France, in the work of French writers
who were familiar with English events; they believed enclosure and the
formation of large farms would improve French farming.[35] In the 1760s the
village communities were generally free from the obligation to follow the same
husbandry practices except in the north-east, but grazing on the stubble and
fallow still persisted, and common land was still subject to common grazing
except in Normandy. In the 1760s and 1770s both national governments and
local *intendants* favoured the enclosure of commons, and *edicts* to enclose
were obtained in Flanders, Alsace-Lorraine and Burgundy. After 1780 there
was little enclosure of common grazing, for both the landless and smallholders
opposed it, while the prosperous peasants feared that the seigneur would
exercise the right of *triage* and claim one-third of the common land. Thus not
only was there little consolidation of plots, but even in the mid-nineteenth
century much of the grazing land was held in common.[36]

The failure to consolidate did not preclude the adoption of rotations
including artificial grasses and root crops, but as has been seen (above, p. 198)
there were few parts of France in 1800 where these new rotations were
followed. As late as 1840 fallow made up 27% of the arable, and rotational
grasses only 6%, while root crops occupied less than 6% of the arable. One
consequence of this was that livestock densities were low and the supply of
manure limited, for in the north there was little waste land left to support
livestock. This in turn helps to account for the comparatively low yields even
in the north in 1840, and *a fortiori* in the south where wheat yields in many
départements in that year were no higher than they had been in the Middle
Ages. Other fertilisers such as marl and lime were used, but were confined
to the north, and their heavy application seems to date only from the 1840s,
as did underdrainage.[37]

Nonetheless, there was undeniable change in the first half of the nineteenth century: oil-cake began to be fed to livestock in the 1830s, guano was imported in the 1840s. The first steam thresher had been imported from England in 1818, and Russian varieties of wheat were adopted in Languedoc in the 1820s. The scythe replaced the sickle in the grain harvest between 1850 and 1870, and the horse drill became more common after 1850, although in 1862 only 7% of even large holdings used it.[38]

There was a very clear difference between the pace of agricultural change in England and France. In England the adoption of roots and rotational grasses, the better feeding of livestock and the higher crop yields resulting from heavy manuring began in the south-east in the seventeenth century, and spread to much of the rest of the country in the eighteenth century.[39] In the early nineteenth century a new series of innovations, associated with the Industrial Revolution and the reduction of sea freights prompted further changes – the import of guano and oil-cake, the use of machinery, the beginnings of artificial fertilisers. This prompted a further series of yield increases, so that the national average yield was continuously increasing between 1650 and 1850. In France, however, the earlier innovations were not adopted until after 1815, and were virtually contemporary with the new inputs, which spread from the 1820s and 1830s, such as sugar-beet and industrial inputs. Although much of this improvement was confined to the north, the advances that had been already made in the north by 1815 and were reflected in the higher yields, spread into central France after 1820. Thus the period after 1815 saw a considerable increase in crop yields, which, combined with an increase in the sown area, ensured that French agricultural production kept ahead of population growth. Although in the 1840s many of the symptoms of overpopulation could be detected in the rural social structure, the age of the subsistence crisis was finally over.

The demographic response to population growth

In England the increase of the rural population between 1750 and 1850 was reduced by a very considerable migration from the countryside to the towns, and to a lesser extent by emigration overseas. In Ireland the decline in the population after the Famine was brought about by massive emigration and increasing celibacy without any fall in marital fertility. In France, however, rural–urban migration had little effect on the rural population until after the 1850s, there was little overseas emigration and the marriage rate was probably higher in the nineteenth century than in the eighteenth century. The slow rate of growth of the French population between 1800 and 1911 was primarily due to a fall in marital fertility.

Overseas migration

Before 1800 there had been emigration from France not only overseas but to other parts of Europe – the persecution of Protestants was one cause of an exodus in the late sixteenth century and again in the late seventeenth century, but probably less than 100 000 left the country between 1650 and 1800.[40] By the beginning of the nineteenth century the failure of French colonial policy left few outlets overseas and, of subsequent acquisitions, only Algeria attracted a significant number. Nonetheless in absolute numbers many left France in the nineteenth century – at least two million – though as a rate emigration was low; it rose from a very low level in the 1820s to a peak in the 1840s and 1850s, a second peak was reached in the 1880s, and the highest on the eve of the First World War. However, in every decade of the nineteenth century, except between 1851–72, immigration *exceeded* emigration, and thus the loss was nullified. In 1851, 379 289 – 1% of the population – had been born abroad, in 1911, 1 159 835, or 3.0%; indeed if naturalised immigrants are included, the foreign-born made up 3.24% of the population as early as 1886.[41] If it had not been for immigration, France's population would have hardly increased at all in the second half of the nineteenth century. Thus while immigration overseas may have locally provided some release from population pressure – particularly in the mountainous areas of the south and south-east – in the country as a whole it had no role to play.[42]

Rural–urban migration

In England the urban population increased much more rapidly than the rural population between 1750 and 1850; this could not be explained by natural increase alone, and there must have been a substantial movement from the countryside to the towns. In France rural birth rates exceeded those in the towns and in most towns mortality exceeded fertility. While there must have been a movement from the countryside to the towns, before 1850 it was on a very limited scale.[43]

Unfortunately official figures on rural, urban and agricultural populations are not available before the 1850s, and are open to a variety of interpretations after that date. However, a recent calculation of the urban population shows how limited rural–urban migration must have been before 1850 (table 40). In 1811 the numbers living in towns of over 3000 formed only 14.3% of the total, in 1841, 15.4%; the rural and urban populations had increased at much the same rate. Thereafter the urban population did increase more rapidly and by 1911 the rural population was less than two-thirds of the total population. According to these figures the rural population reached a peak in 1861 and fell in absolute numbers to the end of the century. J. C. Toutain's calculations (table 41) made on the basis of a different definition of urban

Table 40. *Rural and urban population of France, 1811–1911 (1000s)*

	Total	Urban[a]	Rural	Rural as % of total
1811	29 300	4 201	25 099	85.6
1821	30 460	4 593	25 867	84.9
1831	32 570	5 098	27 472	84.3
1841	34 230	5 281	28 949	84.6
1851	35 780	6 354	29 426	82.2
1861	37 390	7 771	29 619	79.2
1872	36 100	8 249	27 851	77.1
1881	36 670	9 776	26 894	73.3
1891	38 340	10 901	27 439	71.6
1901	38 910	12 375	26 535	68.2
1911	39 610	13 816	25 794	65.1

[a] Urban population comprises those living in communities of more than 3000.
SOURCES: G. Dupeaux, 'La Croissance Urbaine en France aux XIXe siècle', *Revue d'histoire économique et sociale*, 52 (1974), 183; Toutain, *La population de la France de 1700 à 1959*, p. 19.

Table 41. *Agricultural and rural populations of France, 1700–1911*

	Total (millions)	Rural (millions)	%	Urban[a] (millions)	%	Agricultural (millions)
1700	19.25	16.15	83.9	3.1	16.1	—
1801	27.5	22.15	80.5	5.35	19.5	18.8
1811	29.30	23.55	80.4	5.75	19.6	19.4
1821	30.46	24.46	80.3	6.0	19.7	19.7
1831	32.57	26.07	80.0	6.5	20.0	20.5
1841	34.23	26.38	77.1	7.85	22.9	20.1
1851	35.78	26.65	74.5	9.13	25.5	19.72
1861	37.39	26.60	71.1	10.79	28.9	19.87
1872	36.1	24.89	68.9	11.21	31.1	18.5
1881	37.67	24.56	65.2	13.11	34.8	18.25
1891	38.34	24.03	62.7	14.31	37.3	17.44
1901	38.91	22.95	59.0	15.96	41.0	16.17
1911	39.61	22.1	55.8	17.51	44.2	15.07

[a] Urban population comprises those living in communities of more than 2000.
SOURCE: Toutain, *La population de la France de 1700 à 1959*, pp. 54–5.

(places with more than 2000 people) suggest that the rural population reached a peak in 1851 – 26.65 million, and fell to just over 22 million in 1911. His estimates of the numbers dependent upon agriculture show a slow increase from 1801 to 1831 and thereafter a decline.

Whatever figures are accepted, they suggest that there was comparatively little rural–urban migration before the 1830s. Thereafter the numbers leaving the rural districts can be measured; although the absolute numbers were

Table 42. *Loss by migration from rural areas, France 1856–86*

	Number (1000s)	Rate per 100 rural popula-tion, p.a.
1856–61	646 919	0.5
1861–66	661 162	0.5
1866–72	—	—
1872–76	462 871	0.4
1876–81	829 754	0.67
1881–86	449 910	0.4

[a] Taking as rural places with less than 2000 people.
SOURCE: A. Armengaud, 'La rôle de la démographie', in F. Braudel and E. Labrousse (eds.), *Histoire économique et sociale de la France*, vol. 3, part 1 (Paris, 1976), p. 226.

substantial, they were a small proportion of the total (table 42). Indeed, it has been argued, if fertility had not fallen, the French rural population would have not declined.[44] Thus although there was rural–urban migration before the 1850s when the rural population was still increasing, the outflow was not very great. The 1830s, many historians believe, mark the turning-point.[45] If there was population pressure, why was the volume of outflow not greater before then?

In the first place industrial growth in France lagged behind that in Britain and there were, therefore, not enough jobs in the towns to absorb the rural surplus. The growth of heavy urban-located industry only dated from the 1820s and 1830s. In the second half of the nineteenth century wage differentials – industrial wages were double the agricultural labourer's wage – began to attract the rural population to the towns. It was not farmers who left, but agricultural labourers and those engaged in non-agricultural activities in the countryside. Indeed the numbers of farmers in France increased in the second half of the nineteenth century, although the total male agricultural labour force declined.[46]

Second, there was not, as there was in England, any large-scale enclosure movement to loosen ties with the soil. Indeed peasant landownership increased in the nineteenth century. A third factor was the survival of rural industry; in the middle of the nineteenth century a substantial proportion of French industry was still carried out in rural areas, not yet having succumbed to the competition of factory products.[47] A minor factor may have been the importance of seasonal migration in France, which provided the poor in the countryside with supplementary incomes.[48]

Table 43. *Rate of natural increase in France, 1816–90 (average % p.a.)*

1816–20	0.66	1851–55	0.2
1821–25	0.67	1856–60	0.38
1826–30	0.6	1866–69	0.27
1831–39	0.36	1870–71	−0.7
1836–40	0.47	1872–75	0.38
1841–45	0.54	1876–80	0.29
1846–50	0.28	1881–85	0.25
		1886–90	0.1

SOURCE: Armengaud, 'La rôle de la démographie', in Braudel and Labrusse, *Histoire économique et sociale de la France*, vol. 3, part 1 (1976), p. 206.

Declining fertility

The decisive factor in the comparatively slow increase of France's rural population in the first half of the nineteenth century was not overseas migration or rural–urban migration, although obviously this was important, but the decline in fertility. Whereas in England there are no reliable national figures before 1837, and changes before that date must be speculative, in France civil registration dates from 1792; there can be little doubt that the crude birth rate fell from the early nineteenth century (fig. 16). The crude birth rate was 32.9 per thousand in 1816–20, 28.4 per thousand in 1836–40, 26 per thousand in 1872–5 and 23.0 per thousand in 1886–90.[49] The result was a marked decline in the rate of natural increase, which was particularly marked after 1845. This was not due to any decline in the frequency of marriage, which rose markedly from 1792 to 1815, and continuously from 1831, except in the 1880s and 1890s; there is no evidence that the proportion remaining unmarried changed significantly in the nineteenth century.[50]

Thus falling fertility seems to have been due to a fall in marital fertility. The gross reproduction rate (a measure of a generation's capacity to repro-due itself) in 1816–20 was 201, by the 1880s it had fallen to 165.[51] This could have been due to a rise in the age of first marriage of women, but this in fact fell from 1853–7, when it was 24.2 years; it does not seem to have radically changed in the preceding one hundred years.[52] Thus the fall in fertility is generally attributed to the limitation of births within marriage, presumably by the practice of *coitus interruptus*.

It was once thought that the decline in fertility began with the French Revolution; the clergy lost the respect of and, except in remoter areas such as Brittany, had less influence on their congregations. Practices which had hitherto been confined to a few upper-class women now spread among the population in general. Studies of eighteenth-century villages now suggest that there had been some limitation of births within marriage before then, and that marital fertility was declining in some villages before the Revolution.[53]

It was this decline in fertility which was the cause of the decline in the rate of increase of the French population. Bourgeois-Pichat has estimated that if the fertility level of the 1770s had been maintained and mortality had fallen as it did, the population of France in 1880 would have been 88 million instead of 38 million.[54] The decline of the French rural population after 1861 was of course due to the migration from the countryside to the towns. But without the fall in fertility, this exodus would probably not have led to a reduction in numbers.

Conclusions

The most striking feature of French economic change after 1750 is the slow growth of population, particularly after the 1840s, and the importance of declining marital fertility in accounting for this. The early fall in French fertility is regarded as a unique feature in European demography, and there has been much speculation about its effect on French economic development. The slow rate of industrialisation has been attributed to it for, it is argued, French industry did not have the stimulus of rapidly growing demand, nor did it have, until late in the nineteenth century, a supply of cheap labour from the countryside. There is, of course, an alternative view. Far from the French reaction being unique, it would seem to have simply repeated the pattern found in previous centuries. As population grew in the eighteenth century and the symptoms of population pressure appeared, the French rural population responded by limiting its numbers. Indeed perhaps it should be asked, not why the French limited their numbers so early, but why other European populations did not?

CHAPTER 15

SCANDINAVIA IN THE EIGHTEENTH AND NINETEENTH CENTURIES

Between the onslaughts of the Vikings and the rise of the modern welfare state Scandinavia has been on the periphery of European history, political or economic, except in the age of Gustavus Adolphus. But Norway and Sweden have a particular interest in the modern era. Until late in the nineteenth century, they remained overwhelmingly agrarian societies, and much of their early industrial growth was based on the processing of primary produce – fish, timber and iron ore. In the 1830s and 1840s, like much of the rest of Europe, their rural regions suffered from poverty, and as elsewhere, contemporaries were not agreed as to whether this was due to excessive population growth or some defect in their institutions. But Scandinavia has attracted the attention of historians largely because of the excellence of its demographic records. Sweden's first census was taken in 1749, Norway's in 1769, and the registration of vital statistics began in 1749 in Sweden, 1735 in Norway.[1] Agricultural statistics were not collected until much later; in Sweden parish clergy were required to make returns on yields and land use in 1805, and provincial governors made similar returns from 1820, but reliable records did not begin until the formation of the Central Bureau of Statistics in 1865. In Norway some agricultural statistics were obtained at the census of 1835 and at subsequent censuses, but agricultural statistics proper were not collected until 1929.[2]

The growth of population

In 1850 the populations of both Norway and Sweden were two and a half times what they had been in 1700. Norway's population had increased by another 60% by the eve of the First World War, Sweden's by 57%. Norway's pattern of increase was similar to that of much of the rest of Western Europe. The rate of increase was higher after 1750 than before, and reached an average of 0.97% p.a. in 1800–50, and was only a little less in 1850–1900 (table 44). In Sweden the upturn began earlier (after 1720) but the highest rates came after 1810.[3]

The higher rates of increase in both countries after 1810 were due to falling mortality. In the second half of the eighteenth century the crude death rate was still high (table 45 and fig. 17), and there was no downward trend. In

Table 44. *Population growth in Norway and Sweden*

Norway			Sweden		
	Number (1000s)	Average rate of increase (% p.a.)		Number (1000s)	Average rate of increase (% p.a.)
1701	520		1700	1369	
		0.3			0.25
1735	579		1720	1440	
		0.7			0.7
1750	642		1750	1781	
		0.6			0.55
1770	722		1800	2347	
		0.65			0.2
1801	883		1810	2395	
		0.02			0.7
1815	885		1820	2573	
		1.4			1.1
1825	1051		1830	2876	
		1.3			0.8
1835	1194		1840	3123	
		1.1			1.1
1845	1328		1850	3484	
		1.2			0.9
1855	1490		1860	3824	
		1.3			0.85
1865	1701		1870	4164	
		0.6			0.94
1875	1813		1880	4572	
		0.6			0.45
1890	2000		1890	4780	
		1.1			0.72
1900	2240		1900	5136	
		0.65			0.68
1910	2391		1910	5499	
1700	520		1700	1369	
		0.42			0.53
1750	642		1750	1781	
		0.6			0.55
1801	883		1801	2347	
		0.97			0.79
1855	1490		1850	3484	
		0.9			0.78
1901	2240		1901	5136	

SOURCES: S. Dyrvik, 'Historical demography in Norway 1660–1801: a short survey', *Scandinavian Economic History Review*, 20 (1972), 33; Ø. Øyen, 'Norway's population', in N. R. Ramsøy (ed.), *Norwegian society* (Oslo, 1974), p. 11; D. S. Thomas, *Social and economic aspects of Swedish population movements* (New York, 1941), p. 32.

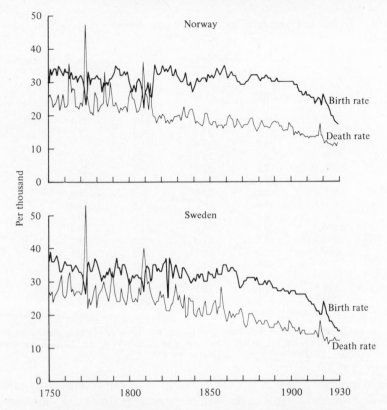

Fig. 17. Crude birth and death rates in Norway and Sweden, 1750–1930. Source: B. R. Mitchell, *European historical statistics, 1750–1970* (London, 1975), pp. 104, 107, 111, 112, 118–19.

both countries there were still frequent crisis years; after 1815 these crises were far less common, and the average crude death rate fell several points. The crude birth rate on the other hand showed no consistent trend, although in Sweden by the 1840s it was somewhat lower than in the eighteenth century. In both countries, births were characterised by bulges in a thirty year cycle.[4]

There is no obvious explanation of the decline of the death rate; in neither country was industrialisation of any significance until the later nineteenth century. As in England there is little evidence of improvement in medicine: inoculation against smallpox was introduced into Bergen in the 1770s and vaccination was made compulsory in Norway in 1810, in Sweden in 1816. But evidence on the causes of death available from Swedish records shows that smallpox accounted for only 8% of all deaths in the late eighteenth century. There were few other improvements in medicine in either country, except possibly in midwifery, until the late nineteenth century. In Norway the state established a system of state-paid doctors in rural areas in the 1820s,

Table 45. *Trends in crude birth and death rates, Norway and Sweden (per thousand)*

	Norway		Sweden	
	CBR	CDR	CBR	CDR
1750–9	33.1	26.8	35.8	27.3
1760–9	31.9	25.4	34.5	27.5
1770–9	29.7	27.9	32.9	29.5
1780–9	33.3	25.3	32.6	27.1
1790–9	33.0	22.5	33.7	25.3
1800–9	25.4	24.4	30.5	28.3
1810–19	29.8	22.3	33.3	26.5
1820–9	33.5	19.0	33.8	23.9
1830–9	30.4	20.6	31.8	23.3
1840–9	30.3	18.4	31.1	20.7
1850–9	32.7	17.0	32.6	22.2
1860–7	31.3	18.5	32.2	19.9
1870–9	30.8	17.1	30.5	18.4
1880–9	30.8	17.0	29.2	17.1
1890–9	30.1	16.5	27.2	16.4
1900–9	27.9	14.4	26.3	15.2

SOURCES: D. Thomas, *Swedish population movements*, pp. 35–8; M. Drake, *Population and society in Norway, 1735–1865* (London, 1969), pp. 184–8, 192–5; B. R. Mitchell, *European historical statistics, 1750–1970* (London, 1975), pp. 86, 118.

but these numbered only 20 in 1824 and 60 in 1848. Improvements in public health date mainly from the second half of the nineteenth century – municipal health boards were established in the towns in 1860, and any improvements in private hygiene from the use of soap and cheap cotton clothes were unlikely to have been widespread before the 1840s when the first cotton factories were established, and the consumption of soap increased significantly.[5]

Another possible cause was the improvement of the food supply: the potato spread rapidly in both countries after 1815, for not only was it high yielding, but it was less susceptible to harvest failure in wet summers. There was also a considerable increase in the area of other crops and some historians believe that food output increased more rapidly than population in the first half of the nineteenth century. However, there is little evidence of improvement in the diet before the 1850s, and real wages were falling until then. Nor had harvest failure been a major cause of death in the eighteenth century, for infectious disease was by far the most important cause.[6]

This had led some writers, unimpressed by the evidence of an increase in food supply or improvements in medicine, to suggest that either some diseases became less virulent, or that the population developed immunity. For this there is, however, no evidence at all, save that, as in the rest of Western Europe, bubonic plague did not appear again after the end of the seventeenth century.[7]

Were Norway and Sweden overpopulated in the nineteenth century?

The rate of population growth in the eighteenth century was not without precedent in either Norway or Sweden. But in the nineteenth century population growth was rapid and sustained. By the 1830s contemporaries were concerned by the growth in the number of landless and the increase in pauperisation, while in Sweden the right to parish settlement and the right to poor relief were discussed in much the same tones as they were in England. There is however no sign of the abject poverty found in Ireland at this time. By the end of the nineteenth century many Swedish writers, notably Knut Wicksell, one of the founders of optimum theory and an early advocate of birth control, believed that Sweden was overpopulated.[8] Among modern writers Michael Drake has denied that Norway was overpopulated as a result of the rapid population growth of 1815–65. He saw no evidence of subdivision or of a fall in the standard of living, a view shared by Ingrid Semmingsen. On the other hand a recent historian of Norway has argued that the country was caught in a Malthusian trap in the middle of the century, and escaped only by emigration and industrialisation. G. A. Montgomery believed that Sweden managed to absorb the great increase in the agricultural population in the first half of the nineteenth century without a fall in the standard of living. On the other hand, there are others who believe that by the 1860s agriculture could provide no more employment, and that the great increase in landlessness was due to population growth. Many share the view of Gustav Sundbärg that 'around 1865 the rural districts of Sweden were overpopulated in comparison with the existing development of the country's resources'.[9]

The symptoms of overpopulation

Any discussion of the symptoms of overpopulation in Norway and Sweden is hampered by the lack of reliable agricultural statistics and the difficulties of estimating the volume of agricultural output. Much the same is true of England and France at this time, but it is probably fair to say that the historiography of Scandinavian agriculture lags behind the historiography of its demography.

Price movements – which have been studied in detail in Sweden – followed much the same pattern as in the rest of Western Europe. Between 1750 and 1800 grain prices rose 500%, livestock prices 300%. Until the 1820s Sweden had to import grain, although this never amounted to more than 15% of consumption needs. Norway, lacking the extensive arable land to be found in southern Sweden, had to import up to 40% of its grain. Grain prices reached a peak in 1815–18 and then collapsed, but grain prices rose continuously from 1825 until the 1870s, and Lennart Jörberg has suggested that this was because of the failure of agricultural production to meet demand. For a period – especially in the 1850s – Sweden was an exporter of cereals, principally oats for the London horse fodder market and barley for the Dutch brewers. This does not necessarily indicate a surplus; it was possibly at the expense of the home market and only made possible by the increased consumption of potatoes. The rise in prices was matched by a rise in the price of land; in Norway peasants were buying up Crown and noble land in the first half of the nineteenth century, but often at ruinous prices. By 1845 two-thirds of the farms in Norway were heavily mortgaged; in Sweden the price of land rose steadily until in the 1850s its price put it beyond the reach of the landless.[10]

The trend in farm size is difficult to establish in the absence of any reliable information before the late nineteenth century, and in the case of Norway, until 1929. In that year Norway's farm structure was dominated by the small farm. Further, little of the total area was farmed in large units: only 2% of the farmland was in farms of more than 50 hectares; according to F. Hodne much the same pattern existed in 1850, although between 1890 and 1929 the number of small farms had increased. In a country where 80% of the farms had less than 5 hectares,[11] it is difficult to avoid the conclusion that there was extreme population pressure. This view, however, must be modified. In the first place the data do not include the common grazing land which Norwegian farmers had in abundance: one-third of Norwegian farmers in 1815 also had *saeters* which provided summer grazing and reduced the need to grow fodder crops. Secondly, many – probably most – farmers combined farming with some other activity. On the west coast farming provided an important source of income, and the crews of fishing ships were drawn from farm families; in southern and south eastern Norway many peasants had forest land, and sold timber to sawmills. Nonetheless there was a considerable increase in the number of farms in the first half of the nineteenth century. In 1802 there were 79 256 *gårds*, by 1860 135 000; many of these were new, reclaimed from land hitherto uncultivated, but many were a result of the subdivision of existing holdings.[12]

In Sweden there were greater possibilities of arable farming, in the low plains of the south-west – Halland and Skåne – and in the plains of the central lake district; farms were larger than in Norway. There was some pressure to subdivide holdings as early as the middle of the eighteenth century – Swedish population growth began in the 1720s – but legislation forbade the subdivision of the *mantal*, a taxation unit considered to be the traditional subsistence holding. This restriction was relaxed in 1749 and again in 1762, and the number of farms increased by 13–21% between 1751 and 1813, partly by subdivision, partly by the creation of new farms.[13]

Subdivision continued in the first half of the nineteenth century, but in parts of the south-west there was a trend to amalgamation and the growth of large farms.[14] In Norway there was no enclosure until after 1857. In Sweden however a series of acts had promoted enclosure, and particularly the consolidation of scattered holdings. In 1757 an act to promote consolidation –

storskifte – was passed but had little effect. In the 1780s Rutgers Maclean, a substantial landlord in Skåne, consolidated his estate with beneficial results, and this prompted a further act to promote enclosure – *enskifte* – in 1803. By the 1860s most of Skåne was enclosed, and the movement had spread to the rest of southern and central Sweden although it was not completed until the end of the nineteenth century. For the most part this did not have adverse consequences for the farming community, for the state paid for the survey and helped with the cost of building new farmhouses, roads and fences. Nor were there many great estates with repressive landlords; peasants had been buying from the Crown and the nobility throughout the eighteenth century. However, in Halland and Skåne half of the land was noble-owned, and in some cases amalgamation proceeded by eviction. In the neighbourhood of Malmo 40% of all tenant farmers were evicted between 1810 and 1850.[15]

The growth of large farms in the south-west was, however, balanced by subdivision elsewhere in the country, and until the 1850s the average size of farm in Sweden was probably falling. But this did not lead to as great a proliferation of smallholdings as it did in Norway. At the end of the nineteenth century only 23% of Sweden's farms were less than 2 hectares, compared with over 50% in Norway.[16]

The *enskifte* not only allowed amalgamation and the extinction of common husbandry and grazing practices, its main purpose was consolidation. Consolidation was particularly vigorously pursued in the south-west, and thus Sweden, like Denmark and England, was spared the progressive fragmentation of farms that population pressure and inheritance practices promoted in much of the rest of Europe. In the mountain and forest areas consolidation into one compact block was not feasible; an act in 1827 recognised this and allowed the retention of holdings in four blocks. But population growth in the nineteenth century did not lead to fragmentation. In Norway an act in 1821 to redistribute scattered holdings had no effect, and it was not until after 1857 that there was any progress towards consolidation, but most fields had been reapportioned by 1900.[17]

While there may have been a growth in the number of small farms in Norway and Sweden in the nineteenth century, subdivision was not as acute as it was in parts of Germany and France, or in Ireland. This was partly because primogeniture prevailed in both countries. Nor was the growth of farms sufficient to provide the rapidly growing rural population with land. One consequence of this was the increase in the number of landless; Sweden has reasonably accurate figures on the structure of its agricultural population from 1751 (table 46). In that year farmers constituted almost half the adult male agricultural population. Crofters, who received a house, land and wages in return for work on a farmer's land, were a small proportion of the population. Cottagers, who had no land and, unlike the crofters, no guarantee of work, were equally unimportant; a large proportion of the labour force was provided by farmer's sons and farm servants who lived in. Between 1751

Table 46. *Male agricultural population: Sweden, 1751–1900*

	Farmers	Crofters	Cottagers and labourers living in	Farmers' sons and farm servants	Statare[a]	Total
			(1000s)			
1751	186.6	27.9	20.0	148.2	—	382.7
1800	209.7	64.7	44.4	235.4	—	554.2
1850	221.2	96.8	89.2	344.7	17.0	768.9
1870	241.9	95.4	101.1	287.8	31.2	757.4
1900	271.5	72.3	54.2	354.8[b]	33.4	786.2
			(%)			
1751	48.8	7.3	5.2	38.7	—	100
1800	37.8	11.7	8.0	42.5	—	100
1850	28.8	12.6	11.6	44.8	2.2	100
1870	31.9	12.6	13.3	38.0	4.1	100
1900	34.5	9.2	6.9	45.1[b]	4.3	100

[a] Labourers not living in.
[b] This figure includes day labourers.
SOURCE: Thomas, *Swedish population movements, 1750–1933*, p. 95.

and 1850 the number of farmers increased by 19%; the number of crofters and cottagers, who had little or no land, quadrupled, and in 1850 were proportionally nearly as important as farmers. The number of farmer's sons and farm servants more than doubled. The landless had risen from 51% to 71% of the male agricultural population.[18] Thus the growth of landlessness may be locally a function of enclosure, but enclosure in Sweden did not reduce peasant landownership. On the contrary the proportion of farmland owned by farmers had been increasing since the early eighteenth century. In 1845 60% of the land was already owned by peasants, and by 1900 only 15% of Swedish farmers were tenants. The rise of a large landless class was mainly a result of population growth outrunning the amount of cultivable land.[19]

Much the same thing happened in Norway. Here there was no enclosure before 1857 and 70% of occupiers owned their farms by 1835.[20]

In 1845 by far the largest class on Norwegian farms was farm servants, often the sons or daughters of other farmers. But the principal change in the preceding century had been the rise of the *husmenn* or *husmaend*, who received land in return for work and were thus analogous with the Swedish crofter. As in Sweden, landlessness had increased as population grew: between 1801 and 1855 the number of farmers in Norway increased by 27%, cottagers doubled and those without any land tripled.[21]

The rapid growth of landlessness had a depressing effect on real wages: in Sweden, real wages declined between 1735 and 1745, were stable from then to 1770, and then declined again to 1810. They rose briefly from 1810 to 1822, but then fell again to the 1840s; after then they rose. The real wage before

Table 47. *Rural social structure in Norway, c. 1845*

	Numbers	%
Bonde	77780	22.0
Tenants	25047	7.1
Farmers	(102827)	(29.1)
Husmaend	58049	16.4
Labourers	47000	13.3
Farm servants	146000	41.2
Landless	(251049)	(70.9)
Total	353876	100.0

SOURCE: T. C. Blegen, *Norwegian migration to America, 1825–1860* (Minneapolis, 1931), p. 5.

1755 was not reached again until the 1850s. By the middle of the nineteenth century it was clear that whatever the performance of Swedish agriculture in terms of output, the land could no longer provide employment for a rapidly increasing rural population. It has been suggested that there was underemployment in Swedish agriculture from the 1830s to possibly as late as the 1870s. Much the same was true in Norway, where by the 1860s, F. Hodne has written, there was a massive surplus of labour in relation to the supply of land and the existing farming techniques.[22]

Thus by the middle of the nineteenth century, by which time there had been virtually no emigration or industrialisation in either country, many of the symptoms of population pressure had appeared: some subdivision, certainly a proliferation of smallholdings, the growth of a landless class, falling or, at best, stagnant real wages, underemployment, debt and pauperisation. On the other hand many authorities believe that the growth of agricultural output at least kept up with population increase. One Norwegian historian has calculated that the output per head of arable produce rose by 70% in the first three decades of the nineteenth century, and, that the rapid expansion of the potato played a major role in this.[23] This seems a prodigious rate of increase for a pre-industrial society to achieve, particularly in view of the literary descriptions of Norwegian agriculture at this time.[24] If this – and equally optimistic estimates of increases in Swedish agricultural output – are accepted, then output per head must have increased in the first half of the nineteenth century; population growth then primarily affected the landless population.

The agrarian response to population growth

Whatever the truth about the growth of agricultural production in the century after 1750, it is certain that a Malthusian crisis was avoided, even though Norway and Sweden were as lacking in industrial development as Ireland;

Table 48. *Population and arable land in Sweden in the nineteenth century*

	Total population (1000s)	Agricultural population (1000s)	Arable land (1000 ha)	Cultivated land per head of		Density per km² of arable land of	
				total population	agricultural population	total population	agricultural population
1805	2352	1856	1500	0.64	0.81	157	124
1860	3824	2960	3200	0.84	1.1	120	93
1900	5117	2828	3600	0.7	1.3	142	79

SOURCES: Thomas, *Swedish population movements 1750–1933*, pp. 93–4; B. Holgersson, 'Cultivated land in Sweden, and its growth, 1840–1939', *Economy and History*, 17 (1974), 21, 47–8.

this suggests that there must have been a considerable change in the agricultural techniques of both countries. In both countries, as in Western Europe in general, the expansion of the cultivated area was of prime importance in increasing output.

The expansion of the arable area

Swedish historians are agreed that the nineteenth century saw a considerable increase in the arable area. Enclosure was an important agent in this transformation. Once common grazing land was divided among individuals, much of it was ploughed up. The precise amount of this increase is in dispute. Gustav Sundbärg used the returns made by the clergy in 1805 to estimate the area under arable, and concluded that the area tripled between 1805 and 1860, and quadrupled between 1800 and 1900. However, it seems that the figures for 1805 were an underestimate, and a modification of the official figures after 1860 suggests that most of the increase was achieved by 1860,[25] that the area under arable increased by 113% between 1800 and 1860, and by a further 12% in the last forty years of the century (table 48).

If these figures are correct they show that the expansion of the arable area kept ahead of the increase in the total population of Sweden and of the growth of the agricultural population in the first half of the nineteenth century. In the second half the decline of the agricultural population combined with a slight increase in cropland led to further increase in arable per head of the agricultural population, but the arable per head of the total population declined. But in spite of the great increase in arable after 1800 the density of the agricultural population on the arable area was nearly a third above that in England in 1851, and a fifth above that in France; it was however less than half that in Ireland in 1841 (see above, p. 121). Figures for the area in arable for Norway are less reliable although there is no doubt that considerable reclamation was going on. Returns made by provincial governors record the addition of substantial areas in 1829–35, in 1846–50 and between 1856 and 1860. It seems possible that the area in arable doubled between 1820 and 1865; there was little further increase in the rest of the century.[26]

A reduction in the area under fallow was a further source of increased output. At the beginning of the nineteenth century the field systems of Scandinavia formed a considerable contrast with the rest of north-western Europe, where the transition from the three-field system, with one year in fallow, to the four-course, with no fallow, was underway. The three-field system was not the norm in Sweden; it predominated only in the south, in Skåne, Kalmar and Vastergotland. In eastern Sweden, the two-field system still prevailed, while over much of the rest of the country land was still cultivated continuously for several years then abandoned.[27] In Norway, the two- and three-field system was found mainly in the area to the north of Oslo, and in the coastal areas of the south and south-east. In the west the infield–outfield system still prevailed.[28] These relatively primitive systems offered the opportunity for a substantial reduction in the area under fallow. In Sweden this may have been as high as 50% of the arable in 1750; it was 25% in 1830, 19% in 1850 and only 7% by 1900. There was thus a very considerable increase in the area sown to crops.[29]

The potato

The potato was grown in Sweden in the second half of the seventeenth century, but does not seem to have been introduced into Norway – from Britain – until the mid-eighteenth century. In neither country was it important before the nineteenth century, but in both countries it expanded rapidly after 1810. In Sweden there were about 7800 hectares in 1801–10, less than 1% of the area under cereals; by 1830 it occupied the equivalent of 6% of the cereal acreage, in 1866 10%, and 5.5% of the total arable. The crop was used for distilling and fodder as well as for human consumption.[30]

In Norway the progress of the crop after 1810 was even more rapid. The first reference to its growth was in 1758 on the south-west coast. Between 1810 and 1835 it was widely adopted. By the 1830s it was said to provide subsistence for one-fifth of the population, and areas which had once relied on the import of grain from Denmark had become self-sufficient in food supplies. Between 1820 and 1865 the area under potatoes is thought to have quadrupled, and in the 1870s occupied 12% of the total arable area, a much higher proportion than in France, England, or Sweden, although much lower than the 38% reached in Ireland before the Famine. It was particularly suited to the small farms of the west, where it was first adopted. There the spade and the hoe were the major implements in use; it helped in freeing the land from weeds, and if properly manured raised the yield of any following cereal crop. But much of the crop did not go to food consumption. In 1816 home distilling was legalised in Norway and until 1845, when it was made illegal,

Table 49. *Crop yields in Sweden 1801–20 to 1891–1900 (kg/ha)*

	All cereals	Autumn wheat	Autumn rye	Barley	Oats
1801–20	1190	1180	1150	1300	1100
1841–60	1310	—	—	—	
1871–80	1330	1390	1370	1460	1300
1891–1900	1380	1560	1450	1430	1310

SOURCE: P. Lundell, 'Agriculture and cattle-breeding', in G. Sundbärg (ed.), *Sweden: its people and industry: a historical and statistical handbook* (Stockholm, 1904), pp. 52–5, 528.

much of the potato crop was diverted to this purpose, the residue used for feeding livestock. By the 1870s the potato was a major part of the Norwegian diet with a consumption of 200 kg per head per year, above the consumption in England although of course well below that in pre-Famine Ireland. Nonetheless, the potato was probably more important in increasing the food supply in Norway than in any country in Europe except Ireland and Belgium.[31]

Changes in agricultural methods

The increase in the area under cultivation, the reduction of fallow and the widespread adoption of the potato must have all substantially increased the output of foodstuffs in Scandinavia in the first half of the nineteenth century. Whether there was a comparable rise in crop yields before the 1860s is more debatable. Estimates of crop yields were made by the parish clergy in Sweden in the early nineteenth century, although they are not thought to have been very accurate (table 49).

The yield of all cereals rose by about 10% in the first half of the nineteenth century and by only 16% in the century as a whole. Estimates of the seed–yield ratio also suggest there was only a limited advance in productivity: between 1802 and 1865–9 it rose from 1:5.4 to 1:6.1 for wheat, from 1:4.2 to 1:5.5 for rye and for oats it fell from 1:4.5 to 1:4.0.[32] At the beginning of the century wheat yields were rather lower than they were in England at the time, but wheat was of minor importance in both Norway and Sweden; barley and oats were the major crops. Comparable figures are not available for the beginning of the century in Norway but there are estimates of the seed–yield ratios from 1835 (table 50), which indicate that yields were low in 1835, but there were substantial advances, particularly for barley and oats, the major crops, between 1835 and 1881.

Environment as much as institutions impeded arable productivity in Scandinavia. Both the shortness of the growing season and the prevalence of steep slopes limited arable farming in Norway to the area north of Oslo,

Table 50. *Seed–yield ratios in Norway, 1835 and 1881*

	1835	1881	% increase
Wheat	7.5	7.7	2.6
Rye	8.8	11.7	14.9
Barley	6.0	8.6	43.3
Oats	4.8	6.7	29.0
Potatoes	7.6	7.0	−7.8

SOURCE: S. Leiberman, *The industrialization of Norway, 1800–1920* (Oslo, 1970), p. 50.

around Trondheim, and a narrow coastal strip south of Stavanger. Sweden was more fortunate and there were lowland areas with good soils in the central lake district and especially in the south-west in Halland and Skåne. In neither country had feudalism or the manorial system ever gained much of a hold, except in the south-west of Sweden, the area most influenced by Denmark, although this system was dissolved at the end of the eighteenth century. The rural nobility had limited power, and their land, and that of the Crown, was being bought by peasants throughout the eighteenth and nineteenth centuries. Although the Scandinavian peasantry did not have to pay the onerous feudal dues that the French peasantry suffered until 1793, they did not have the presence of improving landlords to stimulate innovation as happened in some parts of Britain.[33]

The holdings of farmers were still open and intermixed throughout Norway and Sweden in 1800, and in parts of Norway there was still periodic redistribution of the plots; the rules of collective husbandry were still firmly followed in the west and the north. In Sweden the three-field system was found only in Skåne, Kalmar and Vastergotland. In eastern Sweden the two-field system prevailed, and over much of the rest of the country, as in much of Norway, infield–outfield was practised. In much of western Norway the plough and the harrow were unknown, and the small farms were cultivated with spade and hoe. In Sweden much of the land was cultivated with the ard in the seventeenth and eighteenth centuries; in 1800 the wooden plough and a primitive harrow were the only implements in use in Skåne, although improved ploughs became more common in the first half of the nineteenth century in both countries. Potatoes were rare until the Napoleonic Wars; in the nineteenth century sugar-beet were introduced into the south-west of Sweden, and rotations similar to those in eastern England and northern France were adopted. But in Norway in 1850, provincial governors reported, rational rotations were still only sporadically found. Little arable land was devoted to fodder crops; in Sweden in 1820 only 5% of the arable was so used, although this had risen to 20% by 1840. In 1820 barley and oats were the main crops, with peas and beans in small amounts. By the 1860s the potato was important, but other root crops were never significant. They occupied

Table 51. *Land use in Norway (1870s) and Sweden (1860s) (% of arable)*

	Norway	Sweden
Oats	34.2	20.3
Barley	18.5	9.3
Rye	4.8	13.8
Wheat	1.8	2.2
Mixed cereals	7.0	3.1
Potatoes	13.0	5.3
Peas, beans, vetch	7.0	2.1
Roots		0.4
Temporary grasses	13.7	27.2
Fallow		15.4
Other		0.9
Total	100.0	100.0

SOURCES: Drake, *Population and society in Norway, 1735–1865*, p. 64; H. Osvald, *Swedish agriculture* (Stockholm, 1952), p. 42.

only 0.4% of Sweden's arable in 1866 (table 51). Temporary grasses were, however, very important in Sweden in the 1860s, but had made little advance in Norway, where roots, grasses and fallow together occupied only 13.7% of the arable land in the 1870s.[34]

In both countries at the beginning of the nineteenth century manure was the principal fertiliser. In Sweden in the eighteenth century meadow had been ploughed up to grow cereals, and in the nineteenth century common land when enclosed was often ploughed so the grazing land available declined. This was counterbalanced by the introduction of temporary grasses, and in the 1850s Swedish farmers began to use guano, bones and lime. There was less progress in Norway in the first half of the nineteenth century: however, farm probate inventories show an increase in the number of ploughs, harrows and carts, and the soil was more deeply cultivated. Even so spades were still made of wood in Akerhus diocese in the 1850s. It was not until after the 1840s that there were fundamental changes in the agricultural methods of either country. The slow spread of the railway, the macadaming of roads, and the emulation of Danish innovations – the provision of agricultural credit and the creation of farm education – all led to improvements: in Skåne in the 1850s about half the large farms had adopted the seed drill. In the last two decades the import of American grain enforced a switch to dairy farming, and a return to dependence on imported grain.[35]

It is difficult to determine the extent of improvement in crop yields in the first half of the nineteenth century; Scandinavian historians differ among themselves on this topic. But it seems that most of the increased output of foodstuffs must have come from the increase of the area under cultivation, the reduction of fallow and the adoption of potatoes.

Alternative employment

The rapid growth of population after 1815, the rise of landlessness and the proliferation of small farms, particularly in Norway, suggest that there must have been much poverty in Scandinavia by the 1850s. There was as yet no significant industrial development, and migration to the United States was confined to a very few. The lot of the rural population – particularly in Norway – was ameliorated by the existence of alternative employments. In Norway in 1845 88% of the population lived in rural districts, but only 63% of these directly depended on agriculture for their livelihood. Some of the little industry there was in Norway – there were only 12279 men so employed in 1850 – was found in the country; but far more important sources of employment were fishing, forestry and shipping. Fishing employed 15% of the rural population, and most of the fishermen came from farming families; at the beginning of the century, at least, many combined the two occupations.[36] In the south-west the herring industry was well established in the eighteenth century, but in 1784 the shoals deserted the Norwegian coast, not to return until 1808. Fishing subsequently played an important role in providing both employment and exports; by 1835 80% of the national catch was exported. Timber provided employment for almost as many, some 12% of the rural population. The export of timber was important before the Napoleonic Wars, but during that period Britain – the main market – erected tariffs, and turned to Canada for her supplies. But the trade revived after the reduction of British tariffs in 1842. Until the middle of the nineteenth century saw-mills found it difficult to acquire land for timber, and bought much of their timber from peasant land, providing an important source of income in the south-east. Shipping also provided employment for the farm families. Norway's merchant marine tonnage doubled between 1825 and 1843, and in 1850 there were 19000 sailors in Norway, 60% more than industrial workers. They tripled between 1850 and 1880, when the Norwegian merchant navy stood only third to Britain and the United States, and 40% of the country's export income came from shipping services.[37]

Thus these activities provided important sources of supplementary income for Norwegian farm families, and an outlet for the landless. All three provided an important source of export income; as early as 1800 exports made up nearly one-third of the national income.[38]

In Sweden fishing was of comparatively little importance, but forestry did provide an alternative form of employment in the early nineteenth century. In the second half of the century, when industrialisation got underway, much of the industrial development took place not in the towns, but in the rural areas.

Demographic adjustments

Although there were possibilities of employment in activities other than agriculture for the rural populations of both Norway and Sweden, these were limited. By the 1860s agriculture in both countries could absorb no more. There was, and had been for some time, underemployment in agriculture; in Norway although both fishing and the merchant marine could – and would – absorb more, it was not sufficient. In both countries there were only three possibilities. Numbers could be limited by controlling births, the surplus could emigrate overseas, or industrial growth could provide employment. There was an important difference between the two countries in the second half of the nineteenth century. In Norway industrialisation was somewhat less rapid than in Sweden: in 1910 manufacturing and mining employed 25% of the working population, compared with 32% in Sweden, and in 1865 both countries had 15–16% engaged in industry.[39] Emigration, although less than that from Sweden in absolute terms, was proportionally far greater. Whereas in Sweden rural–urban migration accounted for most of the rural exodus, in Norway overseas emigration was probably as important as rural–urban migration.

Emigration

Neither Norway nor Sweden had played a major role in the early settlement of North America, and made only a minor contribution until the 1850s. Thereafter Scandinavian emigration was considerable both in absolute numbers, as a proportion of total population, and in its effect on population growth in the home countries. Between 1840 and 1914, 1 105 000 left Sweden and 754 000 left Norway, going almost exclusively to the United States.[40] This movement had a far greater effect on Norway than on Sweden (table 52). Although rates of emigration from Britain, Ireland and Germany were far higher than that from Norway before 1860, thereafter until 1891 Norwegian emigration rates exceeded those in any other part of Europe except Ireland; in 1891–1900 Norwegian rates were slightly below those of Italy and in 1901–8 below Ireland and Italy. But in the half century between 1861 and 1911 Norway was consistently second only to Ireland in its rate of emigration. Sweden's rate was more modest: in each decade it was below that of Ireland and Norway, but it consistently exceeded that from Germany, Denmark, and Russia until 1908, Austria-Hungary until 1900, Italy until 1890, and Britain between 1881 and 1900.

The effect of this movement on the home populations was very considerable. Between 1864 and 1914 Norway lost the equivalent of 40% of her natural increase, compared with 25% for Sweden and only 10% from Denmark. In the three great surges of emigration from Norway, 1866–73, 1879–83 and 1900–10, the equivalent of 63%, 66% and 60% of the surplus of births over deaths left the country. This had a considerable effect on the home populations,

Table 52. *Annual overseas emigration per 100000 population*

	1861–70	1871–80	1881–90	1891–1900	1901–8
Denmark	108	205	391	224	282
Sweden	228	234	701	415	428
Norway	581	470	963	454	855
Britain	284	401	566	358	526
Ireland	1465	1024	1492	1010	1108
Germany	167	154	289	101	48
Austria–Hungary	11	31	108	155	450
Italy	—	99	323	491	1039
Russia	1	7	33	51	157

SOURCE: K. Hvidt, *Flight to America: the social background of 300000 Danish emigrants* (London, 1975), p. 14.

as Hofsten and Lundstrom have demonstrated for Sweden. Between 1851 and 1930 1500000 left Sweden and 400000 returned; to the 1100000 who left the country must be added, it is estimated, 1.3 million lost in natural increase. Thus Sweden's population of 6.1 million in 1930 would have been some 8.5 million if there had been no emigration.[41]

Not all the emigrants from Norway and Sweden came from the rural areas; indeed it is often argued that the urban rate of emigration was higher than the rural. This calculation is complicated by the inadequacy of the records; furthermore, many of the emigrants who gave a city as their place of residence may have moved there a short time before from the countryside. Of those who left Bergen in the late nineteenth century, over half had not been born there. A study of three parishes in Stockholm shows that 60% of those who emigrated from them had not been born there; one third of them had lived in Stockholm for less than two years, another third for between two and five years.[42] But whatever the relative rate of rural and urban emigration – and in both countries the latter rose in the course of the century – very large numbers left the countryside in the second half of the nineteenth century. Of those who left Sweden between 1851 and 1920, 800000 had been employed in agriculture, 250000 in industry. In the 1840s and 1850s many of the emigrants were small farmers, who travelled with their families. In the 1850s 60% of all Swedish emigrants were part of a family group, but by 1901–30 only 30%. A similar trend can be detected in Norway. Later in the century it was not farmers who left Sweden, but those farmer's sons and daughters who would not inherit land, crofters, and farm servants. Day-labourers, however, seem to have moved mainly to the cities.[43]

Not all parts of the two countries were equally affected by emigration. In Norway the rate of emigration from the south-east was, in the later nineteenth century, lower than from the west, for Oslo attracted migrants, while Stavanger and Bergen had less attraction for their local populations. In

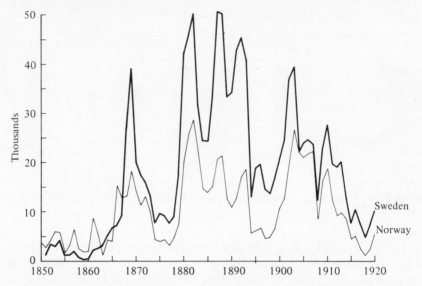

Fig. 18. Emigration from Norway and Sweden, 1850–1920. Source: W. F. Willcox (ed.), *International migrations*, vol. 1, *Statistics* (New York, 1929), pp. 747–53, 756–7.

Sweden there were marked regional variations in the emigration rate, but it was low near the big towns such as Gothenburg, Malmö and Stockholm, where those who left the countryside went to the cities and not overseas.[44]

Thus in both countries the proportion of emigrants coming from rural areas and agricultural occupations declined, and emigrants from the Scandinavian towns grew in numbers. The rate of emigration also varied over time. Before 1865 it was absolutely and proportionally unimportant (fig. 18). In the 1860s harvest failures led to the first mass emigration, and emigration from Sweden exceeded that from Norway for the first time. After a peak in 1869 emigration fell away in both countries to a trough in 1877; emigration in both countries thereafter rose again and remained considerable until a second trough in the late 1890s. A third period of mass emigration extended from 1900 to the First World War.

This chronology – together with the ebb and flow of emigration from other countries in Western Europe – has attracted much attention. The Swede Gustav Sundbärg, who led a government enquiry into Swedish emigration in the early part of this century, thought, as did many others, that the major cause of emigration was the unsatisfactory living conditions in the countryside; this in turn was attributed to population pressure. Since then many writers have argued that Scandinavian – and West European – emigration was more a result of the pull of America than the push of adverse conditions in Europe. H. Jerome, for example, related European emigration to the business cycle in the United States; this view was expanded and modified by Brinley

Thomas, who saw the United States and the countries of Western Europe as part of one great Atlantic economy. Labour movements, he believed, followed cycles in investment in the United States and Europe. Internal and overseas migration in Europe followed fluctuations in investment in the two continents, and the two alternated, so that periods of rural–urban migration in Europe were correlated with high investment at home, emigration overseas was linked to the upturns in the American economy; both were linked to fluctuations in capital flows within the Atlantic economy.[45]

A number of investigations into the relationships between the Scandinavian economy and overseas emigration have proved inconclusive; there seems little relationship between fluctuations in the business cycles in Sweden and the United States; the 'push' from Sweden seems to be stronger than Jerome and his followers would allow.[46] Certainly there would seem to have been a latent propensity to migrate in the Norwegian and Swedish countryside, and this was at least partly a result of population pressure; the first mass emigration in the 1860s was triggered off by a series of harvest failures. It was also possible because cheap crossings of the Atlantic were now available, and information about conditions in the United States was spreading home from earlier migrants. The periods of mass migration also appear to have taken place when the booms in births of two decades earlier were entering the labour market, and finding difficulty in getting jobs.[47]

Whatever the cause of Scandinavian emigration, there is no doubt it played an important role in reducing the rate of increase in the rural populations after 1860. It was particularly important in Norway; in Sweden however, internal migration to the towns played an even more important part in reducing rural population pressure.

Internal migration

When mass emigration began from Scandinavia in the 1860s there were few opportunities for internal migration; manufacturing industry was still of little importance, accounting in 1861–5 for only 13% of the Swedish gross national product, and employing, in 1850, only 10% of the work force, and in Norway in 1865 only 13%.[48] There were few large towns to provide employment opportunities for the rural surplus: in Sweden only Stockholm and Gothenburg exceeded 100000 in 1870, while Oslo, which had overtaken Bergen as the leading Norwegian town, had only 57000 in 1865, Bergen 27000.[49]

Thus, in the first half of the nineteenth century the great increase in population was largely absorbed in the rural sector (table 53). Although the urban population increased more rapidly than the rural between 1800 and 1860, the proportion living in rural areas hardly changed; in mid-century well over 80% lived in rural areas in both countries. As death rates exceeded birth rates in Scandinavian towns at this time, this indicates that there was migration from the countryside but it was very limited in volume. In Norway

Table 53. *Rural and urban populations in Norway and Sweden, 1800–60*

	Sweden				Norway		
	Rural (1000s)	Urban (1000s)	Rural as % of total		Rural (1000s)	Urban (1000s)	Rural as % of total
1800	2118	229	90.2	1801	806	77	91.3
1810	2171	225	90.6	1815	799	87	90.2
1820	2331	254	90.2	1825	937	114	89.2
1840	2835	304	90.3	1835	1066	129	89.2
1850	3131	352	89.9	1845	1167	162	87.8
1860	3425	435	88.7	1855	1292	198	86.7

SOURCES: Thomas, *Swedish population movements, 1750–1933*, p. 42; F. Hodne, *An economic history of Norway, 1815–1970* (Bergen, 1976), p. 25.

Table 54. *External and internal migration from Swedish rural districts, 1816–1900*

	Loss through internal migration		Loss through external migration	
	(1000s)	%	(1000s)	%
1816–40	37	1.45	—	—
1841–50	50	1.67	—	—
1851–60	90	2.75	15	0.47
1861–70	118	3.3	104	2.89
1871–80	136	3.61	121	3.21
1881–90	191	4.92	304	7.85
1891–1900	157	3.97	187	4.74

SOURCE: J. S. Lindberg, *The background of Swedish emigration to the United States* (Minneapolis, 1930), p. 125.

it was the fishing towns of the west coast that experienced most growth; in Sweden, Stockholm and Gothenburg accounted for much of the urban increase.[50]

Industrialisation did not get underway in either country until the 1870s, but from then it was comparatively rapid; in 1870 only 15–16% of their work forces had been engaged in manufacturing and mining, but on the eve of the First World War it had reached 25% in Norway and 32% in Sweden. This had less dramatic consequences for the rural population than had industrialisation, for example, in Britain or Belgium at this time. This was partly because much industrial growth took place in rural areas and not in towns. In Sweden, as late as 1913 60% of all industrial workers lived in rural areas. But there was nonetheless a marked urban growth in the second half of the nineteenth century. In Sweden the urban population tripled between 1860 and

1910, and the proportion living in towns rose from 11.3% to 24.8% while in Norway the urban population more than doubled between 1860 and 1900, rising from 15% of the total population to 28%.[51]

Before 1850 Swedish towns had an excess of deaths over births and owed their increase solely to immigration, but between 1861 and 1891 two-thirds of their increase was attributable to migration, between 1890 and 1910 one-half, and the rest to natural increase.[52] Such figures understate, as they do in most countries, the role of migration, for a substantial proportion of the recorded natural increase was births to rural migrants who had married in the towns. This rural–urban migration was reducing the rate of increase of the rural population; indeed it was more important than overseas emigration, except between 1880 and 1900 (table 54); after 1900 an alternative series of figures shows that loss from internal migration exceeded overseas emigration from rural areas.[53]

Comparable data are not available for Norway, but there was a movement from the countryside to the towns from the middle of the century. In neither country was it simply rural poverty that caused the exodus. In Sweden, in the second half of the nineteenth century, agricultural wages were only 56% of industrial wages although payments in kind reduced the differential; in Norway the differential was even greater.[54] Nor did the rural exodus, whether to the towns or the United States, halt the growth of the rural population. This was partly because so much of Scandinavian industrial growth took place in rural areas. But the exodus kept down the *rate* of rural increase; in Sweden rural population continued to increase until the 1920s (table 55). But whereas the rural population increased by nearly 50% in the first half of the century, it rose only 24% in 1850–80; there was little increase after 1880. The agricultural population rose by 46% 1800–50, but by only 4% in the second half of the nineteenth century; indeed the agricultural population reached a peak in 1880 and has since been in decline.

In Norway neither the massive emigration overseas from the rural districts beginning in the 1860s, nor the urban growth which accelerated after 1855, was sufficient to halt the growth of the rural population but they did reduce the rate of increase; it grew by 60% from 1801 to 1855, and by 25% between 1855 and 1900 (table 56). Statistics on the labour force in Norwegian agriculture are difficult to interpret, as so many farming families combined farming with fishing and forestry; but the proportion engaged in agriculture undoubtedly fell after 1865 and it seems that the numbers employed in agriculture ceased to increase between 1865 and 1920. However, after this the labour force did increase between 1920 and 1930 before beginning a continuous decline.[55]

Thus in neither Sweden nor Norway was the growth of the rural population halted when overseas migration and rural–urban migration got underway after 1860, in contrast to the experience in Britain and France, and in a number of other European countries not discussed in this book – Switzerland,

Table 55. *Rural and agricultural populations in Sweden, 1800–1930*

	Rural		Agricultural	
	1000s	%	1000s	%
1800	2118	90.2	1856	79.1
1850	3131	89.9	2714	77.9
1860	3425	88.7	—	—
1870	3629	87.1	3017	72.4
1880	3875	84.9	3102	67.9
1890	3855	81.2	2973	62.6
1900	4032	78.5	2828	55.1
1910	4155	75.2	2697	48.8
1920	4161	70.4	2596	44.0
1930	4146	67.5	2417	39.4

SOURCE: Thomas, *Swedish population movements, 1750–1933*, pp. 42, 93.

Table 56. *Rural and agricultural populations in Norway, 1801–1910*

	Rural		Agricultural work force	
	1000s	%	1000s	% of total work force
1801	806	91.3	—	—
1855	1292	86.7	—	—
1865	1435	84.4	391	59.8
1875	1479	81.9	381	51.8
1890	1526	76.3	386	49.2
1900	1612	72.0	361	40.7
1910	—	—	359	39.0

SOURCES: T. K. Derry, *A history of modern Norway, 1814–1972* (London, 1973), pp. 97–8, 184; Hodne, *An economic history of Norway, 1815–1970*, p. 167.

Belgium and Germany. This was partly because Scandinavian industrialisation was not only late compared with these countries, but because much of it took place in those areas defined by the Norwegian and Swedish censuses as 'rural' – an administrative rather than an occupational or functional classification. Those who left the countryside after 1860 were not for the most part farmers but crofters, cottagers and labourers. This had a beneficial effect on wages in the agricultural sector, which in money terms doubled between 1850 and 1900 in both countries.[56]

Changes in fertility

If, by the middle of the nineteenth century, the rural districts of Norway and Sweden were suffering from an excess of numbers, and as at that time there was little prospect of industrial growth absorbing the surplus, one might have reasonably expected some signs of a decline in fertility.

In Norway there was no such sign. The crude birth rate showed no sign of continuous decline until after 1900 (fig. 17). Nor do other measures of fertility indicate any decline from the middle of the century: age-specific fertility changed little between 1836 and 1890; samples of family size for those married for between 20 and 29 years conducted in 1855 gave an average size of 6.4; a study in 1903 put it at 6.11. Some of the determinants of fertility were equally unchanging: the proportion of women aged 15–49 who were married was 51% in 1769, 47.9% in 1801 and in 1865, 49.8%; of women aged 41–50 in 1801, 84.7% had been married; in 1865 the figure was 85.5%.[57]

A partial explanation of this lack of adjustment may be that Norwegians were already limiting their numbers in the eighteenth century. The age of marriage was high: in the mid-eighteenth century it averaged 28 years for women in one parish in western Norway, in the 1840s and 1860s when national statistics are available it averaged 28, and 26 for age of first marriage of women. In the eighteenth and nineteenth centuries there is some evidence of attempts to limit marital fertility: primitive condoms, long suckling periods and, presumably, *coitus interruptus* were used. Certainly the Norwegian crude birth rate in the eighteenth century was lower than most estimates which have been made for birth rates in England, Ireland and France at this time, and in the middle of the nineteenth century, when national figures are available for other parts of Europe, Norway's rates are generally lower. Thus it may be that further postponement of marriage was thought impracticable, and the effective control of numbers awaited the wider diffusion of physical methods of contraception.[58]

In Sweden, in contrast, there is evidence of an earlier decline in fertility. The national crude birth rate was rising from the 1840s to 1858–60, thereafter its trend was downward (fig. 17). This may be partly explained by increasing celibacy: in 1850 only 12% of women aged 45–54 had never been married, by 1900 this had risen to 20%. There is also some sign of a decline in marital fertility in some regions after 1860, particularly among women over 30. Swedish fertility, like Norwegian fertility, was already low in the eighteenth century, and there is evidence of attempts to control numbers in the eighteenth century: the average age of marriage of women in 1750 has been estimated to be 26 to 27, in 1890 it was 28; studies of a number of villages in southern Sweden suggest that birth control within marriage was attempted.[59]

The crude birth rate in both countries was characterised by alternating periods of rising birth rates and falling birth rates: declining from 1750 to 1770, rising to 1792 and then falling about 1800, rising again to the mid-1820s, falling 1838–40. The last period of increase was from 1840 to 1860, followed by decline to 1868–70. On previous experience this should have been followed by a boom. The essential difference between Norway and Sweden was that in the latter country there were the beginnings of a boom in 1868–78, followed by decline. In Norway expansion began but was followed not by decline but stagnation until 1900.

Conclusions

In the late eighteenth century both Sweden and Norway were backward peasant societies with little urbanisation or industrial development. It is true that in Sweden the élite groups were familiar with the advances being made in agriculture in Britain. There was a period of 'agromania' in the 1760s and 1770s, comparable with the literary activities of the French *agronomes*, but this had little influence on the peasants themselves; Norway was even more backward. It has been estimated that at the beginning of the nineteenth century only 13% of the population was involved in a commercial economy, in 1845 still less than a fifth.[60] The rapid growth of population in the first half of the century was sustained not by any great advance in farming methods but by a rapid increase in the cultivated area and the adoption of the potato as a foodcrop. But this did not solve the problem of employment and by the 1860s the rural districts had far more people than could be employed. In Sweden there seems to have been some demographic adjustment to this circumstance as early as the 1860s; fertility began to fall both in the towns and the countryside. But in both countries the first major adjustment was mass emigration in the late 1860s. Thereafter industrial growth provided an alternative for the rural population, and in Sweden internal migration played a more important role than overseas migration in relieving rural population pressure. In Norway overseas migration was at a much higher rate than in Sweden, there was less internal migration and there are no signs of any fall in fertility before 1900. Thus the two Scandinavian countries made rather different demographic responses to the challenges of population growth.

CHAPTER 16

CODA TO PART THREE

In the view of many historians the century after 1750 transformed the world. Industrial and agricultural revolutions unleashed an unprecedented population growth in Britain and Western Europe, yet for the first time a rise in income per head was not eaten up by this increase in numbers. David Landes has aptly described the views of many on the changes of the second half of the eighteenth century and the nineteenth century.

> These improvements constitute the Industrial Revolution. They yielded an unprecedented increase in man's productivity and with it, a substantial rise in income per head. Moreover, this rapid growth was self-sustaining. Where previously, an amelioration of the conditions of existence, hence of survival, and an increase in economic opportunity had always been followed by a rise in population that eventually consumed the gains achieved, now for the first time in history, both the economy and knowledge were growing fast enough to generate a continuing flow of investment and technological innovation, a flow that lifted beyond visible limits the ceiling of Malthus's positive checks.[1]

No doubt this is a correct interpretation of events, and no one can doubt that this was a period of unprecedented change in manufacturing industry, commerce and transport. But when we return to the interrelationships of population growth and agrarian change, the abruptness of the contrast with the past is much modified. Indeed rural economic change seems to show many similarities with previous periods.

The century between 1650 and 1750 saw little population increase in Europe. But between 1750 and 1914 populations increased at unprecedented rates. However, *rural* population growth followed much the same course as in the sixteenth and seventeenth centuries. Between 1750 and 1850 *rural* rates of increase were not greatly different from those experienced by *total* populations in the sixteenth century. Thus the rural population of England and Wales rose at 0.5% p.a. between 1750 and 1850, no greater than the rate between 1522 and 1603 of 0.8% p.a. France's overwhelmingly rural population in 1450 had doubled by 1550; but the rural population of 18–19 million in 1750 only increased by 0.46% p.a. between 1750 and 1850.

Elsewhere in Europe the rates of rural and indeed total increase between 1750 and 1850 were not without precedent in the past (tables 4 and 36).

But whereas in the early fourteenth and seventeenth centuries rapid population growth was followed by decline or stagnation, the population of Western Europe continued to increase at high rates after 1850, but not the rural populations, and, more strikingly, the primary rural populations. In the second half of the nineteenth century rural population growth halted in much of Western Europe, in some parts declined, while the numbers in agricultural occupations showed a more abrupt decline. The essential difference from the past was twofold. First there was a massive movement from the countryside to the towns. Secondly, there was an equally dramatic if quantitatively less important movement overseas. Thus the curve of rural population growth did not differ greatly from the two earlier cycles. By the 1850s European agriculture could not absorb any further population growth.

If Europe had escaped from the Malthusian dilemma after 1750 it had certainly not escaped from many of the adverse consequences of rapid population growth. Many of the symptoms of population pressure reappeared in the 1820s and 1830s, so that both contemporary and modern historians believed rural Europe to be overpopulated by mid-century. The price of agricultural products rose steadily between 1750 and the 1870s, when the import of American grain ushered in a period of low prices. The increased competition for land drove rents and the sale price of land upward. Real wages for farm workers stagnated for much of the first half of the nineteenth century, in some areas actually falling. In Ireland, Norway, much of Sweden, parts of France, and in many parts of Western Europe not discussed in this book, particularly in the Rhineland, farms were subdivided and further fragmented. For many Europeans the adoption of the potato was an impoverishment of their diet, not an advance, and in the middle of the nineteenth century milk, meat and vegetables were still a small part of the diet. Until the middle of the nineteenth century the continued growth of the rural population delayed the adoption of labour-saving machinery: nor was this surprising when parts of Sweden, Norway, France and southern England are thought to have been suffering from underemployment in agriculture, as was Ireland.

In terms of the symptoms of population pressure then, the early nineteenth century repeated the experiences of the early fourteenth and early seventeenth centuries in kind if not degree. And the responses to population growth were equally familiar. Until the 1830s in Britain, and later in the rest of Western Europe, the means of increasing agricultural output were much the same as they had been in the past. In Sweden and Norway there were very considerable increases in the area under crops in the first half of the nineteenth century; in France and Britain increases were less dramatic but none the less substantial. In all of Western Europe the fallow was reduced, and new crops grown – potatoes, clover, sugar-beet and maize and fodder roots – so that the sown area increased. Of these new crops, only sugar-beet was unknown before 1750. Potatoes, grown in Western Europe since the sixteenth century, were more widely grown after 1800; roots and clover provided extra fodder, better livestock and increased supplies of manure. But, until the 1830s manure, together with marling and liming, remained the only means of maintaining or increasing crop yields – indeed it is difficult to detect any dramatic increases in crop yields before the 1820s although in England at least there had been steady progress since the 1650s or before. Thus, the wider adoption of traditional practices saw agricultural output increase throughout most of Western Europe between 1750 and 1850; that output per head was maintained there seems little doubt, although whether the increases per head were as spectacular as are sometimes assumed, must be doubted. It was not until the 1820s, and later in most of Western Europe, that the inputs necessary for modern industrialised agriculture were available in the form of machinery, compound feeds, and artificial fertilisers; even later were the advances in crop breeding and the use of pesticides and insecticides. Thus, in the first century of industrialisation increases in agricultural output were achieved with what were still pre-industrial farming methods.

In terms of rural economic change it was the second half of the nineteenth century, not the eighteenth century, that saw the real transformation of rural Europe. The decline in population relieved the direct competition for land, led to increases in real wages, and made necessary the adoption of labour-saving machinery; the import of grain from overseas, and later of meat, relieved the pressure on Europe's agriculture, and the import of cheap feeding stuffs allowed the slow shift to livestock production. The real revolution in European agriculture began only at this time, and did not come to fruition until after the end of the Second World War.

The period after 1750 saw less dramatic change in agriculture than is sometimes thought, and it is apparent that the relief of rural population pressure came from sources outside agriculture itself. The growth of factory industry slowly undermined the domestic industries of the countryside and deprived the cottager of an important source of supplementary income, but the rapid growth of urban industry did now allow for greater opportunities of employment in the towns. Before the nineteenth century there were relatively few outlets in the towns for the impoverished farmer and labourer, but the Industrial Revolution provided the much needed safety-valve. This was above all true in Britain where between 1750 and 1850 there was rapid urbanisation, such that in the second half of the nineteenth century rural migration exceeded rural natural increase. In Scandinavia, industrialisation was much later, and until the 1860s agriculture had to absorb most of the population increase. But from the 1850s emigration afforded an outlet that was sorely needed, particularly in Norway. In France, however, a different solution was chosen; from the beginning of the nineteenth century fertility fell and it was this and not emigration or urbanisation that contained rural population growth, while after the 1830s rural–urban migration and a continued fall in fertility helped to reduce rural population pressure.

Thus it is possible to argue that the simple model of population and agrarian change presented in chapter 5 aids our understanding of rural economic change until well into the nineteenth century. But it is not suggested that there was no fundamental agrarian or institutional change until 1850. On the contrary, Part three does help to explain why parts of Western Europe could break out of the stranglehold numbers had long had over resources. The case of Holland is particularly illuminating, for at the worst it can be said that Dutch economic growth in the sixteenth and seventeenth centuries prevented the fall in income per head that occurred in most of the rest of Europe, at best it increased income per head in a period of rapidly increasing population. The Netherlands, unlike much of the rest of Western Europe, had many of the necessary if not the sufficient conditions for economic growth at the beginning of the sixteenth century. The manorial system had never taken root; the open fields were gone; there was no oppressive nobility or church to tax the farmer as in France. Canals provided the cheap movement of inputs and produce. But it was above all the growth of urban demand that led to the division of labour in rural areas between farmers and the providers of rural services, allowed regional specialisation, encouraged the cultivation of industrial crops and horticultural products, and provided a market for cheese and butter. Urban demand arose largely because of the prosperity from Dutch trade, and the industrial development that was prompted first by the fishing trade, then trade with Eastern Europe, and later the Dutch overseas empire. Above all the impetus for change came from outside rural society. The engines of agrarian change were in the towns of Holland and in its ships.

The case of England seems somewhat different, for the crucial period of early adoption of agricultural innovations seems to have occurred in a period of little population growth 1650–1750, when output was sufficient to allow a considerable export of grain. After 1750 when the innovations continued to spread through the country, output had some difficulty in keeping up with population growth, and by the 1840s, free trade would have been essential to maintain food supplies, let alone allow the improved consumption – both in quality and quantity – that took place in the second half of the nineteenth century. Increases in crop yields were not dramatic until after the 1820s – when industrial inputs first became available. Indeed it seems that in England the traditional view that an agricultural revolution must precede an industrial revolution requires some qualification. There may well have been significant increases in crop yields between 1650 and 1750, although there are no figures to confirm the national trend; it may well be that the prosperity of agriculture in this period prompted industrial expansion at home; but between 1750 and the 1830s the increase in farming productivity was slow, and it was not until the purchase of industrial inputs began in the 1820s and the decline of the labour force in the 1850s that agricultural productivity moved forward again.

PART FOUR
MALTHUS RETURNS?

THE DEVELOPING COUNTRIES TODAY: THE DEMOGRAPHIC RESPONSE

Introduction

In the introduction to this book it was argued that the population pressure to be found in many parts of the underdeveloped world today is not an unprecedented phenomenon; there had been periods of rural overpopulation in the past. These problems were largely overcome in Western Europe by the late nineteenth century. In this and the following chapter an attempt is made to compare the conditions in the present underdeveloped world with Western Europe in the nineteenth century; in this chapter the demographic conditions are considered, in the following chapter production conditions.

Table 57. *Average rates of population increase per annum, 1950–75* (%)

	1950–55	1955–60	1960–65	1965–70	1970–75
Africa	2.1	2.3	2.3	2.6	3.1
Latin America	2.8	2.7	2.9	2.8	2.7
Asia	1.9	2.0	2.2	2.3	1.9
Total	2.0	2.1	2.3	2.4	2.1

SOURCES: United Nations, *Demographic yearbook 1963* (New York, 1964), p. 142; *Demographic yearbook* (New York, 1976), p. 139.

The rate of increase

The rate of population increase in the underdeveloped countries over the last twenty-five years has greatly exceeded that found in Western Europe in the nineteenth century. Between 1950 and 1975 the average rate of increase *per annum* was 2.5% in Africa, 2.7% in Latin America and 2.1% in Asia. Until the 1970s the rate of increase had risen in each successive quinqennium (table 57). No country in Western Europe in the nineteenth century reached such high rates over comparable periods. The fastest rates of growth attained were 1.3% p.a. in Ireland between 1781 and 1831, 1.4% p.a. in England between 1801 and 1831, and 1.4% p.a. in Norway between 1815 and 1835.

It is sometimes implied that prior to 1945 rates of increase were low in Afro-Asia and Latin America, and it is only the dramatic fall in mortality since

Table 58. *Average rates of increase in selected countries, 1900–70* (% *p.a.*)

	1900–10	1910–20	1920–30	1930–40	1940–50	1950–60	1960–70
Egypt[a]	1.5	1.3	1.1	1.2	1.8	2.4	1.3
Mexico	1.1	—	1.6	1.8	2.5	3.0	3.3
Brazil	3.1	2.7	0.9	2.1	2.2	3.1	2.8
Ceylon	—	1.4	0.9	1.7	2.9	2.6	2.5
Thailand[b]	—	1.4	2.2	2.9	1.9	3.6	2.7
Iran	0.7	0.7	1.0	.1.5	1.9	2.6	2.3

[a] Census years 1897, 1907, 1917, 1927, 1937, 1947.
[b] Census years 1911, 1919, 1929, 1937, 1947.
SOURCES: J. Bharier, 'A note on the population of Iran, 1900–1960', *Population Studies*, 22 (1968), 279; O. Onody, 'Quelques traits caractéristiques de l'evolution historique de la population de Brésil', in P. Deprez (ed.), *Population and economics* (Winnipeg, 1970), p. 335; United Nations, *Demographic yearbook 1951* (New York, 1952), pp. 104–18; *Demographic yearbook 1963* (New York, 1964), pp. 148–61; *Demographic yearbook 1973* (New York, 1974), pp. 101–7.

then that has led to high rates of increase. But where evidence on population totals before 1945 is available, quite rapid rates of increase are to be found. Iraq doubled its population between 1905 and 1947, Pakistan between 1901 and 1952, Java increased at an average rate of 1.1% p.a. between 1900 and 1950, Burma at 1.2% p.a. and Malaya at 2.2% p.a.[1] Growth rates were equally high in Latin America: El Salvador more than doubled its population between 1900 and 1950, Costa Rica's numbers rose two and a half times, Honduras tripled its population, and South America increased from 44 million to over 100 million in the same period.[2] Some countries already had high rates of growth in the 1920s and 1930s; not as high as the current rates, but generally as rapid as those achieved in Western Europe in the nineteenth century (table 58).

Before 1900 little is known of populations in much of Afro-Asia or Latin America, and it is often assumed that there was very little increase. Yet J. D. Durand's revision of world population figures suggests that it was not only in Western Europe that population began to grow rapidly after 1750, and certainly after 1800 the rate of increase in parts of Afro-Asia and Latin America was very rapid.[3] Java's population tripled in the nineteenth century, and Egypt's quadrupled.[4] The average rate of increase in the Philippines over the century was 1.4% p.a. and in the second half of the nineteenth century Ceylon, Burma, Malaya, and French Indochina all had rates above 1% p.a. India and China grew more slowly, although between 1750 and 1850 China grew more rapidly than Western Europe.[5] African figures are unreliable, but in Latin America, there was considerable growth, only partly explained by immigration. Central America increased fourfold between 1825 and 1900 and over the same period South America's population rose from nearly 16 million to 44 million.[6] Thus Western Europe's population growth after 1750 was far from unique; nor is the underdeveloped world's increase since 1945 without precedent. Many parts of the underdeveloped world had been growing comparatively rapidly for at least a century; the rapid fall in mortality since 1945 has made worse a problem that already existed, rather than creating an entirely new crisis.

Fertility in the developing countries

The rapid increase in population since 1945 has been due to a fall in mortality without any widespread reduction in fertility; indeed in many countries fertility may have risen.[7] Crude birth rates are remarkably high in Afro-Asia and Latin America: United Nations estimates put the rate per thousand in 1970–3 at 47 in Africa, 44 in South Asia, 38 in Latin America and 32 in East Asia. At the same time the rate in the developed world was 19 per thousand and only 16 per thousand in western and northern Europe. The rates in Africa, South Asia and tropical Latin America are not only well above the crude birth rates in Western Europe today but above those found in Western Europe in the nineteenth century.[8] In mid-nineteenth-century Britain 35 per thousand was the highest rate recorded in any decade; the same figure obtained for Sweden in the mid-eighteenth century. Germany reached 39 per thousand in the 1870s. The only European rates comparable with those now found in Africa, South Asia and tropical Latin America are those for the United States in the first half of the nineteenth century and European Russia throughout the nineteenth century; indeed as late as the 1920s the crude birth rate in Russia was 43 per thousand.[9]

The very high fertility found in the underdeveloped world compared with Western Europe, either in the present or the past, is due to a number of factors. In the first place in the underdeveloped world the great majority of women get married. Evidence on nuptiality is limited, but from studies of 57 countries R. B. Dixon has put the percentage of women aged 40–44 who had never been married at 14.1% in Western Europe and 7.9% in the English speaking countries overseas, but only 2.5% in the Middle East and 2.8% in Asia.[10] Less reliable data suggest that marriage is almost universal in Africa. By the age of 25 only 2.3% of women in Ghana are unmarried, and a study of some nineteen African countries shows that only 1–3% of women aged 50 are unmarried.[11] The percentage of women who marry is thus much higher than in Western Europe at the present time. In nineteenth-century Europe a substantial proportion of women never married: in 1851 12% of women in England aged 45–54 had never married, in 1880 between 8% and 14% of women in Germany aged 40–44 had never married, in the 1870s 18.7% of Swedish women aged 40 were still unmarried, and in 1860 20% of women aged 50 were still single in Switzerland and Belgium, while in 1850 15% of women aged 50 in France and the Netherlands were still single.[12]

Before the nineteenth century there are no national data on the proportion of women married at different ages, although it is commonly assumed that 10–15% of women remained unmarried in the seventeenth and eighteenth centuries. Before then marriage was more universal and thus more like the underdeveloped world today.[13]

Not only do nearly all women eventually marry in the underdeveloped countries, but a high proportion are married when very young. This can be demonstrated from either data on the proportion of women in the youthful age groups who are married, or by calculating the mean age of first marriage for women. Thus in Bangladesh 99% of all women aged 20–24 are married, in west and east Java 75% of women aged 19 are already married, in India in 1971 56% of girls aged between 15 and 19 were already married, and in Iran in 1966 45% of girls of this age group were married; similar ratios have been recorded for Morocco and Algeria.[14] The average age of marriage also indicates how important early marriage is; it is 18 years 4 months in Algeria, 20 years 6 months in rural Thailand, 17 years 7 months in Ghana, 17 years 6 months in Pakistan while in nineteen African countries the modal age of marriage of women is 16–17 years.[15]

In nineteenth-century Western Europe not only were there more never-married women, but women married at much later ages. Whereas in the less developed countries today between 40% and 70% of women aged 15–19 are married, in Western Europe in *c.* 1860 the proportion varied only between 0.6% in the Netherlands and 5.3% in France. Even in the 20–25 age group the variation for eight West European countries was only from 14.4% in Holland to 34.3% in France, whereas in those present-day countries for which data are available, the great majority of this group are married: 99% in Bangladesh, 86% in pre-war Taiwan, 97.7% in Ghana, 89.4% in India in 1971, and just over 70% in Tunisia and Egypt.[16]

Before the nineteenth century there are of course no comprehensive data on the proportions of different age groups who were married. However, calculations of the mean age of marriage of women from various sample populations suggest that the average age of marriage was 25 years or higher in the late seventeenth and eighteenth centuries. Before then the evidence is insubstantial, but suggests that 20–21 was the modal age of marriage in sixteenth-century France and England.

Thus from the seventeenth century Western Europe differed significantly from the present-day underdeveloped world in that a lower proportion of the women in the reproductive age groups were married, either because of late marriage or permanent celibacy. It does not follow from this that marital fertility was necessarily lower. A comparison of fertility in Sweden in the 1870s with India in the 1950s suggests that Swedish age-specific fertility was higher than Indian, and it was thus celibacy that accounted for the lower Swedish crude birth rate. Similarly, comparisons of Crûlai in France and Colyton in England in the seventeenth century with countries in Latin America and Afro-Asia in the mid-twentieth century, show that age-specific marital fertility was higher in Europe than in the modern developing world. Such little evidence as there is on completed family size in modern Afro-Asia suggests this is about 5 or 6: it was about 5.3 in Taiwan in the 1960s, just over 5 in rural China in 1929–31, and 6.5 in Bangladesh in the late 1960s. From what is known of age-specific fertility in the developing countries in the 1960s, it would seem that completed family size would have varied between 5.6 live births per woman in India and Pakistan, and 6.2 in the Middle East. This suggests that marital fertility is not greatly different from much of Western Europe in the nineteenth century or indeed in the seventeenth and eighteenth centuries.[17]

The decline in mortality

The importance of the fall in mortality in the developing countries in the last thirty years needs little emphasis. The reduction of the incidence of certain diseases may have also helped to explain the rise in fertility that has occurred in some parts of the underdeveloped world, as better health may have increased fecundity and falling adult mortality has lengthened marital unions. Nonetheless even in Latin America, where fertility rose significantly between 1930 and 1960, 83% of the enlarged natural increase has been attributed to falling mortality.[18]

The principal difference between the decline in mortality in the present-day underdeveloped world and in Western Europe in the nineteenth century is the speed with which it has happened. There are few long-run series of crude death rates in the developing countries, but where they exist they show a marked decline since the 1940s, to levels almost comparable with those in the developed countries (fig. 19); but crude death rates distort this comparison, for the developed countries have a higher proportion of their populations in the higher age groups. Nonetheless the rapidity of the decline can hardly be denied. The crude death rate in Egypt fell from 25.0 per thousand in 1946 to 13.1 per thousand in 1971; a similar decline in Sweden took from 1800 to 1920.[19] Although most authorities have emphasised the abruptness of the decline since 1945, mortality had been declining earlier in the century. In several countries in Latin America substantial increases in life expectation at birth were made between 1900 and 1940 (table 59). It should be noted that at the beginning of this century life expectation was not only much lower than that which prevailed in Western Europe at that time, but very likely lower than that in Western Europe in the eighteenth century.

The causes of this decline in mortality have been attributed mainly to improvements in public sanitation, the extension of health services, the introduction of drugs that both immunise and cure, and the elimination of the vectors that carry disease; the best example of the latter is the elimination of malaria by spraying mosquito infested areas with D.D.T. The use of antibiotics, sulpha drugs and D.D.T. dates only from the end of the Second

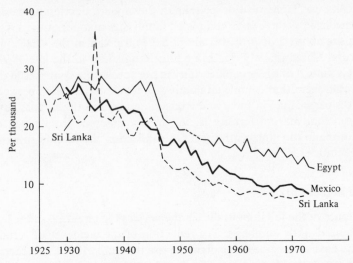

Fig. 19. Decline in the death rate in Egypt, Sri Lanka and Mexico, 1925–73. Source: United Nations, *Demographic yearbooks 1950–1975* (New York, 1951–76).

World War, and other factors must have been operative before then. Thus in British Guiana the crude death rate fell from 28.4 per thousand in the 1920s to 21.7 per thousand in the 1940s. During this period there was little advance in the standard of living but malarial swamps were drained and water supplies were improved.[20] The possibility that some of the decline in mortality in the underdeveloped world has been due to an improved standard of living cannot be excluded;[21] but most authorities believe that the decline has been independent of economic advance and is largely due to imported medical and public health technologies.[22] However, the improved distribution of food supplies probably played a role, so that the incidence of famine has greatly fallen.

Although the decline of mortality has been much more rapid in the developing countries than in Western Europe after 1750, it may be that the causes of decline are not so dissimilar. It is frequently asserted that the declines in mortality in Europe were a result of an improved standard of living, but those obtained in the developing world are independent of economic advance and are a result of introduced medical and public health technologies. Yet it is hard to show that there was any substantial improvement in the standard of living for the majority of the population of Western Europe between 1750 and 1850; the decline in mortality was more rapid after 1890 than between 1850 and 1890 and possibly over a longer period before then.[23] It may be that the fall in mortality after 1750 was due to the recession of bubonic plague, the reduction of smallpox by inoculation, the slow improvement of sewage disposal and clean water supplies after the 1840s, and, only at the end of the

Table 59. *Expectation of life at birth in Latin America (both sexes)*

	c. 1900	*c.* 1920	*c.* 1940	*c.* 1950	*c.* 1960
Brazil	29.3	32.0	36.7	43.0	55.5
Columbia	—	32.0	36.6	49.2	—
Chile	—	30.5	38.1	42.3	57.0
Costa Rica	30.7	—	—	55.5	63.6
Guatemala	23.6	25.9	30.4	40.7	51.3
Mexico	25.3	34.7	38.8	47.6	58.0
Nicaragua	—	24.3	34.5	40.0	51.9

SOURCE: J. Ho, 'La évolution de la mortalité en Amérique Latine', *Population*, 25 (1970), 1103–6.

century, the beginnings of medical advance and improvements in the standard of living. If this is so then the growth of population was independent of economic advance, as it has been in the developing world in the last thirty years.

The density of population

There is no doubt that the current rate of increase in population in the developing world greatly exceeds that in nineteenth-century Europe. It is often argued that the developing world also suffers from the problem of much greater densities, which means that there is less land per head available.[24] The confirmation of this assumption is made difficult by the absence of reliable statistics. Agricultural statistics were not collected in most of Europe until the second half of the nineteenth century, and the early censuses leave much to be desired. At present agricultural censuses have been taken in only a minority of countries in Afro-Asia and Latin America, and for most FAO estimates have to be used. Even the more reliable figures present difficulties of interpretation. Arable land includes land in crops, gardens, temporary grasses, permanent crops such as rubber or coffee and land used for arable but temporarily in fallow. In Africa land in fallow may be a large proportion of the total arable, and thus population densities may be understated. Cultivated land includes arable and permanent grassland. However this latter category includes any herbaceous forage crop, either sown or natural, used for grazing. The distinction between natural vegetation used occasionally for forage, and waste, is a hard line to draw, and seems to be interpreted more liberally in Afro-Asia and Latin America than in Europe. The total cultivated area may thus perhaps be seen as a generous estimate of the *cultivable* area.

The density of the total population to the cultivated area in 1975 averaged 87 per 100 hectares for the world, but there were great variations (fig. 20). The highest densities were to be found in north-west Europe, and south, east and south-east Asia, with elsewhere only a few isolated outliers of very high

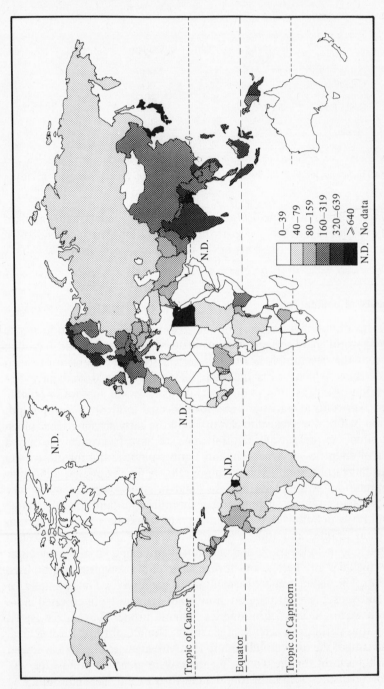

Fig. 20. World population densities, 1975: total population per 100 ha of total cultivated land.
Source: FAO, *Production yearbook 1976*, 30 (Rome, 1977), pp. 45–56, 61–3.

Table 60. *Agricultural densities in Western Europe in the nineteenth century and the developing world* c. *1975*

	Agricultural population as % of total	Total population per 100 ha of cultivated land	Total population per 100 ha of arable land	Agricultural population per 100 ha of cultivated land	Agricultural population per 100 ha of arable land
England and Wales (1700)	70	67	143	47	100
France (1700)	75	51	83	38	62
England and Wales (1808)	33	87	221	29	73
France (1803–12)	66	69	123	46	81
Sweden (1805)	82	—	157	—	129
Ireland (1845)	·70	134	256	94	179
France (1840)	62	82	134	51	83
England (1854)	20	160	318	32	64
Sweden (1860)	75	—	120	—	90
Denmark (1860)	53	65	79	34	42
Prussia	—	119	—	53	—
Africa (1975)	69	40	190	28	131
Asia (1975)	61	219	471	134	287
Latin America (1975)	37	48	230	18	85

SOURCES: E. Jensen, *Danish agriculture: its economic development* (Copenhagen, 1937), p. 389; B. F. Hoselitz, 'Population pressure, industrialization and social mobility', *Population Studies*, 11 (1957), 126; J. C. Toutain, *La population de la France de 1700 à 1959* (Paris, 1963), pp. 54–5; *Le produit de l'agriculture française de 1700 à 1958* (2 vols, Paris, 1961), vol. 2, pp. 36, 48; L. Drescher, 'The development of agricultural production in Great Britain and Ireland from the early nineteenth century', *Manchester School*, 23 (1955), 167; G. E. Barnett (ed.), *Two tracts by Gregory King* (Baltimore, 1936), p. 35; D. S. Thomas, *Swedish population movements*, pp. 93–4; B. Holgersson, 'Cultivated land in Sweden and its growth, 1840–1939', *Economy and History*, 17 (1974), 21, 47–8; P. M. Austin Bourke, 'The agricultural statistics of the 1841 census of Ireland: a critical review', *Economic History Review*, 18 (1965), 382–7; FAO, *Production yearbook 1976*, 30 (1977), pp. 45–56, 61–72.

densities, in Egypt and parts of East Africa. Most of Africa and Latin America had comparatively low densities. In the eighteenth and nineteenth centuries densities ranged between 51 per km² and 160 per km², the latter for England in 1854 when only one-fifth of the population depended on agriculture for a livelihood (table 60). Thus the only major region with densities greatly above those of nineteenth-century Europe is south, east and south-east Asia where they generally exceed 250 per km², reaching 1842 in Japan. But in much of Africa and Latin America population to cultivated area densities are no greater than in nineteenth-century Europe.

If the total population is related to the *arable* area, a different pattern emerges (fig. 21). With a world mean density of 263 per km², the highest densities are to be found in Japan, Korea and Indonesia in Asia and in

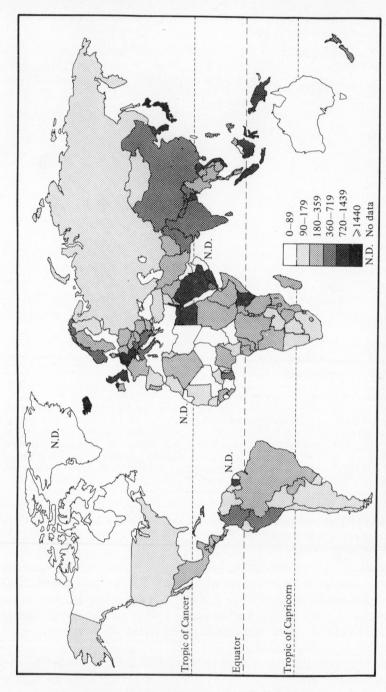

Fig. 21. World population densities 1975: total population per 100 ha of arable land.
Source: FAO, *Production yearbook 1976*, 30 (Rome, 1977), pp. 45–56, 61–9.

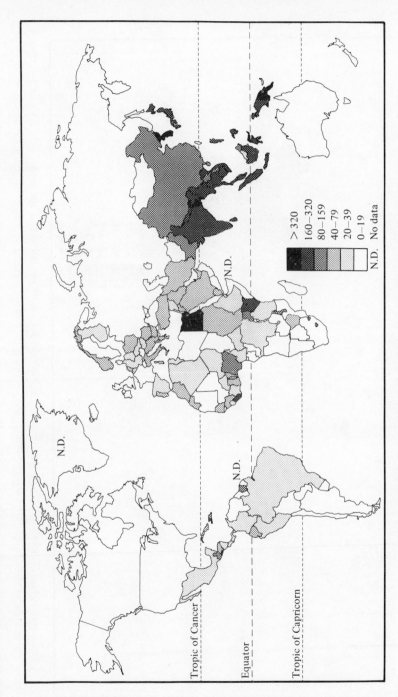

Fig. 22. World population densities, 1975: agricultural population per 100 ha of total cultivated land. Source: FAO, *Production yearbook 1976*, 30 (Rome, 1977), pp. 45–56, 61–9.

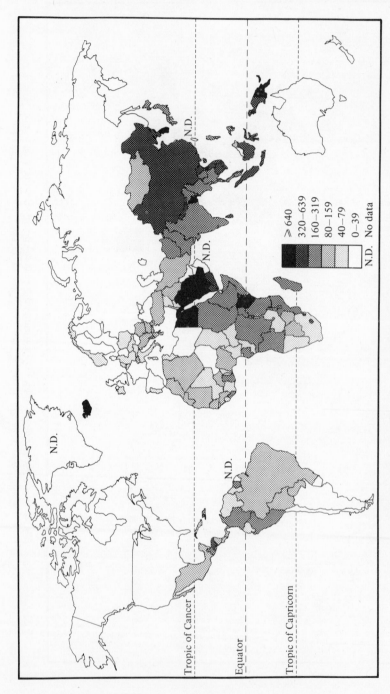

Fig. 23. World population densities, 1975: agricultural population per 100 ha of arable land.
Source: FAO, *Production yearbook 1976*, 30 (Rome, 1977), pp. 45–56, 61–9.

north-west Europe; but parts of the Middle East, east Africa, the Andean republics and Central America have densities well above the average, as does most of south and east Asia. In nineteenth-century Europe the highest densities were in England in 1808 and 1854, and Ireland in 1845, other densities varied between 79 and 143. In terms of this measure most of south and central America, west Africa, central and east Africa, the Middle East and the rest of Asia have densities at present well above those in nineteenth-century Europe.

Figs. 22 and 23 relate only the agricultural population of each country to the cultivated and arable area. The remarkable decline of the agricultural populations in the developed countries over the last century means that in 1975 the densities in Western Europe, North America, Russia and Australasia were remarkably low, but they are also very low in much of Latin America and much of southern Africa. It is Asia, and especially south-east Asia, Japan and Korea that have the highest densities. The density of the agricultural population to the cultivated area was higher in nineteenth-century Europe than it is now, ranging between 29 and 48 if Ireland, with an exceptional density of 100 per km², is excluded. This range falls well short of the density in modern Asia (table 61) but is above the average for both Africa and Latin America at present.

Lastly we turn to consider the relation of the agricultural population to the arable land, possibly the best measure in simple peasant societies (fig. 23). Here there is a clear contrast between most of Europe – the south-east is an exception – Russia, North America, temperate South America, and Australasia, on the one hand, and most of Asia – including the Middle East – most of central, eastern, western and southern Africa, and most of tropical America. In the latter regions densities are well above those in the developed countries, almost without exception, most strikingly in Korea, Bangladesh, Indonesia, the Philippines, Egypt, Kenya and parts of Central America; but densities are also well above those in Western Europe in southern and south-western Asia, most of tropical America and much of Africa. In the nineteenth century this ratio was higher in Europe than it is now, ranging between 42 and 129 with Ireland a striking exception at 179. Comparing this with the present underdeveloped world and excluding Ireland we find comparatively few countries which have densities lower than those in nineteenth-century Europe. Densities in much of Asia are at least twice those of the past, and often four or five times; much of Africa and tropical America also have densities above those obtaining in nineteenth-century Europe.

Reviewing the four measures of density we find that Asia is consistently well above nineteenth-century Europe. In terms of the ratio between total population and total cultivated area, much of Africa and Latin America has densities as favourable as those found in the nineteenth century. If grassland can be regarded as potentially cultivable then these areas do not have

Table 61. *Total population per 100 hectares of arable land*

	1800	1900	1930	1960	1975
Japan	825	866	1122	1609	1984
South Korea	—	500	—	1200	1433
South China	536	600	—	816	—
All China	430	460	505	571	650
North Vietnam	—	230	670	910	—
Java	330	426	491	708	—
All India	—	358	450	376	386
Greater Bengal	—	391	458	559	775[a]
Philippines	—	266	—	388	562
Burma	—	288	—	266	300

[a] Bangladesh.

SOURCES: D. B. Grigg, *The agricultural systems of the world* (Cambridge, 1974), p. 110; FAO, *Production yearbook 1976*, 30 (Rome, 1977), pp. 45–56, 61–72.

excessive problems of population density. But if total population is related to arable land alone, then much of the underdeveloped world has densities above those in the nineteenth century. If agricultural populations are related to the total cultivated land, then again much of Latin America and Africa compare favourably with nineteenth-century Europe; but if agricultural population is related to arable then most of the underdeveloped world has densities above that of the nineteenth century, even in Africa and Latin America. In short, if arable land alone is considered, densities in most of the Third World are well above those of the nineteenth century, those in Asia especially so. If the large areas of natural grazing land included in the areas under cultivation are taken to be potentially cultivable then Latin America and Africa are in a more favourable position than Western Europe was in the nineteenth century. But the arable potential of much of these areas is undoubtedly very limited. All in all it would seem to be true that most parts of the underdeveloped world have a less favourable man:land ratio than nineteenth-century Europe.

It should be noted however that the difference between Asia and Europe is no new feature; densities in much of Asia in the past were much higher than those in Europe. In 1900 densities in Asia were well above anything reached in Western Europe in the mid-nineteenth century, with the exception of England in 1854 and Ireland on the eve of the Famine.

The population densities cited here are not of course any reliable measure of population pressure, for the differences in the quality of land, the type of technology and the intensity of land use all greatly vary. But in simple peasant societies they do give some crude measure of differences in demographic tension. One important qualification must be made. In Europe in the past, multiple cropping was unimportant, and it still is today except in parts of the Mediterranean. Multiple cropping is not of much significance in Africa,

North America or Latin America at present. On the other hand it does add substantially to the gross cropped area in many parts of Asia today. Thus the very high densities of population per hectare of arable recorded for Asia as a whole (table 60) and for individual countries (table 61) need some qualification: but even if Asian agricultural population densities were calculated with reference to the gross cropland rather than arable area, Asian figures would still be above all other parts of the world.

Demographic responses: overseas migration

Until the nineteenth century international migration was not a major means of relieving population pressure, but between the 1820s and 1939 some 60 million people left Europe.[25] By no means all left because of abject poverty at home, nor did all come from rural Europe. Nonetheless emigration was a major factor in reducing the rate of population increase in parts of Western Europe – Ireland, Norway and Italy are perhaps the most notable instances. However emigration was generally less important than rural–urban migration, and in the long run less significant than the decline in fertility.

In the nineteenth century there was some overseas migration from the underdeveloped world. The slave trade from Africa to Latin America continued illegally until the 1880s. More important were outflows from India and China which, however, were more a function of overseas demand for labour than population pressure at home. With the end of slavery in the British colonies in 1834, the system of indentured labour provided labour for the sugar plantations in the West Indies, Mauritius, Natal and Fiji; there was also substantial migration to Ceylon, Burma and Malaysia, and later to East Africa. Between 1834 and 1934 some 30 million left India, of whom four-fifths returned home. The descendants of these settlers now number some 5 million. The other major outflow was from China: although some found their way to the west coast of the Americas, the great majority went to South-East Asia, where 96% of the 30 million overseas Chinese now live.[26]

Although both the Indian and Chinese emigrants had – and continue to have – considerable influence on the economic development of the countries to which they went, they were a minute proportion of the populations of India and China; by the 1920s the countries of overseas European settlement were raising barriers to Asiatic immigration, and since the end of the Second World War many newly independent nations in Asia also began to restrict immigration; indeed in 1961 Indonesia repatriated 100000 Chinese.[27]

Little is known about international migration within the underdeveloped world since 1945. There is undoubtedly much migration within Africa, particularly towards Rhodesia and South Africa but much of it is temporary. In Latin America the principal movement is towards the United States: in the mid-1960s there were 1 million people of Mexican origin living in the United States, and there was also a considerable movement from Central

America and the Caribbean, and a somewhat smaller flow from South America.[28] But the major international movement has been to Western Europe. In 1973 there were 11.5 million foreign workers in the EEC, principally in France and Germany. Few were, however, permanent migrants, although France has had to absorb the return of 400 000 colonists from North Africa, while the Netherlands received refugees from Indonesia after independence. In Britain the principal immigration has been from the West Indies, India and Pakistan but the flow has been much restricted since 1962.[29]

Thus movement from the less developed world has been very small when compared with the great European exodus of the nineteenth century, and it has only had any significant impact in very small countries. Thus between 1955 and 1961 31% of the population of Montserrat left the island and between 1948 and 1967 30% of the 1948 population of Malta emigrated.[30] It seems highly improbable that international migration can make any great impact upon the population problems of the developing world. It must be remembered however that the great European exodus was confined to a very short period of demographic history and had a significant impact on only limited areas of Europe. Europe's problems were eased but not solved by overseas emigration.

Rural–urban migration

In pre-industrial Europe there was a constant movement from the country to the towns; indeed without this movement towns would not have maintained their populations, let alone grown, for deaths consistently exceeded births. But except in the Low Countries, and to a lesser extent England, those living in towns were a small proportion of the total population, and rural–urban migration was only a palliative for rural population pressure, not a cure. But in the nineteenth century the population of the towns began to grow rapidly, and more rapidly than that of the countryside, so that the rural population as a proportion of the total population steadily declined. In France, England and Ireland the *absolute* numbers began to decline in the second half of the nineteenth century. Elsewhere this turning-point came later but certainly everywhere in the later nineteenth century the rate of rural increase was much slower, and by the 1920s the rural populations of most of Western Europe were in absolute decline, and nearly everywhere most people lived in towns. The decline of the primary rural population – those working in agriculture and those servicing it – has continued since the end of the Second World War, although this has been obscured by the rise of commuter populations living in areas defined in national censuses as rural districts, but working in towns.

Although this remarkable change generally attributed to industrialisation is well known, the details of it are still obscure, largely due to the absence of any reliable information on the demographic differences between town and country. In pre-industrial societies towns, and particularly larger towns, are thought to have grown only by migration. But in the late eighteenth century some towns in England, and, in France, Paris began to grow by natural increase, as did some cities in Germany in the first half of the nineteenth century. Before 1841 the towns of Sweden as a whole increased only because of net immigration and Stockholm did not have a surplus of births over deaths until after 1861. As late as 1877 a survey of thirty great cities in Europe showed that seven would have declined in numbers had it not been for migration.[31] Consequently a considerable part of Europe's urban growth in the nineteenth century was due to rural–urban migration. This in turn reduced the rate of increase in the countryside below the national average. Thus in the nineteenth century rates of increase in the countryside were comparatively modest (table 62) and were generally much lower in the second half of the nineteenth century than in the first half.

This is not the place to reopen the question of why there was such a great movement from country to the town. Undoubtedly the towns, with new forms of employment offering wages above those obtaining in the countryside, exercised a powerful attraction. It was in most of Europe the landless and the rural artisan, undercut by factory goods, who left, and not the farmers. But in the first half of the century the push effect must have been significant, for there was widespread underemployment. In the long run industrialisation created enough jobs to absorb the rural surplus, although in some countries in Western Europe this process is only now approaching completion. Two of the characteristics of nineteenth-century industry are worthy of note: first, it was still labour-intensive; second, it expanded the range of possible jobs. The Registrar-General recognised some 7000 different occupations in Britain in 1851, 15000 in 1901.[32] Thus while there was cyclic unemployment in nineteenth-century cities and while there was undoubtedly poverty, and the ranks of domestic servants were doubtless swollen because they could not find more remunerative employment elsewhere, in the long run industrial growth managed to absorb the rural surplus of the early nineteenth century and eventually led to a long-term decline in the primary rural populations of Western Europe.

When in the early 1950s economists and others turned their attention to the problems of population growth and economic development in the developing world, it was natural to think that policies which emphasised industrialisation would not only increase national incomes, but relieve the overpopulation of the countryside. Indeed some models of economic development assumed that there was a labour surplus in the countryside, that this would migrate to the towns to provide the labour force for new industries, and as long as there was underemployment in the countryside this reserve would keep down wages in the factories and allow capital accumulation for further growth.[33]

Indeed at first sight figures of the rural and urban populations of Afro-Asia and Latin America would suggest that these areas are going through a period

Table 62. *Rates of increase of rural and urban populations in Western Europe, 1750–1900 (average % p.a.)*

		1750–1801	1801–1851	1850–1901
England and	Rural	0.5	0.7	−0.3
Wales	Urban	1.4	2.4	1.9
France	Rural	—	0.4	−0.2
	Urban	—	1.1	1.1
Sweden	Rural	—	0.8	0.5
	Urban	—	0.9	2.3
Norway	Rural	—	0.9	0.5
	Urban	—	1.8	2.2
Prussia	Rural	—	1.4	1.0
	Urban	—	1.5	2.3
Netherlands	Rural	—	0.9	0.4
	Urban	—	0.9	1.9
Belgium	Rural	—	—	0.2
	Urban	—	—	1.6

SOURCES: A. Weber, *The growth of cities in the nineteenth century: a study in statistics* (New York, 1899), pp. 82, 113; D. S. Thomas, *Social and economic aspects of Swedish population movements, 1750–1933* (Stockholm, 1941), pp. 93–4; C. M. Law, 'The growth of urban population in England and Wales, 1801–1971', *Transactions of the Institute of British Geographers*, 41 (1967), 130; 'Some notes on the urban population of England and Wales in the eighteenth century', *Local Historian*, 10 (1972), 18; J. C. Toutain, *La population de la France de 1700 à 1959* (Paris, 1963), pp. 54–5; F. Hodne, *An economic history of Norway, 1815–1970* (Bergen, 1976), p. 25.

of urbanisation comparable to that experienced in Europe in the nineteenth and early twentieth centuries. In 1920 Afro-Asia and Latin America were still overwhelmingly rural: in Asia and Africa less than 10% of the population lived in places of more than 20000, and in Latin America 14%, but by 1960 33% of the population in Latin America was living in such cities, 20% in East Asia and 13–14% in Africa and South Asia.[34]

Thus Afro-Asia and Latin America would seem to be repeating the experience of Europe in the past. However, there are important differences. The rate of urban increase is much above that attained in nineteenth-century Europe, when the rate of increase did not exceed 2.5% per annum over any sustained period. But even before 1940 towns were increasing at more than 3% per annum in nearly every part of the developing world (table 63). In the 1940s this rate rose to over 4% p.a., and has remained there until the present. Some of this increase was due to migration from the rural areas, and so the rate of increase in rural areas was somewhat below the rate of rural natural increase between 1920 and 1940. Even so rates of population increase in the countryside were above those for any part of Western Europe in the nineteenth century, save for Prussia in the first half (table 62). The only exception to this was East Asia where rates of rural increase were modest between 1920 and 1950, and indeed have remained so since then. But since

Table 63. *Rates of increase of rural and urban populations, 1920–70*[a]
(*average % p.a.*)

		1920–30	1930–40	1940–50	1950–60	1960–70
Europe	Rural	0.5	0.4	0.2	0.3	−0.5
	Urban	1.7	1.3	0.5	1.6	1.7
North America	Rural	0.5	0.5	0.4	0.4	−1.0
	Urban	2.9	1.0	2.6	3.1	2.0
Soviet Union	Rural	1.5	−0.5	−1.2	0.48	−0.3
	Urban	4.1	7.0	0.6	4.5	2.7
Australasia	Rural	1.6	0.4	0.8	0.6	—
	Urban	2.1	1.7	2.6	3.6	—
East Asia	Rural	0.4	0.4	0.4	0.9	0.8
	Urban	3.8	3.7	2.6	4.3	4.5
South Asia	Rural	1.1	1.2	1.0	1.8	2.3
	Urban	2.5	3.9	4.3	4.2	4.1
Latin America	Rural	1.6	1.6	1.5	1.7	1.2
	Urban	3.4	3.4	4.8	5.3	4.4
Africa	Rural	1.3	1.4	1.2	1.8	1.9
	Urban	3.5	3.6	4.5	5.4	4.6
World	Rural	0.8	0.7	0.6	1.3	1.3
	Urban	2.6	2.7	2.2	3.5	3.3

[a] In the first four columns 'urban' is the number living in places of 20000 or more; in the last column 'urban' is based on the local definition of 'urban'.
SOURCES: United Nations, *Development policies and planning* (New York, 1968), pp. 11–12; *Monthly Bulletin of Statistics*, November (1971), xxiv–xxxiii.

the 1940s the rate of increase in rural Africa and South Asia has steadily mounted; in Latin America, in spite of a great volume of rural–urban migration, the rate of rural increase has been above that of most parts of Europe in the nineteenth century. All this is in spite of unprecedented rates of urban increase.

The explanation of this discrepancy seems to lie in the differing urban–rural differentials. In the early nineteenth century urban growth, except in Britain, was largely a result of rural–urban migration. As urban mortality slowly fell through the century natural increase played an increasingly important role. Much the same situation seems to have obtained in the less developed countries before 1945. Although there was some surplus of births over deaths, rural–urban migration provided most of the urban increase. However, from the 1940s urban death rates began to fall, and fall more rapidly than in the rural areas, thus compensating for the higher fertility in rural areas. Natural increase has sinced then provided an increasing proportion of urban growth. Thus in Calcutta natural increase provided 49% of total increase in 1911–21, 56% by 1951–61; in Mexico migration was the main contributor to urban growth in the 1940s, but was overtaken by natural increase in the 1950s; similarly in Columbia natural increase accounted for 26% of urban growth, 1938–51, but 35%, 1951–64. Natural increase seems then to be providing an

Table 64. *Urban and rural demographic differentials*, c. *1960 (rates per thousand)*

	Developed countries		Developing countries	
	Urban	Rural	Urban	Rural
Crude birth rates	19.8	23.1	38.0	44.1
Crude death rates	9.0	9.5	15.3	21.6
Rate of natural increase	10.8	13.6	22.7	22.5

SOURCE: United Nations, *The determinants and consequences of population trends* (New York, 1973), p. 197.

increasing proportion of total urban increase. In Venezuela in the 1960s it accounted for 66% of the growth of towns of more than 20 000, and in Chile 70%.[35]

Thus a very different situation obtains in the developing world at present from that in Europe in the nineteenth century or indeed in the developing countries before 1945. Although rural fertility is still above that in the towns, urban mortality has fallen more since 1945 than rural mortality. The rate of natural increase in the towns is now much the same as in the countryside. Furthermore, this rate of natural increase, averaging 2.2% p.a., is far above the levels obtaining in nineteenth-century Europe (table 62). Since 1945 cities in the developing world have grown so rapidly because not only is there substantial migration into them but they also have high rates of natural increase.

The consequences of this are well known; the cities of the developing world have had great difficulties in providing employment for these rapidly increasing numbers. Not only do the countries lack capital for industrial growth, but modern industry, unlike nineteenth-century industrial growth, is not labour intensive; it requires high capital inputs and comparatively small numbers of workers. As a result increasing proportions of the urban population are either unemployed or are found in the traditional urban sector of handicrafts and small trading, or in service industries of low productivity. Given a continuing high rate of natural increase, it seems unlikely that the cities will be able to absorb future rural–urban migration in any productive employment, and the rural labourer will exchange underemployment in the countryside for unemployment in the town.[36]

The reduction of fertility

It seems probable that in Western Europe in the later stages of the second and third great cycles of population growth there were attempts to limit fertility; in the seventeenth century later marriage was probably the only mechanism, although it is *possible* that celibacy increased and that there was some attempt to limit the number of births within marriage. In the nineteenth century there is more clearcut evidence: in France there was no increase in celibacy nor any increase in the age of marriage; instead the number of births within marriage was limited, and the crude birth rate fell throughout the nineteenth century. In Ireland marriage began to be postponed in the 1820s and after 1851 the numbers never marrying began to rise without, however, any fall in marital fertility. In England the crude birth rate did not definitely decline until after the 1870s, and this was achieved largely by a fall in the number of births within marriage.

Until the mid-1960s declines in fertility in the less developed world were confined to a few countries mainly in the West Indies and in small and relatively advanced territories in East Asia, such as Singapore, Hong Kong and Taiwan. Elsewhere fertility remained high. Many attempts have been made to explain this persistence. It was argued that as child and infant mortality had traditionally been high, a large number of births were needed to ensure that an adequate number reached maturity. Thus, for example, a survey in Bangladesh in 1968–9 showed that women of over 40 had had an average of 6.5 live births, but only 4.7 had survived to 20. As infant and child mortality had declined in the preceding twenty years lower proportions of those born to preceding generations would have survived. Parents in the underdeveloped world are thought to have wanted large families for two principal reasons: children provide labour on the peasant holding, obviating the need for hired labour, and they ensure that the parents, in the absence of a welfare state, will have some security in their old age. But such explanations, if they are accurate, become less compelling as child mortality has declined over the last thirty years.[37]

Since 1960 a decline in fertility has become far more widespread in the developing countries. Complete registration of vital events are available for only 52 territories, many of which are small islands and include none of the world's most populous states. Nonetheless forty-three of these territories recorded some decline in the crude birth rate between 1956 and 1973, in some cases quite dramatic: the crude birth rate in Costa Rica, for example, fell from 48 per thousand in 1956 to 29.5 per thousand in 1974, and in Trinidad from 37 to 21.6 per thousand. In countries where the registration of vital events is adjudged incomplete, there are nonetheless signs of declining fertility. Thus estimates of the crude birth rate in Brazil put it at an average of 44 per thousand before 1960, but by 1970 it had fallen to 37 per thousand. In Turkey fertility remains high, but an undoubted decline has begun since 1955. In India and Pakistan fertility in the 1960s seems to have been lower than in the 1950s. For China there is little demographic information, and even the total population is not known; one authority, however, has argued that the crude birth rate was 42 per thousand in 1949, 32 per thousand in 1969 and was possibly as low as 26 per thousand in 1975. A comparison of the 1953 census with the population announced by the Chinese government for 1972 yields a growth rate of only 1.2%, which would support the assumption of a dramatic fall in the birth rate.[38]

The decline in fertility which seems to have begun in most parts of the developing world – tropical Africa is an apparent exception – is due to two principal factors. In the first place where information is available – and it is for only a few countries – fewer young women are getting married, and the average age of marriage is rising. Hence a smaller proportion of the women in the reproductive age groups are married, although there are few signs of any change in the proportions who, at 45, have been married at some time. Thus in the Phillipines 54% of the women aged 20–24 were married in 1960, by 1968 only 39%. In India in 1951 75% of women aged 15 to 19 were married, but by 1971 this had fallen to 56%. In Sri Lanka the average age of women at marriage was 20 years 7 months in 1946, 23 years 5 months in 1971; as a consequence, although 65.2% of women in the reproductive age groups were married in 1963, only 60.1% were in 1968–9. The average age of women at marriage has also risen in South Korea. At the beginning of this century it was only 17.2 but for those women born in 1941–5 it had risen to 22.8.[39] Changes such as these are of great importance. It has already been noted that it is age of marriage and celibacy that accounts for the differences in total fertility between the less developed world at present and Europe in the nineteenth century, and probably at times before then. Thus, for example, it has been estimated that if by 1990 no Indian women married before 19 years then the crude birth rate would be reduced by 30%. Indeed some authorities have argued that a rapid reduction in fertility in the less developed countries is only possible if a reduction of marital fertility is combined with a fall in the proportions who do get married. In China the minimum legal age of marriage for women was raised to 18 years, and in recent years it has been suggested that it should be raised to 22 years.[40]

A second presumed reason for the decline in the crude birth rate has been the fall in marital fertility as married couples have attempted to limit the number of children within marriage. Save in Ireland, this was the means by which fertility was reduced in nineteenth-century Europe, and many have thus argued that this is the way in which fertility could be reduced in the less developed countries. Until the 1960s many influential groups – religious and political – were opposed to birth control methods, but since about 1965 this opposition has been less uncompromising, and United Nations agencies have been able to promote the adoption of birth control methods; indeed since 1965 there are few countries in which there have not been attempts to promote the adoption of various means of contraception.[41] No doubt some of the decline in fertility which has occurred in less developed countries may be attributed to a reduction in marital fertility and that this may be due to the use of contraceptive measures. But in some of the better documented cases of fertility decline the fall began before the initiation of family planning programmes; this would seem to be so in Taiwan, for example.[42]

The less developed countries do not differ greatly from nineteenth-century Europe in this respect; the beginning of fertility decline coincided with the much wider discussion of birth control techniques, and the greater commercial availability of physical methods. But it does not follow that the decline was due to the wider adoption of these means. Thus a survey carried out in England in the 1940s showed that only 16% of those women in the sample married before 1910, and who had practised birth control, had used physical appliances. Of those married in 1940–7 the figure had risen, but to only 57%.[43] Thus the decline in fertility after the 1870s was achieved largely with the pre-industrial methods of birth control. This would seem to be true in many less developed countries today.

It is thus the motives for the limitation of numbers which are of greatest interest. It is far from clear why fertility declined in Western Europe from the 1870s (in Ireland and France the decline pre-dates this) but it is generally assumed to be related to *increasing* real income. It is therefore sometimes argued that a decline in fertility in the less developed countries will only come when a certain threshold of economic development is reached.[44] The fact that the earliest declines in fertility did come in such small and relatively prosperous societies as Hong Kong, Singapore and Taiwan would bear this out. But not all Europe's fertility declines can be so easily attributed to *rising* income. France and Ireland's declines can be equally plausibly explained as an attempt to defend living standards that were being eroded by population growth, and the later declines in fertility in Russia and Eastern Europe beginning in the 1920s would bear out this interpretation. It may be then that this may provide a motive for the reduction of fertility in the less developed countries. The case of China would seem to illustrate this point.

Whatever the motives which cause people to limit their families, it is clearly easier for this to be done at present than in the past, for birth control methods are greatly improved and more easily available. Indeed the rate at which fertility declines, once it is underway, has greatly increased since the nineteenth century.

Thus the crude birth rate in England and Wales in the 1870s was 35.6 per thousand; it took more than fifty years for this to be halved. In Bulgaria the crude birth rate was about 38 per thousand in the mid-1920s, but it took little more than thirty years for this to halve. In Japan the birth rate in the first quinqennium after the Second World War averaged 30 per thousand; it fell to an average of 18 per thousand within ten years and has remained at that level to the present day; of the more recent declines Mauritius has fallen from 43.3 per thousand in 1956 to 23 per thousand in 1973, Hong Kong from 37 to 19.8 per thousand over the same period, and Singapore had halved its rate of 44.4 per thousand in 1956 by 1973.[45]

It may be a little premature to argue that a world-wide decline in fertility has begun, and that the less developed countries are making the sort of adjustments that Western Europe did in the nineteenth century; but if the decline has begun, it seems to have come earlier in the population cycle than happened in Europe. It was not until 120 years after the revival of growth in the 1750s that fertility began to decline in most of Western Europe; in contrast the less developed countries have seen the onset of decline only fifty years after the beginnings of modern growth in the 1920s. On the other hand the population of Western Europe only doubled between 1750 and 1870; in comparison the less developed countries have nearly tripled in the half century since 1920. Nor can the possibilities of a rapid reduction in fertility in the future encourage too much optimism. Western Europe managed to bring its growth virtually to a halt between 1880 and 1930, but the very youthful nature of the populations of the less developed world today ensures that they will continue to grow rapidly in the future. Tomas Frejka has calculated that even if the net reproduction rate could be reduced to unity by the 1980s – which is impossible – the populations of the developing world would still increase by about 50% between 1980 and 2000, and by 90% between 1980 and 2050. On the more plausible but still optimistic assumption that unity can be reached by 2000, then the population of the less developed countries in that year will be 80% greater than in 1970, and by 2050 will be 2.5 times greater than in 1970.[46] Thus, however abrupt the decline in fertility in the future there will continue to be a very rapid increase in the populations of the developing world.

Conclusions

In the nineteenth century many parts of rural Western Europe exhibited symptoms of population pressure; in the long run the answer to the problem was technological advance in agriculture. But in many countries there were demographic responses – migration overseas, migration to the towns, and in some cases such as France and Ireland, a reduction in fertility well before the general decline that began in the 1870s. The developing countries today also exhibit symptoms of population pressure, but their circumstances are less favourable for they have smaller amounts of arable per head than did West European countries and rates of population increase are higher. Nor is there much likelihood of overseas migration relieving the problem. Indeed to reduce the rate of natural increase by migration on the scale of Norway and Ireland in the nineteenth century would require the movement of tens of millions of people. Nor does rural–urban migration seem likely to solve the problem. Although this movement has certainly reduced the rate of increase in the rural areas, migrants have great difficulties in finding jobs. Urban unemployment has become a major economic issue in the developing countries. Unless there is some unforeseen alteration in economic conditions in the developing countries, it seems that the only possible demographic response which will help is the reduction of fertility.

CHAPTER 18

THE DEVELOPING COUNTRIES TODAY: THE PRODUCTION RESPONSE

In this chapter an attempt will be made to review the production responses open to rural communities in the developing world, and to compare these with those available in Western Europe in the past. It should be said straightaway that it is difficult to generalise with any confidence about the developing countries, for they vary so greatly in their economic, physical and social characteristics. Thus in terms of population density they range from Bangladesh with 524 per km² to Mauritania with 1 per km²; in terms of economic development they range from countries like Rwanda with a gross domestic product of $68 per head to countries like Brazil or Mexico, with figures twelve times that, while in the last decade the oil-exporting countries have been transformed in terms of income if not in other ways.

The physical environments of these countries also differ profoundly, not only from Western Europe, but between themselves. Much of Western Europe is covered by recent deposits of glacial or alluvial origin which have not been subject to leaching over long periods of time as have much of Africa or South America. Most of Western Europe lacks climatic extremes; only in southern France is drought a limiting factor, and only in northern Scandinavia is the growing season significantly shortened by cold. But most of the developing countries are found in environments where climates are quite different from Western Europe, and where consequently the agricultural technology of Europe is not necessarily easily adopted. Much of northern Africa and south-west Asia has too little rainfall to support permanent agriculture, and what rainfall there is is concentrated in one season and varies unpredictably from year to year. In Saudi Arabia for example, there are no permanent rivers and only 0.2% of the total area is used for crops.[1] In contrast much of South America, central Africa and south-east Asia lies within the humid tropics, where the natural vegetation is rainforest, sustained by high temperatures throughout the year, and by the absence of any dry season. These regions present agronomic problems quite different from most of the rest of the developing world and from Western Europe; as yet only shifting cultivation or the growth of tree crops, both of which simulate the natural vegetation, and wet-rice cultivation, have proved successful farming systems over long periods.[2]

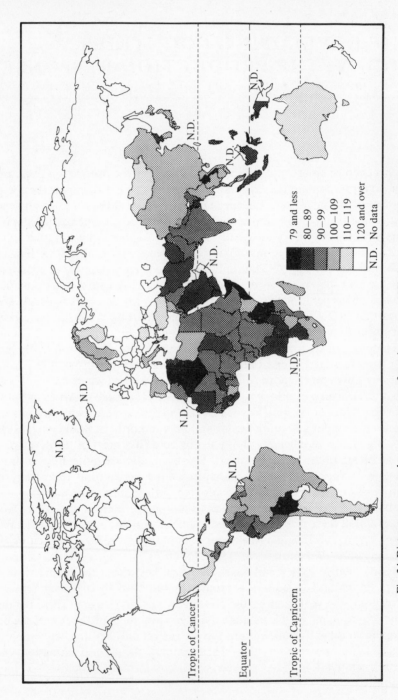

Fig. 24. Dietary energy supply as a percentage of requirements, *c.* 1970. Source: *Monthly Bulletin of Agricultural Economics and Statistics*, 23 (1974), 3–4.

Agricultural progress since 1945

The fact that income per head remains low in the developing world at present and food production is in many countries insufficient to provide minimum food requirements suggests to many that traditional agriculture in the developing world has been unable to increase output. This would seem to be borne out in the critical years in the mid-1960s and the early 1970s. In 1974 world food stocks had fallen to only 33 days, and the majority of developing countries were dependent on imported grain.[3] But this does not mean that there has been no increase in production since 1945; on the contrary between 1948 and 1973 world food output doubled. Over the period 1961–5 to 1976 world food output rose by 40%, that of Africa rose by 31%, Latin America by 55%, the Near East by 57% and the Far East by 45%. These are prodigious increases by nineteenth-century standards. But of course population has also been growing, so that the increase in food output *per head* has been less impressive; since the early 1960s increases in food output in the developing countries as a whole have only managed to maintain output per head. Over a longer period – 1945 to 1974 – output per head has risen in a majority of countries, but in 34 output has failed to keep up with population growth, and these 34 countries included one-quarter of the population of the developing world.[4]

Thus in nearly all the developing world there have been very considerable increases in food production since 1945, but for a quarter of the population of the developing world these increases have been insufficient to match the growth of population. For the remaining three-quarters growth of food output has kept up with population growth, but not sufficiently to provide food supplies which will give the population an adequate diet (fig. 24). In effect much of the world remains on diets which were already poor before the great post-war explosion in population took place.

Having emphasised the diversity of conditions which exist in the developing world, and the fact that agricultural output has increased considerably, it is now necessary to turn to consider the ways in which output has been increased.

The extension of the cultivated area

The extension of the cultivated area has played an important role in increasing food output in the last thirty years, and indeed over a longer period. Land use figures, however, must be used with great caution. In the period since 1950 the area under cultivation in Europe has hardly changed (table 65): in the Soviet Union, North America and Australia there have been marked increases in the area under cereals, fluctuating in response, in the case of the latter two regions, to world demand for grain imports. In the developing continents there have been substantial increases in the arable area in Latin

Table 65. *Arable land 1950–75 (million ha)*

	c. 1950	*c.* 1955	*c.* 1961–5	*c.* 1975	% increase 1950–75
Europe	148	151	152	143	−3.4
USSR	175	220	229	232	+32.6
North America	220	229	222	253	+15.0
Oceania	17	25	35	47	+176
Developed	560	625	638	675	+20.5
Latin America	86	102	116	140	+62.8
Asia	348	426	447	478	+37.4
Africa	228	232	190	211	−7.5
Developing	662	760	753	829	+25.2
WORLD	1222	1385	1391	1504	+23.1

SOURCES: FAO, *Production yearbook 1951*, 5 (Rome, 1952), 3–7; *Production yearbook 1957*, 11 (Rome, 1958), 3–7; *Production yearbook 1976*, 30 (Rome, 1977), 45–6.

Table 66. *Area under major food crops, 1950–75 (million ha)*

	1950	1961–5	1975	% increase 1950–75
Europe	88	88	81	−8
USSR	110	137	134	+22
North America	113	82	95	−15.9
Oceania	6	10	14	+133
Developed	317	317	324	+2.2
Latin America	41	50	86	+110
Asia	335	350	398	+18.8
Africa	57	77	94	+64.9
Developing	433	477	578	33.5

SOURCES: FAO, *Production yearbook 1957*, 11 (Rome, 1958), pp. 31–2; *Production yearbook 1976*, 30 (Rome, 1977), pp. 89–90, 106–7.

America, and less marked but nonetheless considerable increases in Asia. In Africa, apparently, there has been a decline. But these figures are almost certainly misleading. Estimates for arable land for some African countries fluctuate from year to year largely due to the amount of land defined as in fallow, and thus as part of the 'arable' area. The area under food crops may more accurately represent changes in the area under cultivation (table 66) and this shows a striking increase in Africa. Whatever the drawbacks of the data they do suggest that there has been a substantial increase in the area under cultivation in the less developed countries in the last quarter century, and this has been most marked in Latin America, and least marked in Asia, which

Table 67. *Long-term increases in the arable area in parts of Asia*

Year	Arable (1000 km²)	Total population (millions)	Arable per head (ha)
China			
1400	254	70	0.36
1600	335	160	0.21
1760	634	270	0.23
1873	816	350	0.23
1913	917	430	0.21
1933	989	500	0.20
1957	1131	647	0.17
1975	1290	838	0.15
Japan			
1700	30	25	0.12
1800	30	25	0.12
1867	32	27	0.12
1877	41	35	0.12
1905	54	47	0.11
1920	59	55	0.11
1934	60	68	0.09
1960	57	93	0.06
1975	55	110	0.05
Java and Madura			
1815	15	5	0.3
1900	66	28	0.24
1920	80	34	0.24
1930	84	41	0.20
1940	90	48	0.19
1960	88	63	0.14
All India			
1901	795	285	0.28
1911	868	305	0.28
1941	832	388	0.21
1961	1515	570	0.27
1968	1929	647	0.30
1976	1961	750	0.26

SOURCES: D. Grigg, *The agricultural systems of the world* (Cambridge, 1974), pp. 88, 92, 96, 100; FAO, *Production yearbook 1976* (Rome, 1977), pp. 50–3, 64–6.

is the most densely populated of the three developing continents and has less potentially cultivable land.

The expansion of the cultivated area is of course not a new phenomenon in the developing countries. Although reliable data on land use in the past are rare, such estimates as exist suggest a continuous process of expansion (table 67) over the whole period for which figures are available. In other parts of Asia – particularly south-east Asia – there was also a marked increase in the area under rice in the nineteenth century, and also, in more limited areas,

Table 68. *Arable area per head of agricultural and total populations, 1950 and 1975* (*ha*)

	Agricultural		Total	
	1950	1975	1950	1975
Europe	1.2	1.8	0.4	0.3
USSR	1.7	4.5	0.9	0.9
North America	10.0	36.1	1.3	1.1
Oceania	4.3	39.1	1.3	2.8
Latin America	1.0	0.9	0.5	0.4
Asia	0.4	0.3	0.25	0.2
Africa	1.3	0.8	1.2	0.5

SOURCES: FAO, *Production yearbook 1957*, 11 (Rome, 1958), pp. 3–7, 17; *Production yearbook 1976*, 30 (Rome, 1977), pp. 45–56, 61–9.

of plantation crops. In Japan, China and Java arable expansion seems to have kept up with total population growth over very long periods in the past. It is only since the end of the nineteenth century that a progressive decline in arable per head has begun.

Although there have been increases in the cultivated area in many parts of the less developed world in the last twenty-five years, it has for the most part been less than the rate of total population increase. Thus arable per head of total population has fallen slightly in Latin America, and Asia, and probably in Africa, although the figures for total arable for that continent are too inaccurate to be confident about the trend (table 68). But this is no new phenomenon. Arable per head in Java has been falling since the 1920s (and the decline may have begun much earlier), in China since the 1870s (table 67) and in India, South Korea, the Philippines and Vietnam since the beginning of this century.[5] But it should be noted Europe has also had a decline in arable per head of the total population since 1950, as has the United States, and in the USSR the figure has remained constant; it is only in Australasia that it has increased. On the other hand the absolute decline in the agricultural population in this period has meant that arable per head of the agricultural population has risen in all the developed areas (table 68). In the developing nations however, the continued increase in the agricultural population has meant a decline in arable per head of that population as well.

However, this was paralleled in nineteenth-century Europe. Between 1750 and 1850, although the arable area expanded considerably, it did so less rapidly than total population, although Sweden may be an exception to this rule. The fact that agricultural populations grew less rapidly than urban population, however, meant that the fall in arable per head of the agricultural work force was small, except in Ireland, and by the later nineteenth century arable per head of the agricultural population was increasing. The decline in arable per head in the nineteenth century was compensated for by both imports of food and an increase in crop yields, while livestock production also increased.

It is unfortunately difficult to say with any accuracy where the increases in arable in the developing countries have come in the last quarter century, for not only are national figures of land use generally unreliable but few land-use surveys exist; however, there seems no doubt that there has been a considerable expansion of the area under cultivation in Latin America. Indeed until recently arable expansion had kept up with the rapid population growth. Early Spanish settlement took place mainly in the areas of dense indigenous settlement, in the upland areas of central and southern America. The lowlands of the Pacific coast, the Caribbean coasts and the Amazon were sparsely settled by the native inhabitants and largely ignored by early European settlers. In the late nineteenth century there was a remarkable European migration into southern Brazil and the lowlands of the Rio Plata. But since the end of the Second World War the main drive to new settlements has been into the humid tropical lowlands, and to a lesser extent into the drier regions on the Pacific coastlands. This has been prompted by the growing population pressure in the Andean and Central American uplands, where the shortage of land is made worse by an inequitable system of landownership. Approximately half a million people have settled in the *oriente*, the Andean foothills and Amazonian lowlands of Peru, Ecuador and Bolivia, in the last quarter of a century. This has been made possible by the construction of roads, but the marketing of produce in the distant, more populous areas is still difficult. Perhaps more dramatic has been the invasion of the Amazonian lowlands in Brazil: between 1960 and 1970 the population along the highway from Brazilia to Belim rose from 100000 to 2 million.[6] But the settlement of the lowlands of the American humid tropics has presented numerous problems. No more than one-twentieth of the soils are of moderate or better fertility, and the destruction of the forest cover leads to soil impoverishment. Shifting cultivation and the growth of tree crops are still the only successful farming systems, although much forest land has been cleared and put down to pasture.[7]

Asia has been densely settled for a much longer period than either Latin America or Africa, and the increase in cultivation since 1950 has been much slower. In India there have been numerous colonisation schemes, principally in Assam, in the *terai* of Uttar Pradesh and Bihar where malaria once precluded settlement, in Rajasthan where settlement was impossible before the expansion of irrigation, in the hills of the south-west, and in Dandakaranya. In Sri Lanka new land has come largely from the expansion of settlement in the Dry Zone. In the islands of south-east Asia there are remarkable contrasts between the high densities of islands such as Java and Luzon and the sparsely settled islands of Sumatra and Borneo, and there has been some increase in the cultivated area in these frontier zones, particularly on Mindanao in the

Philippines. There have also been increases on the mainland, notably in Malaya and Thailand.[8]

Although there is little comprehensive evidence on the expansion of the arable area in Africa, there have been many state supported colonisation schemes, both in the colonial period and since Independence, a majority in the savanna areas, and thus dependent on the extension of irrigation.[9]

The cultivable area

The expansion of the cultivated area has thus been an important element in the growth of agricultural output in the post-war period in the developing countries; indeed between 1948–52 and 1957–9 it accounted for two-thirds of the increase, and between 1957–9 and 1966–8 one-half. In contrast the increase in the developed world came almost entirely from increases in yields.[10] The countries in the developing world are thus closely comparable with those in Western Europe before the second half of the nineteenth century, when the increases in output which could be obtained from higher yields were probably of less importance than those obtainable from increasing the area under cultivation and reducing the fallow. Not surprisingly many authorities now believe that future increases in output in the developing world will have to come from the adoption of better farming methods and higher yields, on the grounds that there is little cultivable land left in the developing countries. Unfortunately there are few accurate assessments of the potentially cultivable area; it can be said, however, that the costs of clearing land, providing irrigation, and building railways and roads have mounted rapidly in the post-war era, as progressively less fertile land has been developed, and it is argued that such investment would be better placed in raising yields on existing arable areas.

There have been many estimates of the world's potential arable area, ranging from one made in 1945 that put the total potential as 7.2% of the earth's land area, a figure now well exceeded by the area actually in cultivation, to 30% of the earth's land area, made in 1930.[11] A recent attempt by FAO experts based on soil maps and climatic analogies (table 69) puts the developing countries potential arable area at 1145 million hectares, of which 45% was in cultivation in 1962; it is thought that this could be increased to 52% by 1985, with most of the increase coming in Latin America and Africa. Rather less than half the world's arable land is in the developing countries; whether this can be further increased in the next thirty years it is difficult to say, but it seems likely as progressively poorer land is brought into cultivation that the costs of land clearance and the provision of the necessary infra-structure will prove ever more costly. In contrast to Western Europe in the nineteenth century, the developing countries cannot in the long run rely on food imports from abroad to support them in the future, although they have become increasingly dependent on imports over the last thirty

Table 69. *Potential, actual (1962) and proposed (1985) arable areas*

	Estimated potential area		Actual area		Proposed area	
	Million ha	%[a]	Million ha	% of potential	Million ha	% of potential
Africa south of Sahara	304	19	152	50	189	62
Asia and Far East	252	47	211	84	223	88
Latin America	570	29	130	23	169	30
Near East and North[b] West Africa	19	6	19	100	19	100
Total	1145	26	512	45	600	52

[a] Of total land area of each region.
[b] North West Africa only as no estimate of potential arable made for Near East.
SOURCE: FAO, *Provisional indicative world plan for agricultural development* (2 vols, Rome, 1970), vol. 1, p. 49.

years. North America has become the major source of grain exports, and there most of the cultivable land is now under crops.[12]

The reduction of fallow and the spread of multiple cropping

In the medieval period much of Western Europe pursued a cropping system whereby half the arable land in any one season was left fallow; this was thought necessary to conserve soil fertility and to allow weeds to be removed. In the following centuries the two-field system was replaced by the three-field system, whereby only one-third was left fallow in any one year, and eventually the fallow was rendered unnecessary by the introduction of root crops that if drilled allowed cultivation during their growth, and by the growth of clover which helped to maintain soil nitrogen and provided fodder for livestock whose dung, in turn, contributed to the maintenance and indeed increase of soil fertility. In western farming systems weeding has increasingly been achieved by the use of herbicides, and chemical fertilisers have been used to maintain crop yields.

In many parts of the developing world fallowing is a major feature of farming systems, particularly in the humid tropical lowlands and the savannas of Africa and Latin America, and in the upland areas of south-east Asia. The fallow is often long in these regions – up to twenty-five years in some areas. In rainforest areas the clearance of the forest exposes the soil to very high temperatures and the impact of rainstorms; if the land is cropped consecutively for more than three or four years, soil fertility declines, and soil erosion often ensues. However, if secondary forest is allowed to re-establish

Table 70. *Indices of multiple cropping in Asia*

	1880	1900	1910	1920	1930	1940	1950	1960	Nutritional density 1960[a]
North Vietnam	—	—	—	—	—	—	—	147	1130
South Korea	—	—	—	—	—	138[b]	146	150	750
Taiwan	—	—	116	118	132	131	151	180	667
Egypt	100	138	142	145	146	158	159	175	606
East Pakistan	—	—	—	—	—	—	127	126	530
China	—	—	—	—	149[c]	—	131	139	441
South Vietnam	—	—	—	—	—	—	—	112	437
Japan	—	—	—	—	148	—	152	140	391
Philippines	—	—	—	—	—	127	126	136	381
West Pakistan	—	—	—	—	—	—	111	108	236
Thailand	—	—	—	—	—	—	—	101	220
India	—	114[d]	115[d]	112[d]	115[d]	115[d]	113	114	210
Burma	—	—	—	—	—	107	—	107	104

[a] Total population per km² of arable land.
[b] All Korea.
[c] Sample survey.
[d] British India.

SOURCES: D. G. Dalrymple, *Survey of multiple cropping in less developed nations*, US Department of Agriculture, Foreign Economic Development Service (Washington, 1971), 60–97; G. Blyn, *Agricultural trends in India, 1891–1947; output availability and productivity* (Philadelphia, 1966), p. 42; S. McCune, *Korea's heritage: a regional and social geography* (Tokyo, 1957), p. 85.

itself, the nutrient cycle between forest, litter and soil is re-established and the former level of fertility is restored. Such a system is only possible if population density is low; as population increases, the length of the fallow has to be reduced. In many parts of Africa the reduction of the fallow has had adverse effects: soil fertility diminished and soil erosion has destroyed many areas. As yet no satisfactory system has been devised except for the simulation of the forest by the planting of a combination of tree and shrubs. Thus the further reduction of the fallow in parts of Africa – particularly in the savannas – may have adverse effects unless it is accompanied by the expansion of the area under irrigation or the heavy application of fertilisers.[13]

But the tropics – in which most of the developing nations are to be found – do have one major possibility not open to farmers in much of Western Europe either now or in the past. Given an adequate supply of water, the growing season is long enough for two or even three major crops to be grown during one season. Double – or more accurately multiple – cropping is closely associated with the cultivation of rice, and is unimportant outside Asia; generally a summer rice crop is followed by the sowing of wheat or barley in the autumn, more exceptionally two rice crops are grown in the year. The indices of multiple cropping – relating the total area sown to crops in the year to the total arable – are at their highest in Taiwan, where the index is 180. In North Vietnam, China and Korea it is about 150, in Java, the Philippines and East Pakistan in the 130s, but lower than this in most of Asia, and little practised elsewhere except in Egypt (table 70). The increase in multiple cropping might seem to offer considerable prospects of increasing output, but it is not without its problems. Most multiple cropping requires irrigation, and also, if rice is followed by wheat or barley, an efficient method of moving water off the fields. It also needs varieties of cereals which will develop in a short growing season; one of the frequently advertised advantages of the new high yielding varieties of rice and wheat is that they do mature in a shorter period than traditional varieties. Two crops in a year also increases labour demand, but this is sometimes seen as an advantage if it affords employment to the landless. One crop a year, particularly if it is rice, does not make too great demands upon soil fertility, but double cropping necessitates the use of chemical fertilisers. Thus multiple cropping would appear to offer considerable opportunities of expanding the area under crops, and some authorities believe that it offers greater opportunities for increasing output than trying to increase crop yields. Much of Asia still has little multiple cropping, and it is virtually unknown in most of Latin America and Africa. However it does require considerable investment; irrigation is usually a prerequisite but as yet little of the developing world's area is irrigated, only 93 million hectares out of 740 million hectares, some 12%. This suggests that the future expansion of multiple-cropping may not be as rapid as some writers believe.[14]

Multiple cropping is not a new technique. In Egypt and Iraq it has a long history, as it has in most of Asia. It is likely that multiple cropping is a function of population pressure; there is some correlation between population density and the index of multiple cropping (table 70), and the growth of population has often been a cause of a rise in the index. Thus in Java, between 1900 and 1940, farmers only kept up with population growth by increasing the double cropping of not only the irrigated wet-rice lands, the *sawah*, but also the drylands, the *tegalan*.[15]

The adoption of higher yielding crops

Many writers believe that European population growth in the nineteenth century was only possible because of the adoption of two American food plants, the potato and maize, which gave higher yields per hectare than the traditional cereals. Similar possibilities of substitution exist in the developing world at present. The major food crops grown in Africa (table 3) vary greatly in yield: manioc, for example, yields thirteen times the weight of millets, and although the calorific content of manioc is lower, the calorific yield of root crops is well above that of cereals. In Asia the relative importance of crops is different from that in Africa (table 71). The relatively intensive methods

Table 71. *Staple crop yields and calorific output in Asia*

	Average yield, 1948–52 tonnes/ha	Calories per 100 grams	Index of calorific yield
Wheat	0.82	350	207
Maize	0.86	360	224
Millet and sorghum	0.4	345	100
Rice	1.4	359	364
Sweet potatoes and yams	7.8	95	536
Manioc	7.0	109	552
Bananas	12.0	75	652

SOURCES: B. F. Johnston, *The staple food economies of western tropical Africa* (Stanford, 1958), p. 126; FAO, *Production yearbook 1957* (Rome, 1958), pp. 31–2.

of growing rice mean that although crop has a lower calorific yield than the root crops, the latter's advantage is not as great in Asia as in Africa.

Although peasant cultivators are often thought to be conservative in their food preferences and reluctant to grow unfamiliar crops, there is evidence of new crops being adopted quite rapidly in the past. In the sixteenth century American crops were introduced into China both across the Pacific and from India. Groundnuts, sweet potatoes and maize were known in most parts of the country by the end of the seventeenth century. But it was the remarkable population growth of the eighteenth century, when the population grew from 150 million in 1700 to 313 million in 1794 and 430 million in 1850, that accelerated their adoption. The sweet potato did not displace rice, but was grown on upland areas in the south which had hitherto been unused.[16] In Java wet-rice cultivation was the major form of land use at the beginning of the nineteenth century, and the rapid increase in population led to its expansion where irrigation facilities could be extended. But by 1880 little land was left that was suitable for rice, and the Javanese turned to American crops, including sweet potatoes and manioc. At first these crops, known together with maize and groundnuts as *palwidja*, were grown as second crops on the *sawah*, or rice land, but about 1900 they began to be grown on the dry upland areas. Since then the area under dry crops has grown more rapidly than the area under wet-rice, and this led to a fundamental change in the Javanese diet. In 1900 the average supply of food per head consisted of 110 kg of rice, 30 kg of tubers and 3 kg of pulses. By 1940 this had become 85 kg of rice, 40 kg of maize, 180 kg of tubers and 10 kg of pulses. By the 1950s the area under dryland crops exceeded that under rice, an unprecedented change in land use, and one forced on the Javanese by their rapid population growth.[17]

Equally dramatic changes have occurred this century in African food crops.

Before the arrival of Europeans African farmers relied on indigenous crops, and some Asian crops brought to the east coast. In the savannas pearl millet, fonio and sorghum were the staples, on the west coast African rice and yams. Manioc was introduced into Africa by the Portuguese in the sixteenth century, but at the beginning of the present century it was only important in the Congo; since then its use has greatly expanded. Not only does it outyield the preferred African root crop, yams, but it is more tolerant of drought, and will yield well on poor, eroded soils. But there is no doubt that the major cause of its increase in this century is the rapid growth of population. By 1970 it was the major food crop in tropical Africa, accounting for one-third of the volume of output of food crops. The expansion of maize has been equally dramatic; little known at the beginning of this century in southern Africa, it is now the leading crop in a zone south from Lake Victoria to Natal; it has displaced the lower yielding and less reliable millets as population has grown.[18]

Over the last thirty years the area under both roots and cereals has expanded in all parts of the developed world. But in Africa and Latin America where root crops were already widely grown in 1950, cereals have increased more rapidly in area of production than roots and tubers; in Asia on the other hand roots have increased much more rapidly than cereals. Between 1948–52 and 1974–6 the area under cereals increased by only one-fifth, but that under roots tripled.[19] Whether further population growth will further increase the area under root crops remains to be seen, but many authorities believe that they are a neglected way of increasing food output. Although there is a natural resistance to new and nutritionally inferior food crops, as there was in eighteenth-century Europe, necessity may prove a spur as potent as it was in nineteenth-century Europe.

Improving crop yields

It used to be thought that the eighteenth and early nineteenth centuries saw remarkable increases in crop yields in Britain, and somewhat later in Western Europe. As was seen in earlier chapters the absence of reliable series of figures on crop yields makes this difficult to confirm or disprove, but in much of Western Europe the rate of increase in yield per hectare before the 1820s or 1830s seems to have been slow; the expansion of the area under cultivation and the increased frequency of cropping must have been at least as important as rising yields in increasing food output. Before the 1830s the possibilities of increasing output were limited. The main means were the greater application of fertiliser, mainly livestock manure, combined with lesser amounts of a wide variety of materials such as marl, lime, and crushed bones; second was the more careful cultivation of the seed-bed and more frequent and careful weeding during growth. Subsidiary contributions to greater yields may have come from the more careful selection of seed, a subject about which little is known, and the underdraining of heavy soils. But as was argued earlier, traditional agriculture in Western Europe seems to have been incapable, between the thirteenth and the early nineteenth century, of more than doubling crop yields. And this increase, from a national average of 670 kg/ha or slightly less in thirteenth-century England, to 1340 kg/ha or more in the early nineteenth century, did not come in a short period in the eighteenth and nineteenth centuries, but was spread out over a much larger period, with, however, most of the gains coming after 1620. It was not until the middle of the nineteenth century that agriculture began to rely on new inputs from industry: oil-cake concentrates were imported to feed livestock, guano came from Peru, and in the 1840s the artificial fertiliser industry got underway, although the successful production of nitrogenous fertilisers was not possible until the 1920s; cheap and efficient underdrainage with tiles dates only from the 1840s; the use of machinery on any scale for the most part post-dates 1850. Even the adoption of these new inputs was slow, and the later nineteenth century saw few revolutionary increases in crop yields.

Indeed if the term agricultural revolution means a radical increase in farm productivity over a short period, then its use must be confined to the last forty years, when truly revolutionary gains have been made in crop yields; before the 1940s crop yields had risen slowly over a long period. The increase in yields since the 1940s has been primarily due to improvements in the varieties of crop grown, the greater application of chemical fertilisers, and the use of herbicides to eliminate weeds and of pesticides to reduce the loss of crops during growth. All these techniques have their origin in the nineteenth century – although successful plant breeding dates from the very end of the century – but their widespread adoption by farmers has been a relatively recent feature.[20]

It is perhaps not surprising that the rate of increase in agricultural productivity in the century after 1750 was slow; industrial inputs were not yet available to the majority of farmers. But farmers in the less developed world today have two distinct ways of improving crop yields: by improving the existing methods of traditional agriculture, and by using the inputs of modern agricultural technology – chemical fertilisers, herbicides and pesticides, and machinery.

Crop yields 1950–75

In the period after the end of the Second World War there was a major contrast in crop yields between the countries in the developed and the developing world; but there were already marked differences between countries of the developing world. Of the major food crops, wheat yielded in Europe twice what it did in north Africa, the Near East and the Far East. Maize yields in Europe compared unfavourably with those in the United States, but were well above those obtaining in central and southern America, Africa or Asia. Rice yields in Europe were three times the average of Asia; but within Asia there were marked regional differences – yields in China, Korea, Japan, Taiwan and northern Vietnam were well above those in the Indian subcontinent or in mainland south-east Asia.[21]

Between 1948–52 and 1957–9 the average yield of twelve major food crops in the developing nations rose by 11%, and between 1957–9 and 1966–8 by a further 13%; but these increases lagged behind those in the developed world where the increases were, respectively 26% and 29%.[22] Thus in the mid-1960s, in spite of some increase in crop yields, average yields were still well below those in the developed countries. The average yield of all cereals in Western Europe and North America was over twice that in the developing countries. But between 1961–5 and 1974–6 the developing countries have made considerable advances, the yield of all cereals increasing by about a quarter. Thus since 1948–52 cereal yields in the developed countries have doubled, those in the developing world have increased by approximately one-third.[23] Such figures need to be treated with some caution, for yield estimates for the developing countries may be inflated by the inclusion of production from multiple cropping, and by inaccurate reporting, but nonetheless they do suggest widespread gains in crop yields. Further, the rate of increase compares favourably with that achieved in nineteenth-century Europe: the average yield of wheat in Britain increased by less than 50% between 1800 and 1900, that of all crops in France by 36% between 1880 and 1950, with Britain showing the same rate of increase in that period.[24] Since the end of the Second World War an increasing proportion of the total putput of the developing countries has come from yield increases. Between 1948–52 and 1957–9 only 37% of the growth of output came from yield increases, 63% from increases in the area under crops, between 1957–8 and 1966–8 51% came from yield increases, but between 1961–5 and 1974–6 two-thirds of the increase in cereal output was due to an increase in yields.[25]

What was the source of these increases? Traditional agriculture was perfectly capable of increasing output per hectare. Rice yields in China, for example, are estimated to have doubled between 1400 and 1850, a rate of increase comparable to that attained with wheat yields in England over the same period.[26] Increased rice yields in east Asia have been obtained by more careful cultivation, more weeding and greater care in harvesting; soil fertility has been maintained by irrigation, for water brings nutrients in solution, and by the presence of algae in the paddy fields that help fix nitrogen; above all east Asian farmers applied a wide range of organic fertilisers. But in much of the developing world such practices were unknown; livestock farming has not been integrated with crop production as it was in the traditional mixed farming of Western Europe; in some countries, notably in India and the Middle East, dung was used as a fuel. Further, there are few tropical legumes which can play the role that artificial grasses did in Western Europe or the algae did in east Asian paddy fields.

Rapid increases in crop yields only came when industrial technologies were applied to agriculture; before 1945 such advances were most striking in east Asia, and to a lesser extent Egypt, although new technologies were applied to plantation crops in many parts of the developing world. In Japan and Taiwan rice yields rose markedly, especially between 1920 and 1940, and this can be attributed to the adoption of improved varieties and the greater application of chemical fertilisers. But in much of the rest of Asia there were negligible increases in crop yields, indeed in the Indian subcontinent there was a decline in the average yield of all food grains between 1900 and 1940.[27]

In the immediate post-war period there were slow increases in crop yields, but these have accelerated since the mid-1960s with the wider adoption of new hybrid varieties of wheat and rice, and the inputs associated with this programme. The breeding of new varieties of crops is not new, although plant breeding for specific characteristics largely post-dates the rediscovery of Mendel's theories at the beginning of this century. The most striking advance before 1945 was the breeding and rapid diffusion of hybrid corn in the United States. After 1945 semi-dwarf wheats were bred in Mexico, and later new varieties of rice were bred at the International Rice Institute in the Philippines. The variety 1R-8 was released in 1966, and ten further improved rice varieties have since become available. By 1974–5 38% of the wheat area in non-Communist Asia and 26% of the rice was sown with the improved high-yielding varieties. The bulk of this was in India, which accounted for 61% of the improved wheat area and 51% of the rice. Outside of Asia the new rice varieties have made little progress, though some improved wheat is grown in North Africa, and in Mexico the bulk of the wheat area is in improved varieties. The new varieties have been bred to respond to chemical fertilisers; unlike most indigenous varieties they are short-stemmed and do not 'lodge' with a heavy grain. On the other hand their advantage is slight unless they receive heavy applications of chemical fertiliser and are properly irrigated. It is these characteristics which have limited their more widespread adoption. About three-quarters of all improved rice in Asia is grown in areas of irrigation or abundant rainfall. On the other hand in only one-third of Asia is rice irrigated, and the absence of adequate water will limit the further adoption of improved varieties. The need for large applications of chemical fertiliser is a further factor limiting their spread; the cost of purchasing fertilisers – one-third of which have to be imported – limits the adoption of the new technology to the larger farms, and the rise in oil prices in the early 1970s increased fertiliser prices fourfold.[28]

Thus much of the yield increases obtained in the developing countries since 1945 have come from the import of modern scientific technologies; here is a marked contrast with Western Europe between 1750 and 1850, when increases in yield largely came from the wider adoption of traditional techniques. Even after 1850 crop yields increased very slowly. However while crop yields rose slowly, the adoption of machinery, particularly in the United

States and Australia, and to a lesser extent in Britain and some other parts of Western Europe, led to increases in output per man. Thus in France output per hectare rose by only 36% between 1880 and 1950, but output per man doubled, output per man over the same period tripled in Denmark, and nearly quadrupled in the United States.[29]

Such successes convinced many authorities after the Second World War that the successful development of agriculture in the developing world required the mechanisation of agriculture; but over much of Asia and Africa the use of the machinery of Western Europe was impractible as so few of the farms were large enough to use them economically, and few farmers could afford them. Their use was confined to areas of newer settlement. But even in the early 1950s there were some critics of a policy of mechanisation. In Western Europe there was little adoption of labour-saving machinery before 1850, for rural populations were still increasing and there was no shortage of cheap labour. More important was the improvement of implements to undertake tasks that more primitive tools were unable to achieve. It was only after the absolute decline of the agricultural population, and particularly of landless labourers that labour-saving machinery – principally the reaper – was adopted.

In the last decade the policy of mechanising agriculture has been much criticised. As agricultural populations have continued to grow, in spite of much rural–urban migration, so it has been argued that mechanisation creates unemployment and underemployment and agricultural techniques should be adjusted so as to absorb labour. One of the virtues of the new high-yielding varieties is that they sometimes require increases in labour input, particularly where multiple cropping becomes possible. It would however be wrong to argue that no mechanisation should be undertaken, for not all machinery replaces labour, and in some instances it can help to increase yields. Machinery is essential in the more difficult cases of land clearance. Rapid harvesting by machine may increase harvest yields. In Turkey the use of machines to sow winter wheat gained a month in the growing season and has led to a 38% increase in yields.[30] The use of machinery depends very much on local circumstances: in a study of some villages in Uttar Pradesh it was noted that the considerable landless population relied on the two harvests for their food supply, for they got a share of the harvest as reward; thus mechanisation of the harvest would be socially unjust. But irrigation and land preparation had always been undertaken by family labour alone, and the use of power or machinery here would obviate much hardship, do the job more efficiently and not threaten the landless.[31] It is clear that generalisations about the usefulness of mechanisation must be modified to fit local circumstances. But it is worth recalling again the widespread introduction of labour-saving machinery in Western Europe was not profitable until the labour force began to decline; there seems little prospect of this occurring in much of the developing world before the beginning of the next century. It may be that attention should be concentrated on improving existing implements and designing intermediate technologies appropriate to local circumstances.[32]

Rural industries

In pre-industrial Europe there was considerable economic diversity within the rural areas; manufacturing industry was not confined to the towns, and the fact that so many farms were beneath the subsistence level meant that many farmers had to supplement their incomes with work off the farm. In the nineteenth century this economic diversity dwindled. The growth of factory industry, the use of steam power and the gradual realisation of economies of scale with technological advance led to a slow decline of those rural industries whose products could be made with the new methods. Improved transport also helped urban goods to undercut local crafts and trades; in the twentieth century the rise of the bus and lorry led to the concentration of services in the larger rural towns and their decline in the villages.

It was not surprising then that in the post-war period, planning in the underdeveloped world was based on the assumption that industrialisation would be large scale, capital intensive and urban-located. But by the 1960s considerable drawbacks to this policy were apparent. Not only was western technology expensive and labour saving, but the population growth of the 1950s was leading to rapid expansion of the labour force seeking employment in the towns; urban unemployment was becoming a serious problem. But the countryside's difficulties were equally great, for a high rate of natural increase ensured a continued growth in the rural population. As this growth is expected to continue in the developing world until at least the beginning of the next century some means of absorbing the labour surplus had to be found.

Some employment has been found in agriculture itself. The expansion of the cultivated area requires extra labour, as it did in nineteenth-century Europe, the growth of higher-yielding root crops, such as cassava and yams, increases labour demand, as did the potato in Europe. The introduction of high-yielding varieties also requires extra labour, particularly where multiple cropping is established; the greater application of fertilisers requires extra labour, and in traditional agriculture higher yields are invariably a partial result of more careful cultivation of the seed-bed.[33] But agriculture has not been able to absorb the extra labour force, just as European agriculture was unable to absorb all available labour by the 1830s. It has thus been argued that attempts should be made to restrain rural–urban migration and provide employment by encouraging industry in the countryside.

By no means all the rural population of the developing countries depends on agriculture for a livelihood; the non-farm population is already a considerable proportion. In Sri Lanka 38% of the rural population is employed in manufacturing or services, the figure falls as low as 9.5% for Turkey but for most countries for which estimates are available the range is narrower, between 20% and 33%.[34] Furthermore, much of the agricultural population depends on non-farm activities to supplement income. In Iran, for example, the proportion of the agricultural population supplementing income by handicrafts varied by region from 24% to 42%, while in Java 33% of farmers had to resort to off-farm work.[35] It could be that the expansion of industry in the rural areas could not only help to augment the present low incomes, but could also absorb the future growth of the rural population, for there seems little prospect that this will be absorbed in urban industry. It is envisaged that there will be the expansion of existing handicraft industries, producing traditional consumer goods; thus in Iran rural industry already includes the processing of wool and silk, the weaving of carpets and textiles, the making of shoes, and crafts using wood, pottery and embroidery.[36] In many rural areas it should be possible to establish firms processing agricultural products for sale both at home and abroad. Many rural regions in the developing areas lack skilled men in those crafts that service agriculture – notably in metal-working – and the development of small-scale industrial establishments making agricultural implements adapted to local conditions would not only provide employment but benefit agricultural operations. A further possible source of employment lies in the marketing of agricultural produce, a sector which is only weakly developed in many developing countries. The presumption is that industrial development will be small-scale, labour intensive, using local materials, and with low capital costs, using not the sophisticated machinery of Western technologies, but an intermediate technology appropriate to local conditions.[37] Such a policy requires efficient organisation and institutions, and seems to have been most successful in China, where the communes have been the organisational unit for agricultural and industrial development, where technology has been small-scale and labour intensive, and where attempts at developing self-reliance have been successful.[38] Clearly this all contrasts sharply with European experience, where nineteenth-century industrialisation undermined rural society. But it does show many parallels with earlier ways of absorbing labour surpluses in rural Europe.

Conclusions

A majority of the increase in food output in the developing world in the last thirty years has come from increasing the area under crops. This may remain an important remedy in parts of Africa and South America in the coming half century, but in Asia there is little potentially cultivable land left, and increases in yields will have to provide the considerable increases in output which are needed simply to maintain the present poor diets. Gloomy though the prospects may seem, the developing countries do at least have the possibility of adopting high-yielding technologies, costly though these may be. Western Europe did not have such technologies in the early stages of the population boom; not until after 1850 were industro-agricultural technologies available and they were not widely adopted until after 1940. In the intermediate period much of Western Europe relied on imports of food from abroad, and also imported feeding stuffs. In effect it is only recently that Western Europe has ceased to increase output primarily by extending the area under cultivation.

CHAPTER 19

CONCLUSIONS

We may begin by noting that European population history of the last millennium consists not of two phases – slow growth before 1750 and rapid since – but of five. From AD 1000 to 1347 population increased, but between 1347 and 1351 it fell dramatically. From 1450 population began to increase again, and continued to do so in southern Europe until about 1600. In the seventeenth century, populations in many parts of southern Europe declined, and did not begin to grow again until the second half of the eighteenth century. In northern Europe however – particularly in the Netherlands, Scandinavia and Britain – the population growth of the sixteenth century continued until 1650, and only then did it stagnate, to revive, in common with much of the rest of Europe, about 1750.

Within each of these three great periods there were distinctive changes in the rate of increase. Evidence for the period 1000 to 1340 is the least reliable but it is possible that the most rapid rates of increase were in the twelfth century, that rates declined in the late thirteenth century, and that in the early fourteenth century there were actual falls in total numbers in many parts of western Europe – that is, before the catastrophic loss of life in the Black Death between 1347 and 1351. For the period between 1450 and 1650 there is more evidence, although it is far from reliable. From 1450 to 1500 population grew, but slowly, from 1500 to 1550 growth was rapid, but in the second half of the sixteenth century, although population continued to grow, the rate was less rapid than in the first half of the sixteenth century. By the seventeenth century population in southern Europe was declining, while the rate of increase in the Netherlands and England in the first half of the seventeenth century was below the rates attained in the sixteenth century.

The revival in the eighteenth century was at comparatively modest rates of increase; only after 1820 were high rates of increase reached, and these continued throughout the rest of the nineteenth century, although in many, but not all parts of Western Europe, rates were lower in the second half of the nineteenth century than in the first. The extreme cases were France and Ireland, where stagnation and decline respectively occurred after the 1840s. In Britain rates of increase were slightly lower in the second half of the nineteenth century than they were in the first, as they were in Denmark and Norway; on the other hand in Holland, Belgium, Germany and Finland they were higher.[1] By the 1920s however rates of increase had fallen very low everywhere in Western Europe.

Two points are worthy of note here. First, the rates of increase attained in the century of growth 1750–1850 were in many parts of Western Europe not greatly higher than those achieved in the late fifteenth and early sixteenth centuries. Thus the province of Holland grew at 0.8% p.a. between 1514 and 1622, the Netherlands at 0.8% p.a. from 1750 to 1850; France grew at 0.6% p.a. between 1450 and 1550, but only at 0.5% p.a. from 1750 to 1850. No reliable evidence exists for the earliest period of growth, but if England and France grew at about 0.5% p.a. between 1050 and 1340, it seems very possible that there were rates of increase higher than this in the twelfth century.

Secondly, the distinctive curve of growth in each of the periods of increase – slow growth followed by rapid growth, followed by a slowing rate of growth – has attracted the attention of mathematicians and biologists, who have attempted to devise formulae to describe what they call the logistic curve. Most of the attempts made by mathematicians haved used modern population figures and have dealt with fairly short periods – G. U. Yule, for example, used the nineteenth-century census data for England, the United States, France and Finland. Biologists have observed the rate of growth of animals under controlled conditions; most notable are the experiments by R. Pearl with *Drosophila melanogaster*. Subsequently he tested the formula derived from these experiments with the population growth of American cities. More recently Rondo Cameron has noted that in the last thousand years population has had three periods of growth each approximating to a logistic curve; he has suggested that these form more useful periods for the study of economic growth than the more conventional periods based on political history.[2] Indeed schematically European population history can be seen more profitably as three successive logistic curves rather than the more conventional slow increase with a rapid upturn since 1750. This is particularly noticeable if only rural populations are considered in the third period of growth (fig. 25). What is of interest here is, first, the relationship between agricultural change and the logistic curve; and, second, the demographic changes that have caused these variations in the rate of increase.

The logistic curve seems to be explicable in terms of optimum theory. In AD 1000 and in 1450, at the beginning of the first two cycles, Western Europe was relatively sparsely populated and may indeed have been underpopulated, so that once population growth was initiated average output and marginal output rose as more dense populations allowed greater specialisation and division of labour, and spread social overhead costs. Once population was growing, it impelled an expansion of the cultivated area; in both the eleventh and fifteenth centuries there was probably still goodish land available for reclamation. As population continued to grow the simple expansion of the cultivated land was insufficient to maintain output, but the farmers of

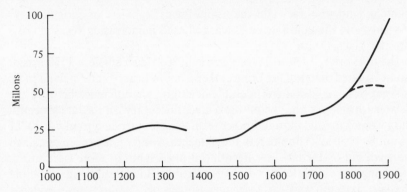

Fig. 25. A schematic representation of population growth in Western Europe. Continuous line, total population; broken line, rural population.

medieval and early modern Europe did not have the techniques radically to increase yields. Thus as population continued to grow, farmers sought to reduce the fallow, to supplement their incomes from non-agricultural activities or migrated to the towns. But as optimum densities for the existing techniques and resources were exceeded, so the production responses available proved inadequate to maintain incomes per head. Not only did the structural and land use symptoms of overpopulation appear, but average output per head began to fall towards the minimum subsistence level; as in Malthusian theory, the preventive and positive checks began to operate. Marriage was deferred so that fertility was reduced, and the erosion of living standards led to a rise in mortality, so that population growth became very slow or even declined.

Such an interpretation seems reasonable, and indeed has been often put forward to explain both the falling rates of population increase about 1300 and 1600, and the failure of medieval and early modern agriculture to maintain income per head or *a fortiori* to increase income per head and achieve sustained economic growth. But what were the demographic trends that accounted for the falling rates of population increase at the end of each of these cycles? There is unfortunately little reliable evidence before the nineteenth century, and little at all in the Middle Ages. If it is accepted that the rate of population increase was falling at the end of the thirteenth century, was this due to falling fertility or rising mortality? It is generally assumed that marriage was early and universal in the Middle Ages; and there is unfortunately no evidence to show whether attempts were being made to limit fertility in the late thirteenth century. It has therefore been assumed that the slower rate of population growth and indeed an apparent absolute decline from 1300 to 1347 – *before* the Black Death – was brought about by rising mortality; but the demographic evidence for such an assumption is fragile. Nonetheless many historians believe that by the thirteenth century population growth had outrun the land resources and the technological capacity of agriculture to raise yields, and the fall in incomes was reflected in increasing years of crisis before the Black Death.

In the next cycle, 1450 to 1650, there is little evidence before 1550 except for some isolated material for France. However, in France and England there does seem to have been a considerable demographic difference between the late sixteenth century and the mid-seventeenth century. In the late sixteenth century women in England and France seem to have married typically at 20–22 years but by 1650 at 25 or older; in the sixteenth century few women remained unmarried, but by the late seventeenth century a tenth or more were single. These changes probably led to a decline in fertility. But if fertility was declining in the late sixteenth and early seventeenth centuries there is also evidence that mortality was rising. Thus the falling rate of population increase seems to have been a result of both declining fertility and rising mortality.

Unfortunately the relationships between the decline in income per head and changes in fertility and mortality are not so easy to substantiate as might seem; this is particularly true of the relationships between income and mortality.[3] Common sense suggests that a fall in income per head towards the minimum level of subsistence would lead to a lower intake of food, less warm clothing, and poorer housing conditions. But studies of mortality in the seventeenth and eighteenth centuries suggest that crisis years – years of very high death rates – were a result either of epidemics of contagious diseases or of harvest failure. Neither of these is necessarily related to population density or the rate of population growth. There are several reasons why mortality could rise.

First, falling output per head could lead to a rise in 'normal mortality', that is to say a long-term process not related to poor climate or pandemics, but to a falling consumption of food and other necessities, and thus giving less immunity to endemic diseases such as dysentery or tuberculosis. There is no need to invoke 'crisis' years in this case.

Secondly, it can be argued that the incidence of harvest failures due to bad weather and pandemics of contagious disease occurred regularly between AD 1000 and the late seventeenth century, that these occurrences were not more frequent at particular periods. However, they caused crisis years – years of exceptionally high death rates – only at times when income per head had fallen so low that the population was malnourished, and thus more likely to catch contagious diseases and less capable of surviving the disease once caught.

Thus although harvest failure or epidemics might have been as common in the early stages of population growth, when output per head was being maintained, as in the later stages, when it was falling, crisis years only appear in the demographic record when the population was suffering from falling living standards.

Thirdly, periods of high mortality could be independent of income per head; harvest failure was primarily a function of climatic accidents, particularly wet summers and autumns, when the harvest was destroyed and the autumn crop had to be sown late, thus reducing yields. It is possible then, that long-term changes in the climate of Western Europe influenced the frequency of crisis years, and thus of periods of high mortality. A similar periodisation of epidemics of contagious disease – particularly bubonic plague – has also been claimed, although not necessarily as a function of climate; its absence in this period of growth between 1000 and 1347, its diminishing significance in the early fifteenth century, its return in the later sixteenth century, and its final disappearance from northern Europe in the late seventeenth century and southern Europe after 1721 has an obvious parallelism with periods of population growth and stagnation. It may be that other diseases had a similar periodisation. Under these circumstances it is not necessary to invoke changes in income per head as a cause of increasing mortality.

Thus the ending of the first two periods of population growth cannot be unequivocally attributed to rising mortality; this is even less true of the third cycle of growth in the eighteenth and nineteenth centuries, and the falling rates of population increase in the first half of the present century. After 1850 – when rates of increase were falling in some parts of Western Europe – there was a universal decline in mortality; there was then no question of population growth being halted by rising mortality. Even the Irish famine, which appears to fit the Malthusian model of falling incomes, with an increasing incidence of crisis years after 1815 and then finally catastrophic mortality, was a result mainly of the potato blight and the maladministration of famine relief. The same is true of the underdeveloped world at present. Although most parts of the underdeveloped world have had rapid rates of population increase since 1920, and, since 1950 at quite unprecedentedly high rates, mortality has not risen to reverse this trend. This is partly of course because in most of the underdeveloped world output of food has kept up with population growth. Further, even where there have been cases of famine they have been due largely to climatic accidents.

Thus there is no sign that rising mortality halted the third cycle of population growth in Europe – quite the reverse indeed. Nor has rising mortality halted the present cycle of growth in the underdeveloped countries since 1920. Again, the reverse is true; population growth has been prompted primarily by a long-term decline in mortality. The previous periods of declining population increase in the early fourteenth century and the seventeenth century *may* have been due to rising mortality, but the data are lacking to prove conclusively that this was so. To what extent then, have the cycles of growth been halted by falling fertility?

The demographic differences in age of marriage and the proportions remaining unmarried suggest a considerable contrast between the sixteenth century, an age of rapid growth, and the seventeenth century, an age of slow growth or decline. But it is difficult to evaluate the effect these changes had on fertility, and even more difficult to determine whether rising mortality or falling fertility was the greater cause of the undoubted falling rates of population increase in the seventeenth century. But given that the late sixteenth century and the early seventeenth century were periods of acute rural poverty for a majority of the rural population of Western Europe – with the possible exception of Holland – it does seem plausible to link the presumed falling incomes of the later sixteenth century with attempts to adjust fertility levels. What is less easy to explain is the considerable lag between the onset of falling incomes and the establishment of the European marriage pattern by the mid-seventeenth century. All that can be said is that there was a similar lag in the two later cycles of growth. In the nineteenth century rural poverty was at its greatest between 1815 and the 1850s. But it was not – with the exception of France and Ireland – until the 1870s that fertility began a continuous decline. This trend has been, almost without exception, attributed not to falling incomes, but to rising incomes and expectations and other allied causes. But it may be that this decline simply represents a delayed adjustment to the poverty of the first half of the nineteenth century.

A similar situation exists in the underdeveloped countries at present. In the nineteenth century population appears to have been growing in many parts of Latin America and Asia. Since 1920 the decline of the death rate has produced progressively higher rates of population increase. But it is only in the last decade that there has been any sign of widespread fertility decline. It would seem that regardless of the technology of birth control, marital habits change slowly in pre-industrial societies, even in those of the present day.

The symptoms of overpopulation

We conclude from the preceding section that there is no Malthusian overpopulation, where mortality rises to halt growth because incomes have fallen below the minimum level of subsistence, in the developing world today, nor did it bring about the slower rates of increase in Western Europe at the end of the nineteenth century and in the early twentieth century; that was due to falling fertility. Rising mortality may have caused the end of the first two cycles of growth, but there is insufficient evidence to confirm this. But this does not mean that there were no periods of overpopulation. In terms of optimum theory overpopulation occurs whenever average output per head falls below the maximum possible with given techniques and resources; although production and demographic responses can arrest the fall below subsistence level, they cannot always prevent the erosion of living standards and the appearance of symptoms of population pressure in the structure of agriculture and in land-use patterns. Thus in the late thirteenth and early fourteenth centuries, in the late sixteenth and seventeenth centuries, in the late eighteenth and early nineteenth centuries, and in the underdeveloped world today a variety of such symptoms appeared. These include the subdivision of farms and their fragmentation, the growth of landlessness both absolutely and as a proportion of the rural population, a growth in unemployment and underemployment; the decline of real wages for farm labourers and the real incomes of small farmers, while prices rise as demand outruns supply and price of land and rents follow prices upwards. Where the supply of land has been limited, there have been adverse consequences for land use. Arable land has been brought into cultivation at the expense of grazing land – on the poorer land this may lead to falling yields. A reduction in the supply of fodder reduces the supply of livestock and thus of manure and hence crop yields. On very poor land soil erosion may occur. Farmers may have to turn to higher-yielding but less palatable crops, such as the potato, and livestock become a progressively smaller part of the farm economy, and their products less important in the diet.

But while these symptoms appear at all periods of rapid population growth, the burden of population pressure has never fallen equally upon all sections of the rural population;[4] indeed at times of apparent rural poverty, with high unemployment, falling real wages and rising food prices, some at least have experienced prosperity. This was true, for example, of the landlords and larger farmers of late Elizabethan England; in sixteenth-century France seigneurial impoverishment was only relative, and the tenant farmers and landlords of early nineteenth-century England were in happier conditions than their constant complaints might suggest. Similarly today, while the lot of the landless and the smaller farmers of India – or indeed of most underdeveloped countries – is pitiful, that of the owners of land or the tenants of larger farms is less so. Such a contrast has led many to argue that population growth is not the true cause of rural poverty, and that it is imperfections in land tenure or the general organisation of society that are the fundamental cause of poverty. There is much truth in this; what, however, is important to notice is that, however equitably rural society is organised, rapid population growth will have adverse effects in the absence of technological and production responses.

The differing responses to population growth

Optimum theory is a static theory; it shows that average and marginal output will decline with population growth in the absence of changes in resources and technology. But population growth itself prompts production and demographic responses; indeed it is an assumption behind this book that the threat of overpopulation stimulates a variety of responses in order to put off a fall in output per head. Much of the interest of such a way of looking at agricultural history is that the responses differ from region to region and at different periods as, it is hoped, has been shown in this book.

The medieval period

In the first cycle of growth – and indeed until much later, the possibilities of both demographic and production responses were very limited. Farming techniques were primitive, and crop yields depended on the supply of manure, which diminished over time as grazing land was ploughed up, and the frequency with which the seed-bed was cultivated and weeded. The fallow afforded the opportunity for the latter, and the replacement of the ox by the horse allowed more frequent cultivations. The only leguminous crops available which helped to maintain soil fertility were peas, beans and vetches, which occupied a small proportion of the arable land before 1300. Thus there were limited possibilities of increasing crop yields between AD 1000 and 1300. Most of the increase in food output must have come from expanding the area under cultivation, but by 1250 there was little good land left, and in some regions intensification took the form of reducing the fallow by shifting from the two-field system to the three-field; this was not always accompanied by adequate means of maintaining soil fertility. By 1300 the technological possibilities of medieval agriculture were largely exhausted.

Demographic responses were equally limited: there was of course no possibility of overseas migration, nor did rural–urban migration offer much of a safety-valve. Only a very small proportion of the population lived in towns, except in the Low Countries and northern Italy, and between 1000 and 1340 rural populations and urban populations grew at much the same rate. Industry was still concentrated in the towns before 1340 and although the eleventh and twelfth centuries did see some growth in the number of craftsmen in the countryside, alternative forms of employment were few. On fertility adjustments little is known; it is perfectly possible that fertility could have been controlled as incomes fell in the thirteenth century, but there is little evidence to substantiate this. Thus the major demographic response to population growth – other than rising mortality – was rural–rural migration. The period from 1000 to 1300 was a great age of expansion in Western Europe, but by 1300 the expansion was over; most villages and hamlets had been founded by then, and there was little good land left.

The early modern period

Between 1450 and 1650 the population of most of Western Europe went through another period of growth followed by stagnation, and in the late sixteenth century most regions were exhibiting symptoms of population pressure; rural poverty seems to have reached a nadir in the 1620s in England, and in France most of the seventeenth century was one of chronic poverty. Nor were there any great advances in agricultural technology. When population began to grow again after 1450 there was land available for reclamation which had been abandoned or laid down to grass in the period of declining population between 1347 and the mid-fifteenth century. But a century of population growth exhausted most of this supply, and by the later sixteenth century only marginal land remained. Nor were there, before 1600, any fundamental advances in farming methods that could have substantially increased crop yields, although the wider adoption of known techniques could have raised average yields, so that by 1600 crop yields may have stood a little above those of the Middle Ages. Undoubtedly in England in the sixteenth century there was less arable in fallow – the two-field system hardly survived – and in the southern Low Countries new methods of replacing the fallow were being devised. But in much of the rest of Europe there was little reduction in fallow and few advances in crop yields. Not surprisingly the seventeenth century – or at least the first half of it – was one of poverty and falling rates of population increase.

However, the peasants of early seventeenth-century Europe did not fall to the abject level of their forebears of the fourteenth century. In the first place the end of the power of the urban guilds – except in Holland – saw a dispersal of manufacturing industry into rural areas, and the sixteenth century was one of rapid growth of rural industry throughout Western Europe; this not only provided employment for the growing numbers without land, but the spread of the domestic organisation of industry provided supplementary incomes on the smaller peasant farms. Improvements in transport also provided – in a few regions – the opportunity of regional specialisation and concentration on high-value products. Even on very small holdings wine-growers and dairy farmers could make a better living than those with larger holdings who still needed to provide most of their own consumption needs. Lastly, there was a greater proliferation of trades and crafts in the sixteenth century than in the medieval period, and thus there were more outlets for productive employment for the landless.

But the seventeenth century is of greatest importance for the widening of the demographic options. In the first place, as noted earlier, it saw the appearance of the West European pattern of late marriage and a comparatively high proportion unmarried. There may too have been some attempt to limit births within marriage. This pattern appears to have emerged between the late sixteenth century and the mid-seventeenth century and it is possible to interpret it as an attempt to defend the erosion of living standards. Overseas migration became, for the first time, possible for relieving population pressure, although it was of little significance except in Spain and England; nor would it be wise to attribute this transatlantic movement simply to poverty at home. More significant was the increasing importance of rural–urban migration. In both medieval and early modern times natural increase in rural areas exceeded that in urban areas. Indeed in most towns, and particularly in the larger towns, death rates exceeded birth rates, and thus urban growth relied on rural–urban migration. In the medieval period this did not help much in relieving rural population pressure, but in the sixteenth and seventeenth centuries the emergence of a number of great cities, and in the Low Countries and England some *urbanisation* of the population, did for the first time offer a significant outlet.

Thus the rural poverty of the late sixteenth and seventeenth centuries was less than that experienced in the fourteenth century. But this was not because of any technological breakthrough in agriculture, which showed little advance on the Middle Ages, it was due more to the adoption of the European marriage pattern and the growth of non-agricultural opportunities of employment in both town and country.

But the seventeenth century has other interests. While much of Europe suffered acute population pressure in the late sixteenth century and poverty was widespread in the first half of the seventeenth century, the Netherlands, and particularly Holland, seem to have weathered the storm, and may indeed have raised income per head in the period between 1500 and 1650. Again, this was not due primarily to a radical advance in agricultural techniques. The most striking feature of the period was the great increase in the area under cultivation, although this came from land remarkably difficult to reclaim. Arable farming made some advance, although most of the new techniques were borrowed from the southern Low Countries; the emergence of specialised areas of horticulture was also of significance. More important were the improvements in dairy farming and the absorption of the growing landless population in productive employments within the countryside, and the ability of the towns to absorb a considerable rural–urban migration. Two underlying themes are noteworthy. First, rural Holland in 1500 was without the institutional obstacles to agricultural improvement which were found in most of the rest of Europe. The feudal system had never taken root, and thus while farmers paid tithe to the church there were no feudal dues. The open fields had largely been extinguished at the beginning of the sixteenth century and so village custom imposed fewer restraints on individual experimentation. Nearly half the farmers were freeholders, and many of the rest had tenancies with customs that compensated them for improvements. But the second point is of more note. The stimulus to rural improvement came largely from outside agriculture. It began with the Dutch control of the North Sea fisheries; from this they assumed command of much of European trade. This led to the rise of industries in the towns, and the growth of a prosperous middle class which could buy high-value agricultural products such as butter and vegetables, while the industries, shipping and fishing, could absorb the rural surplus. Finally, the Dutch control of the European grain trade freed many of their farmers from the need to produce their own grain, and allowed specialisation.

The seventeenth century has a second interest. In England it saw the critical change in farming methods as it did in the Low Countries. Before 1600 there had been little change in farming methods in England, but from then there was experimentation in such techniques as the water-meadow and the beginnings of convertible husbandry; by the 1650s turnips and clover were

Table 72. *The rural population of Europe in the nineteenth century (% of the population living in places of less than 5000)*

	1800	1850	1910
Germany	89.7	84.5	51.2
England and Wales	77.0	50.0	25.2
Belgium	82.1	66.0	43.4
Denmark	83.0	85.4	64.1
Spain	89.0	87.0	58.0
France	87.5	80.5	61.5
Netherlands	65.5	64.1	47.0
Sweden	94.9	93.5	77.4

SOURCE: Paul Bairoch, 'Population urbaine et taille des villes en Europe de 1600 à 1970: présentation de séries statistiques', *Revue d'Histoire Économique et Sociale*, 54 (1976), 312.

being grown, and during the following century were widely diffused through southern and eastern England. But in this century the incentive to improve agriculture in England did not come from the pressures of population growth, for there was little increase in population between 1650 and 1750, but from the necessity to adapt to changing product prices and to reduce production costs.

The eighteenth and nineteenth centuries

The third great period of European population growth began in the 1740s, accelerated in the first half of the nineteenth century, and continued to grow rapidly – except in France and Ireland – after 1850, although in many parts of Europe the second half of the century saw less rapid rates of increase than the first. But it was not until the twentieth century that there was a major decline in the rate of increase.

Historians have for the most part neglected the interrelationships between population growth and agriculture in the century and a half after 1750. This has been seen as an era of agricultural revolution, technological and organisational revolution in industry, of transport revolution, and the growth of a world economy focussed on Western Europe. Above all it is thought to have seen the end of the Malthusian connection between population and resources; output per head did not inevitably fall as population grew beyond resources. Instead incomes per head rose steadily throughout Western Europe. However, the analysis presented in the later chapters of this book conflicts with some of these accepted generalisations. The major points are restated here.

First, most of Western Europe remained overwhelmingly rural until the second half of the nineteenth century, and most of the increase in population between 1750 and 1850 had to be absorbed in the rural economy (table 72).

Only in Britain and Belgium was there any significant *urbanisation* or growth of the industrial population before 1850.

Secondly, with the exception of Britain and Ireland, the rates of population increase between 1750 and 1850 did not *greatly* exceed those found in the sixteenth century; it was the continued rapid growth beyond 1850, except in France and Ireland, that sets this period apart from the earlier periods. However if *rural* populations alone are considered then the curve of growth differs little from the two earlier cycles, for after 1850 the rural population declined in Ireland, France and Britain, and rose only very slowly elsewhere in Western Europe (fig. 25). This was due to the increase in rural–urban migration throughout Europe in the second half of the nineteenth century as industrial growth began to absorb the rural surplus. The *rural* populations of Western Europe thus repeated the pattern of stagnation or decline that had occurred in the fourteenth and seventeenth centuries, if for different reasons.

Thirdly, no clear reason can be given for the growth of population after 1750; neither demographic trends nor the underlying causes are sufficiently well documented before the middle of the nineteenth century. But the growth was universal in Western Europe and thus industrialisation can be excluded as a general causal factor and the belief that growing opportunities of employment in industry encouraged earlier marriage and greater fertility can hardly be true outside Britain, Belgium and a few parts of France and Germany. This does not exclude the possibility that there was an increase in fertility for other reasons; but the Scandinavian data suggest that from about 1810 there was a clear fall in the death rate. The precise cause of this decline is not easily determined.

Whatever the causes of population growth, there was rural population pressure in much of Western Europe by the 1820s, though the symptoms varied from country to country. In France and Ireland there was subdivision of farms; in England the growth of landlessness led to unemployment and underemployment; in most parts of Western Europe the real incomes of the landless and those with small farms fell. Contemporaries believed that inequitable land-tenure systems, as in Ireland, or the Poor Laws, as in England, were the main cause of poverty. But the universality of the phenomenon, in areas with quite different land-tenure systems suggests that the rural population had grown too large to provide farms of adequate size for all the rural population, or employment for all the landless.

How had this population growth been sustained? Here our analysis differs from most interpretations. What evidence there is on crop yields – the only quantifiable index of productivity change in agriculture at this time – suggests that there was no radical increase in the period between 1750 and 1850.

The upward trend in crop yields does not become significant in England until after 1830, although there had been slow improvements in the national average between 1650 and 1830. There is general agreement among historians that in France any increase in yields was delayed until after 1815, and possibly until later, while in Scandinavia the increase in crop yields in the nineteenth century was slow. Thus much of the increase in food output to sustain the doubling of population in Western Europe came from the increase in the area under crops, either by bringing new land into cultivation, or by reducing the area under fallow; neither of these techniques was new. On the other hand the adoption of the potato was new and the fact that – with the possible exception of Ireland – it only became a major food crop after 1800 suggests that it was adopted because of population pressure rather than being a cause of population growth. The combination of some increase in crop yields, the extension of the area under crops and the introduction of the high-yielding potato was sufficient to sustain the growth of population; but there are few signs of an improvement in the diet – either in quantity or quality – for the mass of the urban and rural populations before the 1840s. Nor is there much sign of any great advance in output per head within European agriculture, except possibly in limited parts of eastern England and northern France. A characteristic feature of the new farming methods in England was the greater labour inputs needed. In the mid-nineteenth century the flail and the scythe, or in many places still the sickle, were used to harvest the cereal crop. Only in England was the drill found in any numbers. Improved ploughs were more common, and doubtless helped to improve the preparation of the seed-bed. The implication of this analysis is that it is difficult to argue that there was a radical change in farming productivity in Western Europe before 1850, and thus difficult to see how agricultural progress could be a necessary pre-requisite to industrial revolution, as it is invariably assumed to be.

Thus the demographic responses to population growth are far more important than they are often allowed to be. In the 1820s, 1830s and 1840s there was a labour surplus in much of rural Europe, and it was difficult to find land or employment. Real wages were at best stagnant, more commonly falling. Whereas in the sixteenth and seventeenth centuries the dispersal of industry into the country provided employment for the rural poor, in the nineteenth century the rise of factory produced goods in England was already destroying rural industries in the British Isles, and was to do so later in much of the rest of Western Europe, while the extraordinary proliferation of trades and crafts in the countryside in mid-century is more a symptom of overpopulation than a sign of the 'soundness' of rural life.

The countries of Western Europe made a variety of demographic responses to population pressure. In France births were limited within marriage, but the marriage rate increased; there was no increase in celibacy. Overseas migration was of little significance, and even rural–urban migration was at a low rate, and would not have led to a decline in numbers had there not been a fall in fertility. In Ireland on the other hand, marriage began to be postponed from the 1820s, but marital fertility remained unchanged. In Norway there was little change in fertility until after 1900, but very considerable proportions of the natural increase emigrated as they did from Ireland. In Sweden there are some signs of both increasing celibacy and declining marital fertility from the middle of the nineteenth century; there was also emigration on a sizeable scale, and rural–urban migration. In England it is possible that there was a fall in fertility in the very early nineteenth century although it is more common to date it from the 1870s; there was also a large emigration, although as a proportion of the population this was small. What was of greatest importance in England was migration from the rural areas to the towns, which by the 1860s was so great that the absolute size of the rural population began to decline. In France rural–urban migration combined with falling fertility also led to a decline in the rural population from the 1860s, while a similar decline began in much of the rest of Western Europe by the end of the nineteenth century. Rates of increase in the rural population were low throughout the West in the second half of the nineteenth century and Western Europe was never again to be faced with the difficulties of a rapidly rising rural population.

The decline or stagnation of the rural populations of Western Europe marks the end of the pre-industrial economy. Not only did the rural and agricultural populations decline absolutely and as a proportion of the population, but industrialisation began to transform agriculture. New inputs became available which could greatly increase output per man – although they were only adopted when the labour force began to decline. New technologies allowed great increases in output per acre. Even so it took more than a century for these changes to bring about a real agricultural revolution in Western Europe. The new technologies had their beginnings in the 1820s and 1830s, when the steam thresher was spreading through Britain, and the reaper was being perfected in America, and the artificial fertiliser industry was in its infancy. The full impact of these changes has not come until the last fifty years.

Thus the various countries of Western Europe solved – or perhaps more accurately ameliorated – the problems of rural population pressure in a variety of ways in the nineteenth century. Some were new – the absorption of the rural surplus in industry, mass emigration, the adoption of the potato. Some traditional methods had less impact – factory goods destroyed rural industries, and the improvements in transport concentrated services and crafts in the larger rural towns, and made the earnings of extra income in these trades more difficult. Increased agricultural output came from the expansion of the cultivated area, the reduction of fallow, and the adoption of the potato. But before the 1830s it is difficult to detect widespread increases in crop yields or output per man. It was the second half of the nineteenth century that saw these increases, and also the import into Europe of grain and other agricultural products from abroad, in return for the export of manufactured goods.

The developing world

Has Europe's past any lessons for the developing countries today? At least we can point out similarities and differences in the growth of population and the possible demographic and production responses.

First it should be recalled that rapid population growth dates back at least to the 1920s and is not simply a post-war phenomenon; indeed in many parts of the developing world growth as rapid as that in Western Europe occurred in much of the nineteenth century.

Secondly, this increase, at rates well above those found in Western Europe in the nineteenth century, has produced acute rural population pressure in many parts of the developing world and not all the demographic responses open to nineteenth-century Europeans are available in Asia, Africa and Latin America. There seems little prospect of overseas emigration playing any significant role in relieving population pressure. Rural–urban migration has helped to reduce rural rates of increase, but has also helped to cause massive urban problems. Unlike the nineteenth century, urban rates of *natural* increase are high, indeed as high as rural rates. Further, rural populations are likely to continue to increase; on the most optimistic assumptions they will not reach a peak until the second decade of the next century. This leaves the possibility of fertility decline. Most of the developing world still has demographic patterns which are more like sixteenth- than nineteenth-century Europe, and a rapid reduction in fertility will require not only a decline in marital fertility but an increase in celibacy and the deferment of marriage to later ages. There are signs that the medieval pattern is breaking up in parts of Asia, most notably in China; but even if the developing world is on the brink of fertility decline this of course will not halt the continued rapid growth of population.

Thus even if family planning campaigns are successful, the need for successful production responses is imperative. In spite of the gloomy accounts given of agriculture in the developing world there has been a remarkable expansion of food output over the last thirty years. Indeed over the last fifty years the growth of food output has just about matched population growth. In the long run, the developing world is doing as well as Western Europe did at any time until the 1830s. But of course this has not been enough, for the expectations of the peoples and politicians of the developing world are far higher than those of Europeans before the nineteenth century. Whether these will be fulfilled is not a proper subject for an essentially historical work, but we can be sure they will not be achieved in the same way as they were in nineteenth-century Europe.

NOTES

CHAPTER 1

1 J. de Vries, *The Dutch rural economy in the Golden Age, 1500–1700* (New Haven, 1974), pp. 84–7; N. L. Tranter, *Population since the Industrial Revolution: the case of England and Wales* (London, 1973), pp. 41–2; K. H. Connell, *The population of Ireland, 1750–1845* (Oxford, 1950), p. 25.

2 FAO, *Production yearbook 1956*, 11 (Rome, 1957), pp. 16–22; *Production yearbook 1975*, 29 (Rome, 1976), pp. 57–9.

3 M. B. Nanavati and J. J. Anjaria, *The Indian rural problem* (Bombay, 1965), p. 221; L. Nulty, *The green revolution in West Pakistan; implications of technological change* (New York, 1972), p. 32; B. N. Floyd, *Changing patterns of African land use in Southern Rhodesia* (Lusaka, Zambia, 1959), p. 117.

4 A. T. Grove, 'Soil erosion and population problems in south east Nigeria', *Geographical Journal*, 117 (1975), 291–306; J. M. Hunter, 'Population pressure in a part of the West African savanna; a study of Nangodi, north east Ghana', *Annals of the Association of American Geographers*, 57 (1967), 101–14.

5 E. H. Jacoby, *Man and land: the fundamental issue in development* (London, 1971).

6 E. H. Tuma, *Twenty-six centuries of agrarian reform: a comparative analysis* (Berkeley, 1965).

7 D. H. Perkins, *Agricultural development in China, 1368–1968* (Edinburgh, 1969); P. Ho, *Studies in the population of China, 1368–1953*, Harvard East Asian Studies, no. 4 (Cambridge, Mass., 1959).

CHAPTER 2

1 J. A. Field, *Essays on population*, University of Chicago, Studies in Economics, No. 1 (Chicago, 1931), p. 250.

2 G. T. Bettany (ed.), T. R. Malthus, *An essay on the principle of population or a view of its past and present effects on human happiness* (London, 1890).

3 J. S. Mill, *Principles of political economy*, 6th edn (London, 1873), pp. 108–22.

4 L. Robbins, 'Malthus as an economist', *Economic Journal*, 77 (1967), 257–8; G. F. McCleary, *The Malthusian population controversy* (London, 1953), p. 45.

5 G. F. McCleary, *Population controversy*, pp. 113, 117, 128, 130.

6 A. Carr-Saunders, *The population problem: a study in human evolution* (London, 1922), p. 198.

7 K. Smith, 'Some observations on modern Malthusianism', *Population Studies*, 6 (1952), 92–105.

8 A. T. Peacock, 'Theory of population and modern economic analysis', *Population Studies*, 6 (1952), 114–22; K. E. Boulding, 'The Malthusian model as a general system', *Social and Economic Studies*, 4 (1955), 195–205.

9 J. E. Meade, *The theory of international economic policy: trade and welfare* (London, 1955), pp. 83–5; A. T. Peacock, 'Economic theory and the concept of an optimum', in J. B. Craggs and N. W. Pirie (eds), *The numbers of man and animals*, Institute of Biology (London, 1955), pp. 1–7.

10 Meade, *International economic policy*, pp. 84–6; M. Gottlieb, 'The theory of optimum population for a closed economy', *Journal of Political Economy*, 53 (1945), 293; H.

Leibenstein, *A theory of economic demographic development* (Princeton, New Jersey, 1954), pp. 173–5; J. D. Pitchford, *Population in economic growth* (Amsterdam, 1974), pp. 87–9.

11 Colin Clark, *Population growth and land use* (London, 1967), pp. 60, 253–76; E. Boserup, *The conditions of agricultural growth: the economics of agrarian change under population pressure* (London, 1965); A. O. Hirschman, *The strategy of economic development* (New Haven, 1959), pp. 172–8.

12 A. Sauvy, *General theory of population* (London, 1969), p. 283; United Nations, *The determinants and consequences of population trends* (2 vols., New York, 1973), vol. 1, p. 455; G. C. Zaidan, 'Population growth and economic development', *Finance and Development*, 1 (1969), 2–8; A. J. Coale and E. M. Hoover, *Population growth and economic development in low-income countries: a case study of India's prospects* (London, 1959).

13 L. M. Fraser, 'On the concept of an optimum in population theory', *Population*, 1 (London, 1933), 38; Lord Robbins, *The theory of economic development in the history of economic thought* (London, 1968), p. 41; H. Dalton, 'The theory of population', *Economica*, 8 (1928), 45; M. Gottlieb, 'Optimum population, foreign trade and world economy', *Population Studies*, 3 (1949), 115–69.

14 A. Carr-Saunders, *The population problem: a study in human evolution* (London, 1922), p. 271; Fraser, *Population*, 1 (1933), 38; Sauvy, *General theory*, p. 93.

15 J. N. Sinha, 'Population and agriculture', in L. Tabah (ed.), *Population growth and economic development in the Third World* (2 vols., Dolhain, Belgium, 1976), p. 256.

16 R. Bićanić, 'Three concepts of agricultural overpopulation', in R. N. Dixey (ed.), *International explorations of agricultural economics* (Ames, Iowa, 1964), pp. 8–20.

17 P. Sen Gupta, 'Population and resource development in India', in W. Zelinsky, L. Kosinski and R. Mansell Prothero (eds.), *Geography and a crowding world* (Oxford, 1970), pp. 424–41.

18 B. Kenadjian, 'Disguised unemployment in underdeveloped countries', *Zeitschrift für Nationalökonomie*, 21 (1961), 216–23; D. Warriner, *The economics of peasant farming*, 2nd edn (London, 1964); W. E. Moore, *The economic demography of Eastern and Southern Europe* (League of Nations, Geneva, 1945); Political and Economic Planning, *Economic development in South Eastern Europe* (London, 1945); Royal Institute of International Affairs, *South Eastern Europe: a brief survey*, Information Department Papers, No. 26 (London, 1940).

19 Warriner, *Peasant farming*, pp. 67–72.

20 Moore, *Economic demography*, pp. 63, 71.

21 J. Poniatowski, 'Le problème du surpeuplement dans le agriculture Polonaise', *L'Est Europe en Agricole*, 17 (1936), 21–60. Quoted in C. J. Robertson, 'Population and agriculture with special reference to agricultural overpopulation', in International Institute of Agriculture, *Documentation for the European Conference on Rural Life, 1939* (Rome, 1939), pp. 11–70.

22 W. C. Robinson, 'Types of disguised rural unemployment and some policy implications', *Oxford Economic Papers*, 21 (1969), 373–86.

23 D. Jorgensen, 'Testing alternative theories of the development of a dual economy', in I. Adelman and E. Thorbecke (eds.), *The theory and design of economic development* (Baltimore, 1966), pp. 41–66; B. Kenadjian, *Zeitschrift für Nationalökonomie*, 21 (1961), 216–23; R. W. M. Johnson, 'Disguised unemployment and the village economy', *African Social Research*, 3 (1967), 220–3; K. S. Kim, 'Labour force structure in a dual economy: a case study of South Korea', *International Labour Review*, 101 (1970), 35–48.

24 F. Dovring, 'Unemployment in traditional agriculture', *Economic Development and Cultural Change*, 15 (1967), 165.

25 P. N. Rosenstein-Rodan, 'Problems of industrialisation of Eastern and Southern Europe', *Economic Journal*, 53 (1943), 202–11; K. Mandelbaum, *The industrialisation of backward areas*, Institute of Statistics, Monograph No. 2 (London, 1945); R. Nourske, *Problems of capital formation in underdeveloped countries* (London, 1953); W. A. Lewis, 'Economic development with unlimited supplies of labour', *The Manchester School*, 22 (1954), 139–91.

26 M. Gollas, 'Surplus labour and economic efficiency in the traditional sector of a dual

economy: the Guatemalan case', *Journal of Development Studies*, 8 (1972), 411–23: N. Islam, 'Concept and measurement of unemployment and underemployment in developing countries,' *International Labour Review*, 89 (1964), 240–56; W. C. Robinson, 'Population change and agricultural productivity in East Pakistan, 1951–1961', in Zelinsky, Kosinski and Mansell Prothero (eds.), *Crowding world*, pp. 467–83; N. Sarkar, 'A method of estimating surplus labour in peasant agriculture in overpopulated underdeveloped countries', *Journal of the Royal Statistical Society*, Series A, 120 (1957), 209–14; K. Abercrombie, 'Agricultural mechanisation and employment in Latin America', *International Labour Review*, 106 (1972), p. 14.

27 P. N. Rosenstein-Rodan, 'Disguised unemployment and underemployment in agriculture', *Monthly Bulletin of Agricultural Economics and Statistics*, 6 (1957), 1–7.

28 N. Georgescu-Roegen, 'Economic theory and agrarian economics', *Oxford Economic Papers*, 12 (1960), p. 13.

CHAPTER 3

1 R. Bićanić, 'Excess population', *Advancement of Science*, 2 (1942), 141.

2 W. A. Lewis, *The theory of economic growth* (London, 1963), pp. 320–30; D. R. Kamerschen, 'On an operational index of overpopulation', *Economic Development and Cultural Change*, 13 (1965), 169–87.

3 W. C. Robinson, 'The development of modern population theory', *American Journal of Economics and Sociology*, 23 (1964), 384.

4 J. N. Sinha, 'Population and agriculture', in L. Tabah (ed.), *Population growth and economic development in the Third World* (2 vols., Dolhain, Belgium, 1976), vol. 1, p. 256.

5 C. J. Robertson, 'Population and agriculture with special reference to agricultural overpopulation', in International Institute of Agriculture, *Documentation for the European Conference on Rural Life, 1939* (Rome, 1939), p. 29.

6 FAO, *World agricultural structure*, Study no. 1 (Rome, 1961), pp. 40–1; D. Grigg, 'The geography of farm size: a preliminary survey', *Economic Geography*, 42 (1966), 205–35.

7 M. B. Nanavati and J. J. Anjaria, *The Indian rural problem* (Bombay, 1965), p. 281; K. S. Kim, 'Labour force structure in a dual economy: a case study of South Korea', *International Labour Review*, 101 (1970), 35–48; M. A. W. Ezzat, 'The land tenure system of Egypt', in K. H. Parsons, R. J. Penn, and P. M. Raup (eds.), *Land tenure* (Madison, Wisconsin, 1956), pp. 100–1; A. Fuentes-Mohr, 'Land settlement and agrarian reform in Guatemala', *International Journal of Agrarian Affairs*, 2 (1955–6), 29; Sie Kwat Soen, *Prospects for agricultural development in Indonesia, with special reference to Java* (Wageningen, 1968), pp. 57–60; J. L. Buck, *Land utilization in China* (2 vols., New York, 1964), vol. 1, p. 269; D. R. F. Taylor, 'Agricultural change in Kikuyuland', in M. F. Thomas and G. W. Whittington (eds.), *Environment and land use in Africa* (London, 1969), pp. 470–1; E. H. Jacoby, *Man and land: the fundamental issue in development* (London, 1971), p. 205.

8 M. Paglin, '"Surplus" agricultural labour and development: facts and theories', *American Economic Review*, 55 (1965), 816; M. J. Sternberg, 'Agrarian reform and employment, with special reference to Latin America', *International Labour Review*, 95 (1967), 12.

9 T. W. Freeman, *Pre-famine Ireland* (Manchester, 1957), p. 58; D. Warriner, *The economics of peasant farming*, 2nd edn (London, 1964), p. 153.

10 D. H. Penny, 'Indonesia', in R. T. Shand (ed.), *Agricultural development in Asia* (Canberra, 1969), p. 264; H. Bowen-Jones, 'Agriculture', in W. B. Fisher (ed.), *The Cambridge history of Iran*, vol. 1, *the land of Iran* (Cambridge, 1968), p. 587.

11 A. M. Lambert, 'Farm consolidation in Western Europe', *Geography*, 48 (1963), 31–48; B. Binns, 'The consolidation of fragmented holdings', *FAO Agricultural Studies*, 11 (1950); E. H. Jacoby, *Land consolidation in Europe* (Wageningen, 1959).

12 J. Naylon, 'Progress in land consolidation', *Annals of the Association of American Geographers*, 51 (1961), 335–46; D. J. Shaw, 'The problem of land fragmentation in the Mediterranean area: a case study', *Geographical Review*, 53 (1963), 40–51; D. N. McCloskey, 'The persistence of English common fields', in W. N. Parker and E. L. Jones (eds.), *European peasants and their markets* (Princeton, New Jersey, 1975), pp. 114–15.

13 J. Thirsk, 'The common fields', *Past and Present*, 29 (1964), 3–25.

14 P. V. John, *Some aspects of the structure of the Indian agricultural economy, 1947–8 to 1961–2* (London, 1968), p. 111.
15 B. H. Slicher van Bath, *The agrarian history of Western Europe A.D. 500–1850* (London, 1963), pp. 77, 102, 103; W. Abel, *Crises agraires en Europe (XIIIe–XXe siècles)* (Paris, 1973); E. H. Phelps-Brown and S. V. Hopkins, 'Seven centuries of building wages', *Economica*, 22 (1955), 195–206; 'Seven centuries of the prices of consumables, compared with builders' wage rates', *Economica*, 23 (1956), 296–314; 'Wage rates and prices: evidence for population pressure in the sixteenth century', *Economia*, 24 (1957), 289–306.
16 A. J. Bauer, 'Chilean rural labour in the nineteenth century', *American Historical Review*, 76 (1971), 1059–82; M. Mörner, 'A comparative study of tenant labor in parts of Europe, Africa and Latin America 1700–1900: a preliminary report of a research project in social history', *Latin American Research Review*, 5 (1970), 3–15.
17 W. C. Robinson, 'The economics of work-sharing in peasant agriculture', *Economic Development and Cultural Change*, 20 (1971), 131–41.
18 A. R. Bridbury, 'The Black Death', *Economic History Review*, 26 (1973–4), 557–92; R. D. Crotty, *Irish agricultural production: its volume and structure* (Cork, 1966), p. 44.
19 E. J. T. Collins, 'Labour supply and demand in European agriculture, 1800–1880', in E. L. Jones and S. J. Woolf (eds.), *Agrarian change and economic development: the historical problems* (London, 1969), pp. 61–94.
20 D. Grigg, 'Trends in the world's agricultural population', *Geography*, 56 (1971), 320–4; 'The world's agricultural labour force 1800–1970', *Geography*, 60 (1975), 194–202.
21 Slicher van Bath, *Agrarian history*, pp. 7–25.
22 J. M. Street, 'An evaluation of the concept of carrying capacity', *Professional Geographer*, 21 (1969), 104–7.

CHAPTER 4

1 R. Firth, *Primitive Polynesian society* (London, 1939); R. Firth and B. S. Yamey (eds.), *Capital, saving and credit in peasant societies* (London, 1964); G. Dalton, 'Economic theory and peasant society', *American Anthropology*, 63 (1961), 1–25; 'Traditional production in primitive African economies', *Quarterly Journal of Economics*, 76 (1962), 360–78; J. H. Boeke, *Economics and economic policy of dual societies* (New York, 1953); Polly Hill, 'A plea for indigenous economics; the West African example', *Economic Development and Cultural Change*, 15 (1966), 10–20; A. V. Chayanov, *The theory of peasant economy* (Homewood, Illinois, 1966).
2 J. W. Mellor, 'The subsistence farmer in traditional economies', in C. R. Wharton, Jr. (ed.), *Subsistence agriculture and economic development* (London, 1976), p. 209; D. Thorner, 'Peasant economy as a category in economic history', in T. Shanin (ed.), *Peasants and peasant societies; selected readings* (Harmondsworth, 1971), p. 206.
3 A. Everitt, 'Farm labourers', in J. Thirsk (ed.), *The agrarian history of England and Wales*, vol. 4, *1500–1640* (Cambridge, 1967), p. 425; Chayanov, *Peasant economy*, p. 24.
4 E. R. Wolf, *Peasants* (Englewood Cliffs, New Jersey, 1966), pp. 2–15; T. Shanin, 'The nature and logic of the peasant economy', *Journal of Peasant Studies*, 1 (1973), 63–80; G. Foster, 'Introduction: what is a peasant?' in J. M. Potter, M. N. Diaz and G. M. Foster (eds.), *Peasant society* (Boston, Mass., 1967), p. 4; G. Dalton, 'How exactly are peasants exploited?', *American Anthropologist*, 76 (1974), 553–61.
5 M. N. Diaz, 'Introduction: economic relations in peasant society', in Potter, Diaz and Foster, *Peasant society*, pp. 57–9; W. Goldschmidt and E. J. Kunkel, 'The structure of the peasant family', *American Anthropologist*, 73 (1971), 1058–76; B. F. Johnston and G. S. Tolley, 'Strategy for agriculture in development', *Journal of Farm Economics*, 47 (1965), 370.
6 M. Lipton, 'The theory of the optimising peasant', *Journal of Development Studies*, 4 (1968), 331; A. Parik, 'Market responsiveness of peasant cultivators: some evidence from pre-war India', *Journal of Development Studies*, 8 (1972), 209–36; W. C. Neale, 'Economic accounting and family farming in India', *Economic Development and Cultural Change*, 7 (1959), 286–321.
7 D. Gale Johnson, *World agriculture in disarray* (London, 1973), pp. 61–71.
8 D. Grigg, 'The growth and distribution of the world's arable land, 1870–1970', *Geography*, 59 (1974), 104–10.

9 Grigg, *Geography*, 59 (1974), p. 109.
10 B. H. Slicher van Bath, *The agrarian history of Western Europe, A.D. 500–1850* (London, 1963), p. 60; G. Duby, *Rural economy and country life in the medieval West* (London, 1968), p. 98.
11 Ester Boserup, *The conditions of agricultural growth: the economics of agrarian change under population pressure* (London, 1965); D. Grigg, 'Ester Boserup's theory of agrarian change: a critical review', *Progress in Human Geography* (1979).
12 W. O. Jones, 'Manioc: an example of innovation in African economies', *Economic Development and Cultural Change*, 5 (1956), 100–10.
13 G. Borgstrom, *Too many: a study of earth's biological limitations* (London, 1969), p. 42.
14 W. Langer, 'American foods and Europe's population growth 1750–1850', *Journal of Social History* (1975), 51–66; K. H. Connell, *The population of Ireland 1750–1845* (Oxford, 1950).
15 M. Morineau, 'La pomme de terre au XVIIIe siècle', *Annales ESC*, 25 (1970), 1767–85; L. M. Cullen, 'Irish history without the potato', *Past and Present*, 40 (1968), 72–83.
16 D. Grigg, 'The impact of industrialization upon world agriculture since 1800', *Acta Museorum Agriculturae Pragae 1976*, vol. 9, no. 1–2, pp. 25–33.
17 Ministry of Agriculture, Fisheries and Food, *A century of agricultural statistics: Great Britain 1866–1966* (London, 1968), p. 108; M. R. Healey and E. L. Jones, 'Wheat yields in England 1815–59', *Journal of the Royal Statistical Society*, Series A, 125 (1962), 578.
18 J. Z. Titow, *Winchester yields: a study in medieval agricultural productivity* (Cambridge, 1972), p. 12; P. F. Brandon, 'Cereal yields on the Sussex estates of Battle Abbey during the later Middle Ages', *Economic History Review*, 25 (1972–3), 417.
19 B. H. Slicher van Bath, 'Yield ratios 1810–1820', *A.A.G. Bijdragen*, 10 (1963), 16–17.
20 J. de Vries, *The Dutch rural economy in the Golden Age, 1500–1700* (New Haven, 1974), pp. 1–10.
21 J. P. Pousson, 'Les mouvements migratoires en France a partir de la fin du XVe siècle au début du XIXe siècle; approches pour un synthèse', *Annales de Démographie Historique* (1970), 11–78.

CHAPTER 5

1 V. C. Wynne-Edwards, 'Self-regulating systems in populations of animals', *Science*, 147 (1965), 1543–8; L. Thompson, 'A self-regulating system of human population control', *Transactions of the New York Academy of Sciences*, Series 11, 32 (1970), 262–70; D. H. Stott, 'Cultural and natural checks on population growth', in M. F. Ashley-Montagu (ed.), *Culture and the evolution of man* (New York, 1962), pp. 355–76; B. Benedict, 'Population regulation in primitive societies', in A. Allison (ed.), *Population control* (Harmondsworth, 1970), pp. 165–80; B. Hayden, 'Population control among hunter-gatherers', *World Archaeology*, 4 (1973), 205–21.
2 M. Drake, *Population and society in Norway, 1735–1865* (Cambridge, 1969); P. C. Matthiessen, *Some aspects of the demographic transition in Denmark* (Copenhagen, 1970); E. Hofsten and H. Lundström, *Swedish population history: main trends from 1750 to 1970* (Stockholm, 1976).
3 P. Goubert, 'Historical demography and the re-interpretation of early modern French history: a research review', *Journal of Interdisciplinary History*, 1 (1970), 37–48; E. A. Wrigley (ed.), *An introduction to English historical demography from the sixteenth to nineteenth century* (London, 1966).
4 J. Hajnal, 'European marriage patterns in perspective', in D. V. Glass and D. E. C. Eversley (eds.), *Population in history* (London, 1965), pp. 101–43.
5 R. E. Kennedy, Jr., *The Irish: emigration, marriage and fertility* (Berkeley, 1973), pp. 138–42.
6 E. A. Wrigley, 'Family limitation in pre-industrial England', *Economic History Review*, 19 (1966–7), 82–109.
7 Wrigley, *Economic History Review*, 19 (1966–7), 82–109; D. Gaunt, 'Family planning and the pre-industrial society: some Swedish evidence', in K. Ågren, D. Gaunt, I. Eriksson, J. Rogers, A. Norberg and S. Akerman, *Aristocrats, farmers, proletarians: essays in Swedish demographic history*, Studia Historia Upsaliensia, 47 (Uppsala, 1973), pp. 28–59; J.

Dupâquier and M. Lachiver, 'Sur les débuts de la contraception en France ou les deux malthusianismes', *Annales ESC*, 24 (1969), 1391–406.

8 E. A. Wrigley, *Population and history* (London, 1969), pp. 108–14; J. Dupâquier, 'De l'animal à l'homme: le mécanisme autorégulateur des populations traditionnelles', *Revue de l'institut de sociologie*, 2 (1972), 177–211.

9 C. T. Smith, *An historical geography of Western Europe before 1800* (London, 1967), pp. 171–82; A. Den Hollander, 'The great Hungarian plain: a European frontier area', *Comparative Studies in Society and History*, 3 (1960), 755–69.

10 E. E. Lampard, 'The urbanizing world', in H. J. Dyos and M. Wolff (eds.), *The Victorian city: images and reality* (2 vols., London, 1973), vol. 1, pp. 3–57.

11 E. M. Carus-Wilson, 'The first half-century of the borough of Stratford-upon-Avon', *Economic History Review*, 18 (1965–6), 46–63; M. Anderson, *Family structure in nineteenth century Lancashire* (Cambridge, 1971), p. 37; D. B. Grigg, 'E. G. Ravenstein and the "laws of migration"', *Journal of Historical Geography*, 3 (1977), 41–54.

12 D. B. Grigg, 'The world's agricultural labour force 1800–1970', *Geography*, 60 (1975), 194–202; 'Agricultural populations and economic development', *Tijdschrift voor Economische en Sociale Geografie*, 65 (1974), 414–20.

13 D. A. Harkness, 'Irish emigration', in W. F. Willcox (ed.), *International migrations*, vol. 2, *Interpretations* (New York, 1931), p. 269; B. Thomas, *Migration and economic growth: a study of Great Britain and the Atlantic economy* (Cambridge, 1954), p. 95; US Bureau of the Census, *Historical statistics of the United States: colonial times to 1957* (Washington, 1960). pp. 82–3.

14 E. Hofsten and H. Lundström, *Swedish population history: main trends from 1750 to 1970* (Stockholm, 1976), p. 16.

15 Drake, *Population and society*, p. 39.

16 L. Widen, 'Mortality and causes of death in Sweden during the eighteenth century', *Statistik Tidskrift*, 2 (1975), 100; A. E. Imhof and B. J. Lindskog, 'Les causes de la mortalitié en Suède et en Finlande entre 1749 et 1773', *Annales ESC*, 29 (1974), 932; E. Juttikala and M. Kauppinen, 'The structure of mortality during catastrophic years in a pre-industrial society', *Population Studies*, 25 (1971), 283–5.

CHAPTER 6

1 T. H. Hollingsworth, *Historical demography* (London, 1969), pp. 72–4.

2 J. C. Russell, *British medieval population* (Albuquerque, 1948), pp. 10, 52–4; H. C. Darby, *Domesday England* (Cambridge, 1977), pp. 57–94; J. T. Krause, 'The medieval household: large or small?', *Economic History Review*, 9 (1956–7), 420–32.

3 J. C. Russell, *Medieval population*, pp. 94, 146; 'The pre-plague population of England', *Journal of British Studies*, 5 (1966), 19.

4 J. Cornwall, 'English population in the early sixteenth century', *Economic History Review*, 23 (1970–1), 32–44.

5 Cornwall, *Economic History Review*, 23 (1970–1), 32–44; Russell, *Medieval population*, pp. 120–46; Hollingsworth, *Historical demography*, pp. 79–88.

6 D. V. Glass, 'Two papers on Gregory King', in D. V. Glass and D. E. C. Eversley (eds.), *Population in history* (London, 1965), pp. 159–220.

7 C. Clark, *Population growth and land use* (London, 1967), p. 64.

8 Russell, *Medieval population*, pp. 52–4; *Journal of British Studies*, 5 (1966), 1–3; M. M. Postan, 'Agrarian society in its prime: England', in M. M. Postan (ed.) *Cambridge economic history of Europe*, vol. 1, *The agrarian life of the Middle Ages* (2nd edn, Cambridge, 1966), pp. 561–2; J. Z. Titow, *English rural society 1200–1350* (London, 1969), pp. 67–8.

9 J. C. Russell, 'Late ancient and medieval population', *Transactions of the American Philosophical Society*, 48 (1958), 105; G. Fourquin, 'La population de la région parisienne aux environs 1328', *Le Moyen Age*, 62 (1956), 63–91; 'Vers une histoire quantitative', in G. Duby and A. Wallon (eds.), *Histoire de la France rurale*, vol. 1, *La formation des campagnes françaises des origines au XIVe siécle* (Paris, 1975), pp. 554–60.

10 W. Abel, *Crises agraires en Europe (XIIIe–XXe siècles)* (Paris, 1973), pp. 34–6; G. Ohlin, 'No safety in numbers: some pitfalls of historical statistics', in H. Rosovsky (ed.),

Industrialisation in two systems; Essays in honour of Alexander Gerschenkron (New York, 1966), pp. 68–90.

11 J. C. Russell, 'Population in Europe, 500–1500', in C. M. Cipolla (ed.), *The Fontana economic history of Europe*, vol. 1, *The Middle Ages* (London, 1972), pp. 20–2.

12 P. Riché, 'Problèmes de démographie historique du haut moyen âge (Ve–VIIe siècles)', *Annales de Démographie Historique* (1966), 47; J. C. Russell, 'That other plague', *Demography*, 5 (1968), 174–84.

13 G. Duby, *The early growth of the European economy* (London, 1974), pp. 113, 116–17.

14 Duby, *The early growth*, p. 5.

15 Abel, *Crises agraires*, p. 37.

16 K. F. Helleiner, 'The population of Europe from the Black Death to the eve of the vital revolution', in E. E. Rich and C. H. Wilson (eds.), *The Cambridge economic history of Europe*, vol. 4, *The economy of expanding Europe in the sixteenth and seventeenth centuries* (Cambridge, 1967), p. 9; M. Reinhard, A. Armengaud and J. Dupâquier, *Histoire generale de la population mondiale* (Paris, 1968), p. 98.

17 I. Blanchard, 'Population changes, enclosure and the early Tudor economy', *Economic History Review*, 23 (1970–1), 427–45; Hollingsworth, *Historical demography*, pp. 385–7; J. M. W. Bean, 'Plague, population and economic decline in the later Middle Ages', *Economic History Review*, 15 (1962–3), 423–37.

18 Abel, *Crises agraires*, p. 136; H. Neveux, 'La restuaration démographique et économique, 1450–1560', in E. Le Roy Ladurie (ed.), *Histoire de la France rurale*, vol. 2, *L'âge classique des paysans* (Paris, 1975), p. 101; F. Braudel, *The Mediterranean and the Mediterranean world in the age of Phillip II*, vol. 1 (London, 1972), p. 142.

19 E. A. Wrigley, 'Family reconstitution' in E. A. Wrigley (ed.), *An introduction to English historical demography* (London, 1966), pp. 96–159; D. E. C. Eversley, 'Exploitation of Anglican parish registers by aggregative analysis', in Wrigley, *English historical demography*, pp. 44–95; P. Goubert, 'Recent theories and research in French population between 1500 and 1700', in Glass and Eversley, *Population in history*, pp. 457–73; 'Registres paroissiaux dans la France du XVIe siècle', *Annales de Démographie Historique* (1965), 43–8; F. Lebrun, 'Registres paroissiaux et démographie en Anjou au XVIe siècle', *Annales de Démographie Historique* (1965), 49–50; A. Croix, *Nantes et les pays nantais au XVIe siècle; étude démographique* (Paris, 1974).

20 R. Burr Litchfield, 'Demographic characteristics of Florentine patrician families, sixteenth to nineteenth centuries', *Journal of Economic History*, 29 (1969), 191, 205; J. Kintz, 'Démographie en pays Lorraine au XVIe siècle', *Annales de Démographie Historique* (1975), 411; E. Le Roy Ladurie, 'Les paysans français au XVIe siècle', in B. Kopeczi and E. H. Balázs (eds.), *Paysannerie française, paysannerie hongroise XVIe–XXe siècles* (Budapest, 1973), p. 37; E. A. Wrigley, 'Family limitation in pre-industrial England', *Economic History Review*, 19 (1966–7), 87; T. H. Hollingsworth, 'The demography of the British peerage' *Population Studies*, 18 (Supplement) (1965), 7; L. Henry, *Anciennes familles Genevoises* (Paris, 1956), p. 55.

21 E. Gautier and L. Henry, *La population de Crûlai paroisse Normande; étude historique* (Paris, 1958), p. 75; P. Goubert, *Beauvais et le Beauvaisis de 1600 à 1730: contribution à l'histoire sociale de la France du XVIIe siècle* (Paris, 1960), p. 43; Croix, *Nantes et les pays Nantais*, p. 79.

22 Croix, *Nantes et les pays Nantais*, pp. 86–90; J. C. Polton, 'Coulommiers et Chailly-en-Brie (1557–1715)', *Annales de Démographie Historique* (1969), 14–32; H. Neveux, 'L'expansion démographique dans un village du Cambrésis; Saint Hilaire (1450–1575)', *Annales de Démographie Historique* (1971), 265–98; A. R. H. Baker, 'Changes in the later Middle Ages', in H. C. Darby (ed.), *A new historical geography of England* (Cambridge, 1973), p. 195; A. R. Dyer, *The city of Worcester in the sixteenth century* (Leicester, 1973), p. 20; W. G. Howson, 'Plague, poverty and population in parts of north west England, 1580–1720', *Transactions of the Historic Society of Lancashire and Cheshire for 1960*, 112 (1961), 45–6; E. A. Wrigley, *Population and history* (London, 1969), p. 87; Hollingsworth, *Population Studies*, 18 (1965), 30–2.

23 Neveux, 'La restuaration démographique', p. 99; Helleiner, 'The population of Europe', p. 76; Bean, *Economic History Review*, 15 (1962–3), 423–47.

24 R. Davis, *The rise of the Atlantic economies* (London, 1973), p. 16; J. T. Rosenthal,

'Medieval longevity and the secular peerage, 1350–1500', *Population Studies*, 27 (1973), 288.

25 Neveux, 'La restuaration démographique', p. 99; Helleiner, 'The population of Europe', p. 76; B. Bennassar and J. Jacquart, *Le XIVe siècle* (Paris, 1972), pp. 10–11; E. Le Roy Ladurie, *Times of feast, times of famine* (London, 1972), p. 58.

26 Guy Bois, cited in E. Le Roy Ladurie, 'Population and subsistence in sixteenth century France', *Peasant Studies Newsletter*, 1 (1972), 60–5.

27 R. Mols, 'Population in Europe, 1500–1700', in C. M. Cipolla (ed.), *The Fontana economic history of Europe*, vol. 2, *The sixteenth and seventeenth centuries* (London, 1974), p. 28; Colin Clark, *Population growth and land use* (London, 1967), p. 65.

28 Helleiner, 'Population of Europe', pp. 47–52.

29 H. Kamen, 'The economic and social consequences of the Thirty Years war', *Past and Present*, 39 (1968), 44–61; E. Le Roy Ladurie, 'De la crise ultime à la vraie croissance, 1660–1789', in G. Duby and A. Wallon, *Histoire de la France rurale*, vol. 2, *L'âge classique des paysans, 1340–1789* (Paris, 1975), p. 576; Abel, *Crises agraires*, p. 263.

30 J. A. Faber, H. K. Roessingh, B. H. Slicher van Bath, A. M. van der Woude and H. J. van Xanten, 'Population changes and economic developments in the Netherlands: a historical survey', *A.A.G. Bijdragen*, 12 (1965), 37–44; E. Hofsten and H. Lundström, *Swedish population history: main trends from 1750 to 1970* (Stockholm, 1976), p. 13; A. Lassen, 'The population of Denmark in 1660', *Scandinavian Economic History Review*, 13 (1965), 4, 29; 'The population of Denmark', *Scandinavian Economic History Review*, 14 (1966), 134–57; S. Dyrvik, 'Historical demography in Norway 1660–1801: a short survey', *Scandinavian Economic History Review*, 20 (1972), 27.

31 Wrigley, *Economic History Review*, 19 (1966–7), 82–109; J. Ravensdale, *Liable to floods: village landscape on the edge of the Fens, A.D. 450–1850* (Cambridge, 1974); M. Spufford, *Contrasting communities: English villages in the sixteenth and seventeenth centuries* (Cambridge, 1974), pp. 18–19, 25–6; R. Speake, 'The historical demography of the ancient parish of Audley, 1538–1801', *North Staffordshire Journal of Field Studies*, 11 (1971), 68; A. R. Dyer, *The city of Worcester in the sixteenth century* (Leicester, 1973), p. 23.

32 P. Goubert, *Louis XIV and twenty million Frenchmen* (London, 1970), pp. 22–3; E. Gautier and L. Henry, *La population de Crûlai paroisse Normande: étude historique* (Paris, 1958), p. 193.

33 Hollingsworth, *Population Studies*, 18 (1965), 56.

34 E. Le Roy Ladurie, 'L'histoire immobile', *Annales ESC*, 29 (1974), 684–5; C. H. Wilson, *England's apprenticeship, 1603–1768* (London, 1965), p. 108.

35 R. S. Schofield, '"Crisis" mortality', *Local Population Studies* 9 (1972), 10–21.

36 Hollingsworth, *Population Studies*, 18 (1965), 32; Wrigley, *Economic History Review*, 19 (1966–7), 89, 107.

37 P. Goubert, *Louis XIV*, pp. 21–2.

38 R. Lee, 'Estimating series of vital rates and age structures from baptisms and burials: a new technique with applications to pre-industrial England', *Population Studies*, 28 (1974), 495–512.

CHAPTER 7

1 C. Cipolla, *Before the Industrial Revolution: European society and economy, 1000–1700* (London, 1976), p. 153.

2 W. Abel, *Crises agraires en Europe (XIIIe–XXe siècles)* (Paris, 1973), p. 60.

3 H. Dubled, 'Conséquences économiques et sociales des "mortalités" du XIVe siècle, essentiellement en Alsace', *Revue d'histoire économique et sociale*, 37 (1959), 278: B. H. Slicher van Bath, *The agrarian history of Western Europe, A.D. 500–1850* (London, 1963), pp. 58–9.

4 G. Duby, *Rural economy and country life in the medieval West* (London, 1962), pp. 123, 286; E. Perroy, 'At the origin of a contracted economy: the crisis of the fourteenth century', in R. Cameron (ed.), *Essays in French economic history* (Homewood, Illinois, 1970), p. 92; D. C. North and R. P. Thomas, *The rise of the Western world: a new economic history* (Cambridge, 1973), pp. 12, 59.

5 M. M. Postan, 'Moyen Age: rapport', *IXe Congrès International des Sciences Historiques*, 1 (Paris, 1950), p. 235; 'Agrarian society in its prime: England', in M. M. Postan (ed.) *The Cambridge economic history of Europe*; vol. 1, *The agrarian life of the Middle Ages* (Cambridge, 1966), pp. 549–632; *The medieval economy and society: an economic history of Britain in the Middle Ages* (Harmondsworth, 1975).

6 H. Lucas, 'The great European famine of 1315, 1316 and 1317', *Speculum*, 5 (1930), 343–77; H. van Werveke, 'Le famine de l'an 1316 en Flandre et dans les regions voisines', *Revue du Nord*, 41 (1959), 5–14; M. M. Postan and J. Z. Titow, 'Heriots and prices on Winchester Manors', in M. M. Postan, *Essays in medieval agriculture and general problems of the medieval economy* (London, 1973), pp. 150–85; North and Thomas, *The rise of the Western world*, pp. 51, 59.

7 W. Abel, *Crises agraires*, p. 60.

8 T. H. Hollingsworth, *Historical demography* (London, 1969), pp. 263–5.

9 H. Hallam, 'Population density in the medieval fenland', *Economic History Review*, 14 (1961–2), 72; 'The Postan thesis', *Historical Studies* (Melbourne), 15 (1972), 204; J. R. Strayer, 'Economic conditions in the county of Beaumont-le-Roger, 1261–1313', *Speculum*, 26 (1951), 277–87; L. Génicot, 'Crisis: from the Middle Ages to modern times', in Postan, *The agrarian life of the Middle Ages*, p. 669; N. J. G. Pounds, 'Overpopulation in France and the Low Countries in the late Middle Ages', *Journal of Social History*, 3 (1969–70), 241; *An economic history of medieval Europe* (London, 1974), p. 188; D. Herlihey, *Medieval and Renaissance Pistoia: the social history of an Italian town, 1200–1430* (New Haven, 1967), pp. 112–13; H. Neveux, 'Déclin et reprise: la fluctuation biseculaire', in G. Duby and A. Wallon (eds.), *Histoire de la France rurale*, vol. 2, *L'âge classique des paysans, 1340–1789* (Paris, 1975), p. 20.

10 Dubled, *Revue d'histoire économique et sociale*, 37 (1959), 277.

11 Pounds, *An economic history*, p. 53; Duby, *Rural economy*, p. 31.

12 Duby, *Rural economy*, p. 282; L. Génicot, 'L'étendue des exploitations agricoles dans le comté de Namur à la fin du XIIIe siècle', *Etudes Rurales*, 5 (1962), 20–2; Neveux, 'Déclin et repris', p. 29.

13 Neveux, 'Déclin et repris', p. 29; G. Fourquin, 'Paysannerie et féodalité', in Duby and Wallon (eds.), *Histoire de la France rurale*, vol. 1, *Les formations des campagnes françaises des origines au XIVe siècle* (Paris, 1975), p. 572.

14 R. H. Hilton, 'Lord and peasant in Staffordshire in the Middle Ages', *Staffordshire Journal of Field Studies*, 10 (1970), 10; *A medieval society: the west Midlands at the end of the thirteenth century* (London, 1966), pp. 114, 122; Dubled, *Revue d'histoire économique et sociale*, 37 (1959), 277; G. Duby 'The French countryside at the end of the 13th century', in R. Cameron (ed.), *Essays in French economic history* (Homewood, Illinois, 1970), pp. 38–9; J. Z. Titow, 'Some evidence of the thirteenth century population increase', *Economic History Review*, 14 (1961–2), 222; Postan, 'Agrarian society', p. 564; H. E. Hallam, 'The agrarian economy of medieval Lincolnshire before the Black Death', *Historical Studies* (Melbourne), 11 (1964), 163–9.

15 Pounds, *Journal of Social History*, 3 (1969–70), 241; J. Z. Titow, *English rural society 1200–1350* (London, 1969), p. 251; H. E. Hallam, 'The Postan Thesis', *Historical Studies* (Melbourne), 15 (1972), 221.

16 J. Z. Titow, 'Some differences between manors and their effects on the condition of the peasant in the thirteenth century', *Agricultural History Review*, 10 (1962), 3.

17 A. R. Bridbury, 'The Black Death', *Economic History Review*, 26 (1973–4), 578; John Hatcher, *Plague, population and the English economy 1458–1530* (London, 1977), pp. 33–4.

18 Postan, *The medieval economy*, p. 149.

19 P. R. Hyams, 'The origins of a peasant land market in England', *Economic History Review*, 23 (1970–1), 26–7; C. G. Reed and T. L. Anderson, 'An economic explanation of English agricultural organization in the twelfth and thirteenth centuries', *Economic History Review*, 26 (1973–4), 134–7; S. Fenoaltea, 'Authority, efficiency and agricultural organization in medieval England and beyond: a hypothesis', *Journal of Economic History*, 35 (1975), 693–718.

20 Postan, 'Agrarian society', p. 566.

21 D. L. Farmer, 'Some price fluctuations in Angevin England', *Economic History Review*, 9 (1956–7), 34–43; 'Some grain price movements in thirteenth century England', *Economic History Review*, 10 (1957–8), 207–20; P. D. A. Harvey, 'The English inflation of

1180–1220', *Past and Present*, 61 (1973), 4, 16; Abel, *Crises agraires*, p. 33; W. C. Robinson, 'Money, population and economic change in late medieval Europe', *Economic History Review*, 12 (1959–60), 63–78.

22 Hyams, *Economic History Review*, 23 (1970–1), 26–7; D. Herlihy, 'Population, plague and social change in rural Pistoia, 1201–1430', *Economic History Review*, 18 (1965–6), 238; *Pistoia*, pp. 131–4, 144.

23 L. Génicot, *Le XIIIe siècle Européen* (Paris, 1968), p. 343; M. M. Postan, 'Village livestock in the thirteenth century', in M. M. Postan, *Medieval agriculture*, p. 233; G. Fourquin, 'Paysannerie et féodalité', pp. 428, 513; J. Z. Titow, *Winchester yields; a study in medieval agricultural productivity* (Cambridge, 1972), pp. 14–15, 20.

24 Duby, *Rural economy*, p. 147; B. H. Slicher van Bath, 'Mark, manor and village in the eastern Netherlands', *Speculum*, 21 (1946), 115–28; A. R. Lewis, 'The closing of the medieval frontier 1250–1350', *Speculum*, 33 (1958), 479; Postan, *The medieval economy*, p. 23; J. Steane, 'The forests of Northamptonshire in the early Middle Ages', *Northants Past and Present*, 5 (1973), 7–17.

25 Joan Thirsk, 'The common fields', *Past and Present*, 29 (1964), 3–25; Duby, *Rural economy*, pp. 46, 156–63; R. C. Hoffman, 'Medieval origins of the common fields' in W. N. Parker and E. L. Jones (eds.), *European peasants and their markets* (Princeton, 1975), pp. 23–72.

26 Fourquin, 'Paysannerie et féodalité', pp. 430–50; H. Aubin, 'The lands east of the Elbe and German colonization eastwards', in Postan, *Agrarian life of the Middle Ages*, pp. 449–86; Duby, *Rural economy*, pp. 81–6; G. T. Beech, *A rural society in medieval France: The Gâtine of Poitu in the eleventh and twelfth centuries* (Baltimore, 1964), pp. 26–9.

27 Fourquin, 'Paysannerie et féodalité', pp. 428–9.

28 B. Lyon, 'Medieval real estate development and freedom', *American Historical Review*, 63 (1957), 43–63; A. Verhulst, *Histoire du paysage rurale en Flandre de l'epoque romaine au XVIIIe siècle* (Brussels, 1966); Slicher van Bath, *Speculum*, 21 (1946), 115–28; J. Foekema Andrae, 'Embanking and drainage authorities in the Netherlands during the Middle Ages', *Speculum*, 27 (1952), 158–67; F. L. Ganshof and A. Verhulst, 'Medieval agrarian society in its prime: France, the Low Countries and Germany', in Postan, *Agrarian life*, p. 291; Abel, *Crises agraires*, p. 42; H. E. Hallam, *Settlement and society* (Cambridge, 1965); H. C. Darby, *The medieval fenland* (Cambridge, 1940), *Rural economy*, p. 70; P. L. Jones, 'The agrarian development of medieval Italy', *Second International Conference of Economic History, Aix-en-Provence 1962: Congrès et Colloques*, 8 (1965), 69–86.

29 Fourquin, 'Paysannerie et féodalité', pp. 437, 444–5.

30 H. C. Darby, 'The clearing of the woodland', in W. L. Thomas, Jr. (ed.), *Man's role in changing the face of the earth* (Chicago, 1956), p. 202; M. Bloch, *French rural history* (London, 1966), pp. 6–17; M. Le Mené, 'La fôret du Lattay au Moyen Âge; défrichement de sa partie occidentale entre la Loire, l'Evre et L'Hyrome', *Le Moyen Age*, 25 (1970), 27–60; R. Latouche, 'Défrichement et peuplement rural dans La Maine du IXe an XIIIe siècle', *Le Moyen Âge*, 3 (1948), 77–87; Verhulst, *Histoire du paysage rurale*, p. 551; Slicher van Bath, *The agrarian history*, p. 133; Pounds, *An economic history*, p. 174; Postan, 'Agrarian society', p. 551; Fourquin, 'Paysannerie et féodalité', p. 429.

31 A. R. H. Baker, 'Evidence in the "Nonarum Inquisitions" of contracting arable lands in England during the early fourteenth century', *Economic History Review*, 19 (1966–7), 518–32; 'Some evidence of a reduction in the acreage of cultivated lands in Sussex during the early fourteenth century', *Sussex Archaeological Collections*, 104 (1966), 1–5; Hallam, *Historical Studies*, 11 (1964), 4; Duby, *Rural economy*, p. 87.

32 H. C. Darby, *Domesday England* (Cambridge, 1977), pp. 129–33; Titow, *English rural society*, p. 72.

33 Duby, *Rural economy*, p. 94; D. Roden, 'Demesne farming in the Chiltern Hills', *Agricultural History Review*, 17 (1965), 17; P. F. Brandon, 'Demesne arable farming in coastal Sussex during the later Middle Ages', *Agricultural History Review*, 19 (1971), p. 119; Abel, *Crises agraires*, p. 38; Hallam, *Historical Studies*, 15 (1972), 219; G. Duby, 'Medieval agriculture, 900–1500', in C. M. Cipolla (ed.), *The Fontana economic history of Europe*, vol. 1, *The Middle Ages* (London, 1972), pp. 175–220; North and Thomas, *The rise of the Western world*, p. 43; Titow, *English rural society*, pp. 39–40; Fourquin, 'Paysannerie et féodalité', p. 424; Postan, *The medieval economy*, p. 62.

34 Titow, *Winchester yields*, pp. 82–9.

35 Fourquin, 'Paysannerie et féodalité', pp. 451–4; G. Duby, 'Techniques et rendements agricoles dans les Alpes du Sud en 1338', *Annales du Midi*, 70 (1958), 404–13.

36 P. F. Brandon, 'Cereal yields on the Sussex estates of Battle Abbey during the later Middle Ages', *Economic History Review*, 25 (1972–3), 413, 417; 'Arable farming in a Sussex scarp-foot parish during the late Middle Ages', *Sussex Archaeological Collections*, 100 (1962), 60–72; Titow, *Winchester yields*, p. 148.

37 Duby, *Rural economy*, pp. 25–6; B. H. Slicher van Bath, 'The yields of different crops (mainly cereals) in relation to the seed c. 810–1820', *Acta Historiae Neerlandica*, 2 (1967), 32–64.

38 B. Wailes, 'Plow and population in temperate Europe', in B. Spooner (ed.), *Population growth: anthropological implications* (Cambridge, Mass., 1972), pp. 155–79; Duby, *Rural economy*, p. 208; Lynn White, Jr., *Medieval technology and social change* (Oxford, 1962), p. 64; J. Moore, 'The ox in the Middle Ages', *Agricultural History*, 35 (1961), pp. 90–3.

39 Fourquin, 'Paysannerie et féodalité', pp. 406–12; G. Duby, *Rural economy*, p. 104; *The early growth of the European economy* (London, 1974), pp. 192–4.

40 Duby, *Rural economy*, p. 104; Titow, *Winchester yields*, p. 30; Roden, *Agricultural History Review*, 17 (1969), 16; Postan, *The medieval economy*, p. 56; P. F. Brandon, *Economic History Review*, 25 (1972–3), 407; 'Agriculture and the effects of floods and weather at Barnhorne, Sussex during the late Middle Ages', *Sussex Archaeological Collections*, 109 (1971), 76; Fourquin, 'Paysannerie et féodalité', pp. 417–18.

41 Fourquin, 'Paysannerie et féodalité', p. 418; Titow, *Winchester yields*, p. 30; Duby, *Rural economy*, p. 97; Brandon, *Sussex Archaeological Collections*, 109 (1971), 76; Hallam, *Historical Studies*, 15 (1972), 219; Postan, *The medieval economy*, p. 56; Roden, *Agricultural History Review*, 17 (1969), 15.

42 R. A. Donkin, 'Changes in the early Middle Ages', in H. C. Darby (ed.), *A new historical geography of England* (Cambridge, 1973), p. 116; Neveux, 'Déclin et reprise', p. 29; Fourquin, 'Paysannerie et féodalité', pp. 454–72.

43 Duby, 'The French countryside', p. 36; Fourquin, 'Paysannerie et féodalité', p. 400; J. Birrell, 'Peasant craftsmen in the medieval forests', *Agricultural History Review*, 17 (1969), 91–107; Neveux, 'Déclin et reprise', p. 29.

44 Pounds, *An economic history*, p. 100.

45 N. J. G. Pounds, *An historical geography of Europe 450 BC–AD 1330* (Cambridge, 1973), p. 358; J. C. Russell, *Medieval regions and their cities* (Newton Abbot, 1972), pp. 44, 64, 116, 122, 148; *British medieval population* (Albuquerque, 1948), p. 142.

46 Pounds, *An historical geography*, p. 358; D. Herlihy, 'The Tuscan town in the Quattrocento: a demographic profile', *Medievalia et Humanistica*, 1 (1970), 84.

47 Donkin, 'Changes in the early Middle Ages', p. 77; Russell, *Medieval population*, p. 65; Hilton, *The west Midlands*, pp. 183–4; H. S. Fox, 'Going to town in thirteenth century England'. in A. R. H. Baker and J. B. Harley (eds.), *Man made the land: essays in English historical geography* (Newton Abbot, 1973), p. 70; Duby, *The early growth*, p. 242; *Rural economy*, pp. 128, 307; Herlihy, *Economic History Review*, 18 (1965–6), 25–6; *Medievala et Humanistica*, 1 (1970), 86–7, 98–9; *Pistoia*, p. 96; L. Génicot, 'On the evidence of growth of population in the West from the eleventh to the thirteenth century', in S. Thrupp (ed.), *Change in medieval society: Europe north of the Alps, 1050–1500* (New York, 1964), p. 18; Fourquin, 'Paysannerie et féodalité', p. 530.

48 E. M. Carus-Wilson, 'The first half-century of the borough of Stratford-upon-Avon', *Economic History Review*, 18 (1965–6), 45–63; Pounds, *An historical geography*, pp. 269, 340; *An economic history*, pp. 268–9; J. C. Russell, 'Medieval Midland and Northern migrants to London 1100–1365', *Speculum*, 34 (1959), 641–5.

49 Hallam, *Historical Studies*, 15 (1972), 207–9; *Economic History Review*, 14 (1961–2), 71–81; Génicot, 'Crisis', p. 669; Pounds, *An economic history*, p. 145; *Journal of Social History*, 3 (1969–70), 239; D. Herlihy, *Pistoia*, pp. 112–13; 'Santa Maria Improventa: a rural commune in the late Middle Ages', in N. Rubinstein (ed.), *Florentine studies* (Evanston, Illinois, 1968), p. 270.

50 Russell, *Medieval population*, pp. 231–2; Postan and Titow, 'Heriots and prices', p. 161; G. Ohlin, 'No safety in numbers: some pitfalls of historical statistics', in H. Rosovsky, *Industrialization in two systems: essays in Honour of Alexander Gerschenkron* (New York, 1966), pp. 70–6, 85–9.

51 M. M. Postan, 'Some evidence of declining population in the later Middle Ages', *Economic History Review*, 2 (1949–50), 221–46; Ian Kershaw, 'The great famine and agrarian crisis in England, 1315–22', *Past and Present*, 59 (1973), 3–50.

52 B. Harvey, 'The population trend in England 1300 to 1348', *Transactions of the Royal Historical Society*, 16 (1966), 23–42; D. G. Watts, 'A model for the early fourteenth century', *Economic History Review*, 20 (1967–8), 547.

53 J. Scammell, 'Freedom and marriage in medieval England', *Economic History Review*, 27 (1974–5), 530; Duby, *The early growth*, p. 182.

54 W. Abel, *Crises agraires*, p. 60.

55 J. C. Russell, 'The pre-plague population of England', *Journal of British Studies*, 5 (1966), 19.

56 R. H. Hilton, 'Rent and capital formation in feudal society', *Second Conference of Economic History, Aix en Provence; Congrès et colloques* (12 vols., Paris, 1965), vol. 8, pp. 33–68; M. Postan, 'Investment in medieval agriculture', *Journal of Economic History*, 27 (1967), 579–81.

CHAPTER 8

1 J. H. M. Salmon, *Society in crisis: France in the sixteenth century* (London, 1975), p. 32; K. Helleiner, 'The population of Europe from the Black Death to the eve of the vital revolution', in E. E. Rich and C. H. Wilson (eds.), *The Cambridge economic history of Europe*, vol. 4, *The economy of expanding Europe in the sixteenth and seventeenth centuries* (Cambridge, 1976), pp. 25–30.

2 Mildred Campbell, 'A people too few or too many', in W. A. Aiken and B. D. Hemming (eds.), *Conflict in Stuart England: essays in honour of Wallace Notestein* (London, 1960), pp. 172–96.

3 G. S. L. Tucker, 'English pre-industrial population trends', *Economic History Review*, 16 (1963–4), 212; T. H. Hollingsworth, *Historical demography* (London, 1969), p. 87; D. V. Glass, 'Gregory King's estimate of the population of England and Wales, 1695', in D. V. Glass and D. E. C. Eversley (eds.), *Population in history: essays in historical demography* (London, 1965), pp. 183–220.

4 Carl Bridenbaugh, *Vexed and troubled Englishmen, 1590–1642* (Oxford, 1968), p. 397; D. C. Coleman, 'Labour in the English economy of the seventeenth century', in E. M. Carus-Wilson (ed.), *Essays in economic history*, vol. 2 (London, 1962), p. 291.

5 R. H. Tawney, *The agrarian problem in the sixteenth century* (London, 1912); 'The rise of the gentry 1558–1640', *Economic History Review*, 11 (1941), 1–38.

6 M. W. Beresford, 'A review of historical research (to 1968)', in M. W. Beresford and J. G. Hirst (eds.), *Deserted medieval villages; studies* (London, 1971), p. 17; F. J. Fisher, 'The sixteenth and seventeenth centuries: the Dark Ages in English economic History', *Economica*, 24 (1957), 16; P. Corfield, 'Economic issues and ideologies', in C. Russell (ed.), *The origins of the English Civil War* (London, 1973), p. 199; A. B. Appleby, 'Agrarian capitalism or seigneurial reaction? The north west of England, 1500–1700', *American Historical Review*, 80 (1975), 578; E. A. Wrigley, 'Family limitation in pre-industrial England', *Economic History Review*, 19 (1966–7), 106–7; S. Pollard and D. W. Crossley, *The wealth of Britain 1085–1966* (London, 1968), p. 95.

7 W. K. Jordan, *Philanthropy in England, 1480–1660; a study of the changing pattern of English social aspirations* (London, 1955), p. 13.

8 Y. S. Brenner, 'The inflation of prices in early sixteenth century England', *Economic History Review*, 14 (1961–2), 228–37; 'The inflation of prices in England, 1551–1630', *Economic History Review*, 15 (1962–3), 266–84; P. Ramsey (ed.), *The price revolution in sixteenth century England* (London, 1971); H. A. Miskimin, 'Population growth and the price revolution in England', *Journal of European Economic History*, 4 (1975), 179–86.

9 P. J. Bowden, 'Agricultural prices, farm profits and rents', in J. Thirsk (ed.), *The agrarian history of England and Wales*, vol. 4, *1500–1640* (Cambridge, 1967), pp. 605–6.

10 B. A. Holderness, *Pre-industrial England: economy and society 1500–1750* (London, 1976), p. 71.

11 J. Thirsk, 'The farming regions of England', in Thirsk, *The agrarian history*, p. 75; J. F. Cliffe, *The Yorkshire gentry from the Reformation to the Civil War* (London, 1969), p. 47;

L. Stone, *The crisis of the aristocracy 1558–1641* (Oxford, 1965), p. 327; A. Simpson, *The wealth of the gentry, 1540–1660: East Anglian studies* (Cambridge, 1961), pp. 207, 222; E. Kerridge, 'The movement of rent, 1540–1640', *Economic History Review*, 6 (1953–4), 16–34.

12 R. A. Tawney, *The agrarian problem*, p. 71.

13 B. Murphy, *A history of the British economy 1086–1970* (London, 1973), p. 199; L. A. Clarkson, *The pre-industrial economy in England* (London, 1971), p. 66.

14 Tawney, *Economic History Review*, 11 (1941), 1–38; L. Stone, 'The Elizabethan aristocracy – a restatement', *Economic History Review*, 4 (1951–2), 302–21; H. Trevor-Roper, 'The Elizabethan aristocracy; an anatomy anatomized', *Economic History Review*, 3 (1950–1), 279–98; J. Hexter, 'Storm over the gentry' in J. Hexter, *Reappraisals in History* (London, 1962), pp. 117–62.

15 M. Spufford, *Contrasting communities: English villages in the sixteenth and seventeenth centuries* (Cambridge, 1974), pp. 46–51, 65–70, 118, 165; J. Thirsk, 'The farming regions of England' in Thirsk, *The agrarian history*, pp. 9, 24; V. Skipp, 'Economic and social change in the Forest of Arden, 1530–1649', *Agricultural History Review*, 18 (1970), Supplement, pp. 89, 98; C. W. Chalklin, 'The rural economy of a Kentish Wealden parish 1650–1750', *Agricultural History Review*, 11 (1962), pp. 34–5.

16 J. Cooper, 'The social distribution of land and men in England, 1436–1700', *Economic History Review*, 20 (1967–8), p. 426; M. E. James, *Family, lineage and civil society: a study of society, politics and morality in the Durham region, 1500–1640* (Oxford, 1974), p. 74; Thirsk, *The agrarian history*, p. 9.

17 P. J. Bowden, 'Agricultural prices', in Thirsk, *The agrarian history*, p. 590; Coleman, 'Labour in the English economy', pp. 294–5; A. Everitt, 'Farm labourers', in Thirsk, *The agrarian history*, pp. 398–400; D. Hey, *An English rural community: Myddle under the Tudors and Stuarts* (Leicester, 1974), p. 53; Skipp, *Agricultural History Review*, 18 (1970), 109; A. J. and R. H. Tawney, 'An occupational census of the seventeenth century', *Economic History Review*, 5 (1934–5), 25–64.

18 Bowden, 'Agricultural prices', pp. 599–600; J. D. Hatcher, *Plague, population and the English economy, 1348–1530* (London, 1977), pp. 47–54.

19 A. L. Beirer, 'Vagrants and the social order in Elizabethan England', *Past and Present*, 64 (1974), 5.

20 B. Manning, 'The peasantry and the English Revolution', *Journal of Peasant Studies*, 2 (1975), 138; A. Appleby, 'Agrarian capitalism or seigneurial reaction? The north-west of England, 1500–1700', *American Historical Review*, 80 (1975), 578; 'Common land and peasant unrest in sixteenth century England: a comparative note', *Peasant Studies*, 4 (1975), pp. 21–2; J. Thirsk, *The agrarian history*, pp. 12, 32; 'The common fields', *Past and Present*, 29 (1964), 7; K. J. Allison, 'The sheep and corn husbandry of Norfolk in the sixteenth and seventeenth centuries', *Agricultural History Review*, 5 (1957), 12–30.

21 Appleby, *American Historical Review*, 80 (1975), 575; G. Elliot, 'The system of cultivation and evidence of enclosure in the Cumberland open fields in the sixteenth century', *Transactions of the Cumberland and Westmorland Antiquarian and Archaeological Society*, 59 (1960), 85–104; James, *Family, lineage and civil society*, p. 8; Cliffe, *The Yorkshire gentry*, pp. 36–7; J. Cornwall, 'Agricultural improvement, 1560–1640', *Sussex Archaeological Collections*, 98 (1960), 125–6; W. G. Hoskins, 'The reclamation of the waste in Devon, 1550–1800', *Economic History Review*, 13 (1943), 82, 87, 89; 'The rebuilding of rural England, 1570–1640', *Past and Present*, 4 (1953), 48; E. Kerridge, *The agricultural revolution* (London, 1967), pp. 194, 222–7; Chalklin, *Agricultural History Review*, 11 (1962), pp. 29–30; Bowden, 'Agricultural prices', pp. 607, 639; Thirsk, *The agrarian history*, p. 100.

22 F. J. Fisher, 'Tawney's century', in F. J. Fisher (ed.), *Essays in the economic and social history of Tudor and Stuart England* (Cambridge, 1961), pp. 4–5.

23 F. V. Emery, 'England circa 1600' in H. C. Darby (ed.), *A new historical geography of England* (Cambridge, 1973), p. 296.

24 J. Shepherd, 'Field systems of Yorkshire' in A. R. H. Baker and R. A. Butlin (eds.), *Field systems of the British Isles* (Cambridge, 1973), p. 152; J. Thirsk, 'Field systems of the East Midlands', in Baker and Butlin, *Field systems*, p. 257.

25 M. K. Bennett, 'British wheat yield per acre for seven centuries', *Economic History*, 3 (1935), 22–3; P. Deane and W. A. Cole, *British economic growth 1688–1950* (Cambridge,

2nd edn, 1962), p. 67; I am grateful to Mark Overton of the Department of Geography, Cambridge, for the information on East Anglian yields.

26 B. A. Holderness, *Pre-industrial England*, p. 73; G. E. Fussell, 'Introduction', (ed.) *Robert Loder's farm accounts 1610–1620*, Camden 3rd Series, vol. 53 (London, Royal Historical Society, 1936), p. xvii.

27 Thirsk, *The agrarian history*, pp. 167–8, 188, 199; T. B. Dicks, 'Farming in Elizabethan Pembrokeshire', *National Library of Wales Journal*, 15 (1967), 222; J. Cornwall, 'Agricultural improvement 1560–1640', *Sussex Archaeological Collections*, 98 (1960), 121–3; G. E. Fussell, 'Crop nutrition in Tudor and Stuart England', *Agricultural History Review*, 3 (1955), 95–106; 'Four centuries of farming systems in Hampshire, 1500–1900', *Papers and Proceedings of the Hampshire Field Club and Archaeological Society*, 17 (1952), 270; M. Havinden, 'Lime as a means of agricultural improvement; the Devon example', in C. W. Chalklin and M. A. Havinden (eds.), *Rural change and urban growth 1500–1800* (London, 1974), p. 111.

28 S. Pollard and D. W. Crossley, *The wealth of Britain*, p. 95.

29 E. L. Jones, 'Agriculture and economic growth in England, 1660–1750: agricultural change', in E. L. Jones (ed.), *Agriculture and economic growth in England, 1650–1815* (London, 1967), p. 156; Kerridge, *The agricultural revolution*, pp. 39, 180–217.

30 E. Kerridge, *The farmers of Old England* (London, 1973), pp. 110–15; J. H. Bettey, 'Sheep, enclosures and water meadows in Dorset agriculture in the sixteenth and seventeenth centuries', in M. Havinden (ed.), *Husbandry and marketing in the South West 1500–1800*, Exeter Papers in Economic History, 8 (1973), 11–12; E. L. Jones, 'Agricultural conditions and changes in Hereford, 1660–1815', *Transactions of the Woolhope Naturalists Field Club*, 37 (1961), 40.

31 F. J. Fisher, 'The development of the London food market, 1540–1640', *Economic History Review*, 5 (1934–5), 46–64; 'London as an "Engine of Economic Growth"', in J. S. Bromley and E. H. Kossman (eds.), *Britain and the Netherlands; metropolis, dominion and province* (The Hague, 1971), pp. 3–16; R. Webber, 'London's market gardens', *History Today*, 23 (1973), 871–8; Thirsk, *The agrarian history*, p. 176.

32 G. E. Fussell, 'Four centuries of farming systems in Dorset, 1500–1900', *Proceedings of the Dorset Natural History and Archaeological Society*, 73 (1951), 120; J. Thirsk, 'Seventeenth century agriculture and social change', *Agricultural History Review*, 18 (1970), Supplement, 157–62.

33 A. R. Dyer, *The city of Worcester in the sixteenth century* (Leicester, 1973), p. 34; P. Clark and P. Slack, *English towns in transition, 1500–1700* (Oxford, 1976), p. 85.

34 Clark and Slack, *English towns*, pp. 84–5; I. G. Doolittle, 'The effects of the plague on a provincial town in the sixteenth and seventeenth centuries', *Medical History*, 19 (1975), 333–41.

35 S. Peyton, 'The village population in the Tudor lay subsidy rolls', *English Historical Review*, 30 (1915), 234–50; P. Laslett and J. Harrison, 'Clayworth and Cogenhoe', in H. E. Bell and R. L. Ollard (eds.), *Historical essays 1600–1750 presented to David Ogg* (London, 1964), p. 174; J. Cornwall, 'Evidence of population mobility in the seventeenth century', *Bulletin of the Institute of Historical Research*, 39 (1966), 150; R. F. Peel, 'Local intermarriage and the stability of rural population in the English Midlands', *Geography*, 27 (1942), 22–30.

36 J. Patten, 'Patterns of migration and movement of labour in three pre-industrial East Anglian towns', *Journal of Historical Geography*, 2 (1976), 118; P. Clark, 'The migrant in Kentish towns 1580–1640', in P. Clark and P. Slack (eds.), *Crisis and order in English towns 1500–1700* (London, 1972), p. 125; E. J. Buckatzsch, 'Places of origin of a group of immigrants into Sheffield 1624–1799', *Economic History Review*, 2 (1949–50), 303–6; D. F. McKenzie, 'Apprenticeship in the Stationer's Company, 1550–1640', *The Library*, 13 (1958), 292–8; D. V. Glass, 'Socio-economic status and occupations in the City of London at the end of the seventeenth century', A. E. J. Hollaender and W. Kellaway (eds.), *Studies in London History* (London, 1969), pp. 373–85.

37 D. C. Coleman, *Industry in Tudor and Stuart England* (Oxford, 1975), pp. 12–13, 20–21, 25, 27.

38 Everitt, 'Farm labourers', pp. 425–6.

39 L. A. Clarkson, 'The leather crafts in Tudor and Stuart England', *Agricultural History Review*, 14 (1966), 25–39.

40 M. Campbell, *The English yeoman under Elizabeth and the early Stuarts* (London, 1942), pp. 156–7.
41 Holderness, *Pre-industrial England*, p. 83.
42 A. J. and R. H. Tawney, *Economic History Review*, 5 (1934–5), 25–64.
43 E. L. Jones, 'The condition of English agriculture 1500–1640', *Economic History Review*, 21 (1968–9), 618–19.
44 Bridenbaugh, *Vexed and troubled Englishmen*, p. 395.
45 T. H. Breen and S. Foster, 'Moving to the New World: the character of early Massachusetts immigration', *William and Mary Quarterly*, 30 (1973), 187–222; M. Campbell, 'Social origins of some early Americans' in J. M. Smith (ed.), *Seventeenth century America: essays in colonial history* (Chapel Hill, North Carolina, 1959), pp. 63–89.
46 E. A. Wrigley, 'Family limitation in pre-industrial England', *Economic History Review*, 19 (1966–7), 82–109; J. Ravensdale, *Liable to floods: village landscape on the edge of the fens AD 450–1850* (Cambridge, 1974), p. 168; Dyer, *The city of Worcester*, p. 2; R. Speake, 'The historical demography of the ancient parish of Audley, 1538–1801', *North Staffordshire Journal of Field Studies*, 11 (1971), 68; M. Spufford, *Contrasting communities*, pp. 18–19, 25–6.
47 D. C. Coleman, *The economy of England, 1450–1750* (Oxford, 1977), p. 16.
48 T. H. Hollingsworth, 'The demography of the British peerage', *Population Studies*, 18 (1965), Supplement, p. 56.
49 R. S. Schofield, '"Crisis" mortality', *Local Population Studies*, 9 (1972), 10–21; M. W. Flinn, 'The stabilisation of mortality in pre-industrial Western Europe', *Journal of European Economic History*, 3 (1974), 285–318; C. Morris, 'The plague in Britain', *Historical Journal*, 14 (1971), 205–24.
50 R. Lee, 'Estimating series of vital rates and age structures from baptisms and burials; a new technique with applications to pre-industrial England', *Population Studies*, 28 (1974), 495–512.
51 Hollingsworth, *Population Studies*, 18 (1965), 32.
52 Wrigley, *Economic History Review*, 19 (1966–7), 89, 101.
53 Hollingsworth, *Population Studies*, 18 (1965), 7; Wrigley, *Economic History Review*, 19 (1966–7), 86–7.
54 P. E. Razell, 'Population change in eighteenth century England; a re-appraisal', *Economic History Review*, 18 (1965–6), 315–16; N. J. R. Crafts and N. J. Ireland, 'A simulation of the impact of changes in age at marriage before and during the advent of industrialization in England', *Population Studies*, 30 (1976), 495–510.

CHAPTER 9

1 E. Le Roy Ladurie, 'Les paysans français au XVI siècle', in Béla Köpeczi and Eva H. Balázs, *Paysannerie française, paysannerie hongroise, XVIe–XXe siècles* (Budapest, 1973), p. 35.
2 E. Le Roy Ladurie, *The peasants of Languedoc* (Urbana, Illinois, 1974), p. 52.
3 Ladurie, 'Les paysans français au XVI siècle', pp. 33–4.
4 F. Braudel, *Capitalism and material life 1400–1800* (London, 1974), p. 23; R. Davis, *The rise of the Atlantic economies* (London, 1973), p. 213; B. Bennassar and J. Jacquart, *Le XVIe siècle* (Paris, 1972), p. 33.
5 P. Goubert, 'Recent theories and research in French population between 1500 and 1700', in D. V. Glass and D. E. C. Eversley (eds.), *Population in history* (London, 1965), p. 458.
6 Ladurie, *The peasants of Languedoc*, pp. 52, 213.
7 J. Jacquart, 'Immobilisme et catastrophes', in G. Duby and A. Wallon (eds.), *Histoire de la France rurale*, vol. 2, *L'âge classique des paysans, 1340–1789* (Paris, 1975), pp. 109, 190–2; H. Neveux, 'La restuaration démographique et économique, 1450–1560', in Duby and Wallon, *Histoire de la France rurale*, vol. 2, pp. 100, 119; Ladurie, 'Les paysans français au XVIe siècle', p. 35.
8 E. Le Roy Ladurie, 'Première esquisse d'une conjuncture du produit décimal et domanial: fin du Moyen Âge – XVIIIe siècle', in E. Goy and E. Le Roy Ladurie (eds.), *Les fluctuations du produit de la dîme: conjuncture décimale et dominale de la fin du Moyen Âge au XVIIIe siècle* (Paris, 1972), pp. 337–572.

9 E. Le Roy Ladurie, 'L'histoire immobile', *Annales ESC*, 29 (1974), 673–92; 'Les paysans français au XVIe siècle', pp. 35–53.

10 W. Abel, *Crises agraires en Europe (XIIIe–XXe siècles)* (Paris, 1973), p. 161; Neveux, 'La restuaration démographique', p. 95.

11 J. Jacquart, 'Immobilisme et catastrophes', pp. 190–1.

12 P. Goubert, *The ancien regime: French society, 1600–1750* (London, 1969), pp. 83–4; J. H. M. Salmon, *Society in crisis: France in the sixteenth century* (London, 1975), pp. 29, 40; Jan De Vries, *The economy of Europe in an age of crisis 1600–1750* (Cambridge, 1976), p. 63; D. Bitton, *The French nobility in crisis 1560–1640* (Stanford, 1969), pp. 1–2, 72.

13 Abel, *Crises agraires*, p. 177; J. Jacquart, 'La productivité agricole dans la France du nord aux XVIe et XVIIe siècles', *Third International Conference of Economic History*, vol. 2, *Production et productivité agricoles* (Paris, 1969), p. 68; 'Immobilisme et catastrophes', pp. 251–2.

14 E. S. Teal, 'The seigneur of renaissance France: advocate or oppressor', *Journal of Modern History*, 38 (1965), 147.

15 Neveux, 'La restuaration démographique', pp. 267–73.

16 J. Jacquart, 'Immobilisme et catastrophes', pp. 182–218; 'French agriculture in the seventeenth century', in P. Earle (ed.), *Essays in European economic history, 1500–1800* (Oxford, 1974), pp. 165–8; P. Goubert, 'The French peasantry of the seventeenth century; a regional example', *Past and Present*, 10 (1956), 56, 59, 67; E. Le Roy Ladurie, *The peasants of Languedoc*, pp. 85–7.

17 Neveux, 'La restuaration démographique', pp. 151–3; Ladurie, *The peasants of Languedoc*, pp. 43–4, 98–9, 103; H. Kamen, *The age of iron* (London, 1971), p. 69; Davis, *The rise of the Atlantic economies*, p. 217.

18 Ladurie, *The peasants of Languedoc*, p. 138; H. D. Clout, 'Retreat of rural settlement', in H. D. Clout (ed.), *Themes in the historical geography of France* (London, 1977), p. 119.

19 H. D. Clout, 'Retreat of rural settlement', p. 119.

20 Bennassar and Jacquart, *Le XVIe siècle*, pp. 2–3; R. Boutrouche, 'The devastation of rural areas during the Hundred Years War and the agricultural recovery of France', in P. S. Lewis (ed.), *The recovery of France in the fifteenth century* (London, 1971), pp. 48, 51.

21 Jacquart, 'French agriculture', p. 178; 'Immobilisme et catastrophes', p. 182; Ladurie, *The peasants of Languedoc*, p. 56; J. Meyer, 'Le paysan français pendant les guerres de la ligne', in Köpeczi and Balázs (eds.), *Paysannerie français, paysannerie hongroise*, p. 59; Neveux, 'La restuaration démographique', pp. 194–6; B. H. Slicher van Bath, *The agrarian history of Western Europe, AD 500–1850* (London, 1963), p. 204; H. D. Clout, 'Reclamation of coastal marshland', in Clout, *Themes in the historical geography of France*, pp. 194–6.

22 Jean Meuvret, 'Agronomie et jardinage aux XVe et XVIIe siècles', in J. Meuvret, *Études d'histoire économique*, Cahiers des Annales, 32 (Paris, 1971), pp. 153–5.

23 P. Goubert, *Beauvais et les Beauvaisis de 1600 à 1730* (Paris, 1960), 94; H. D. Clout and A. D. M. Phillips, 'Fertilisants mineraux en France au XIXe siècle', *Etudes Rurales*, 45 (1972), 12.

24 Bennassar and Jacquart, *Le XVIe siècle*, p. 39; Jacquart, 'French agriculture', pp. 170–2; 'Immobilisme et catastrophes', pp. 236–38; Ladurie, 'Les paysans français au XVI siècle', p. 39; J. L. Goldsmith, 'Agricultural specialisation and stagnation in early modern Auvergne', *Agricultural History*, 47 (1973), 219; J. Goy, 'Les rendements du blé au pays d'Arles, XVIIe–XVIIIe siècles', in Ladurie and Goy, *Les fluctuations du produit de la dîme*, pp. 249–50.

25 P. Goubert, *Louis XIV and twenty million Frenchmen* (London, 1970), p. 32; 'Les techniques agricoles dans le pays picards au XVIIe et XVIIIe siècles', *Revue d'Histoire Économique et Sociale*, 35 (1957), 24–40; Ladurie, *The peasants of Languedoc*, p. 236; Jacquart, 'Immobilisme et catastrophes', pp. 214–18; Neveux, 'La restuaration démographique', p. 112.

26 Jacquart, 'Immobilisme et catastrophes', pp. 227, 229, 236; Neveux, 'La restuaration démographique', p. 119.

27 Jacquart, 'French agriculture', pp. 165, 175; 'Immobilisme et catastrophes', pp. 225, 229; Ladurie, *The peasants of Languedoc*, pp. 57–62, 71; R. Gascon, 'La France du mouvement: les commerces et les villes', in F. Braudel and E. Labrousse, *Histoire*

economique et sociale de la France, vol. 1, *De 1450 à 1660; l'etat et la ville* (Paris, 1977), pp. 261–2; Neveux, 'La restuaration démographique', pp. 90, 144.

28 C. S. L. Davies, 'Peasant revolt in France and England: a comparison', *Agricultural History Review*, 21 (1973), 124–5.

29 R. Mols, 'Population in Europe, 1500–1700', in C. M. Cipolla (ed.), *The Fontana economic history of Europe*, vol. 2, *The sixteenth and seventeenth centuries* (London, 1974), pp. 59–60, 67, 77.

30 R. Gascon, 'La France du mouvement', p. 398; A. Croix, *Nantes et le pays Nantais au XVIe siècle: étude démographique* (Paris, 1974), pp. 167–70.

31 H. D. Clout, 'Urban growth, 1500–1900', in Clout, *Themes in the historical geography of France*, p. 486; E. Gautier and L. Henry, *La population de Crûlai paroisse Normande: étude historique* (Paris, 1958), p. 197.

32 Gascon, 'La France du mouvement', p. 396.

33 Clout, 'Urban growth', p. 485.

34 Gascon, 'La France du mouvement', p. 396; L. Bernard, *The emerging city: Paris in the age of Louis XIV* (Durham, North Carolina, 1970), pp. 284–5; Bennassar and Jacquart, *Le XVIe siècle*, p. 32.

35 Clout, 'Urban growth', p. 483; Gascon, 'La France du mouvement', p. 396.

36 Neveux, 'La restuaration démographique', p. 122.

37 Goubert, *The ancien regime*, pp. 53–5; Gascon, 'La France du mouvement', p. 406.

38 Goubert, 'French population', p. 466; Gascon, 'La France du mouvement', p. 265.

39 J. Pousson, 'Les mouvements migraitoires en France et à partir de la France de la fin du XVe siècle au début du XIXe siècle; approches pour un synthèse', *Annales de Démographie Historique* (1972), 42; F. Braudel, *Capitalism and material life*, p. 24.

40 E. Le Roy Ladurie, 'L'Histoire immobile', *Annales ESC*, 29 (1974), 673–92; Jacquart, 'Immobilisme et catastrophes', pp. 180–229; Neveux, 'La restuaration démographique', pp. 89–159.

41 Goubert, *Louis XIV*, pp. 22–3; E. Gautier and L. Henry, *La population du Crûlai*, p. 193; J. Meuvret, 'Demographic crisis in France from the sixteenth to the eighteenth centuries', in D. V. Glass and D. E. C. Eversley (eds.), *Population in history* (London, 1965), pp. 511–21.

42 E. Le Roy Ladurie, 'Famine amenorrhoea (seventeenth to twentieth centuries)' in R. Forester and O. Ranum (eds.), *Biology of man in history* (Baltimore, 1975), pp. 167–78; Meuvret, 'Demographic crisis', pp. 511–21; Goubert, *Louis XIV*, pp. 11, 21; Bennassar and Jacquart, *Le XVIe siècle*, p. 32.

43 Bennassar and Jacquart, *Le XVIe siècle*, p. 33; Croix, *Nantes et les pays Nantais*, p. 169; Goubert, *The ancien regime*, p. 37; Jacquart, 'Immobilisme et catastrophes', pp. 186, 191; E. Le Roy Ladurie, *Times of feast, times of famine* (London, 1972), pp. 66–8, 78, 119, 234, 282, 288; *The peasants of Languedoc*, pp. 684–5.

44 P. Benedict, 'Catholics and Huguenots in sixteenth century Rouen: the demographic effects of the Religious Wars', *French Historical Studies*, 9 (1975), 217–19; Croix, *Nantes et les pays Nantais*, pp. 80–90; P. Goubert, 'Registres parissoiux dans la France du XVIe siècle', *Annales de Démographie Historique* (1965), 44; J. C. Polton, 'Coulommiers et Chailly-en-Brie (1557–1715)', *Annales de Démographie Historique* (1969), 15–18.

45 Ladurie, *The peasants of Languedoc*, p. 37; J. P. Kintz, 'Démographie en pays Lorraine au XVIe siècle', *Annales de Démographie Historique* (1975), 309–15; Gautier and Henry, *La population de Crûlai*, pp. 75, 83, 84, 156; Croix, *Nantes et les pays Nantais*, p. 79; P. Goubert, 'Les fundaments démographiques', in E. Labrousse and P. Goubert (eds.), *Histoire economique et sociale de la France*, vol. 2, *Des derniers temps de l'âge seigneurial aux préludes de l'âge industriel (1660–1789)* (Paris, 1970), pp. 24–37; J. Dupâquier, 'Villages et petites villes de la géneralité de Paris', *Annales de Démographie Historique* (1969), pp. 11–13; P. Goubert, 'Historical demography and the reinterpretation of early modern French history; a research review', *Journal of Interdisciplinary History*, 1 (1970), 37–48.

CHAPTER 10

1 G. O'Tuathaigh, *Ireland before the Famine 1798–1848* (Dublin, 1972), pp. 203–4.

2 J. C. Beckett, *The making of modern Ireland, 1603–1923* (London, 1966), p. 343.

3 M. Drake, 'Population growth and the Irish economy', in L. M. Cullen (ed.), *The formation of the Irish economy* (Cork, 1968), p. 72.

4 K. H. Connell, 'The potato in Ireland', *Past and Present*, 23 (1962), 64.

5 P. Froggatt, 'The census of Ireland of 1813–14', *Irish Historical Studies*, 14 (1965), 227–35; K. H. Connell, *The population of Ireland, 1750–1845* (Oxford, 1950), pp. 1–3.

6 M. Drake, 'The Irish demographic crisis of 1740–41', *Historical Studies*, 6 (1968), 101–24.

7 G. Talbot Griffith, *Population problems of the age of Malthus* (Cambridge, 1926), p. 50.

8 Connell, *Population of Ireland*, pp. 29–43, 188–195; V. Morgan, 'Mortality in Magherafelt, County Derry', *Irish Historical Studies*, 19 (1974), 123–5.

9 G. Talbot Griffith, *Population problems*, p. 58.

10 Connell, *Population of Ireland*, pp. 191–5, 220, 237.

11 Connell, *Population of Ireland*, pp. 30, 36; G. S. L. Tucker, 'Irish fertility ratios before the Famine', *Economic History Review*, 23 (1970–1), 267–84; J. Lee, 'Irish agriculture', *Agricultural History Review*, 17 (1969), 65.

12 Connell, *Population of Ireland*, p. 51; M. Drake, 'Marriage and population growth in Ireland, 1750–1845', *Economic History Review*, 21 (1968–9), 283–95; P. E. Razell, 'Population growth and economic change in eighteenth and early nineteenth century England and Ireland', in E. L. Jones and G. E. Mingay (eds.), *Land, labour and population in the Industrial Revolution: essays presented to J. D. Chambers* (London, 1967), pp. 260–81; R. E. Kennedy, Jr., *The Irish: emigration, marriage and fertility* (Berkeley, 1973), p. 142.

13 K. H. Connell, *Population of Ireland*, pp. 122–5; 'The potato in Ireland', *Past and Present*, 23 (1962), 57–63; M. Drake, 'Marriage and population growth in Ireland, 1750–1845', *Economic History Review*, 16 (1963–4), 311–12.

14 P. M. A. Bourke, 'The use of the potato in pre-famine Ireland', *Journal of the Statistical and Social Inquiry Society of Ireland*, 21 (1967–68), 81; L. M. Cullen, 'Irish history without the potato', *Past and Present*, 40 (1968), 80; R. F. Salaman, *The history and social influence of the potato* (Cambridge, 1949), p. 189; K. H. Connell, 'Essays in bibliography and criticism; the history of the potato', *Economic History Review*, 3 (1950–1), 389; *Population of Ireland*, pp. 122–38, 143–56, 158–62.

15 Cullen, *Past and Present*, 40 (1968), 75–7; P. E. Razell, 'Population growth and economic change in eighteenth and early nineteenth century England and Ireland' in Jones and Mingay, *Land, labour and population*, pp. 260–81.

16 P. M. A. Bourke, 'The use of the potato in pre-famine Ireland', p. 87; C. M. Law, 'The growth of urban population in England and Wales, 1801–1911', *Transactions of the Institute of British Geographers*, 41 (1967), 142; P. Deane and W. A. Cole, *British economic growth 1688–1959* (Cambridge, 1962), p. 142; T. W. Freeman, *Pre-Famine Ireland* (Manchester, 1957), pp. 18, 25.

17 Connell, *Population of Ireland*, pp. 163–9, 174.

18 J. S. Donnnelly, Jr., *The land and the people of nineteenth century Cork: the rural economy and the land question* (London, 1975), p. 16; Freeman, *Pre-Famine Ireland*, pp. 54–5, 58; P. M. A. Bourke, 'The use of the potato in pre-famine Ireland', p. 81.

19 Bourke, 'The use of the potato in pre-famine Ireland', p. 81; R. M. Buchanan, 'Field systems of Ireland', in A. R. H. Baker and R. A. Butlin (eds.), *Studies of field systems in the British Isles* (Cambridge, 1973), p. 617; Cullen, *Past and Present*, 40 (1968), 80; E. R. R. Green, 'Agriculture', in R. D. Edwards and T. D. Williams (eds.), *The Great Famine; studies in Irish history, 1848–52* (Dublin, 1956), pp. 113.

20 L. M. Cullen, *An economic history of Ireland since 1660* (London, 1968), p. 121; 'The Irish economy in the eighteenth century', in Cullen, *The formation of the Irish economy*, p. 16; G. E. Christianson, 'Population, the potato and depression in Ireland: 1800–1830', *Eire-Ireland*, 7 (1972), 81–2; Green, 'Agriculture', pp. 92, 96; R. D. Crotty, *Irish agricultural production: its volume and structure* (Cork, 1966), p. 44; T. P. O'Neill, 'Fever and public health in pre-famine Ireland', *Journal of the Royal Society of Antiquaries of Ireland*, 103 (1973), 4; Donnelly, *Land and people of Cork*, pp. 25, 47; P. M. A. Bourke, 'The agricultural statistics of the 1841 census of Ireland; a critical review', *Economic History Review*, 18 (1965–6), 382–3; 'The use of the potato in pre-famine Ireland', p. 93.

21 Crotty, *Irish agricultural production*, p. 44.

22 D. Large, 'The wealth of the greater Irish landlords, 1750–1815', *Irish Historical Studies*, 15 (1966), 28, 32; Crotty, *Irish agricultural production*, p. 25; Connell, *Population of Ireland*, p. 69; G. O'Brien, *The economic history of Ireland from the Union to the Famine* (London, 1918), p. 71; J. H. Johnson, 'The two Irelands at the beginning of the nineteenth century', in N. Stephens and R. E. Glasscock (eds.), *Irish geographical studies in honour of E. Estyn Evans* (Belfast, 1970), p. 229; Donnelly, *Land and people of Cork*, pp. 17–19.

23 K. H. Connell, 'The colonization of waste land in Ireland, 1700–1845', *Economic History Review*, 3 (1950–1), 44–7; *Population of Ireland*, pp. 90, 92, 99; Green, 'Agriculture', p. 98; Crotty, *Irish agricultural production*, p. 42; T. Jones Hughes, 'Society and settlement in nineteenth century Ireland', *Irish Geographer*, 5 (1964–68), 84; Bourke, 'The use of the potato in pre-famine Ireland', p. 11; R. B. McDowell, 'Ireland in the eighteenth century British Empire', *Historical Studies*, 9 (1974), 62.

24 Crotty, *Irish agricultural production*, p. 50: R. D. Collinson Black, *Economic thought and the Irish question 1817–1870* (Cambridge, 1960), pp. 178, 180, 187–90; Bourke, *Economic History Review*, 18 (1965–6), 380.

25 Crotty, *Irish agricultural production*, p. 26; Bourke, *Economic History Review*, 18 (1965–6), 385; Buchanan, 'Field systems of Ireland', pp. 587, 597; Connell, *Population of Ireland*, p. 76; Green, 'Agriculture', pp. 110–13.

26 Bourke, 'The use of the potato in pre-famine Ireland', pp. 72, 83; *Economic History Review*, 18 (1965–6), pp. 382–3, 387; Donnelly, *Land and people of Cork*, p. 43.

27 Crotty, *Irish agricultural production*, p. 28; Connell, *Population of Ireland*, p. 123.

28 M. Drake, *Population and society in Norway, 1735–1865* (Cambridge, 1969), p. 59.

29 Connell, *Population of Ireland*, pp. 120–36; *Past and Present*, 23 (1962), 57–71; Cullen, *Past and Present*, 40 (1968), 75–7.

30 Donnelly, *Land and people of Cork*, p. 36; O'Brien, *The economic history of Ireland from the Union*, pp. 27–8; Green, *The Great Famine*, p. 90.

31 Crotty, *Irish agricultural production*, pp. 53–4; P. M. A. Bourke, 'The average yields of food crops in Ireland on the eve of the Great Famine', *Journal of the Department of Agriculture and Fisheries*, 66 (Dublin, 1969), 26–39; M. Healey and E. L. Jones, 'Wheat yields in England, 1815–59', *Journal of the Royal Statistical Society*, Series A, 125 (1962), 574–9.

32 R. A. Butlin, 'The population of Dublin in the late seventeenth century', *Irish Geographer*, 5 (1965), 55.

33 Freeman, *Pre-Famine Ireland*, pp. 27, 75; Cullen, *An economic history of Ireland*, p. 121.

34 Kennedy, *The Irish*, p. 32.

35 Connell, *Population of Ireland*, p. 184; S. H. Cousens, 'The restriction of population growth in pre-Famine Ireland', *Proceedings of the Royal Irish Academy*, 64 C (1966), 88.

36 S. H. Cousens, 'The regional variation in emigration from Ireland between 1821 and 1841', *Transactions of the Institute of British Geographers*, 37 (1965), 16–17.

37 Beckett, *Making of modern Ireland*, pp. 167, 169, 241–2, 290; Freeman, *Pre-Famine Ireland*, pp. 75, 77, 83–7; Cullen, *An economic history of Ireland*, pp. 64, 90, 94, 120.

38 Cullen, *An economic history of Ireland*, pp. 123, 142–3; J. Lee, 'The provision of capital for early Irish railways, 1830–1853', *Irish Historical Studies*, 16 (1968), 33–63.

39 J. Lee, 'Capital in the Irish economy', in Cullen, *The formation of the Irish economy*, pp. 53–63; E. Larkin, 'Economic growth, capital investment and the Roman Catholic Church in nineteenth century Ireland', *American Economic Review*, 72 (1966), 852–84.

40 E. J. T. Collins, 'Migrant labour in British agriculture in the nineteenth century', *Economic History Review*, 29 (1976–7), 48–9; C. Ó Gráda, 'Seasonal migration and post-famine adjustment in the west of Ireland', *Studia Hibernia*, 13 (1973), 51; B. Kerr, 'Irish seasonal migration to Great Britain, 1800–1836', *Irish Historical Studies*, 3 (1943), 372.

41 J. H. Johnson, 'Harvest migration from nineteenth century Ireland', *Transactions of the Institute of British Geographers*, 41 (1967), 100, 105; Ó Gráda, *Studia Hibernica*, 13 (1973), 56.

42 Collinson Black, *Economic thought*, pp. 203, 213–14; D. A. Harkness, 'Irish emigration', in W. F. Willcox (ed.), *International migrations*, vol. 2, *Interpretations* (New York, 1931), p. 126.

43 Beckett, *Making of modern Ireland*, p. 176; Donnelly, *Land and people of Cork*, p. 21.
44 Connell, *Population of Ireland*, p. 28, US Bureau of the Census, *Historical statistics of the United States: colonial times to 1957* (Washington, DC, 1960), pp. 56–7.
45 Harkness, 'Irish emigration', p. 2.
46 C. Ó Gráda, 'A note on nineteenth century Irish emigration statistics', *Population Studies*, 29 (1975), 148.
47 S. H. Cousens, 'The regional variation in emigration from Ireland between 1821 and 1841', *Transactions of the Institute of British Geographers*, 37 (1965), 15–30.
48 S. H. Cousens, 'The regional pattern of emigration during the Great Irish Famine, 1846–1851', *Transactions of the Institute of British Geographers*, 28 (1960), 119–134; *Transactions of the Institute of British Geographers*, 37 (1965), 23–6; Donnelly, *Land and people of Cork*, pp. 124, 228.
49 Cullen, *Economic history of Ireland*, p. 137; Donnelly, *Land and people of Cork*, p. 178.
50 S. H. Cousens, 'The regional variations in population changes in Ireland, 1861–1881', *Economic History Review*, 17 (1964–5), 301–21; 'Emigration and demographic change in Ireland, 1851–61', *Economic History Review*, 14 (1961–2), 275–88; B. M. Walsh, 'Marriage rates and population pressure: Ireland, 1871 and 1911', *Economic History Review*, 23 (1970–1), 148–62.
51 Lee, *Agricultural History Review*, 17 (1969), 65; Connell, *Population of Ireland*, p. 51; M. S. Teitelbaum, 'Birth underregistration in the constituent counties of England and Wales: 1841–1910', *Population Studies*, 28 (1974), 335.
52 K. H. Connell, 'Peasant marriage in Ireland: its structure and development since the Famine', *Economic History Review*, 14 (1961–2), 502–23; 'Peasant marriage in Ireland after the Great Famine', *Past and Present*, 12 (1957), 76–9; 'Marriage in Ireland after the Famine; the diffusion of the Match', *Journal of the Statistical and Social Inquiry Society of Ireland*, 19 (1955–6), 82–103.
53 Walsh, *Economic History Review*, 23 (1970–1), 148–9; Donnelly, *Land and people of Cork*, p. 223.
54 Cousens, *Proceedings of the Royal Irish Academy*, 64C (1966), 83–99; Connell, *Population of Ireland*, p. 46; J. H. Johnson, 'Marriage and fertility in nineteenth century Londonderry', *Journal of the Statistical and Social Inquiry Society of Ireland*, 20 (1957–8), 99–117.
55 Donnelly, *Land and people of Cork*, p. 223.
56 E. E. McKenna, 'Marriage and fertility in post-famine Ireland: a multivariate analysis', *American Journal of Sociology*, 80 (1975), 688–705.
57 Connell, *Population of Ireland*, pp. 144, 231; O'Neill, *Journal of the Royal Society of Antiquaries of Ireland*, 103 (1973), 2, 3, 8, 17, 21.
58 Razell, 'Population growth', p. 268; S. H. Cousens, 'Regional death rates in Ireland during the Great Famine from 1846 to 1851', *Population Studies*, 14 (1960), 62.
59 Drake, 'Population growth and the Irish economy', p. 75.
60 N. D. Palmer, 'Irish absenteeism in the eighteen seventies', *Journal of Modern History*, 12 (1940), 357–66; A. P. W. Macolmson, 'Absenteeism in eighteenth century Ireland', *Irish Economic and Social History*, 1 (1974), 15–35; Cullen, *An economic history of Ireland*, p. 83.
61 W. Burn, 'Free trade in land: an aspect of the Irish question', *Transactions of the Royal Historical Society*, 31 (1949), 61–74; C. Ó Gráda, 'The investment behaviour of Irish landlords 1850–75; some preliminary findings', *Agricultural History Review*, 23 (1975), 39–55. G. E. Christianson, 'Landlords and land tenure in Ireland, 1790–1830', *Eire-Ireland*, 9 (1974), 25–58; Crotty, *Irish agricultural production*, p. 44.

CHAPTER 12

1 J. A. Faber, H. K. Roessingh, B. H. Slicher van Bath, A. V. Van der Woude and R. J. Xanten, 'Population changes and economic developments in the Netherlands; a historical survey', *A.A.G. Bijdragen*, 12 (1965), 47–114; H. Wansink, 'Holland and six allies: the Republic of the Seven United Provinces', in J. S. Bromley and E. H. Kossman (eds.), *Britain and the Netherlands*, vol. 4, *Metropolis, dominion and province* (The Hague, 1971), pp. 139–40.

2 J. de Vries, *The Dutch rural economy in the Golden Age, 1500–1700* (New Haven, 1974), p. 111.

3 W. Abel, *Crises agraires en Europe* (*XIIIe–XXe siècles*) (Paris, 1973), p. 161; De Vries, *Dutch rural economy*, pp. 181–3; D. C. North and R. P. Thomas, *The rise of the Western world: a new economic history* (Cambridge, 1973); J. L. Price, *Culture and society in the Dutch Republic during the seventeenth century* (London, 1974), p. 117; I. Schoffer, 'Did Holland's Golden Age coincide with a period of crisis?', *Acta Historiae Neerlandica*, 1 (1966), 93.

4 Abel, *Crises agraires*, p. 220; Faber *et al.*, *A.A.G. Bijdragen*, 12 (1965), 17; De Vries, *Dutch rural economy*, p. 189.

5 De Vries, *Dutch rural economy*, pp. 127–36; Faber *et al.*, *A.A.G. Bijdragen*, 12 (1965), p. 79.

6 J. de Vries, 'Peasant demand and patterns of economic development: Friesland 1550–1750', in W. Parker and E. L. Jones (eds.), *European peasants and their markets* (Princeton, New Jersey, 1975), pp. 205–66; Colin Clark, *Population growth and land use* (London, 1967), pp. 254–5.

7 P. Wagret, *Polderlands* (London, 1968), p. 75; B. H. Slicher van Bath, *The agrarian history of Western Europe, AD 500–1850* (London, 1963), pp. 197, 211, 213; J. P. Bakker, 'The significance of physical geography and pedology for historical geography in the Netherlands', *Tijdschrift voor Economische en Social Geographie*, 49 (1958), 214–20.

8 Wagret, *Polderlands*, pp. 75–85; De Vries, *Dutch rural economy*, p. 192; A. Lambert, *The making of the Dutch landscape* (London, 1971), pp. 212–15; C. T. Smith, 'Dutch peat-digging and the origin of the Norfolk Broads', *Geographical Journal*, 132 (1966), 70.

9 B. H. Slicher van Bath, 'The rise of intensive husbandry in the Low Countries', in Bromley and Kossman (eds.), *Britain and the Netherlands*, vol. 1 (London, 1960), p. 149; A. Friis, 'An inquiry into the relations between economic and financial factors in the sixteenth and seventeenth centuries; the two crises in the Netherlands in 1557', *Scandinavian Economic History Review*, 1 (1953), 200; J. A. Faber, 'The decline of the Baltic grain trade in the second half of the seventeenth century', *Acta Historiae Neerlandica*, 1 (1966), 117.

10 J. de Vries, *Dutch rural economy*, p. 33; 'On the modernity of the Dutch Republic', *Journal of Economic History*, 33 (1973), 193, 200; H. van der Wee, *The growth of the Antwerp market and the European economy* (3 vols., The Hague, 1962), vol. 2, p. 169.

11 C. Vanderbroeke, 'Cultivation and consumption of the potato in the 17th and 18th centuries', *Acta Historiae Neerlandica*, 5 (1971), 15–39.

12 B. H. Slicher van Bath, 'Agriculture in the Low Countries', *Relazioni del X Congresso Internazionale di Scienze Storiche, Storia Moderna*, 4 (1955), 169–203; 'The rise of intensive husbandry', p. 133; De Vries, *Dutch rural economy*, p. 147.

13 Slicher van Bath, 'The rise of intensive husbandry', p. 133.

14 Slicher van Bath, 'The rise of intensive husbandry', pp. 133–4.

15 Slicher van Bath, 'The rise of intensive husbandry', pp. 145–6; 'The yields of different crops (mainly cereals) in relation to the seed *c.* 810–1820', *Acta Historiae Neerlandica*, 2 (1967), p. 64; *The agrarian history*, p. 176.

16 Slicher van Bath, 'The rise of intensive husbandry', p. 136; *The agrarian history*, pp. 179–180; Lambert, *The Dutch Landscape*, pp. 193, 208.

17 Slicher van Bath, 'The rise of intensive husbandry', p. 136; *The agrarian history*, pp. 184, 188, 200; De Vries, *Dutch rural economy*, p. 154; Lambert, *The Dutch landscape*, p. 221; C. T. Smith, *An historical geography of Western Europe before 1800* (London, 1967), pp. 522–4.

18 De Vries, *Dutch rural economy*, pp. 136–44, 166–8, 174–82.

19 W. G. Hoskins, *The age of plunder: the England of Henry VIII, 1500–47* (London, 1976), p. 89: H. D. Clout, 'Urban growth, 1500–47', in H. D. Clout (ed.), *Themes in the historical geography of France* (London, 1977), p. 483.

20 De Vries, *Dutch rural economy*, p. 115.

21 De Vries, *Dutch rural economy*, pp. 95, 260 note 20; G. Parker, 'War and economic change: the economic cost of the Dutch Revolt', in J. M. Winter (ed.), *War and economic development* (Cambridge, 1975), pp. 50, 52, 59.

22 De Vries, *Dutch rural economy*, pp. 112–13.

23 De Vries, *Dutch rural economy*, pp. 117–18.

24 Lambert, *The Dutch landscape*, pp. 171, 185–7; C. Wilson, *Profit and power; a study of England and the Dutch Wars* (London, 1957), pp. 2, 32–4; J. L. Price, *Culture and society in the Dutch Republic*, pp. 41–5.

25 J. G. Van Dillen, 'Amsterdam's role in seventeenth century Dutch politics and its economic background' in Bromley and Kossman (eds.), *Britain and the Netherlands*, vol. 2 (Groningen, 1964), pp. 134–6; Lambert, *The Dutch landscape*, pp. 171, 187; Faber, *Acta Historiae Neerlandica*, 1 (1966), 108–17; V. Barbour, 'Dutch and English merchant shipping in the seventeenth century', in E. M. Carus-Wilson (ed.), *Essays in economic history* (vol. 1, London, 1954), pp. 231–40, 244, 247; M. Bogucka, 'Amsterdam and the Baltic in the first half of the seventeenth century', *Economic History Review*, 26 (1973–4), 433–47; Price, *Culture and society*, pp. 43–4.

26 E. H. Kossman, 'The Low Countries', in J. P. Cooper (ed.), *New Cambridge modern history*, vol. 4, *The decline of Spain and the Thirty Years War, 1609–48* (Cambridge, 1970), pp. 368–70.

27 J. A. Van Houtte, 'Economic development of Belgium and the Netherlands from the beginning of the modern era', *Journal of European Economic History*, 1 (1972), 109; Kossman, 'The Low Countries', p. 368; Lambert, *The Dutch landscape*, p. 193.

28 Lambert, *The Dutch landscape*, pp. 195–6, 203; F. L. Jones and K. W. Swart, 'Survey of recent historical works in Belgium and the Netherlands published in Dutch', *Acta Historiae Neerlandica*, 9 (1976), 207.

29 De Vries, *Dutch rural economy*, pp. 106–7.

30 De Vries, *Dutch rural economy*, pp. 119–36.

31 De Vries, *Dutch rural economy*, pp. 110–13; H. Van Dijk and D. J. Roorda, 'Social mobility under the regents of the Republic', *Acta Historiae Neerlandica*, 9 (1976), 85–6.

32 E. Hobsbawm. 'The general crisis of the European economy in the seventeenth century', *Past and Present*, 5 (1954), 33–53; 6 (1954), 44–65.

33 B. H. Slicher van Bath, 'Study of historical demography in the Netherlands', in P. Harsin and E. Hélin (eds.), *Problèmes de mortalité: actes du Colloque International de démographie historique* (Liege, 1965), p. 191; F. Spooner, 'The European economy 1609–50', in Cooper (ed.), *New Cambridge modern history*, vol. 4, p. 75.

34 De Vries, *Dutch rural economy*, pp. 113, 118.

35 D. C. North and R. P. Thomas, *The rise of the Western World: a new economic history* (Cambridge, 1973), pp. 131–4; B. Lyon, 'Medieval real estate developments and freedom', *American Historical Review*, 63 (1957), 58; B. H. Slicher van Bath, 'The economic and social conditions in the Frisian districts from 900 to 1300', *A.A.G. Bijdragen* 13 (1965), 106; *The agrarian history*, p. 146; De Vries, *Dutch rural economy*, p. 50.

36 J. C. G. M. Jansen, 'Agrarian development and exploitation in South Limburg in the years 1650–1850', *Acta Historiae Neerlandica*, 5 (1971), 244–5; De Vries, *Dutch rural economy*, pp. 16, 197; *Journal of Economic History*, 33 (1973), 193, 200.

CHAPTER 13

1 P. Deane and W. A. Cole, *British economic growth 1688–1959* (Cambridge, 1962), p. 78.

2 S. Pollard and D. W. Crossley, *The wealth of Britain, 1085–1966* (London, 1968), pp. 180–2.

3 P. K. O'Brien, 'Agriculture and the Industrial Revolution', *Economic History Review*, 30 (1977–8), 173.

4 J. T. Coppock, *An agricultural geography of Great Britain* (London, 1971), pp. 12, 16.

5 N. F. R. Crafts, 'English economic growth in the eighteenth century: a re-examination of Deane and Cole's estimates', *Economic History Review*, 29 (1976–7), 235.

6 J. T. Krause, 'The changing adequacy of English registration, 1690–1837', in D. V. Glass and D. E. C. Eversley (eds.), *Population in history* (London, 1965), 379–93.

7 T. H. Hollingsworth, *Historical demography* (London, 1969), p. 349.

8 N. L. Tranter, *Population since the Industrial Revolution: the case of England and Wales* (London, 1973), p. 53.

9 J. Brownlee, 'The history of the birth and death rates in England and Wales, taken as a whole from 1570 to the present time', *Public Health*, June (1916), 211–22; July (1916), 228–38; D. V. Glass, 'Population and population movements in England and Wales 1700

to 1850', in Glass and Eversley, *Population in history*, pp. 159–220; J. T. Krause, 'Changes in English fertility and mortality, 1781–1850', *Economic History Review*, 11 (1958–9), 52–7; G. T. Griffith, *Population problems in the age of Malthus* (Cambridge, 1967); Deane and Cole, *British economic growth*, pp. 99–106.

10 T. H. Hollingsworth, 'The demography of the British peerage', *Population Studies*, 18 (1969), Supplement, p. 56; P. E. Razell, 'Population change in eighteenth century England; a reappraisal', *Economic History Review*, 18 (1965–6), 133; M. W. Beaver, 'Population, infant mortality and milk', *Population Studies*, 27 (1973), 244; F. West, 'Infant mortality in the East Fen parishes of Leake, Wrangle', *Population Studies*, 13 (1974), 41–4; R. E. Jones, 'Infant mortality in rural North Shropshire, 1561–1810', *Population Studies*, 30 (1976), 309.

11 J. T. Krause, 'Some aspects of population change 1690–1790', E. L. Jones and G. E. Mingay (eds.), *Land, labour and population in the Industrial Revolution* (London, 1967), p. 193; Hollingsworth, *Historical demography*, p. 30; E. A. Wrigley, 'Family limitation in pre-industrial England', *Economic History Review*, 19 (1966–7), 82–109; D. Levine, 'The demographic implications of rural industrialization: a family reconstitution study of Shepshed, Leicestershire from 1600–1851', *Social History*, 2 (1976), 185.

12 E. S. Lee, 'Estimating series of vital rates and age structures from baptisms and burials; a new technique, with applications to pre-industrial England', *Population Studies*, 28 (1974), 495–512.

13 G. T. Griffith, *Population problems*; T. McKeown and R. G. Brown, 'Medical evidence related to changes in the eighteenth century', *Population Studies*, 9 (1955), 119–41; T. McKeown and R. G. Record, 'Reasons for the decline of mortality in England and Wales during the nineteenth century', *Population Studies*, 16 (1962), 94–122; T. McKeown, R. G. Brown and R. G. Record, 'An interpretation of the modern rise of population in England and Wales', *Population Studies*, 26 (1972), 345–82; T. McKeown, *The modern rise of population* (London, 1976); Razell, *Economic History Review*, 18 (1965–6), 312–32; 'Population growth and economic change in eighteenth and early nineteenth century England', in Jones and Mingay, *Land, labour and population*, pp. 260–81; 'An interpretation of the modern rise of the population in England – a critique', *Population Studies*, 28 (1974), 5–17; S. Cherry, 'The role of a provincial hospital; the Norfolk and Norwich Hospital, 1771–1880', *Population Studies*, 26 (1972), 291–306; E. M. Sigsworth, 'Gateways to death? Medicine, hospitals and mortality 1700–1850', in P. Mathias (ed.), *Science and society, 1600–1900* (Cambridge, 1972), pp. 97–110; M. W. Flinn, 'The stabilisation of mortality in pre-industrial Europe', *Journal of European Economic History*, 3 (1974), 287–317; K. F. Helleiner, 'The vital revolution reconsidered', in Glass and Eversley, *Population in history*, pp. 79–86; J. D. Chambers, *Population, economy and society in pre-industrial England* (London, 1972), pp. 85–7.

14 J. D. Chambers, *The Vale of Trent, 1670–1800: a regional study of economic change*. *Economic History Review Supplement*, 3 (1957), pp. 20–1.

15 J. D. Chambers and G. E. Mingay, *The agricultural revolution, 1750–1880* (London, 1966), p. 115; J. T. Coppock, *An agricultural geography*, p. 12.

16 A. J. Peacock, 'Village radicalism in East Anglia, 1800–1850', in J. P. D. Dunbabin (ed.), *Rural discontent in nineteenth century Britain* (London, 1974), p. 59.

17 P. K. O'Brien, *Economic History Review*, 30 (1977–8), 174–5; H. J. Habakkuk, 'Population problems and European economic development in the late eighteenth and nineteenth centuries', *American Economic Review, Papers and Proceedings*, 53 (1963), 613, 616.

18 Lord Ernle, *English farming, past and present* (6th edn, London, 1961), p. 488; Chambers and Mingay, *Agricultural revolution*, pp. 39, 111; Pollard and Crossley, *The wealth of Britain*, p. 176.

19 T. W. Fletcher, 'The agrarian revolution in arable Lancashire', *Transactions of the Lancashire and Cheshire Antiquarian Society*, 7 (1962), 102; G. Hueckel, 'English farming profits during the Napoleonic Wars, 1793–1815', *Explorations in Economic History*, 13 (1976), 331–2; Chambers and Mingay, *The agricultural revolution*, p. 112; R. A. C. Parker, *Coke of Norfolk: a financial and agricultural study, 1707–1842* (Oxford, 1975), p. 39; G. E. Mingay, 'The agricultural depression 1730–1750', *Economic History Review*, 8 (1955–6), 323–38.

20 H. Levy, *Large and small holdings* (Cambridge, 1911).

21 H. J. Habakkuk, 'English landownership, 1680–1740', *Economic History Review*, 10 (1940), 2–17; F. M. L. Thompson, 'Landownership and economic growth in England in the 18th century', in E. L. Jones and S. J. Woolf (eds.), *Agrarian change and economic development* (London, 1969), pp. 43–4.

22 Sir John Clapham, 'The growth of an agrarian proletariat, 1688–1832: a statistical note', *Cambridge Historical Journal*, 1 (1923), 92–5; *An economic history of modern Britain*, vol. 1, *The early railway age, 1820–1850* (Cambridge, 1926), p. 452; D. Grigg, 'Large and small farms in England and Wales: their size and distribution', *Geography*, 48 (1963), 268–79.

23 G. E. Mingay, 'The size of farms in the eighteenth century', *Economic History Review*, 14 (1961–2), 469–88; J. R. Wordie, 'Social change on the Leveson-Gower estates, 1714–1832', *Economic History Review*, 27 (1974–5), 593–609; D. Grigg, *The agricultural revolution in South Lincolnshire* (Cambridge, 1966), pp. 88–94; D. C. Barnett, 'Allotments and the problem of rural poverty in 1780–1840', in Jones and Mingay, *Land, labour and population*, pp. 162–83.

24 M. G. Turner, 'Parliamentary enclosure and population change in England, 1750–1830', *Explorations in Economic History*, 13 (1976), 463.

25 E. J. T. Collins, 'Harvest technology and labour supply in Britain, 1790–1870', *Economic History Review*, 22 (1969–70), 467.

26 A. W. Coates, 'The relief of poverty, attitudes to labour and economic change in England 1660–1782', *International Review of Social History*, 21 (1976), 110; Dunbabin, *Rural discontent*, p. 18; D. E. Williams, 'Were hunger rioters really hungry? Some demographic evidence', *Past and Present*, 71 (1976), 70–5.

27 C. P. Timmer, 'The turnip, the new husbandry and the English agricultural revolution', *Quarterly Journal of Economics*, 83 (1969), 392; E. L. Jones, 'The agricultural labour market in England, 1793–1872', *Economic History Review*, 17 (1964–5), 325.

28 G. E. Mingay, 'The transformation of agriculture', in Institute of Economic Affairs, *The long debate on poverty* (London, 1972), pp. 34–6; J. D. Marshall, 'The Lancashire rural labourer in the early nineteenth century', *Transactions of the Lancashire and Cheshire Antiquarian Society*, 71 (1961), 98; E. H. Hunt, 'Labour productivity in English agriculture, 1850–1914', *Economic History Review*, 20 (1967–8), 280; J. R. Bellerby, 'The distribution of manpower in agriculture and industry, 1851–1951', *The Farm Economist*, 9 (1958), 3; E. Richards, 'Captain Swing in the West Midlands', *International Review of Social History*, 19 (1974), 86–99.

29 T. L. Richardson, 'The agricultural labourer's standard of living in Kent, 1790–1840', in D. J. Oddy and D. Miller (eds.), *The making of the modern British diet* (London, 1970), 103–16; A. Digby, 'The rural poor law', in D. Fraser (ed.), *The new poor law in the nineteenth century* (London, 1976), p. 165; J. Burnett, *Plenty and want: a social history of diet in England from 1815 to the present day* (Harmondsworth, 1966), p. 27; 'Trends in bread consumption', in T. C. Barker and J. C. Mackenzie (eds.), *Our changing fare* (London, 1966), p. 69.

30 Chambers and Mingay, *Agricultural revolution*, pp. 18–19; Marshall, *Transactions of the Lancashire and Cheshire Antiquarian Society*, 71 (1961), 97; D. W. Howell, 'The agricultural labourer in nineteenth century Wales', *Welsh History Review*, 6 (1972), 262; Burnett, *Plenty and want*, p. 15.

31 N. Gash, 'Rural unemployment, 1815–34', *Economic History Review*, 6 (1935–6), 90–3; E. J. Hobsbawm and G. Rudé, *Captain Swing* (London, 1969), p. 19; E. J. T. Collins, *Economic History Review*, 22 (1969–70), 454–69; *Sickle to combine* (Reading, 1969), pp. 6–7; 'The diffusion of the threshing machine in Britain, 1790–1800', *Tools and Tillage*, 2 (1972), 16–33.

32 J. P. Huzel, 'Malthus, the Poor Law and population in early nineteenth century England', *Economic History Review*, 22 (1969–70), 430–52.

33 M. Blaug, 'The myth of the old poor law and the making of the new', *Journal of Economic History*, 23 (1963), 154–5; A. Digby, 'The rural poor law', in D. Fraser (ed.), *The new poor law in the nineteenth century*, pp. 149–70; 'The labour market and the continuity of social policy after 1834: the case of the eastern counties', *Economic History Review*, 28 (1975–6), 70–1; Chambers and Mingay, *Agricultural revolution*, p. 133; Clapham, *Cambridge Historical Journal*, 1 (1923), 92–5; Clapham, *An economic history of modern Britain*, vol. 1, p. 452.

34 A. J. Peacock, 'Village radicalism in East Anglia, 1800–1850', in Dunbabin, *Rural discontent*, p. 63; D. Jones, 'Thomas Campbell Foster and the rural labourer: incendiarism in East Anglia in the 1840s', *Social History*, 1 (1976), 5–37.
35 Lord Ernle, *English farming*, pp. 148–223.
36 E. Kerridge, *The agricultural revolution* (London, 1967); 'The agricultural revolution reconsidered', *Agricultural History*, 43 (1969), 463–75; *The farmers of old England* (London, 1973).
37 M. Havinden, 'Agricultural progress in open-field Oxfordshire', *Agricultural History Review*, 11 (1961), 73–83.
38 M. Williams, 'The enclosure and reclamation of wasteland in England and Wales in the eighteenth and nineteenth centuries', *Transactions of the Institute of British Geographers*, 51 (1970), 57–9.
39 A. Harris, *The rural landscape of the East Riding of Yorkshire 1700–1850; a study in historical geography* (London, 1961), p. 86; Grigg, *South Lincolnshire*, p. 157.
40 R. N. Salaman, *The history and social influence of the potato* (Cambridge, 1949), p. 613.
41 C. Davenant, *The political and commercial works of C. D. 'Avenant, Ll.D.* (5 vols., London, 1771), vol. 2, p. 217.
42 H. D. Prince, 'England *circa* 1800', in H. C. Darby (ed.), *A new historical geography of England* (Cambridge, 1973), p. 417; L. Drescher, 'The development of agricultural production in Great Britain and Ireland from the early nineteenth century', *Manchester School*, 23 (1955), 167.
43 Kerridge, *The agricultural revolution*, p. 277; H. J. Henderson, 'Agriculture in England and Wales in 1801', *Geographical Journal*, 118 (1952), 342; Grigg, *South Lincolnshire*, p. 77; Burnett, *Plenty and want*, p. 69; E. J. Evans, 'Some reasons for the growth of English rural anti-clericalism, *c.* 1750 – *c.* 1830', *Past and Present*, 66 (1975), 92; Salaman, *The history and social influence of the potato*.
44 Kerridge, *The agricultural revolution*, pp. 215, 278, 280, 281; F. V. Emery, 'The mechanics of innovation: clover cultivation in Wales before 1750', *Journal of Historical Geography*, 2 (1976), 34, 36, 38.
45 A. H. John, 'The course of agricultural change, 1660–1760', in L. S. Pressnell (ed.), *Studies in the Industrial Revolution* (London, 1960), pp. 125–55; 'Agricultural productivity and economic growth in England, 1700–1760', *Journal of Economic History*, 25 (1965), 19–34; E. L. Jones, 'Agriculture and economic growth, 1660–1750: agricultural change', *Journal of Economic History*, 25 (1965), 1–18; 'Introduction', in E. L. Jones (ed.), *Agriculture and economic growth in England 1650–1815* (London, 1967), 1–48.
46 J. A. Venn, 'An inquiry into British methods of crop estimating', *Economic Journal*, 36 (1925), 394–418; H. D. Vigor, 'Crop estimates in England', *Journal of the Royal Statistical Society*, 51 (1928), 1–49.
47 R. Lennard, 'English agriculture under Charles II: the evidence of the Royal Societies "Enquiries"', *Economic History Review*, 4 (1951–2), 41.
48 G. E. Fussell, quoted in Deane and Cole, *British economic growth*, pp. 62, 67.
49 M. K. Bennett, 'British wheat yields per acre over seven centuries', *Economic History*, 10 (1935), 22–6.
50 J. A. Yelling, *Common field and enclosure in England 1450–1850* (London, 1977), p. 172; P. G. Craigie, 'Statistics of agricultural production', *Statistical Journal*, 46 (1883), 21; Grigg, *South Lincolnshire*, pp. 59, 152; J. A. Perkins, 'The prosperity of farming on the Lindsey uplands, 1813–1837', *Agricultural History Review*, 27 (1976), 129.
51 M. J. R. Healey and E. L. Jones, 'Wheat yields in England, 1815–1859', *Journal of the Royal Statistical Society*, Series A, 125 (1962), 108–9; Grigg, *South Lincolnshire*, p. 152; J. A. Perkins, *Agricultural History Review*, 27 (1976), 129.
52 Jones, *Journal of Economic History*, 25 (1975), 1–18; 'Introduction', in Jones, *Agriculture and economic growth*, pp. 1–48; Kerridge, *The agricultural revolution*.
53 A. H. John, 'English agricultural improvement and grain exports, 1660–1765', in D. C. Coleman and A. H. John (eds.), *Trade, government and economy in pre-industrial England: essays presented to F. J. Fisher* (London, 1976), p. 48.
54 D. E. C. Eversley, 'The home market and economic growth in England, 1750–1780', in Jones and Mingay, *Land, labour and population*, pp. 206–59; A. H. John, 'The course of agricultural change', in Pressnell, *Studies*, pp. 125–55.
55 A. Harris, *The rural landscape of the East Riding*, p. 61.
56 Deane and Cole, *British economic growth*, p. 65.

57 F. M. L. Thompson, 'The second agricultural revolution, 1815–1880', *Economic History Review*, 21 (1968–9), 62–77.
58 Sir John Clapham, *An economic history of modern Britain*, vol. 2, *Free trade and steel, 1850–1886* (Cambridge, 1932), p. 22.
59 P. Horn, *Labouring life in the Victorian countryside* (Dublin, 1976), pp. 90–2, 106–8; J. B. Harley, 'England – *circa* 1850', in H. C. Darby (ed.), *A new historical geography of England* (Cambridge, 1973), p. 568; J. Saville, *Rural depopulation in England and Wales, 1851–1951* (London, 1957), pp. 4–5, 22, 25, 28; A. Harris, 'Changes in the early railway age 1800–1850', in Darby, *New historical geography*, p. 415.
60 Saville, *Rural depopulation*, p. 21; B. Kerr, *Bound to the soil* (London, 1968), p. 133; R. J. Olney, 'Labouring life on the Lincolnshire Wolds: a study of Binbrook in the mid-nineteenth century', *Occasional Papers in Lincolnshire History and Archaeology*, 2 (1975), 12.
61 C. M. Law, 'Some notes on the urban population of England and Wales in the eighteenth century', *Local Historian*, 10 (1972), 13–26; 'The growth of urban population in England and Wales, 1801–1911', *Transactions of the Institute of British Geographers*, 41 (1967), 125–44.
62 Clapham, *An economic history of modern Britain*, vol. 1, pp. 536–7.
63 D. Grigg, 'E. G. Ravenstein and the laws of migration', *Journal of Historical Geography*, 3 (1977), 50–1.
64 T. Mansell Hodges, 'The peopling of the hinterland and Port of Cardiff, 1801–1914', in W. E. Minchinton (ed.), *Industrial South Wales 1750–1914* (London, 1969), pp. 5, 8; J. F. C. Harrison (ed.), *The early Victorians, 1832–1851* (London, 1971), p. 142; R. Lawton, 'The population of Liverpool in the mid-nineteenth century', *Transactions of the Historic Society of Lancashire and Cheshire*, 107 (1955), 99; R. A. Church, *Economic and social change in a Midland town; Victorian Nottingham 1815–1900* (London, 1966), p. 234.
65 *Census of England and Wales, 1861: 3. General Report, Sessional Papers* (1863), 53 (Cd 3221); H. A. Shannon, 'Migration and the growth of London, 1841–91', *Economic History Review*, 5 (1934–5), 79–86.
66 J. D. Chambers, 'Population change in a provincial town: Nottingham 1700–1800', in Pressnell, *Studies in the Industrial Revolution*, pp. 97–124; R. Lawton, 'Genesis of population', in W. Smith (ed.), *A scientific survey of Merseyside* (Liverpool, 1953), pp. 120–31; J. E. Williams, 'Hull 1700–1835', in K. J. Allison (ed.), *The Victoria county history of the East Riding*, vol. 1, *The city of Kingston-upon-Hull* (London, 1960), p. 191.
67 J. R. Bellerby, *Agriculture and industry, relative income* (London, 1956), p. 223.
68 B. Thomas, *Migration and economic growth: a study of Great Britain and the Atlantic economy* (Cambridge, 1954), 36–55; N. H. Carrier and J. R. Jeffrey, *External migration: a study of the available statistics 1815–1950* (London, 1953), 139; M. A. Jones, 'The background to emigration from Great Britain in the nineteenth century', *Perspectives in American History*, 7 (1973), 23.
69 C. J. Erickson, *Invisible immigrants: the adaptation of English and Scottish immigrants in the nineteenth century* (London, 1972); S. C. Johnson, *A history of emigration from the United Kingdom to North America, 1763–1912* (London, 1913), p. 48; W. A. Carrothers, *Emigration from the British Isles with special reference to the development of the overseas dominions* (London, 1929), p. 182; W. S. Shepperson, 'Agrarian aspects of early Victorian emigration to North America', *Canadian Historical Review*, 33 (1952), 254–64; Jones, *Perspectives in American History*, 7 (1973), 38, 45, 49.
70 Carrier and Jeffrey, *External migration*, p. 139; Jones, *Perspectives in American History*, 7 (1973), 49, 57, 60.
71 T. H. Hollingsworth, *Historical demography* (London, 1969), pp. 345–7; Krause, *Economic History Review*, 11 (1958–9), 52–7; J. P. Huzel, *Economic History Review*, 22 (1969–70), 430–52.
72 Pollard and Crossley, *The wealth of Britain*, p. 210.

CHAPTER 14

1 M. Reinhard, A. Armengaud and J. Dupâquier, *Histoire générale de la population mondiale* (Paris, 1968), pp. 252, 291; A. Armengaud, *La population française au XIXe siècle* (Paris, 1971), pp. 6, 41–2.

2 J. Dupâquier, 'French population in the 17th and 18th centuries', in R. Cameron (ed.), *Essays in French economic history* (Homewood, Illinois, 1970), p. 157.
3 J. Bourgeois-Pichat, 'The general development of the population of France since the eighteenth century', in D. V. Glass and D. E. C. Eversley (eds.), *Population in history* (London, 1965), p. 484.
4 R. Denie and L. Henry, 'La population d'un village du Nord de la France, Sainghin-en-Mélantois, de 1665 à 1851', *Population*, 20 (1965), 562–602; A. Chamoux and C. Dauphin, 'La contraception avant la révolution française; l'example de Châtillon-sur-Seine', *Annales ESC*, 24 (1969), 666, 677; J. Dupâquier and M. Lachiver, 'Sur les débuts de la contraception en France ou les deux malthusianismes', *Annales ESC*, 24 (1969), 1391–1406; J. Godechat and S. Moncassin, 'Démographie et subsistences en Languedoc', *Bulletin d'Histoire Économique et Sociale de la Révolution Française* (1964), 21–60; E. Le Roy Ladurie, 'Démographie et funestes secrets; le Languedoc (fin XVIIIe–début XIXe siècle)', *Annales Historiques de la Révolution Française*, 37 (1965), 395; L. Henry and J. Houdaille, 'Fécondité des marriages dans le quart nord-ouest de la France de 1670 à 1829', *Population*, 28 (1973), 873–924.
5 Reinhard, Armengaud and Dupâquier, *Histoire générale*, p. 331.
6 P. Goubert, 'Les fondements démographique', in E. Labrousse and P. Goubert, (eds.), *Histoire économique et sociale de la France*, vol. 2, *Des Dernier temps de l'âge seigneurial aux préludes de l'âge industriel, 1660–1789* (Paris, 1970), pp. 55–66; L. Henry, 'The population of France in the eighteenth century', in Glass and Eversley, *Population in history*, p. 44; E. Le Roy Ladurie, 'De la crise ultime à la vraie croissance', in E. Le Roy Ladurie (ed.), *Histoire de la France rurale*, vol. 2, *L'âge classique des paysans, 1340–1789* (Paris, 1975), p. 582; Reinhard, Armengaud and Dupâquier, *Histoire générale*, p. 258.
7 Reinhard, Armengaud and Dupâquier, *Histoire générale*, p. 329; Proudhon quoted in *Encyclopedia Brittanica; Macropaedia* (Fourteenth Edition, Chicago, 1973), vol. 14, p. 819.
8 M. Agulhon, G. Désert and R. Specklin, *Histoire de la France rurale*, vol. 3, *Apogée et crise de la civilisation paysanne, 1789–1914* (Paris, 1976), p. 10; R. Laurent, 'Les cadres de la production agricole: propriété et modes d'exploitation', in F. Braudel and E. Labrousse (eds.), *Histoire économique et sociale de la France*, vol. 3, *L'avenement de l'ère industrielle (1789 annes 1880)* (Paris, 1976), p. 621; R. Price, *The economic modernisation of France, 1730–1880* (London, 1975), p. 56; A. Armengaud, *La population français au XIXe siècle* (Paris, 1971), p. 26.
9 O. H. Hufton, *The poor of eighteenth century France 1750–1789* (Oxford, 1974), p. 16; W. Abel, *Crises agraires en Europe (XIIIe–XXe siècle)* (Paris, 1973), pp. 304–32; Laurent, 'Les cadres de la production agricole', p. 718; R. Forster, 'Obstacles to agricultural growth in eighteenth century France', *American Historical Review*, 75 (1970), 1603.
10 G. V. Taylor, 'Non-capitalist wealth and the French Revolution', *American Historical Review*, 72 (1967), 474; G. Désert and R. Specklin, 'Victoire sur la disette', in Agulhon, Désert and Specklin, *Histoire de la France rurale* vol. 3, p. 114.
11 E. Labrousse, 'The evolution of peasant society in France from the eighteenth century to the present', in E. M. Acomb and M. L. Brown, Jr. (eds.), *French society and culture since the Old Regime* (New York, 1966), pp. 44–6.
12 A. Davies, 'The origins of the French peasant revolution in 1789', *History*, 49 (1964), 29; T. Kemp, *Economic forces in French history* (London, 1971), p. 19.
13 Ladurie, *Histoire de la France rurale*, vol. 2, p. 417.
14 G. Lefebvre, *The great fear of 1789: rural panic in revolutionary France* (London, 1973), pp. 8–9; H. Sée, 'The peasants and agriculture', in R. M. Greenlaw (ed.), *The economic origins of the French Revolution: poverty or prosperity* (Boston, 1958), p. 50; T. F. Sheppard, *Lourmarin in the eighteenth century: a study of a French village* (Baltimore, 1971), p. 15.
15 Laurent, *Histoire économique et sociale*, vol. 3, p. 364.
16 Labrousse, *French society and culture*, p. 56.
17 Laurent, *Histoire économique et sociale*, vol. 3, pp. 651–2.
18 G. Lefebvre, 'The French revolution and the peasants', in Greenlaw, *The economic origins*, p. 77; *The great fear*, p. 9.
19 G. Désert, 'Vers le surpeuplement?', in *Histoire de la France rurale*, vol. 3, p. 60; M. Agulhon, 'La pauvreté et les classes sociales', in *Histoire de la France rurale*, vol. 3, p. 97; Laurent, *Histoire économique et sociale*, vol. 3, p. 658.

20 R. Forster, 'The noble wine producers of the Bordelais in the eighteenth century', *Economic History Review*, 14 (1961–2), 26; Davies, *History*, 49 (1964), 30; Désert and Specklin, *Histoire de la France rurale*, vol. 3, p. 107; F. Langois, *Les salariés agricoles en France* (Paris, 1962), p. 7.

21 E. J. T. Collins, 'Labour supply and demand in European agriculture, 1800–1880', in E. L. Jones and S. J. Woolf (eds.), *Agrarian change and economic development: the historical problems* (London, 1969), p. 72.

22 Price, *Economic modernization of France*, p. 205; W. Camp, *Marriage and the family in France since the Revolution* (New York, 1961), p. 25; E. Weber, *Peasants into Frenchmen: the modernization of rural France, 1870–1914* (London, 1977), pp. 132–44.

23 Désert, *Histoire de la France rurale*, vol. 3, pp. 63–6.

24 J. C. Toutain, *Le produit de l'agriculture française de 1700 à 1958* (Paris, 1961), p. 215; W. H. Newell, 'The agricultural revolution in nineteenth century France', *Journal of Economic History*, 33 (1973), 699–700; J. Marczewski, 'Some aspects of the economic growth of France, 1660–1958', *Economic Development and Cultural Change*, 9 (1961), 375; Ladurie, *Histoire de la France rurale*, vol. 2, pp. 395–417.

25 F. Sigaut, 'Pour une cartographie des assolements en France au début du XIXe siècle', *Annales ESC*, 31 (1976), 631–43.

26 Laurent, *Histoire économique et sociale*, vol. 3, p. 672.

27 Laurent, *Histoire économique et sociale*, vol. 3, p. 717.

28 H. D. Clout, 'Agrarian changes in the eighteenth and nineteenth centuries', in H. D. Clout (ed.), *Themes in the historical geography of France* (London, 1977), p. 411; Désert and Specklin, *Histoire de la France rurale*, vol. 3, pp. 118, 126.

29 H. D. Clout and A. D. M. Phillips, 'Sugar-beet production in the Nord department of France during the nineteenth century', *Erdkunde*, 27 (1973), 105–19.

30 M. Augé Laribé, *L'evolution de la France agricole* (Paris, 1912); *La révolution agricole* (Paris, 1955), pp. 7–8; D. Faucher, 'La révolution agricole du XVIIIe–XIXe siècle', *Bulletin de la Societé d'Histoire Moderne*, 20 (1956), 2–11; M. Bloch, *French rural history; an essay on its characteristics* (London, 1966), pp. 198–227; M. Morineau, 'Ya-t-il eu une révolution agricole en France au XVIIIe siècle?' *Revue Historique*, 239 (1968), 299–326; *Le faux-semblants d'un démarrage économique: agriculture et démographie en France au XVIIIe siècle* (Paris, 1970); Newell, *Journal of Economic History*, 33 (1973), 697–731; O. Festy, *L'agriculture pendant la Révolution français: les conditions de production et de récolte des céréales: étude d'histoire économique* (Paris, 1947); A. Armengaud, 'Agriculture et démographie au XVIIIe siècle: réflexions sur un livre récente,' *Revue d'Histoire Économique et Sociale*, 49 (1971), 406–15.

31 Morineau, *Revue Historique*, 239 (1968), 308.

32 Clout, *Themes in the historical geography of France*, p. 420.

33 Laurent, *Histoire économique et sociale*, vol. 3, p. 682.

34 Newell, *Journal of Economic History*, 33 (1973), 697–73; J. Pautard, *Les disparités régionales dans la croissance de l'agriculture française* (Paris, 1965), p. 30.

35 A. J. Bourde, *The influence of England on the French agronomes, 1750–1789* (Cambridge, 1953); D. J. Brandenburg, 'Agriculture in the Encyclopédie: an essay in French intellectual history', *Agricultural History*, 24 (1950), 96–108.

36 M. Bloch, *French rural history*, pp. 206, 210, 219, 226; A. Davies, 'The new agriculture in Lower Normandy 1750–1789', *Transactions of the Royal Historical Society*, 8 (1958), 139, 141–2; A. Soboul, 'The French rural community in the eighteenth and nineteenth centuries', *Past and Present*, 10 (1956), 82.

37 Price, *Economic modernization of France*, p. 47; H. D. Clout and A. D. M. Phillips, 'Fertilisants minéraux en France au XIXe siècle', *Etudes Rurales*, 45 (1972), 12–16; A. D. M. Phillips and H. D. Clout, 'Underdraining in France during the second half of the nineteenth century', *Transactions of the Institute of British Geographers*, 51 (1970), 55–70.

38 Laurent, *Histoire économique et sociale*, vol. 3, pp. 620, 673–4, 675, 680; A. Chatelaine, 'La lente progression de la faux', *Annales ESC*, 11 (1956), 485–99; J. H. Clapham, *The economic development of France and Germany 1815–1914* (Cambridge, 1961), pp. 26, 170.

39 Newell, *Journal of Economic History*, 33 (1973), 697–731.

40 J. P. Pousson, 'Les mouvement migratoires en France et a partir de la France de la fin du XVe siècle au début du XIXe siècle: approches pour une synthèse', *Annales de Démographie Historique* (1970), 55.

41 A. Armengaud, *La population français*, pp. 87, 93; 'La rôle de la démographie', in Braudel and Labrousse, *Histoire économique et sociale de la France*, vol. 3, pp. 208–10; H. Bunle, 'Migratory movements between France and foreign lands', in W. F. Willcox (ed.), *International migrations*, vol. 2, *Interpretations* (New York, 1931), p. 207.
42 Armengaud, *La population français*, p. 87.
43 A. Armengard, *La population français*, p. 27; 'Industrialisation et démographie dans la France du XIXe siècle', in P. Léon, F. Crouzet and R. Gascon (eds.), *Colloques Internationaux du C.N.R.S.*, no. 540 (Paris, 1970), p. 191; F. Crouzet, 'Agriculture et révolution industrielle: quelques réflexions', *Cahiers d'Histoire*, 12 (1967), 72; Désert, *Histoire de la France rurale*, vol. 3, p. 62.
44 P. Hohenburg, 'Migration et fluctuations démographiques dans la France rurale, 1836–1901', *Annales ESC*, 29 (1974), 461–97.
45 Désert, *Histoire de la France rurale*, vol. 3, p. 80; Armengaud, *La population français*, p. 70; C. H. Pouthas, *La population français pendant la prèmiere moitie du XIXe siècle* (Paris, 1956), p. 95.
46 G. Désert, 'Prospéritié de l'agriculture', in *Histoire de la France rurale*, vol. 3, p. 222; P. Barral, *Les agrariens français de Meline à Pisani* (Paris, 1968), p. 19; Jean Bouvier, 'Le mouvement d'une civilisation nouvelle', in G. Duby (ed.), *Histoire de la France*, vol. 3, *Les temps nouveaux de 1852 à nos jours* (Paris, 1972), p. 17; Pauthard, *Les disparités régionales*, p. 120; T. Zeldin, *France 1848–1945*, vol. 1 (Oxford, 1973), p. 170; R. Price, 'The onset of labour shortage in nineteenth century French agriculture', *Economic History Review*, 28 (1975–6), 264–6, 271.
47 Armengaud, *Histoire économique et sociale*, vol. 3, p. 26; Lefebvre, *The great fear*, p. 10; C. Fohlen, 'France, 1700–1914' in C. M. Cipolla (ed.), *The Fontana economic history of Europe*, vol. 4, *The emergence of industrial societies* (London, 1973), part 1, pp. 27, 64.
48 A. Chatelain, 'Les migrations temporaires françaises aux XIXe siècle', *Annales de Démographie Historique* (1967), 9–28.
49 Armengaud, *Histoire économique et sociale*, vol. 3, p. 190.
50 E. van de Walle, *The female population of France in the nineteenth century* (Princeton, New Jersey, 1974), p. 182; W. D. Camp, *Marriage and the family in France*, pp. 21, 34, 36; Armengaud, *Histoire économique et sociale*, vol. 2, p. 178.
51 Armengaud, *Histoire économique et sociale*, vol. 3, p. 191.
52 Camp, *Marriage and the family*, p. 52.
53 See the references in note 4 above.
54 Bourgeois-Pichet, *Population in history*, p. 490.

CHAPTER 15

1 M. Drake, *Population and society in Norway, 1735–1865* (London, 1969), pp. 2–17.
2 L. Jörberg, 'The Nordic countries, 1850–1914', in C. M. Cipolla (ed.), *The Fontana economic history of Europe*, vol. 4, *The emergence of industrial societies* (London, 1973), part 2, p. 404; S. Lieberman, *The industrialization of Norway 1800–1920* (Oslo, 1970), p. 15.
3 S. Dyrvik, 'Historical demography in Norway 1660–1801; a short survey', *Scandinavian Economic History Review*, 20 (1972), p. 34.
4 Drake, *Population and society*, pp. 39, 71.
5 Drake, *Population and society*, pp. 49, 54; G. Guteland, I. Holmberg, T. Hagerstrand, A. Karlqvist, B. Rundbad, *The biography of a people: past and future population changes in Sweden* (Stockholm, 1974), p. 62; F. Hodne, *An economic history of Norway 1815–1970* (Bergen, 1976), p. 191; S. Lieberman, 'Norwegian population growth in the nineteenth century', *Economy and History*, 11 (1968), 52–66; B. J. Hovde, *The Scandinavian countries, 1720–1865*, vol. 2, *The rise of the middle classes* (New York, 1943), p. 741.
6 G. Fridlizius, 'Some new aspects on Swedish population growth: II, a study at parish level', *Economy and History*, 18 (1975), 149–50; S. Dyrvik, 'Infant mortality about 1800 – a preliminary exploration into Norwegian local material', *Scandinavian Population Studies*, 3 (Helsinki, 1974), 134; Drake, *Population and society*, p. 59; C. J. O'Neill, 'A fresh look at Norway's pre-industrial population growth using stable population theory', *Conference of the International Union for the Scientific Study of Population* (Liege, 1973, mimeographed), pp. 4–5.

7 Fridlizius, *Economy and History*, 18 (1975), 149–50.
8 Ann-Sofie Kälvemark, 'Reactionen mot utvendringe: emigrationsfrågan; svensk debatt och politik 1901–1904', *Studia Historica Upsaliensis*, 41 (1972), 225–37; L. Ljungmark, 'For Sale – Minnesota organized promotion of Scandinavian emigration 1860–73', *Studia Historica Gothenburgensia*, 13 (1971), 4; G. A. Montgomery, *The rise of modern industry in Sweden* (Stockholm, 1939), p. 50; T. Gårdlind, *The life of Knut Wicksell* (Uppsala, 1958), pp. 257–8.
9 Drake, *Population and society*, p. 174; I. Semmingsen, 'Emigration from Scandinavia', *Scandinavian Economic History Review*, 20 (1972), 46; Hodne, *An economic history of Norway*, p. 364; Montgomery, *The rise of modern industry*, p. 61; J. S. Lindberg, *The background of Swedish emigration to the United States* (Minneapolis, 1930), p. 101; Guteland *et al.*, *Biography of a people*, p. 60; L. Jörberg, 'Structural change and economic growth: Sweden in the 19th century', *Economy and History*, 8 (1965), 13.
10 L. Jörberg, *A history of prices in Sweden, 1732–1914*, vol. 1, *Description, analysis* (Lund, 1972), pp. 183, 196, 199–200; G. Fridlizius, 'Sweden's exports 1850–1960', *Economy and History*, 6 (1963), 8–9, 12, 16, 18; 'The Crimean War and the Swedish economy', *Economy and History*, 3 (1960), 65, 96–7; Drake, *Population and society*, p. 59; S. Akerman, 'Rural and urban immigration', *Scandinavian Economic History Review*, 20 (1972), 100; T. C. Blegen, *Norwegian migration to America, 1825–1860* (Minneapolis, 1931), p. 70.
11 Hodne, *An economic history of Norway*, p. 135.
12 Blegen, *Norwegian migration*, pp. 167–8; T. K. Derry, *A history of modern Norway, 1814–1972* (London, 1973), p. 100; Drake, *Population and society*, p. 81.
13 E. Heckscher, *An economic history of Sweden* (London, 1954), pp. 162, 165.
14 Fridlizius, *Economy and History*, 18 (1975), 128; Jörberg, *Economy and History*, 8 (1965), 13; Montgomery, *The rise of modern industry*, p. 56; D. S. Thomas, *Social and economic aspects of Swedish population movements, 1750–1933* (New York, 1941), p. 68.
15 O. Bjurling, 'The Baron's revolution', *Economy and History*, 2 (1959), 23–35; S. Helmfrid, 'The storskifte, enskifte and laga skifte in Sweden – general features', *Geografiska Annaler*, 43 (1961), 114–29.
16 P. Lundell, 'Agriculture and cattle-breeding', in G. Sundbärg (ed.), *Sweden, its people and industry: a historical and statistical handbook* (Stockholm, 1904), p. 518.
17 Helmfrid, *Geografiska Annaler*, 43 (1961), 122; Montgomery, *The rise of modern industry*, pp. 53–5; *An economic history of Sweden*, pp. 158–9; Hodne, *An economic history of Norway*, p. 154.
18 Thomas, *Social and economic aspects*, pp. 53–66.
19 Lundell, 'Agriculture and cattle-breeding', p. 522; S. Carlsonn, 'The dissolution of the Swedish estates, 1700–1865', *Journal of European Economic History*, 1 (1972), 574–624.
20 A. Holmsen, 'The Norwegian peasant community; a general survey and historical introduction', *Scandinavian Economic History Review*, 4 (1956), 21; 'The transition from tenancy to freehold peasant ownership in Norway', *Scandinavian Economic History Review*, 9 (1961), 153, 160, 162; 'Landowners and tenants in Norway', *Scandinavian Economic History Review*, 6 (1958), 119.
21 S. Lieberman, *The industrialisation of Norway*, p. 71; Hodne, *An economic history of Norway*, p. 27.
22 L. Jörberg, 'The development of real wages for agricultural workers in Sweden during the eighteenth and nineteenth centuries', *Economy and History*, 16 (1972), 41–57; 'The Nordic countries, 1850–1914', p. 186; *Growth and fluctuations of Swedish industry, 1868–1912* (Stockholm, 1961), p. 10; H. A. Gemery, 'Absorption of population pressure in 19th century Sweden', *International Population Conference, London, 1969* (3 vols., Liege, 1971), vol. 3, p. 1693; Hodne, *An economic history of Norway*, p. 41.
23 F. Valen-Sendstad, *Norske Landbruksredskaper 1800–1850 årene* (Lillehammer, 1964), quoted in Drake, *Population and society*, p. 60.
24 T. C. Smout, 'The lessons of Norwegian agrarian history: a review of S. Tveite, *Jord og Gjerning. Trekk av Norsk landsbruk i 150 ar. Dt. Knglselscap for Norges Vel, 1809–1959*', *Scottish Historical Review*, 53 (1974), 72.
25 B. Holgersson, 'Cultivated land in Sweden, and its growth, 1840–1939', *Economy and History*, 17 (1974), 21, 47–8.

26 Drake, *Population and society*, p. 13; Hodne, *An economic history of Norway*, pp. 26, 147; Hovde, *The Scandinavian countries*, p. 296.
27 S. Erixon, 'Swedish villages without systematic regulation', *Geografiska Annaler*, 43 (1961), 73–4.
28 L. Jörberg, 'The Nordic countries, 1850–1914', p. 402.
29 H. Osvald, *Swedish agriculture* (Stockholm, 1952), p. 41; Thomas, *Social and economic aspects*, p. 75.
30 Hecksher, *An economic history of Sweden*, pp. 150–81; Lindberg, *The background of Swedish emigration*, p. 76; Thomas, *Social and economic aspects*, pp. 70–2; Osvald, *Swedish agriculture*, p. 42.
31 Drake, *Population and society*, pp. 56–63; Dyrvik, *Scandinavian Economic History Review*, 20 (1972), 41; Hodne, *An economic history of Norway*, p. 26; Derry, *A history of modern Norway*, p. 100; Blegen, *Norwegian migration*, pp. 172–3; C. Vandenbroeke, 'Cultivation and consumption of the potato in the 17th and 18th centuries', *Acta Historia Neerlandica*, 5 (1971), 15–39.
32 Holgersson, *Economy and History*, 17 (1964), 21, 25; Hovde, *The Scandinavian countries*, p. 298.
33 Carlsson, *Journal of European Economic History*, 1 (1972), 593; Montgomery, *The rise of modern industry*, pp. 56, 58.
34 Holmsen, *Scandinavian Economic History Review*, 9 (1961), 163; Derry, *A history of modern Norway*, p. 100; Jörberg, 'The Nordic countries, 1850–1914', p. 402; Lieberman, *The industrialization of Norway*, pp. 59, 66, 69; Smout, *Scottish Historical Review*, 53 (1974), 72–4; Fridlizius, *Economy and History*, 3 (1960), 25; Hecksher, *An economic history of Sweden*, pp. 153–9; Osvald, *Swedish agriculture*, p. 54; Lindberg, *The background of Swedish emigration*, p. 105; C. Winberg, 'Folkökning och proletarisering', *Meddelanden Från Historiska Institutionen*, no. 10 (Gothenburg, 1973), English summary, pp. 331–44; Hovde, *The Scandinavian countries*, p. 293.
35 Lundell, 'Agriculture and cattle-breeding', p. 516; Lindberg, *The background of Swedish emigration*, pp. 138–9; T. Moe, 'The history of economic growth in Norway', *Scandinavian Economic History Review*, 20 (1972), 174–81; Smout, *Scottish Historical Review*, 53 (1974), 72–3; Hodne, *An economic history of Norway*, pp. 137, 203, 209; J. Kuuse, 'Mechanisation, commercialisation, and the protectionist movement in Swedish agriculture, 1860–1910', *Scandinavian Economic History*, 19 (1971), 32; Derry, *A history of modern Norway*, p. 122; Hovde, *The Scandinavian countries*, p. 257.
36 Hodne, *An economic history of Norway*, pp. 25, 290; I. Semmingsen, 'The dissolution of estate society in Norway', *Scandinavian Economic History Review*, 2 (1954), 179.
37 Derry, *A history of modern Norway*, p. 10; Hodne, *An economic history of Norway*, pp. 20, 73, 74, 79, 101, 290; Jörberg, 'The Nordic countries, 1850–1914', pp. 425–6; Smout, *Scottish Historical Review*, 53 (1974), 69–71; Drake, *Population and society*, p. 81; E. Bull, 'Industrialisation as a factor in economic growth: Norway', *First International Conference of Economic History, Stockholm, 1960: contributions* (Paris, 1960), p. 263.
38 Hodne, *An economic history of Norway*, p. 20.
39 Jörberg, 'The Nordic countries, 1850–1914', p. 392.
40 K. Hvidt, *Flight to America: the social background of 300000 Danish emigrants* (London, 1975), p. 8.
41 K. Hvidt, 'Danish emigration prior to 1914: trends and problems', *Scandinavian Economic History Review*, 14 (1966), 166; I. Semmingsen, 'Norwegian emigration in the nineteenth century', *Scandinavian Economic History Review*, 8 (1960), 150; E. Hofsten and H. Lundstrom, 'Swedish population history: main trends from 1750–1970', *Urval*, 8 (Stockholm, 1976), 76.
42 I. Semmingsen, *Scandinavian Economic History Review*, 8 (1960), 156–7; 'Emigration from Scandinavia', *Scandinavian Economic History Review*, 2 (1972), 53–4; 'Family emigration from Bergen, 1874–93', *Americana Norvegica*, 3 (1971), 60–1; F. Nilsson, *Emigrationen från Stockholm til Nord Amerika, 1880–1893: en studie i urban utvandring* (Stockholm, 1970), English summary, p. 365.
43 Lindberg, *The background to Swedish emigration*, p. 195; Hofsten and Lundstrom, *Swedish population history*, p. 72; Semmingsen, *Americana Norvegica*, 3 (1971), 60; S. Carlsonn, 'Chronology and composition of Swedish emigration to America', in H. Runblum and H. Norman (eds.), *From Sweden to America: a history of the migration* (Stockholm, 1976), p. 142.

44 Carlsonn, 'Chronology and composition', pp. 134–7; Semmingsen, *Scandinavian Economic History Review*, 8 (1960), 153–4.
45 H. Jerome, *Migration and business cycles* (New York, 1926), pp. 205–6; B. Thomas, *Migration and economic growth: a study of Great Britain and the Atlantic economy* (London, 1954), pp. 127–130.
46 J. M. Quigley, 'A model of Swedish emigration', *Quarterly Journal of Economics*, 86 (1972), 111–26; J. A. Tomaske, 'International migration and economic growth; the Swedish experience', *Journal of Economic History*, 25 (1965), 696–9; H. Wilkinson, 'Evidence of long swings in the growth of Swedish population and related economic variables, 1860–1965', *Journal of Economic History*, 27 (1967), 17–38.
47 T. Moe, 'Some economic aspects of Norwegian population movements 1740–1940: an econometric study', *Journal of Economic History*, 30 (1970), 267–76; Thomas, *Social and economic aspects*, pp. 88–90.
48 P. J. Bjerve, *Langtidslinger i norsk økonomi 1865–1960* (Oslo, 1965), p. 54; E. Dahmen, *Entrepreneurial activity and the development of Swedish industry* (Stockholm, 1970), p. 13; Jörberg, 'The Nordic countries, 1815–1914', p. 437.
49 Montgomery, *The rise of modern industry*, p. 108; Hovde, *The Scandinavian countries*, p. 709.
50 Hodne, *An economic history of Norway*, p. 25; Montgomery, *The rise of modern industry*, p. 108; Thomas, *Migration and economic growth*, p. 23; Guteland, *The biography of a people*, p. 20.
51 Jörberg, 'The Nordic countries, 1850–1914', p. 392; Thomas, *Social and economic aspects*, pp. 42, 136; Blegen, *Norwegian emigration*, p. 21.
52 Guteland, *The biography of a people*, p. 200.
53 Thomas, *Social and economic aspects*, p. 27.
54 Jörberg, 'The Nordic countries, 1850–1914', p. 345; G. R. Allen, 'A comparison of real wages in Swedish agriculture and secondary and tertiary industries, 1870–1949', *Scandinavian Economic History Review*, 3 (1955), 85–107; Hodne, *An economic history of Norway*, p. 141.
55 B. R. Mitchell, *European historical statistics, 1750–1970* (London, 1975), p. 139; Lieberman, *The industrialization of Norway*, p. 48; Montgomery, *The rise of modern industry*, p. 142; Hodne, *An economic history of Norway*, pp. 72–4; Thomas, *Social and economic aspects*, pp. 62–6.
56 B. Mitchell, *European historical statistics*, pp. 191–2.
57 Lieberman, *Economy and History*, 11 (1968), 61–3; M. Drake, 'Fertility controls in pre-industrial Norway', in D. V. Glass and R. Revelle (eds.), *Population and social change* (London, 1972), pp. 186–8.
58 Lieberman, *Economy and History*, 11 (1968), 61–3; Drake, 'Fertility controls', pp. 187–8; *Population and society*, pp. 77, 95.
59 Guteland, *The biography of a people*, p. 53; Hofsten and Lundström, *Swedish population history*, p. 97; D. Gaunt, 'Family planning and the pre-industrial society: some Swedish evidence', in *Aristocrats, farmers, proletarians: essays in Swedish demographic history. Historia Upsaliensia*, 47 (Uppsala, 1973), pp. 28–59; Fridlizius, *Economy and History*, 18 (1975), 140; Winberg, *Folkökning och proletarisering*, pp. 339–40; G. Carlsonn, 'The decline of fertility: innovation or adjustment process', *Population Studies*, 20 (1966), 149–74.
60 R. Østensjø, 'The spring herring fishing and the industrial revolution in Western Norway in the nineteenth century', *Scandinavian Economic History Review*, 2 (1963), 135–6; Hovde, *The Scandinavian countries*, p. 73.

CHAPTER 16

1 D. S. Landes, *The unbound Prometheus: technological change and industrial development in Western Europe from 1750 to the present* (London, 1970), p. 41.

CHAPTER 17

1 G. Myrdal, *Asian drama* (2 vols., London, 1968), vol. 1, p. 435; R. I. Lawless, 'Iraq: changing population patterns', in J. I. Clarke and W. B. Fisher (eds.), *Populations of the Middle East and North Africa* (London, 1972), p. 97; L. L. Bean and A. D. Bhatti,

'Pakistan's population in the 1970s: problems and prospects', *Journal of Asian and African Studies*, 8 (1973), 263.

2 R. Barón Castro, 'El desarrollo de la poblacion Hispano americana (1492–1950)', *Journal of World History*, 5 (1959), 339.

3 J. D. Durand, 'A long range view of world population growth', *Annals of the American Academy of Political and Social Science*, 369 (1967), 1–9.

4 D. C. Mead, *Growth and structural change in the Egyptian economy* (London, 1967), p. 20; B. Peper, 'Population growth in the nineteenth century in Java', *Population Studies*, 24 (1970), 83.

5 Myrdal, *Asian drama*, vol. 1, p. 435; Durand, 'A long range view', p. 38.

6 Castro, *Journal of World History*, 5 (1959), 339.

7 E. E. Arriaga, 'The nature and effects of Latin America's non-Western trend in fertility', *Demography*, 7 (1970), 483–501.

8 United Nations, *Demographic yearbook 1973* (New York, 1974), p. 81; M. S. Teitelbaum, 'Relevance of demographic transition theory for developing countries', *Science*, 188 (1975), 421–2; United Nations, *The determinants and consequences of population trends* (New York, 2 vols., 1973), vol. 1, p. 65.

9 D. V. Glass and E. Grebenik, 'World population, 1800–1950', in H. J. Habakkuk and M. Postan, *Cambridge economic history of Europe*, vol. 6, *The industrial revolutions and after* (Cambridge, 1965), part 1, pp. 68–9.

10 R. B. Dixon, 'Explaining cross-cultural variations in age at marriage and proportions never marrying', *Population Studies*, 25 (1971), 217.

11 A. A. Armar and A. S. David, *Ghana*, Country Profiles: a publication of the Population Council (New York, 1977), p. 3; F. Genderau, 'La démographie des pays d'Afrique: revue et synthèse', *Population*, 32 (1977), 917.

12 R. E. Kennedy, Jr., *The Irish: emigration, marriage and fertility* (London, 1973), p. 143; E. A. Wrigley, *Population and history* (London, 1969), p. 159; J. Kumar, 'A comparison between current Indian fertility and late nineteenth century Swedish and Finnish fertility', *Population Studies*, 25 (1971), 269; E. van de Waale, 'Marriage and marital fertility', in D. V. Glass and R. Revelle (eds.), *Population and social change* (London, 1972), p. 144.

13 H. J. Hajnal, 'European marriage patterns in perspective', in D. V. Glass and D. E. C. Eversley (eds.), *Population in history* (London, 1965), pp. 101–46.

14 I. Sirageldin, D. Norris and M. Ahmad, 'Fertility in Bangladesh; facts and fancies', *Population Studies*, 29 (1975), 209; G. W. Jones, 'Fertility levels and trends in Indonesia', *Population Studies*, 31 (1977), 34; A. Adlakha and D. Kirk, 'Vital rates in India, 1961–71, estimated from 1971 census data', *Population Studies*, 28 (1974), 398; B. D. Clark, 'Iran: changing population patterns', in J. I. Clarke and W. B. Fisher (eds.), *Populations of the Middle East: a geographical approach* (London, 1972), p. 77; J. Vallin, 'Les populations de l'Afrique au Nord du Sahara; Maroc, Algérie, Tunisie, Libye, Egypte', *Population*, 25 (1970), 1227.

15 J. Vallin, *Population*, 25 (1970), 1228; Armar and David, *Ghana*, p. 3; Bean and Bhatti, *Journal of Asian and African Studies*, 8 (1973), 270; Gendereau, *Population*, 32 (1977), 907; J. Knodel and V. Prachuabmuh, 'Demographic aspects of fertility in Thailand', *Population Studies*, 28 (1974), 438.

16 M. Drake, 'Fertility controls in pre-industrial Norway', in Glass and Revelle, *Population and social change*, p. 196; Sirageldin, Norris and Ahmad, *Population Studies*, 29 (1975), 209; A. J. Coale, 'Age patterns of marriage', *Population Studies*, 25 (1971), 195; Armar and David, *Ghana*, p. 3; Adlakha and Kirk, *Population Studies*, 28 (1974), 358; Vallin, *Population*, 25 (1970), 1227.

17 Kumar, *Population Studies*, 25 (1971), 273; Wrigley, *Population and history*, p. 91; United Nations, *The determinants and consequences*, vol. 1, p. 73; Y. Blayo and J. Veron, 'La fécondité dans quelques pays d'Asie orientale', *Population*, 32 (1977), 1945–75; S. Kuznets, 'Fertility differentials between less developed and developed regions: components and implications', *Proceedings of the American Philosophical Society*, 119 (1975), 364–5; G. W. Barclay, A. J. Coale, M. A. Stoto, and T. J. Toussell, 'A reassessment of the demography of traditional rural China', *Population Index*, 42 (1976), 613.

18 Arriaga, *Demography*, 7 (1970), 487.

19 E. Hofsten and H. Lundström, *Swedish population history: main trends from 1750 to 1970*, Urval, No. 8 (Stockholm, 1976), p. 16.

20 J. R. Mandle, 'The decline in mortality in British Guiana, 1911–1960', *Demography*, 7 (1970), 301–15.

21 H. Frederiksen, 'Feedbacks in economic and demographic transition', *Science*, 166 (1969), 837–47.

22 S. H. Preston, 'The changing relation between mortality and level of economic development', *Population Studies*, 29 (1975), 231–48; G. J. Stolnitz, 'Recent mortality trends in Latin America, Asia and Africa: review and re-interpretation', *Population Studies*, 19 (1965), 117–38.

23 G. J. Stolnitz, 'A century of international mortality trends: part 1', *Population Studies*, 9 (1955), 30.

24 B. F. Hoselitz, 'Population pressure, industrialization and social mobility', *Population Studies*, 11 (1957), 123–35.

25 United Nations, *The determinants and consequences*, vol. 1, p. 225.

26 J. I. Clarke, *Population geography and the developing countries* (London, 1971), pp. 197, 232; H. Tinker, *The banyan tree: overseas emigrants from India, Pakistan and Bangladesh* (London, 1977), p. 4.

27 United Nations, *The determinants and consequences*, vol. 1, pp. 233–4.

28 G. Trewartha, *The less developed realm* (London, 1972), pp. 65, 72.

29 J. Power, 'Europe's army of immigrants', *International Affairs*, 51 (1975), 372–86; C. Peach, *West Indian migration to Britain: a social geography* (London, 1968), pp. 51–61; S. Paine, *Exporting workers: the Turkish case* (Cambridge, 1974), p. 27.

30 Peach, *West Indian migration*, p. 15; H. R. Jones, 'Modern emigration from Malta', *Transactions of the Institute of British Geographers*, 60 (1973), 103.

31 A. Weber, *The growth of cities in the nineteenth century: a study in statistics* (New York, 1899), pp. 232–9; E. E. Lampard, 'The urbanizing world', in H. J. Dyos and M. Wolff (eds.), *The Victorian city: images and realities* (2 vols., London, 1973), vol. 1, pp. 12–14.

32 J. A. Banks, 'Population change and the Victorian city', *Victorian Studies*, 11 (1967), 281.

33 W. A. Lewis, 'Economic development with unlimited supplies of labour', *Manchester School*, 22 (1954), 139–91.

34 United Nations, *Urbanization: development policies and planning*, International Social Development Review, No. 1 (New York, 1968), p. 9.

35 J. Beaujeu-Garnier, 'Large overpopulated cities in the underdeveloped world', in W. Zelinsky, L. A. Kosinski and R. Mansell Prothero (eds.), *Geography and a crowding world* (New York, 1970), p. 269; L. Unikel, 'Mexico' in R. Jones (ed.), *Essays in world urbanization* (London, 1975), p. 289; C. Stadel, 'Columbia', in Jones, *Essays in world urbanization*, p. 240; E. E. Arriaga, 'Components of city growth in selected Latin American countries', *Milbank Memorial Fund Quarterly*, 46 (1968), 242.

36 J. E. Annable, Jr., 'Internal migration and urban employment in low-income countries: a problem in simultaneous equations', *Oxford Economic Papers*, 24 (1972), 399–412; J. Friedman and F. Sullivan, 'The absorption of labour in the urban economy: the case of the developing countries', *Economic Development and Cultural Change*, 22 (1974), 385–413.

37 I. Sirageldin, D. Norris and M. Ahmad, 'Fertility in Bangladesh; facts and fancies', *Population Studies*, 29 (1975), 211; M. Mamdani, *The myth of population control; family, caste and class in an Indian village* (London, 1972); P. A. Neher, 'Peasants, procreation and pensions', *American Economic Review*, 61 (1971), 380.

38 United Nations, *Demographic yearbook 1975* (New York, 1976), pp. 486–506; T. W. Merrick, 'Interregional differences in fertility in Brazil, 1950–1970', *Demography*, 2 (1974), 423–40; G. M. Farooq and B. Tuncer, 'Fertility and economic and social development in Turkey: a cross-sectional and time series study', *Population Studies*, 28 (1974), 268; Adlakha and Kirk, *Population Studies*, 28 (1974), 383; S. Chandrasekhar, 'Population policy perspectives in Communist China', *Population Review*, 19 (1975), 89; R. L. Morrison and J. D. Salman, 'Population control in China', *Asian Survey*, 13 (1973), 876–88; Y. Blayo and J. Veron, 'La fecondité dans quelques pays d'Asie orientale', *Population*, 32 (1977), 945–75.

39 Blayo and Verron, *Population*, 32 (1977), 956, 966; Adlahka and Kirk, *Population Studies*, 28 (1974), 398; D. F. S. Fernando, 'Recent fertility decline in Ceylon', *Population Studies*, 26 (1972) 187; 'Changing nuptiality patterns in Sri Lanka, 1901–1971', *Population Studies*, 29 (1975), 185.

40 United Nations, *The determinants and consequences*, vol. 1, p. 79; R. Lesthaeghe,

'Nuptiality and population growth', *Population Studies*, 25 (1971), 430; V. H. Whitney, 'Population planning in Asia in the 1970s', *Population Studies*, 30 (1976), 347.

41 R. Symonds and M. Carder, *The United Nations and the population question 1945–1970* (London, 1973), p. 140.

42 W. L. Li, 'Temporal and spatial analysis of fertility decline in Taiwan', *Population Studies*, 27 (1973), 98.

43 E. A. Wrigley, *Population and history* (London, 1969), p. 190.

44 D. Kirk, 'A new demographic transition', in National Academy of Sciences, *Rapid population growth: consequences and policy implications*, vol. 2 (Washington, 1972), p. 140; H. Frederikson, 'Feedbacks in economic and demographic transition', *Science*, 166 (1969), 837–47.

45 N. L. Tranter, *Population since the Industrial Revolution: the case of England and Wales* (London, 1973), p. 53; United Nations, *Demographic yearbook, 1955* (New York, 1956), p. 617; *1963* (New York, 1964), p. 499; *1975* (New York, 1976), pp. 488–98.

46 T. Frejka, *The future growth of world population* (New York, 1973), pp. 71–7.

CHAPTER 18

1 P. Beaumont, 'Water and development in Saudi Arabia', *Geographical Journal*, 143 (1977), 43.

2 D. Grigg, *The harsh lands: a study in agricultural development* (London, 1970), pp. 194–227; P. H. Nye and D. J. Greenland, *The soil under shifting cultivation*, Technical Communication no. 51 (Harpenden, 1960).

3 L. R. Brown, 'The world food prospect', *Science*, 190 (1975), 1053.

4 FAO, *Production yearbook 1976*, 30 (Rome, 1977), pp. 78–9; 'Population, food supply and agricultural development', *Monthly Bulletin of Agricultural Economics and Statistics*, 23 (1974), 3–4.

5 D. B. Grigg, *The agricultural systems of the world: an evolutionary approach* (Cambridge, 1974), p. 110.

6 E. Allan, 'New settlement in the Upper Amazon basin', *Bank of London and South America Review*, 9 (1975), 622–8; W. M. Denevan, 'Development and the imminent demise of the Amazon rainforest', *Professional Geographer*, 25 (1973), 130–5.

7 J. Kirby 'Agricultural land use and the settlement of Amazonia', *Pacific Viewpoint*, 17 (1976), 105–32.

8 B. H. Farmer, *Agricultural colonization in India since Independence* (London, 1974), p. 36; *Pioneer peasant colonization in Ceylon* (London, 1957); *Agricultural colonization in south and south east Asia* (Hull, 1969); R. Ng, 'Land settlement projects in Thailand', *Geography*, 53 (1968), 179–82; R. Wikkramatileke, 'State aided rural land colonization in Malaya; an appraisal of the F.L.D.A. program', *Annals of the Association of American Geographers*, 55 (1965), 377–403.

9 R. J. Harrison Church, 'Problems and development of the dry zone of West Africa', *Geographical Journal*, 127 (1961), 187–204; 'Observations on large scale irrigation development in Africa', *Agricultural Economics Bulletin for Africa*, 4 (1963), 1–48.

10 FAO, *World agriculture: the last quarter century* (Rome, 1970), p. 26.

11 C. B. Fawcett, 'The extent of the cultivable land', *Geographical Journal*, 76 (1930), 504–9; F. A. Pearson and F. A. Harper, *The world's hunger* (New York, 1945); G. C. Anderson, 'An agricultural view of the world population food crisis', *Journal of Soil and Water Conservation*, 27 (1972), 54.

12 Brown, *Science*, 190 (1975), 1054–5.

13 Grigg, *Agricultural systems*, pp. 57–74.

14 D. G. Dalrymple, *Survey of multiple cropping in less developed nations*, US Department of Agriculture, Foreign Economic Development Service (Washington, 1971); FAO, *The state of food and agriculture 1974* (Rome, 1975), p. 132.

15 C. Geertz, *Agricultural involution: the process of ecological change in Indonesia* (Berkley, 1970), p. 96.

16 D. H. Perkins, *Agricultural development in China, 1368–1968* (Edinburgh, 1969), pp. 25, 216; P. Ho, 'The introduction of American food plants into China', *American Anthropologist*, 57 (1955), 191–201.

17 Geertz, *Agricultural involution*, p. 96.

18 W. Jones, 'Manioc; an example of innovation in African economies', *Economic Development and Cultural Change*, 5 (1957), 100–10; G. P. Murdock, 'Staple subsistence crops of Africa', *Geographical Review*, 50 (1960), 523–40.

19 FAO, *Production yearbook 1957*, 11 (Rome, 1958), pp. 56–7, 74–8; *Production yearbook 1976*, pp. 80–6.

20 L. R. Brown, *Increasing world food output*, Foreign Agriculture Economic Report, 25 (Washington, 1965), p. 16; A. N. Duckham, 'Forty years on: agriculture in retrospect and prospect', *Journal of the Royal Agricultural Society*, 127 (1966), 7–16; 'The current agricultural revolution' *Geography*, 44 (1959), 71–8.

21 FAO, *Production yearbook 1957*, pp. 31–2.

22 FAO, *World agriculture*, p. 26.

23 FAO, *Production yearbook 1957*, pp. 31–2; *Production yearbook 1976*, pp. 89–92.

24 Y. Hayami and V. W. Ruttan, *Agricultural development: an international perspective* (Baltimore, 1971), pp. 329–31.

25 FAO, *Production yearbook 1976*, p. 91.

26 Perkins, *Agricultural development in China*, pp. 20–2, 27.

27 Yhi-Min Ho, *Agricultural development of Taiwan, 1903–60* (Kingsport, Tennessee, 1966), pp. 85–7; Y. Hayami, *A century of agricultural growth in Japan* (Tokyo, 1975), p. 120; G. Blyn, *Agricultural trends in India, 1891–1957; output, availability, and productivity* (Philadelphia, 1966), p. 154.

28 D. G. Dalrymple, *Development and spread of high-yielding varieties of wheat and rice in the less developed nations*, US Department of Agriculture, Foreign Development Division (Washington, D.C., 1976), pp. 88, 108; FAO, *The state of food and agriculture, 1974* (Rome, 1975), p. 131; B. H. Farmer (ed.), *Green revolution? Technology and change in rice-growing areas of Tamil Nadu and Sri Lanka* (London, 1977).

29 Hayami and Ruttan, *Agricultural development*, pp. 327–30.

30 C. Voss, 'Agricultural mechanization, production and employment', *Monthly Bulletin of Agricultural Economics and Statistics*, 23 (1974), 1–7.

31 J. A. Allan, 'Appropriate technology and labour supply in rural India', *Journal of Tropical Geography*, 43 (1876), 1–8.

32 L. Emmerij, 'A new look at some strategies for increasing productive employment in Africa', *International Labour Review*, 110 (1974), 199–218; E. F. Schumacher, 'The work of the intermediate technology development group in Africa', *International Labour Review*, 106 (1972), 75–92.

33 R. J. Ward, 'Absorbing more labour in L.D.C. agriculture', *Economic Development and Cultural Change*, 17 (1968), 178–88.

34 L. Naiken, 'Estimation of rural participation in non-agricultural employment', *Monthly Bulletin of Agricultural Economics and Statistics*, 26 (1977), 1–12.

35 M. W. Leiserson, 'Employment perspectives and policy approaches in Indonesia', *International Labour Review*, 109 (1974), 333–58; S. Guha, 'The contribution of non-farm activities to rural employment promotion: experience in Iran, India and Syria', *International Labour Review*, 109 (1974), 235–50.

36 Guha, *International Labour Review*, 109 (1974), p. 242.

37 Emmerij, *International Labour Review* 110 (1974), 199–218; K. Marsden, 'Progressive technologies for developing countries', *International Labour Review*, 101 (1970), 475–502.

38 B. Stavis, 'China's rural local institutions in comparative perspective', *Asian Survey*, 16 (1976), 381–96.

CHAPTER 19

1 N. L. Tranter, *Population since the Industrial Revolution: the case of England and Wales* (London, 1973), p. 43; D. V. Glass and E. Grebenik, 'World population, 1800–1950', in H. J. Habakkuk and M. M. Postan (eds.), *The Cambridge economic history of Europe*, vol. 6, *The Industrial Revolutions and after: incomes, population and technological change* (Cambridge, 1965), part 1, p. 62.

2 G. U. Yule, 'The growth of population and the factors that control it', *Journal of the Royal Statistical Society*, 88 (1925), 1–58; D. O. Cowgill, 'The theory of population growth cycles', *American Journal of Sociology*, 55 (1949), 163–70; R. Cameron, 'The logistics of European economic growth: a note on a historical periodization', *Journal of*

European Economic History, 2 (1973), 145–8; R. Pearl, *The biology of population growth* (New York, 1930).

3 D. J. Loschky, 'Economic change, mortality and Malthusian theory', *Population Studies*, 30 (1976), 439–52.

4 H. E. Daly, 'A Marxian–Malthusian view of poverty and development', *Population Studies*, 25 (1971), 25–37.

INDEX

Abel, W., 65, 67, 81
age of marriage, 40, 41, 59, 63, 77, 285: in
  developing countries, 240; in England,
  100, 167, 184; in France, 57, 113, 284; in
  Ireland, 118, 136; in the Netherlands, 159;
  in Norway, 229; in Sweden, 229; in
  Western Europe, 240
age specific fertility, 229: in Sweden and
  India, 240
agricultural labourers, *see* labourers,
  agricultural
agricultural output, 233: in developing
  countries, 263
agricultural population densities in
  nineteenth-century Europe, 245–51
agricultural populations, 2, 6, 27, 60: in
  England, 164; in France, 202–4; in
  Norway and Sweden, 214–15, 227–8
agricultural prices, 46, 123–4, 168, 232: in
  France, 103–4; in Holland, 146, 149; in
  Sweden, 211–12
agricultural revolution, 54, 62, 176, 179, 274:
  in France, 199
agricultural statistics, 177, 179, 243: in
  Sweden, 243
agronomes, French, 230
Akershus, 104, 220
Algeria, French emigration to, 202
allotments, 25, 171
Alps, 39, 72, 77, 199
Alsace, 65, 106, 197: farm size, 68
amalgamation, 89, 135, 170, 213
Amiens, 78, 110
Amsterdam, 144, 150, 154, 156, 158, 159:
  plague, 160
Antwerp, 147, 158: population decline, 156
apprentices in London, 96
Aquitaine, 113: fertility, 59
arable: expansion, 143; per head, 266;
  stubble, 90; in Africa, 264; in East Asia,
  265–6; European, 32; in France, 198; in
  Sweden, 216
ard, 32, 37, 108
Arden, Forest of, 88, 89
Artois, 153: legumes, 75

Bakewell, Robert, 176
Baltic: grain exports, 59, 148–9, 152; timber
  exports, 91
Bangladesh, 240: family size, 257
baptisms, 56, 58, 167
barley, 34, 73
Barnstaple, natural increase, 95
beans, 35, 38, 75, 92, 153, 219
Beauvais, 78, 107, 113: farm size, 105
Beauvrequem farm size, 68
beer, in the Netherlands, 158
Belfast, industry in, 128–9
Belgium, 27, 43, 218
Bennett, M. K., 180–1
Bergen, 225, emigration, 225
birth control, 12, 29; physical methods, 40;
  see also coitus interruptus, contraception
birth place of brides and grooms, 96
birth rate, 78–80, 257: in developing
  countries, 239–40, 257–9; in England, 166,
  188; in France, 192, 205; in Ireland, 118,
  135–7; in Norway, 62, 209–10; in Sweden,
  62, 240; urban, 77
births: illegitimate, 113; registration of, 41,
  60–2
Black Death, 7, 24, 26, 53, 60, 66, 69, 72, 78,
  79, 82, 83, 87, 102, 105, 110, 111, 142,
  143, 147, 150, 283
Bordeaux, 67, 108, 109
Bordelais, 106, 196: farm size, 68
Boserup, Ester, 34
Bourgeois-Pichat, J., 193, 206
Bourke, P. M. A., 122
Brabant, 67, 150, 156
Brazil, birth rate, 257
brewing: in Ireland, 129; in the Low
  Countries, 154, 158
Bridbury, A. R., 69
Brittany, 72, 106, 107, 113: fertility, 59; cider,
  108
bubonic plague, 47, 53, 54, 57, 59, 63, 65,
  95, 99, 112, 167, 193, 210, 242, 285; *see
  also* Black Death
buckwheat, 35, 105, 107
building workers' wages, 24

Burma, population increase, 238
Bury St Edmunds farm size, 68
business cycle and migration, 225
butter in the Netherlands, 155

calorific content of crops, 34–5, 272
Cameron, R., 282
Canada, 132, 185, 221
canals, 234: in the Netherlands, 154–5
Canterbury: farm size, 68; migrants, 96
capital, 15; in Ireland, 129; and tenure, 172
Carr-Saunders, A., 13
cassava, 28; *see also* manioc
celibacy, 41, 80, 113, 240, 257, 258; in
    Ireland, 137
censuses, 51: British, 51, 164, 183, 184, 188;
    French, 51, 190; Irish, 51, 135, 116–17;
    Swedish, 51, 228
cereals: prices, 69, 194; yields, 67, 93;
    imports into Holland, 151; in the
    Netherlands, 155; *see also* crop yields,
    prices, *and under individual crops*
Ceylon, 251: population increase, 238;
    underemployment, 18
charcoal, 71, 97
checks, Malthusian, 12
cheese, 39: in the Netherlands, 155
chestnuts, in Cevennes, 197
child mortality: in Ireland, 128; in London,
    166
child–woman ratio, 118, 136–7
China: American crops in, 272; farm size,
    22; emigration, 251; fertility, 257; legal
    age of marriage, 258; population increase,
    7
Cipolla, C., 65
Cistercians, 71
civil registration: in England, 166; in
    France, 191
Clapham, Sir John, 182
Clark, Colin, 52, 53
clay soils, 33, 179: and the ard, 37
climate: and mortality, 284; and population,
    54; in seventeenth century, 112
clover, 33, 75, 93, 155, 177, 179, 232: in
    England, 92; in the Netherlands, 153
coal, 91, 97, 129
coitus interruptus, 42, 59, 100, 205, 229
Coke of Holkham, rents, 169
Colchester, plague, 95
collective regulations, 23, 31, 70, 200, 213;
    see also common fields, open fields
colonisation, 42–3, 84
Columbia, migration in, 255
Colyton, 41, 56, 59, 99, 100, 117, 240
common fields, 23, 27, 70, 90, 162, 200; *see
    also* collective regulations, open fields
conacre land, 122–3, 124, 134

Connell, K. H., 117, 118, 119
consolidation, 23, 176, 200: in England, 172;
    in France, 195; in Sweden, 212–13
consumption approach to overpopulation,
    16
contraception, 229, 258–9
convertible husbandry, 107, 181: in England,
    93, 179; in the Low Countries, 153
copyholders, 87
Cork, 121, 128, 131
Cork Co., 123, 126, 136–7
Corn Laws, 182, 189
Cornwall, Julian, 51
Costa Rica, birth rate, 257
Cotswolds, 97, 181
cottagers, 122–3, 213–15
cotton: in Ireland, 129; and mortality, 167,
    210
craftsmen, 30, 38–9, 81, 110, 183
crisis mortality, 56, 63, 79, 81, 139, 284; in
    France, 112, 193; in Scandinavia, 209; *see
    also* mortality, weather and harvests
crop yields, 67, 75, 78, 92, 93, 233; in
    developing countries, 273–7; in France,
    107, 201; in Sweden, 218; *see also* yields
    and under individual crops
Crotty, R. D., 123
Crulâi, 112, 113, 240
cultivated land, 17: in medieval period,
    71–3; in sixteenth century, 90; in
    developing countries, 5, 243–51, 263–8; in
    England, 176–8; in France, 198–9; in
    Scandinavia, 216–17; *see also* arable, land
    reclamation
Cumberland farm size, 88
currency debasement, 69, 85

dairy prices, 85, 155
dairying: in Cheshire, 94; in the
    Netherlands, 154–5; in Sweden, 220
Dartmoor, 72, 91
Davenant, Charles, 177–8
death rate, 58–9, 66, 78–80, 166; in British
    Guiana, 242; in Egypt, 241; in England,
    44, 165–9, 188; in France, 44, 192–3; in
    Ireland, 117–19; in Norway, 207–9,
    229–30; in Sweden, 144, 229–30, 241;
    urban, 77; *see also* mortality
deaths: registration of, 60–2; violent, 56
Delft, 150, 154
demesne, 69, 73, 81, 83: decline of farming,
    87
Denmark, 29, 41, 53, 219
Derry Co., 136
Devon Commission, 122
diet, 5, 62, 75, 105, 142, 232: in East Anglia,
    173; in Ireland, 119, 173; in Java, 272; in
    Norway, 218; world pattern, 262

disease, infectious, 47, 62–3, 99, 112, 119, 284: in Ireland, 138–9; *see also* Black Death, bubonic plague
disease of plants, 33
division of labour, 38, 158–9
Dixon, R. B., 239
doctors in Norway, 209
Domesday Book, 51, 53, 72, 77
domestic servants, 43, 183, 253
Dorset water meadows, 93
dowries, 31, 136
Drake, M., 211
drill, seed, 26, 36, 154, 176, 220
Dubled, H., 65
Dublin, 127–8, 130, 131
Duby, G., 65, 74
dues, peasant, 69
Durand, J. D., 238
Durham, 51, 88
Dutch East India Company, 157
Dutch West India Company, 157
dwarf wheats in Mexico, 276
dye plants, 108
dysentery, 138

East Asia, fertility decline in, 257
Eastern Europe, 16–17, 43
Elbe, 32, 42, 71, 72, 80
emigration, 28, 29, 80–1, 144, 233; statistics, 185–6; from developing countries, 251–2; from England, 98, 164, 185–8; from France, 111, 202; from Ireland, 128, 131–5; from Norway, 222–5; from Sweden, 222–5
enclosure, 23, 26, 28, 84, 106, 123, 171, 176; by agreement, 179; and farm size, 89; Parliamentary, 170, 172, 173, 176; in France, 200, 204; in Norway, 212–13; Sweden, 212–13, 214, 216
England, 2, 22, 53–5, 65, 67, 68, 69, 70, 71, 72, 75, 83–101, 117, 118, 121, 124, 126, 127, 130–1, 135, 149, 151, 153, 161, 163–89
entry fines, 24, 69, 87
Estonia, 149, 152
European Economic Community, 252
eviction: in Ireland, 135; in sixteenth-century England, 88; in Sweden, 213
expectation of life, 79, 167: in England, 166; in France, 112; in Latin America, 241; *see also* death rates, mortality

factory system, 118, 257
fallow, 5, 23, 27, 33, 34, 37–8, 66, 70, 74, 93, 125, 143, 152–3, 177; in Africa, 264; in developing countries, 269–70; in England, 178, 199; in France, 198, 200; in Sweden, 217

family limitation, 59, 80
family reconstitution, 4, 58, 191
family size, 80, 167: in Afro-Asia, 241; in Colyton, 56; of English peers, 56, 100; in England, 95, 100; in Norway, 229
famine, 12–13, 65: Irish, 26, 115, 125, 127, 131–5, 137, 138–9, 144, 250; of 1315–17, 79, 81, 82
farm servants, 69: in Norway and Sweden, 214
farm size, 21–2, 25, 26, 179: medieval, 68–9; and ploughs, 167; in England, 170–2; in France, 104–5, 194–6; in India, 5; in Ireland, 122, 129, 134–5; in Norway and Sweden, 212–13
farming methods, 33–8; in developing countries, 273–8; in England, 90–4, 179–82; in France, 106–8, 199–201; in Holland, 150–5; in Ireland, 124–7; in medieval Europe, 73–6; in Scandinavia, 218–22
fenlands, English, 33, 90: population density, 67; steam-pumping, 177
fertilisers, 37, 179, 201
fertility, 59, 41, 283: and employment, 167; medieval, 55–7, 78–80; rural and urban, 95, 256; in developing countries, 239–41, 256–60; in England, 100–1, 188; in France, 113–14, 204–6; in Holland, 159–60; in Ireland, 135–8; in Norway and Sweden, 229–30
feudalism, 57, 61, 64, 69, 81, 104, 141, 161, 196, 219, 290
Field, J. A., 11
fishing in Norway, 212, 221
Fitzwilliam estates, 174
flail, 26, 36–7, 177
Flanders, 31, 32, 39, 65, 67, 68, 72, 79, 82, 107, 150, 155, 156, 196
flax, 39, 94, 97, 108, 110, 128–9, 194
Florence, 55, 77
fold-course, 90, 92
forestry, 71–3, 91, 212
Forez, 78, 110
Fourquin, G., 68
fragmentation, 22–3, 32, 70, 71; in France, 196; in Sweden, 213
France, 22, 26, 27, 43, 52, 58, 82, 102–14, 190–206; emigration, 202; farm size, 68, 194–6; fertility decline, 205–6; landlessness, 196–7; migration, 202–4; new farming methods, 199–201; overpopulation, 193–7; population, 53–4, 102–3, 124, 160, 190–3
Frank, S., 83
freeholders: in Holland, 161; in Scandinavia, 214–15
Frejka, T., 260
Fussell, G. E., 92, 180

Gantoise region, farm size, 68
Geneva, 55, 196
Germany, 43, 58, 132: emigration, 43;
　enclosure, 23; overpopulation, 65, 83;
　population, 54
Ghent, 77
Gilbert, Sir Humphrey, 83
glass, 76, 129
Glastonbury farm size, 68
Gloucestershire, 89, 97
Godwin, W., 12, 193
Graham, Sir James, 182
grain exports: North American, 269;
　Swedish, 212; English, 181
grain imports, 266; England, 168; Europe,
　233
Gray, R., 83
grazing, 70, 82, 90, 107
Griffith, G. Talbot, 62, 117, 166, 167
Griffith, R., 125
gross reproduction in France, 205
guano, 37, 182, 220
Guatemala: farm size, 5; underemployment,
　18
guilds, 39, 76, 80, 97, 143: in Netherlands,
　158
Gupta, Sen, 16
Gustavus Adolphus, 207

Haarlem, 154, 158
Haarlemmermeer, 151
Hallam, H. E., 68
Harrison, W., 92
harrow, 74, 126, 219
harvest failure, 56, 57, 68, 81, 167, 284–5
Healey, M. J., 180
hemp, 94, 97, 108, 110, 154
herrings, 157, 221
Hertfordshire: life expectation, 166; straw
　hats, 183
Hodne, F., 212, 215
Holderness, field system, 91
Holland, 2, 32, 54, 147–62, 234; *see also*
　Low Countries, Netherlands
Hollingsworth, T. H., 165, 188
homeostasis, 142, 188
Honduras population increase, 238
hops, 39; in Low Countries, 154
horses, 37: for ploughing, 74
horticulture in the Netherlands, 154–5
hospitals, 62, 167
Hundred Years War, 56, 105–6, 112
Hungary, 17, 42
Hutten, Ulrich von, 83
Huzel, J. P., 188

Île de France, 65, 79: crop yields, 74; farm
　size, 68

incendiarism, in England, 175
India, 2; age of marriage, 240; birth rate,
　257; colonisation, 267; emigration, 251;
　farm size, 5, 22, 23; indentured labour,
　251; overpopulation, 16
Industrial Revolution, 42, 43, 62, 164, 175,
　201, 231, 233
industrialisation, 44, 147, 222, 253
industry, 39: in medieval towns, 70; in
　Dutch towns, 158–9; in France, 204; in
　Ireland, 127–9; in Norway and Sweden,
　226–7
infant mortality, 109; and fertility, 257; in
　France, 111–12, 193
infectious disease, *see* disease
infield–outfield in Norway, 217, 219
inflation, 69, 141, 245
inheritance, 23, 213: in Ireland, 136
inoculation, 167, 193, 209
intercommoning, 70, 90
inventories of Dutch farms, 150
investment: in the Industrial Revolution,
　163; in medieval estates, 81; and
　migration, 225
Ireland, 35, 115–40, 142, 168, 218;
　age-specific fertility, 41; emigration, 43,
　98; population, 2, 7, 59–60, 166
irrigation: in Africa, 268; and multiple
　cropping, 270
Ivwy farm size, 68

Java, 28, 279: age of marriage, 240;
　American crops in, 272; farm size, 22;
　population increase, 238, 271
Jenner, E., 62
Jerome, H., 224, 229
Jones, E. L., 180
Jörberg, L., 211
Jordan, W. K., 85

Kalmar, 217, 219
Kempsey farm size, 68
Kent, 91: wages, 173
Kerry, 121, 131
King, Gregory, 51, 89, 92, 148, 165, 177
kings, English, family size, 80
Korea, South, 22: age of marriage, 258
Krause, J. T., 166, 188

labour surplus, 17–18, 26, 63, 127, 277: in
　England, 172–5, 182
labourers, agricultural, 3, 4, 17, 25, 76, 79,
　89, 130, 168, 185, 197
Labrousse, E., 195
Lancashire, 91, 174: poll tax, 51; potatoes,
　178
land reclamation, 42–3, 53, 90–1, 150–2,
　267–8

land tenure, 7: in Ireland, 139
land use: symptom of population pressure, 27–8; in developing countries, 243; in Norway and Sweden, 220
land values, 69–70, 79, 80, 85–6, 109; in France, 103–4, 194; in Norway, 212, 232
Landes, D., 231
landlessness, 25–6, 65, 68–9, 89–90, 97, 98, 109, 127–8, 142, 158–9, 277: in England, 170, 172–5; in France, 105, 196; in Ireland, 122–3; in Norway and Sweden, 213, 214–15
landownership, 5, 15, 25, 67, 170, 287; in England, 88, 90, 172; in France, 104–5, 194–5; in Ireland, 123–4, 126
Languedoc, 39, 102, 105, 106, 108
Laon, 67, 76, 195
Latin America, 18; emigration, 251; landownership, 5; population increase, 1
Law, C. M., 184, 185
Le Roy Ladurie, E., 197
legumes, 33, 73, 75, 275; *see also* beans, clover, peas, vetch
Leiden, 158: plague, 160
Leveson-Gower estate, 170, 172
lime, 75, 82, 107, 154, 220
Limousin, 109, 195
Lincolnshire: potato, 178; Wolds, 18, 176, 180
linen, Ulster, 128–9, 132
Liverpool, 130, 184
livestock, 27, 70, 75, 85, 126, 181
Loder, Robert, 92
Loire, 72, 102, 108
London, 43, 77, 144, 184: market, 93–4; migration, 96
Lorraine, 72, 197
Louis XIV, 112
Lourmarin, 72, 195
Low Countries, 38, 58, 77, 108
Lyons, 56, 108, 109, 110

McCormick, C., 174
McCulloch, J. R., 180
machinery, agricultural, 7, 26, 31, 126, 174, 232, 277
Maclean, Rutgers, 213
madder, 39, 154
maize, 27, 35, 106, 107–8, 153, 271: in Africa, 273; in France, 199
malaria, 106, 241
Malaya, population increase, 238
Mälmo, 213, 224
malnutrition, 66, 79, 284
Malthus, T. R., 11–13, 20, 44, 47, 131, 174, 193, 231
Malthusian crisis, 65, 66, 67, 81, 103, 142, 164, 211, 215, 232

Malthusian theory, 40, 283, 285
manioc, 34, 271, 273
manure, 27, 31, 38, 65, 74–5, 82, 107, 142, 154, 201, 220
marginal land, 65, 72, 91, 169
marginal productivity of labour, 14, 18, 20, 30, 142, 179
marital fertility, 212, 257; in developing countries, 258; in France, 205; in Ireland, 135–7; in Sweden, 229
market gardening near London, 94; *see also* horticulture
marl, 75, 82, 92, 107, 154, 182, 200
marriage, 55: early, 80, 118, 167; pattern of, 286, 289; postponement, 116, 136, 229; rates, 205, 229; in France, 59, 113; Ireland, 42, 130; *see also* age of marriage, fertility, marital fertility, nuptiality
marshland, reclamation, 71–2
Massif Central, 39, 109, 199
Mayo, 121, 123, 131
medicine, 62, 107, 117–18, 167
Midi, 112: soil erosion, 105
migration, 42–4, 76–8: rural–urban, 42–3, 96–7, 128–9, 143–4, 155–9, 183–5, 202–4, 225–8, 252–6; seasonal, 130–1, 204; temporary, 39; in Africa, 251–2
milk, 38, 119, 142
Mill, J. S., 12
minifundia, 22, 101
Mitchel, J., 116
mobility, 42, 43: in Elizabethan England, 96
Mols, R., 58
monasteries, 54, 71; dissolution of, 88
Montgomery, G. A., 211
Montserrat, emigration, 252
Moore, W. E., 17–18
Morineau, M., 200
mortality, 44, 54, 57, 58, 283; causes of, 44; crisis, 44; infant and child, 58, 160; medieval, 78–80; normal, 44; in developing countries, 241–3, 256; in England, 99–100, 167; in France, 111–12; in Holland, 156, 160; in Ireland, 138; in Scandinavia, 44, 229–30
Moselle, 53, 70, 72, 76
multiple cropping, 250–1

Namur farm size, 68
Nantes, 56, 109, 113
Napoleonic Wars, 124, 132, 163, 168, 177, 180, 219
Natal, 251
natural increase, 59, 77, 109, 117; in developing countries, 256; in Sweden, 227–30
Netherlands, 42, 51, 59–60, 147–62, 252, 290: farming methods, 152–5; fertility and

Netherlands (cont.)
  mortality, 159–60; land reclamation,
  150–2; population growth, 147–50;
  urbanisation and migration, 155–9
Norfolk, 173, 175
Normandy, 106, 110, 113: age of marriage,
  55; population, 79
Northamptonshire, 96, 166
Norway, 41, 43, 58, 59, 126, 207–30:
  emigration, 222–5; farm size, 212–13;
  farming changes, 215–20; fertility, 229–30;
  industry, 221–2; migration (internal),
  225–8; overpopulation, 211–15;
  population, 207–10; potato in, 217–18
Norwich, 96, 97, 184
Nottinghamshire family size, 167
nuptiality: in developing countries, 239; in
  Europe, 239; *see also* marriage

oats, 35, 73, 212
oil-cake, 37, 176, 181, 201
open fields, 101, 234: in Holland, 153; *see
  also* collective regulations, common fields
optimum density, 80, 135
optimum population, 13, 18, 29, 141
optimum theory, 13–16, 20, 282–3
Oslo, 218, 223, 225
Overijssel, 148, 153
overpopulation, 33, 44, 141–2, 232, 284, 292:
  definition, 11–19; and migration, 42–4,
  96–7; symptoms of, 20–8, 66–71, 286–7; in
  England, 85–90, 168–70; in France, 102–5,
  201; in Ireland, 120–4; in Scandinavia,
  211–15
oxen, 22, 36, 37, 74

Pakistan: farm size, 5; population, 238;
  underemployment, 18
Paris, 45, 68, 76, 77, 95, 104, 110, 144:
  migration, 109; natural increase, 253
Parish Register Abstracts, 165, 166, 167
partible inheritance, 21, 122
Peacock, A. J., 168
Pearl, R., 282
peas, 35, 75, 92, 153, 219
peasants, 21, 38–9, 194–6
Peel, Sir Robert, 182
peers, British demography, 56, 58–9, 99,
  166–7
Petty, Sir William, 150
Philippines: nuptiality, 258; population, 2,
  238
Phytophthora infestans, 115
Picardy farm size, 68, 106
pigs in Ireland, 175
place of birth statistics, 184
plague, *see* bubonic plague
plant breeding, 274

plants, American, introduced into China,
  272
plough, 33, 36, 37–8, 126: Brabant, 154;
  iron, 74, 176
Poitu, 104, 106
Pollard, Sydney, 189
Poor Law: in England, 122, 133, 172, 174–5,
  181; in Ireland, 131; in Sweden, 211
population density, 38; and plague, 284; in
  medieval Europe, 66–8; in developing
  countries, 243–51, 261; in France, 197; in
  Ireland, 120–1, 135
population growth: in medieval Europe,
  65–6; in England, 83–5, 164–8; in Europe,
  51–63, 83–4, 231–2, 281–2; in France,
  102–3, 190–3; in Holland, 148–50; in
  Ireland, 126, 137; in Norway and Sweden,
  207–10
population pressure, 5, 8, 15, 24, 65, 73: in
  medieval Europe, 66–72; in France,
  103–5; *see also* overpopulation
positive checks, 12–13
Postan, M., 65, 79
potatoes, 27, 35, 63, 107, 115, 118, 127, 142,
  143, 173, 174, 177, 232, 271; in England,
  178–9; in France, 199–200; in Holland,
  153; in Ireland, 116, 119–20, 124–6, 131;
  in Norway, 126, 215, 217–18; Sweden,
  217–18
Pounds, N. J. G., 68, 77
Presbyterians, 131, 133
Preston, 43, 184
prices, agricultural, 24–5, 69, 80, 85, 169,
  177, 181
primogeniture, 21, 25: in Sweden and
  Norway, 213
printing, 83; in the Netherlands, 158
productivity, agricultural, 31, 179, 182
Protestants: in France, 202; in Ireland, 116
Provence, 106: population, 79, 102
Prussia, 148, 151
Pyrenees, 72, 80, 107: emigration, 109

Queen's County, 124

railways, 220; in Ireland, 129
rainforest, 261, 269
Ramsay farm size, 68
reclamation, 32, 125, 173; in Holland,
  150–2, 161
regional specialisation, 38, 93–4, 234
registration of births and deaths, 164: in
  Ireland, 135
rents, 24–5, 68, 69–70, 87–8, 141, 149, 170:
  in France, 104, 194; in Ireland, 123–4,
  126, 129, 139–40
Revolution, French, 190, 193, 205
Ricardo, D., 20

rice, 22, 23, 28, 265, 270, 275
Rickman, J., 165
Robertson, C. J., 21
Rogers, J. Thorold, 67
root crops, 33, 93, 220, 232–3, 272; *see also* turnips
Rosenstein-Roden, P., 18
rotations, 33, 38, 91, 198
Rouen, 109, 113, 194
Rundale, 123, 125
rural industry, 98, 144: in developing countries, 278–9; in England, 183; in France, 110–11, 202–4; in Sweden, 226–7
rural population, 60; in England, 164, 168, 173, 182, 184–6; in Europe, 291; in France, 196; in Ireland, 128–9; in the Netherlands, 158–9; in Norway and Sweden, 226–7; in Western Europe, 231–2
Russell, J. C., 53, 79, 81
Russia, 30, 201, 239
rye, 73, 152, 200
rye grass, 179, 181

sainfoin, 93, 107, 179
St Hilaire family size, 56
Salaman, R. N., 175, 177
sanitation, public, 62, 242: in Ireland, 117
Saudi Arabia, 261
savannas, African, 269–70
Scotland, 37, 79, 131, 174
scythe, 27, 126, 201
sea level, in Holland, 150
seaweed, 3, 92
Seebohm, F., 67
seed-bed, 37–8, 74
seed–yield ratio, 36, 74: in Norway, 219; in Sweden, 218; *see also* crop yields
seigneur, 67, 104, 110–11
Seine, 76
self-sufficiency, 29–30
Semmingsen, I., 211
serfdom, 36, 69, 77–8, 161: in France, 104
severalty, 70
sheep, 92, 98, 127: folding, 75; stealing, 175
Sheffield, 96, 184
Shepshed, 167
shifting cultivation, 261, 267
shipbuilding: in Ireland, 129; in the Netherlands, 158
shipping, 157, 221
sickle, 27, 127, 201
silk, 110: Amsterdam, 158; Lyons, 108
silver, 24, 85
Skåne, 212, 217, 219; enclosure, 220
slavery, 54, 251
Slicher van Bath, B. H., 36, 65, 74
Sligo, 121, 131, 133
smallpox, 47, 62, 112, 118, 167, 193, 209

soil, 33: acidity, 38; erosion, 5, 27, 33, 105, 269; fertility, 5, 37–8, 271; nitrogen, 75, 92, 93; structure, 93; texture, 38
South Africa: emigration to, 187
spade, in Norway, 219–20
Spain, 42, 71, 148: French, 111; population, 58
specialisation, regional, 158–9, 161
squatting, 70, 89
Sri Lanka, 258, 267, 279; *see also* Ceylon
stall-feeding, 75, 92, 181
standard of living, 15, 67, 89, 160, 242: in developing countries, 2; Dutch, 160; Irish, 138; *see also* wages
starvation, in Ireland, 115
Stavanger, 219, 223
Stockholm, 223, 224, 225, 253
subdivision, of farms, 21–2, 28, 68, 90, 119, 141, 149: in France, 194–6; in Ireland, 121–2, 136–7; in Sweden, 212; *see also* farm size
subsistence crisis, 112, 149, 201
subsistence level, 20, 65, 68, 69, 141, 189
suckling periods, 42, 229
Suffolk, 87, 97
sugar, 157: plantations, 251
sugar-beet, 33, 232: in Sweden, 219; France, 201
Sundbärg, G., 211, 216, 224
Sussex, 72, 74, 90, 96
Sweden, 23, 41, 58, 59, 79, 207–30: arable, 216–17; emigration, 222–5; farming methods, 218–20; fertility, 229–30; migration (internal), 225–8; overpopulation, 211–15; population, 207–10; potato, 217–18; rural industry, 221
Switzerland, 27, 43

Taïwan, family planning, 258
Taunton farm size, 68
tenancy, 5, 25, 28: in Ireland; 121–2; in Sweden, 213
tenant right: in Holland, 161; in Ulster, 133
textiles, 39, 97, 98, 275
Thirsk, Joan, 70
Thirty Years War, 55
Thomas, B., 225
Thompson, F. M. L., 181
three-field system, 33–4, 66, 73, 74, 75, 219; in England, 91; in France, 198; in Ireland, 125; in Sweden, 217
threshing machine, 26, 36–7, 127, 174: in France, 201
tithe, 104, 161: in France, 103
Titow, J. Z., 68, 79, 91
tobacco, in Holland, 184
Tonbridge, 88
Toulouse, 78, 102, 109

Tours, 110
Toutain, J. C., 193, 197, 198, 202
towns: English, 77; medieval, 77; plague in,
    54; *see also* urban growth, urban
    mortality, urban population
trade, 39: British, 163; Dutch, 157
transport, 38–9, 63, 76, 108
trefoil, 93
Trinidad, birth rate, 257
tulips, in Holland, 155
Tull, Jethro, 176
Turgot, A.-R.-J., 12
Turkey, 42, 83, 257, 277, 279
turnips, 38, 93, 125, 173, 179: in East
    Anglia, 181; in Low Countries, 153; in
    Netherlands, 155
Tuscany, 77: population, 67, 79; rents, 70
two-field system, 66, 73, 74, 106, 143: in
    England, 91; in France, 198; in Sweden,
    217, 219
typhus, 110, 112

Ulster, 131, 132–3, 137
underdrainage, 127, 200–1
underemployment, 18, 26, 63, 69, 142: static
    and dynamic, 18; in Chile, 18; in England,
    175; in Ireland, 125; in Sweden, 215
unemployment, 18, 26, 174, 232: in France,
    196
Union, of Britain and Ireland, 116, 129
United Provinces, 148; *see also* Holland,
    Netherlands
United States, 26, 43, 132–3, 135
urban growth, 77–8, 144; in developing
    countries, 254–6; in England, 94–6, 184–6;
    in France, 109–10; in the Netherlands,
    155; in Norway, 225–6
urban mortality, 95, 160
urban population, 76; England, 183–5;
    France, 202–4; Ireland, 128; Netherlands,
    155–7
urbanisation, 42–4, 60; medieval, 77; in
    developing countries, 254–6; in England,
    94–6; in France, 109–11; in Holland, 160

vaccination, 62, 119–20
vagrancy, 28: in England, 89–90; in France,
    105
Vastergotland, 217, 219

Veluwe, population increase, 148–9
Venezuela, urban growth, 236
Venice, 77, 157
vetch, 38, 75, 92, 107, 153
Vikings, 54, 207
viticulture, 76, 108
Völkerwanderung, 65

wages, 18, 24, 26, 56, 69, 78, 79, 89, 90, 97,
    99, 105, 141–2, 149, 204, 214, 253; in
    England, 172–3; in France, 196–7; in
    Ireland, 123
Warriner, D., 17, 18, 66
war: and disease, 56; Sweden v. Denmark, 58
Wars of Religion, 102–3
Wars of the Roses, 56
waste, 176–7
water-meadows, 38, 93, 179
water supplies and mortality, 167
Weald, 91, 181
weather and harvests, 31, 37, 54, 65, 80
weeding, 22, 36–8, 107
wheat, 34, 124–5; consumption, 179;
    imports, 182; prices, 86, 90; yields, 67, 73,
    82, 91–2, 180
Wicklow, 124, 133
Wicksell, K., 211
William of Orange, 139
wills: family size, 95; farmers, 30
Winchester estates, 36, 73, 75, 87, 91
windmills, 150
wine, 76, 108
woad, 39
wool, 39, 94, 97: prices, 85, 86, 90; woollen
    industry, 154, 158, 183
Worcester, 56, 99
work-sharing, 175

yams, 28
Yelling, J. A., 180
yields, crop, 27–8, 31–2, 36–7, 63, 65, 179,
    182: decline of, 70; potatoes, 127; wheat
    in France, 199–200
Yorkshire Wolds, 176, 181
Young, A., 122, 126
Yule, G. U., 282

Zeeland, 150, 153